Alice
IN THE
COUNTRY OF
Hearts

Love Labyrinth
of Thorns

STORY:
QuinRose

ART:
Aoi Kurihara

SEVEN SEAS ENTERTAINMENT PRESENTS

Alice IN THE COUNTRY OF Hearts

LOVE LABYRINTH OF THORNS

art by AOI KURIHARA / story by QUINROSE

TRANSLATION
Angela Liu

ADAPTATION
Shanti Whitesides

LETTERING
Roland Amago

LAYOUT
Bambi Eloriaga-Amago

LOGO DESIGN
Courtney Williams

COVER DESIGN
Nicky Lim

PROOFREADER
Rebecca Scoble

MANAGING EDITOR
Adam Arnold

PUBLISHER
Jason DeAngelis

Seven Seas books may be purchased in bulk for educational, business, or promotional use. For information on bulk purchases, please contact Macmillan Corporate & Premium Sales Department at 1-800-221-7945 (ext 5442) or write specialmarkets@macmillan.com.

ISBN: 978-1-626920-54-5

Printed in Canada

First Printing: May 2014

10 9 8 7 6 5 4 3 2 1

FOLLOW US ONLINE: ***www.gomanga.com***

READING DIRECTIONS

This book reads from ***right to left***, Japanese style. If this is your first time reading manga, you start reading from the top right panel on each page and take it from there. If you get lost, just follow the numbered diagram here. It may seem backwards at first, but you□ll get the hang of it! Have fun!!

1
2
3
4
5
6
7
8
9

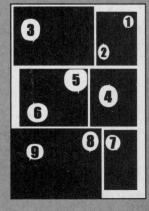

Alice in the Country of Hearts
ハートの国の
アリス
~Wonderful Wonder World~

- STORY -

This is a love adventure game. It is based on *Alice in Wonderland*, but evolves into a completely different story.

The main character is far from a romantic. In fact, she's especially sick of love relationships.

She's pulled (against her will) into the dangerous Country of Hearts, which is not as peaceful as the name makes it sound. The Hatters are a mafia family, and even the employees of the Amusement Park carry weapons.

The leaders of the three domains are constantly trying to kill each other. Many of the skirmishes are the result of territory grabs by three major powers trying to control more land: the Hatter, the Queen of Hearts, and Gowland.

After drinking some strange medicine (again, against her will), the main character is unable to return to her world. She quickly decides that she's trapped in a dream and allows herself to enjoy(?) the extraordinary experience she's been thrown into.

What territory will she stay with and who will she interact with to get herself home?
And will this girl, so jaded about love, fall into a relationship she doesn't expect?

Alice in Country of Hearts
Character Information

Elliot March
VA: Tsuguo Mogami

The No. 2 of the Hatter Family and Blood's right-hand man, Elliot is an ex-criminal and an escaped convict. Very short-tempered, he used to be a "very bad guy" who shot before asking questions. After partnering up with Blood, he rounded out and changed to a "slightly bad guy" who thinks for about three seconds before shooting. In his mind, this is a vast improvement.

Blood Dupre
VA: Katsuyuki Konishi

The dangerous leader of the crime syndicate known as the Hatter Family. Since he enjoys plotting more than working directly, he controls everything from the shadows. He's incredibly smart, but due to his temperamental moods and his desire to keep things "interesting," he often digs his own grave in his secret plans.

Alice Liddell
VA: Rie Kugimiya

She grew up to be a responsible young woman after losing her mother early, but Alice still carries a complex toward her older sister. She respects her older sister very much, but is frustrated about always being compared to her. Since her first love fell for her older sister, she has no confidence in herself when it comes to romance.

Vivaldi
VA: Yuuko Kaida

Ruthless and cruel, the Queen of Hearts is an arrogant beauty with a wild temper. She's enemies with the Hatter and Gowland. Impatient at heart, Vivaldi takes her fury out on everyone around her, including her subordinates, whom she considers pawns. Anyone **not** working for her doesn't even register as existing.

Tweedle Dum
VA: Jun Fukuyama

The second "Bloody Twin" and a dead ringer for his brother—in both appearance and personality. As they often change places, it's uncertain which one is the older twin.

Tweedle Dee
VA: Jun Fukuyama

Gatekeeper of the Hatter territory, and one of the dark, sneaky twins. They sometimes show an innocent side, but they usually have a malicious agenda. Also known as the "Bloody Twins" due to their unsavory activities.

Ace
VA: Daisuke Hirakawa

The knight of Hearts and the ex-subordinate of Vivaldi. He's left the castle and is currently wandering. He's a very unlucky and unfortunate man, yet he remains strangely positive, thus he tends to plow forward and make mistakes that only worsen his situation. He's one of the few friends of the clockmaker, Julius.

Julius Monrey
VA: Takehito Koyasu

The clockmaker, a gloomy machine expert who easily falls into depression. He lives in the Clock Tower and doesn't get out much. He always thinks of everything in the most negative way and tends to distrust people, but he gets along with Ace. He had some part in the imprisonment of the March Hare, Elliot, and is thus the target of Elliot's hatred.

Peter White
VA: Kouki Miyata

Don't be fooled by the cute ears—Peter is the dangerous guide who dragged Alice to Wonderland in the first place. He claims to always be worried about the time, despite having a strange grasp on it. Rumors say his heart is as black as his hair is white.

Nightmare
VA: Tomokazu Sugita

A sickly nightmare. He appears in Alice's dream, sometimes to guide her— and other times, to **misguide** her.

Mary Gowland
VA: Kenyuu Horiuchi

The owner of the Amusement Park. He hides his hated first name, Mary, but pretty much everyone already knows it. His full name is a play on words that sounds like "Merry Go Round" when said quickly. If his musical talent was given a numerical value, it would be closer to negatives than zero.

Boris Airay
VA: Noriaki Sugiyama

A riddle-loving cat with a signature smirk. He sometimes gives hints to his riddles, but the hints usually just cause more confusion. He also has a tendency to pose questions and never answer them.

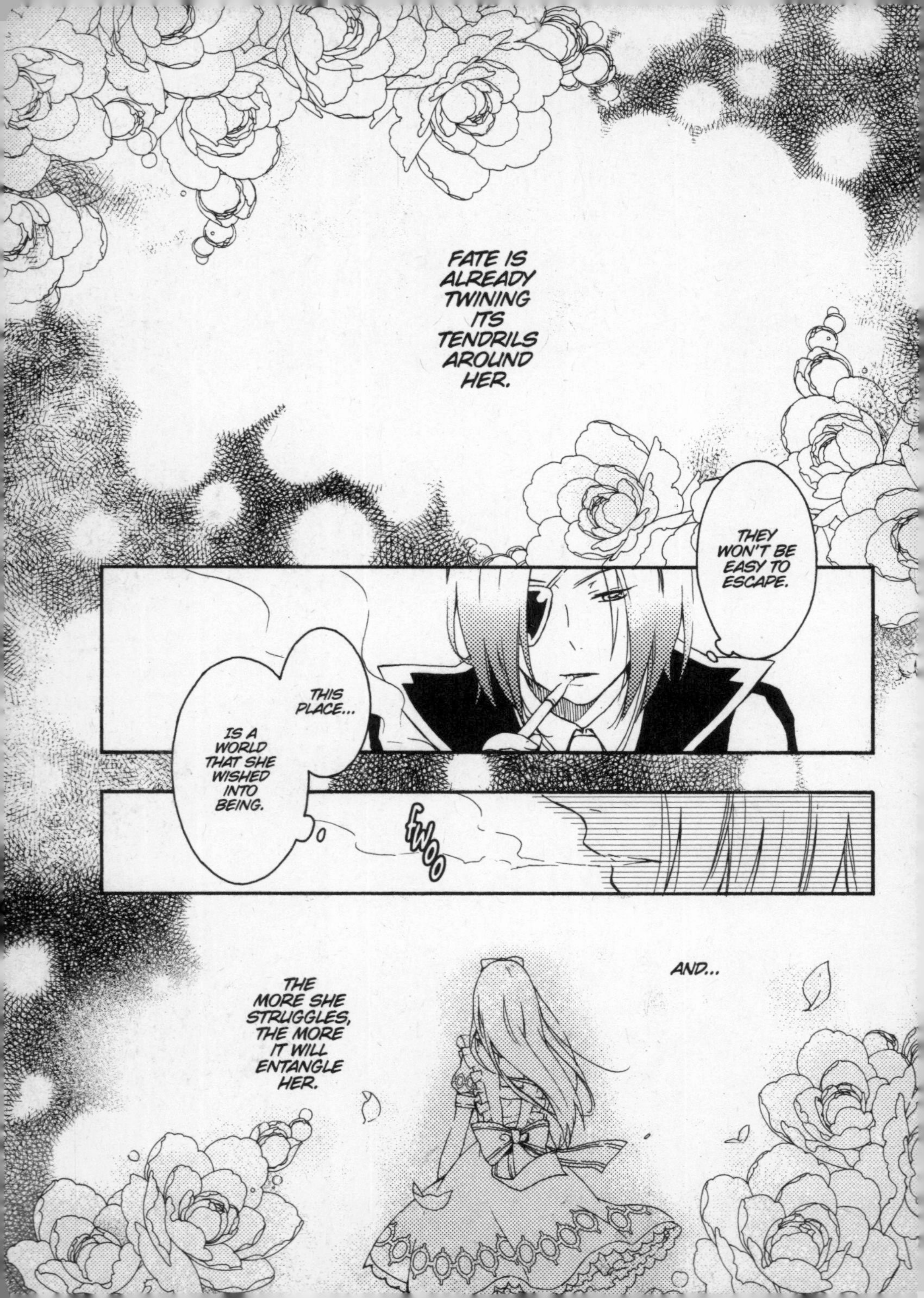
FATE IS ALREADY TWINING ITS TENDRILS AROUND HER.
THEY WON'T BE EASY TO ESCAPE.
THIS PLACE...
IS A WORLD THAT SHE WISHED INTO BEING.
FWOO
AND...
THE MORE SHE STRUGGLES, THE MORE IT WILL ENTANGLE HER.

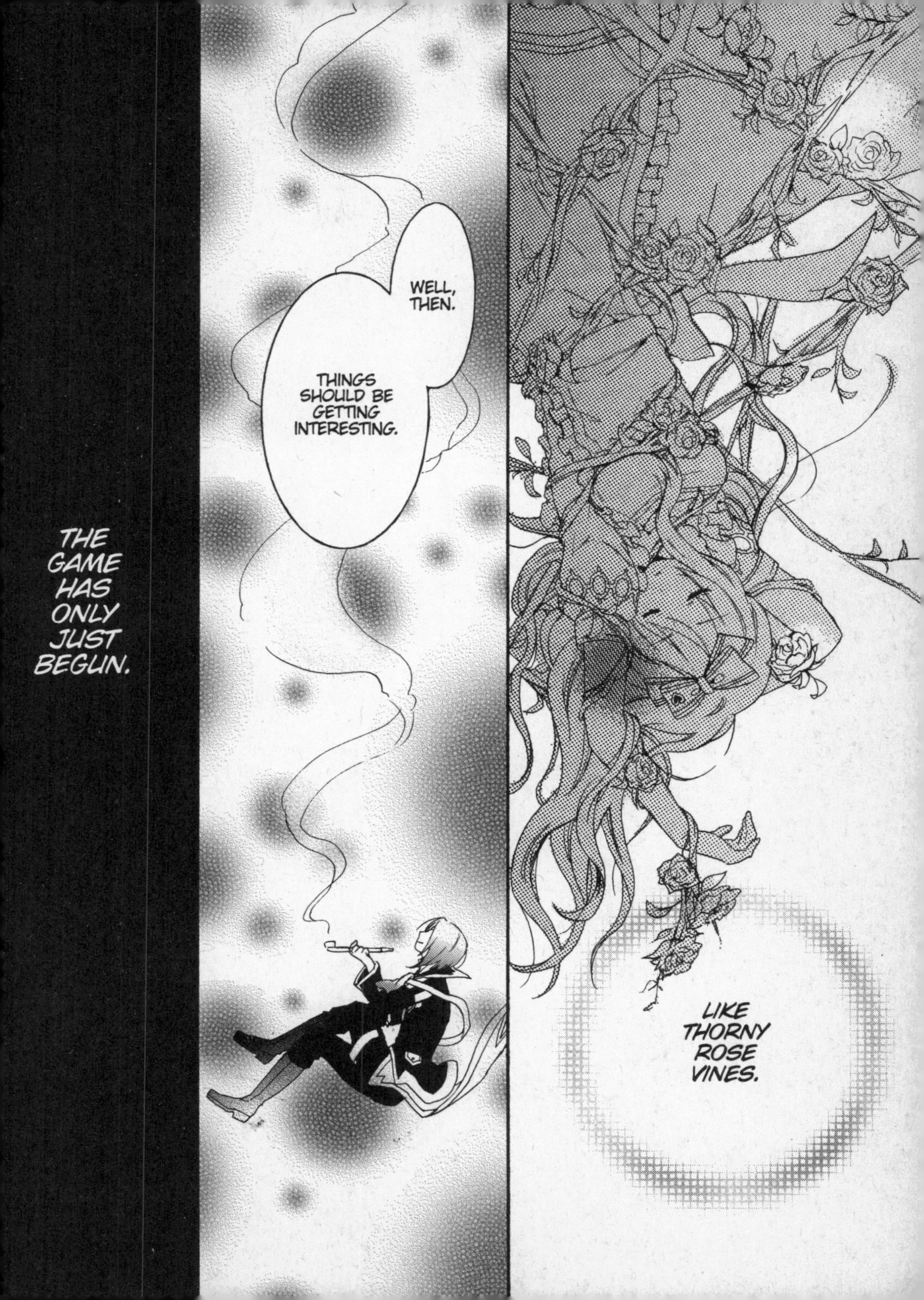
LIKE THORNY ROSE VINES.
WELL, THEN.
THINGS SHOULD BE GETTING INTERESTING.
THE GAME HAS ONLY JUST BEGUN.

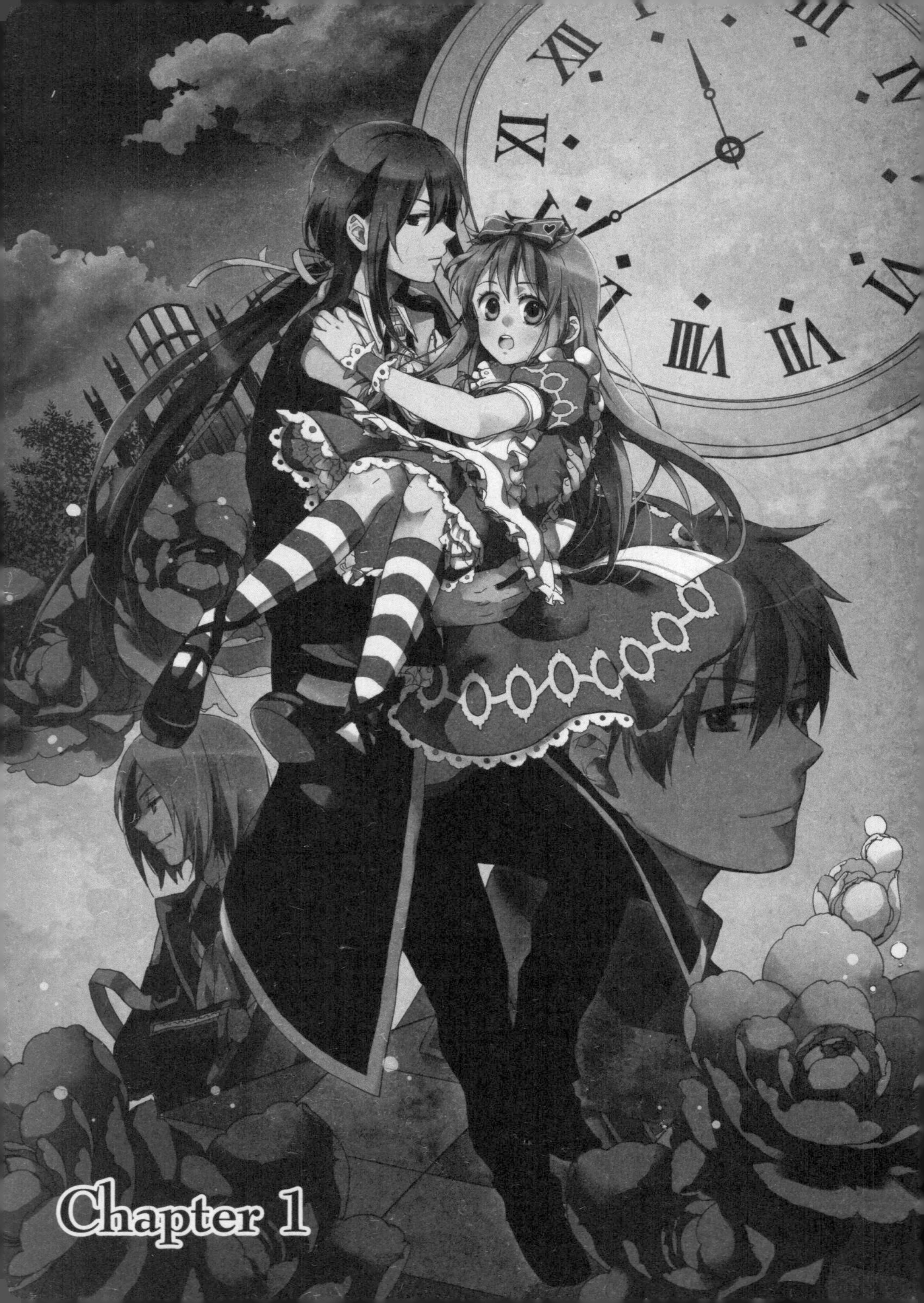
Chapter 1

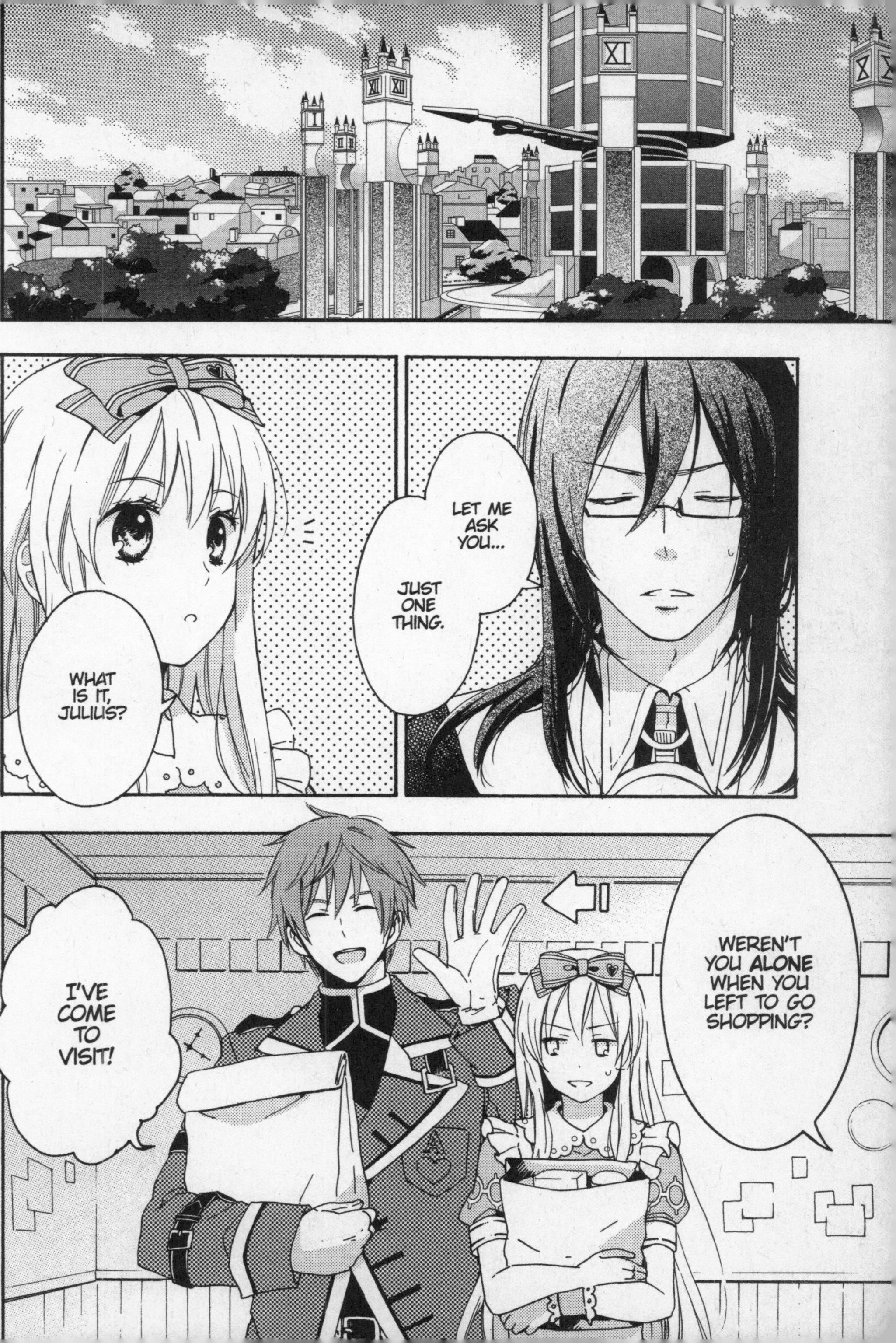
LET ME ASK YOU...
JUST ONE THING.
WHAT IS IT, JULIUS?
WEREN'T YOU ALONE WHEN YOU LEFT TO GO SHOPPING?
I'VE COME TO VISIT!

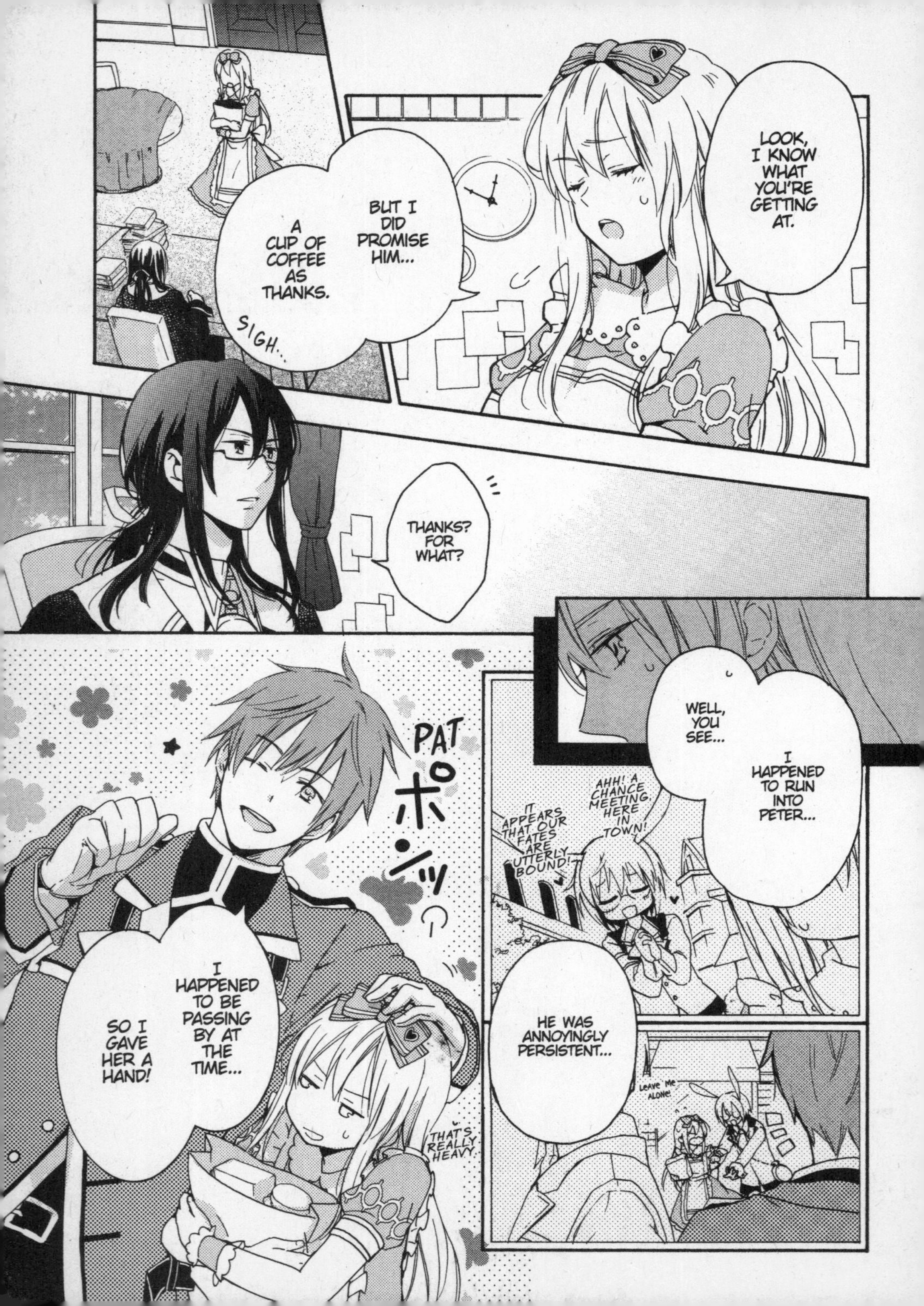
LOOK, I KNOW WHAT YOU'RE GETTING AT.
BUT I DID PROMISE HIM...
A CUP OF COFFEE AS THANKS.
SIGH...
THANKS? FOR WHAT?
WELL, YOU SEE...
I HAPPENED TO RUN INTO PETER...
AHH! A CHANCE MEETING, HERE IN TOWN!
IT APPEARS THAT OUR FATES ARE UTTERLY BOUND!
HE WAS ANNOYINGLY PERSISTENT...
LEAVE ME ALONE!
PAT
ポンッ
I HAPPENED TO BE PASSING BY AT THE TIME...
SO I GAVE HER A HAND!
THAT'S REALLY HEAVY.

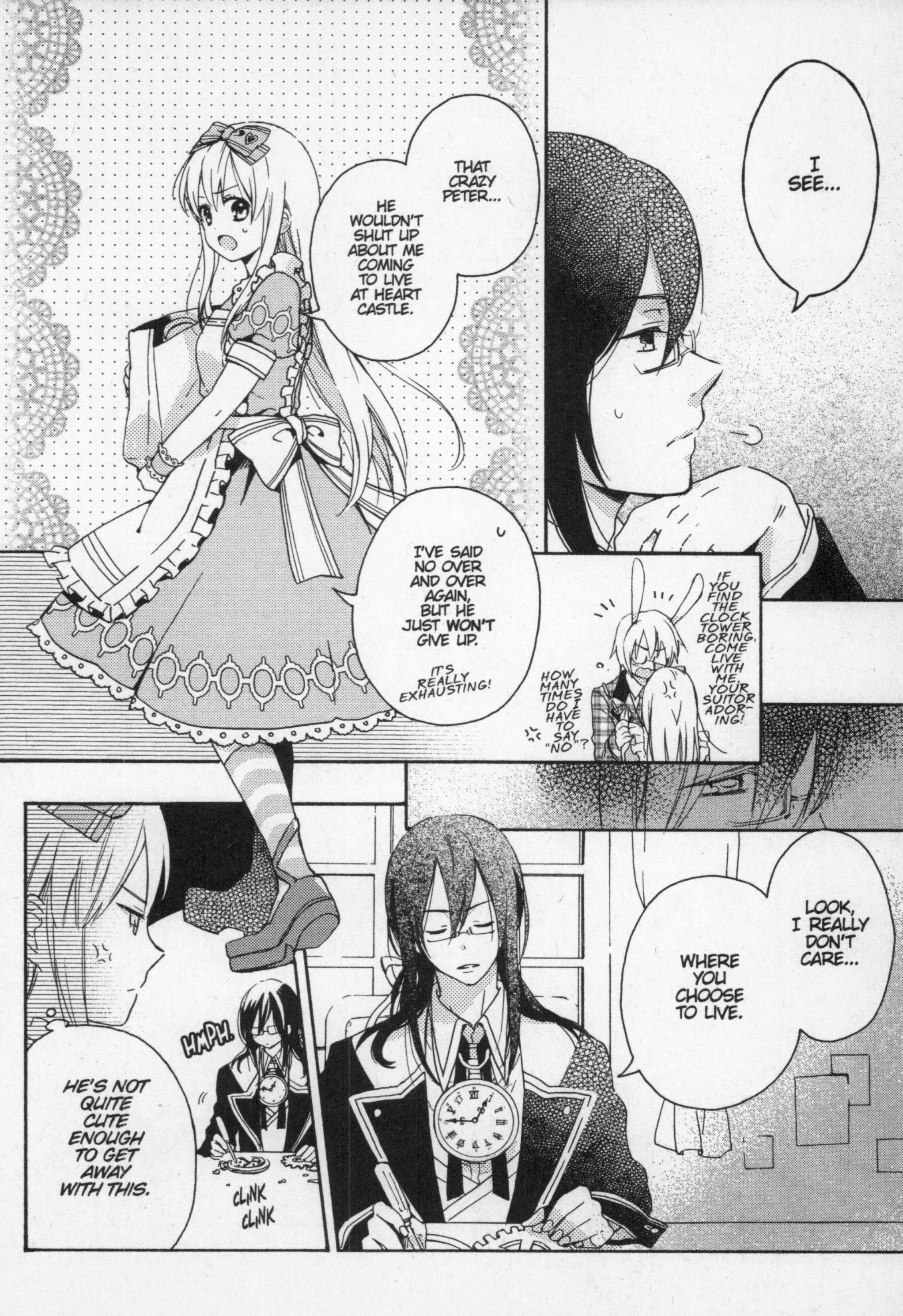
THAT CRAZY PETER...
HE WOULDN'T SHUT UP ABOUT ME COMING TO LIVE AT HEART CASTLE.
I SEE...
I'VE SAID NO OVER AND OVER AGAIN, BUT HE JUST WON'T GIVE UP.
IT'S REALLY EXHAUSTING!
IF YOU FIND THE CLOCK TOWER BORING, COME LIVE WITH ME, YOUR SUITOR ADORING!
HOW MANY TIMES DO I HAVE TO SAY "NO"?
LOOK, I REALLY DON'T CARE...
WHERE YOU CHOOSE TO LIVE.
HMPH.
HE'S NOT QUITE CUTE ENOUGH TO GET AWAY WITH THIS.
CLINK
CLINK

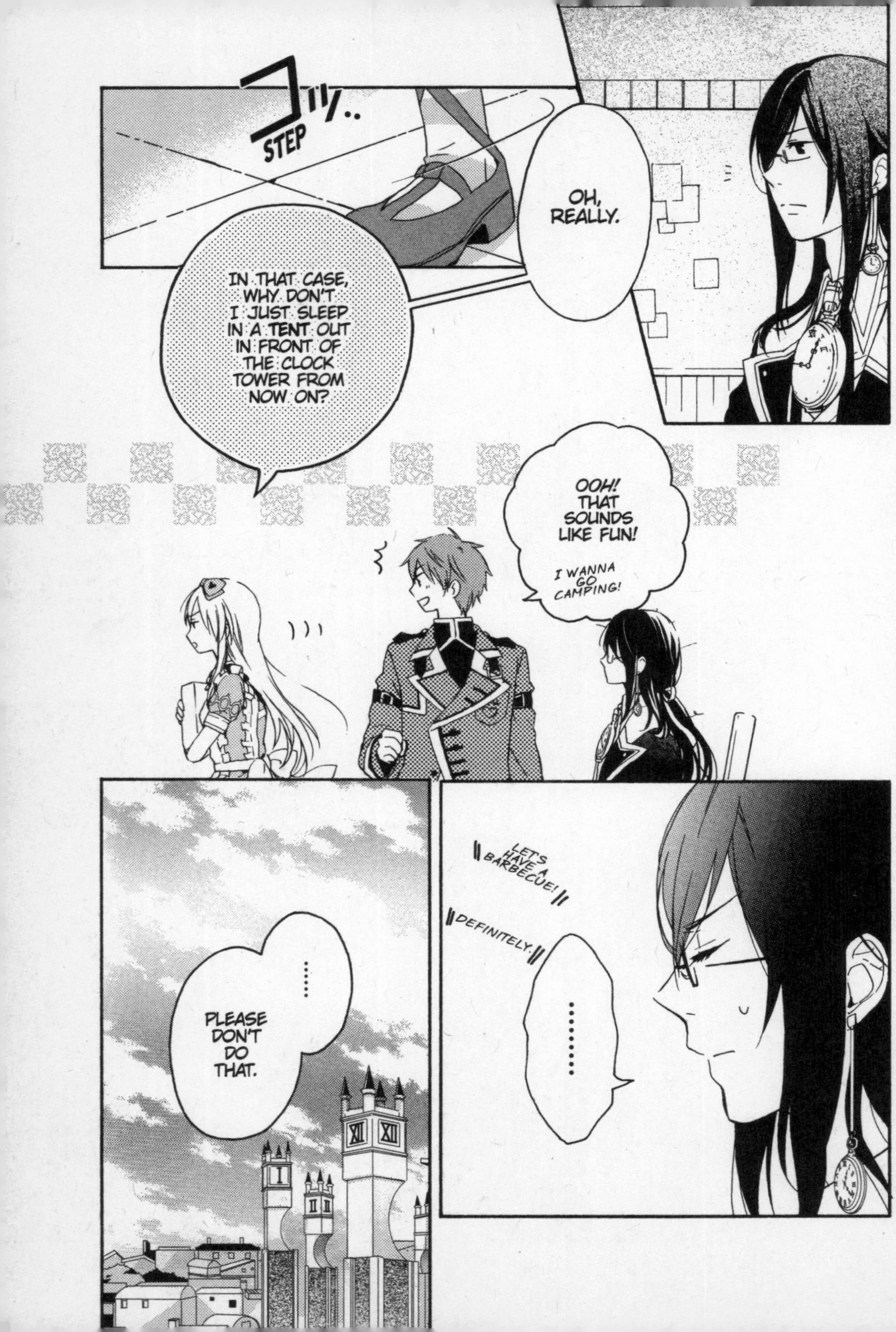
OH, REALLY.
STEP
IN THAT CASE, WHY DON'T I JUST SLEEP IN A TENT OUT IN FRONT OF THE CLOCK TOWER FROM NOW ON?
OOH! THAT SOUNDS LIKE FUN!
I WANNA GO CAMPING!
LET'S HAVE A BARBECUE!
DEFINITELY.
....
...... PLEASE DON'T DO THAT.

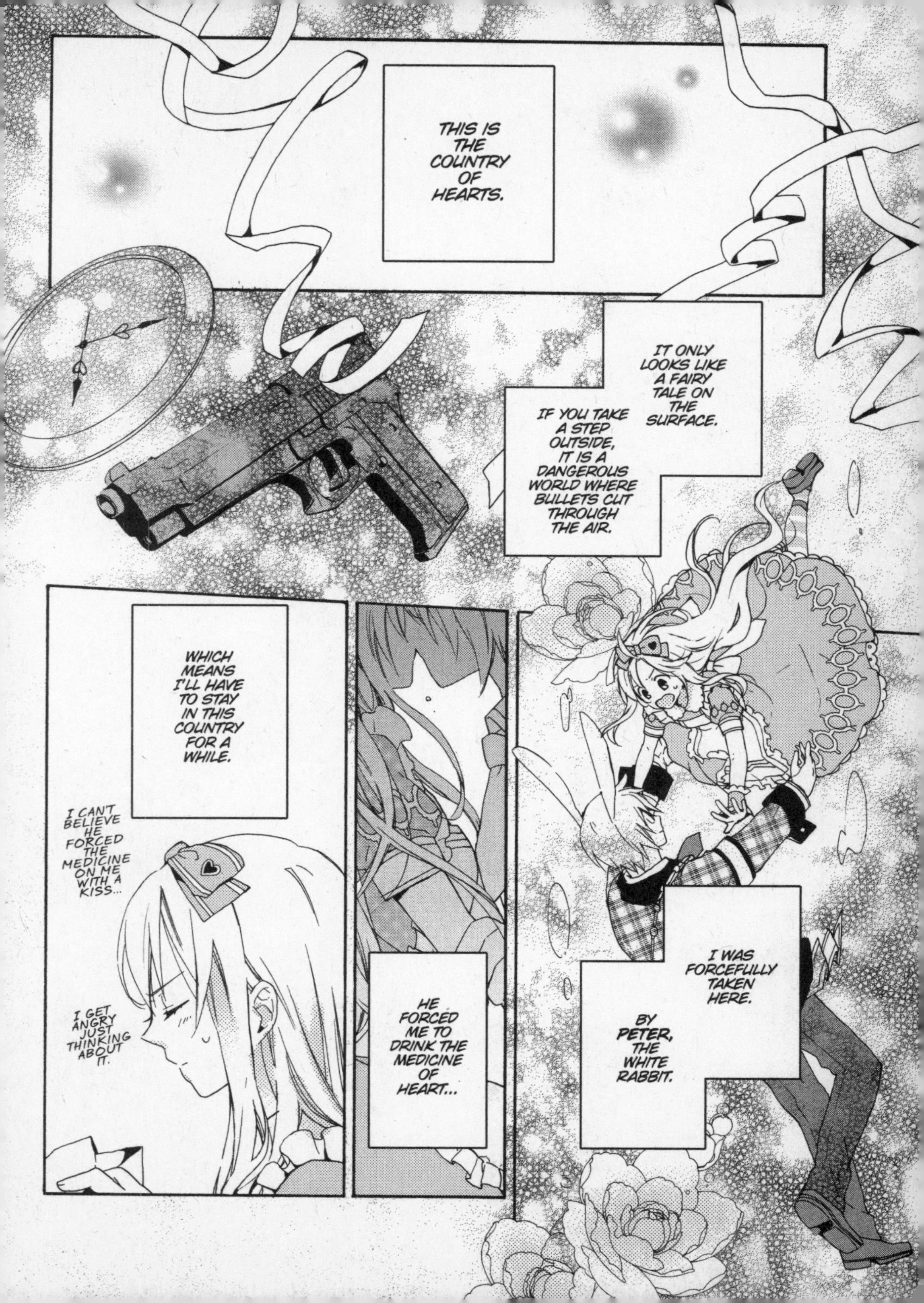
THIS IS THE COUNTRY OF HEARTS.
IT ONLY LOOKS LIKE A FAIRY TALE ON THE SURFACE.
IF YOU TAKE A STEP OUTSIDE, IT IS A DANGEROUS WORLD WHERE BULLETS CUT THROUGH THE AIR.
I WAS FORCEFULLY TAKEN HERE.
BY PETER, THE WHITE RABBIT.
HE FORCED ME TO DRINK THE MEDICINE OF HEART...
WHICH MEANS I'LL HAVE TO STAY IN THIS COUNTRY FOR A WHILE.
I CAN'T BELIEVE HE FORCED THE MEDICINE ON ME WITH A KISS...
I GET ANGRY JUST THINKING ABOUT IT.

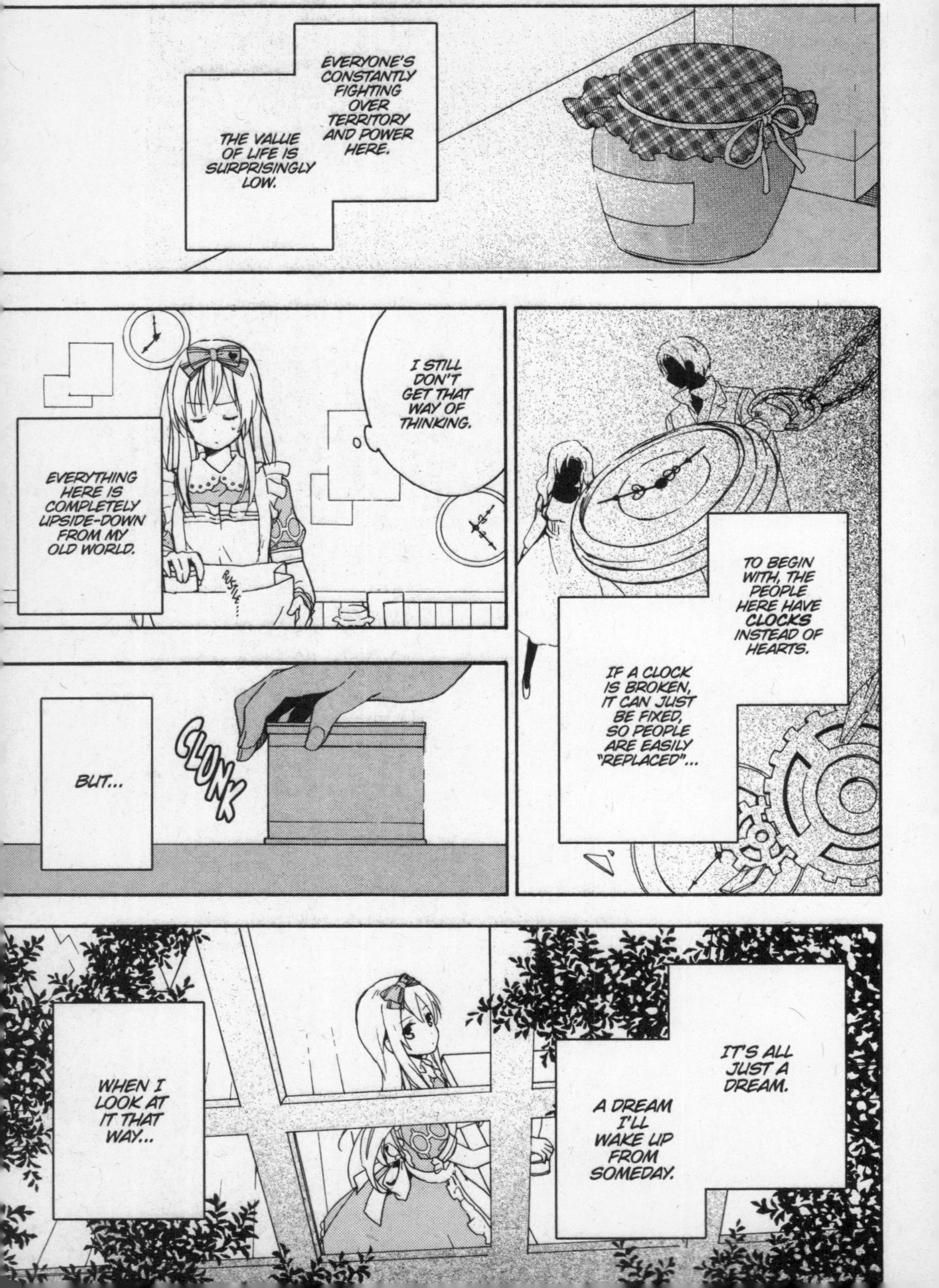
EVERYONE'S CONSTANTLY FIGHTING OVER TERRITORY AND POWER HERE.
THE VALUE OF LIFE IS SURPRISINGLY LOW.
TO BEGIN WITH, THE PEOPLE HERE HAVE CLOCKS INSTEAD OF HEARTS.
IF A CLOCK IS BROKEN, IT CAN JUST BE FIXED, SO PEOPLE ARE EASILY "REPLACED"...
I STILL DON'T GET THAT WAY OF THINKING.
RUSTLE...
EVERYTHING HERE IS COMPLETELY UPSIDE-DOWN FROM MY OLD WORLD.
CLUNK
BUT...
IT'S ALL JUST A DREAM.
A DREAM I'LL WAKE UP FROM SOMEDAY.
WHEN I LOOK AT IT THAT WAY...

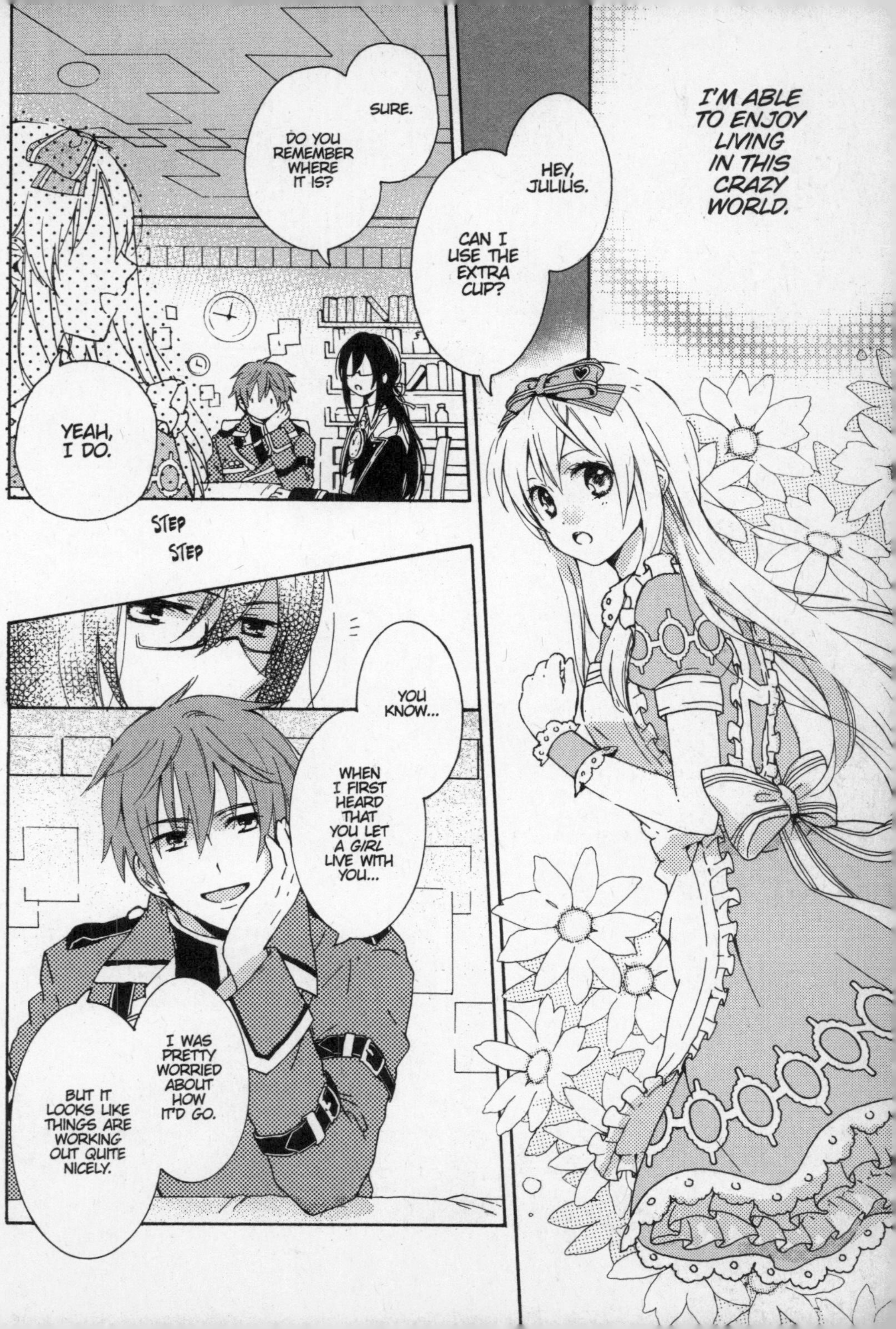
I'M ABLE TO ENJOY LIVING IN THIS CRAZY WORLD.
HEY, JULIUS.
CAN I USE THE EXTRA CUP?
SURE.
DO YOU REMEMBER WHERE IT IS?
YEAH, I DO.
STEP
STEP
YOU KNOW...
WHEN I FIRST HEARD THAT YOU LET A *GIRL* LIVE WITH YOU...
I WAS PRETTY WORRIED ABOUT HOW IT'D GO.
BUT IT LOOKS LIKE THINGS ARE WORKING OUT QUITE NICELY.

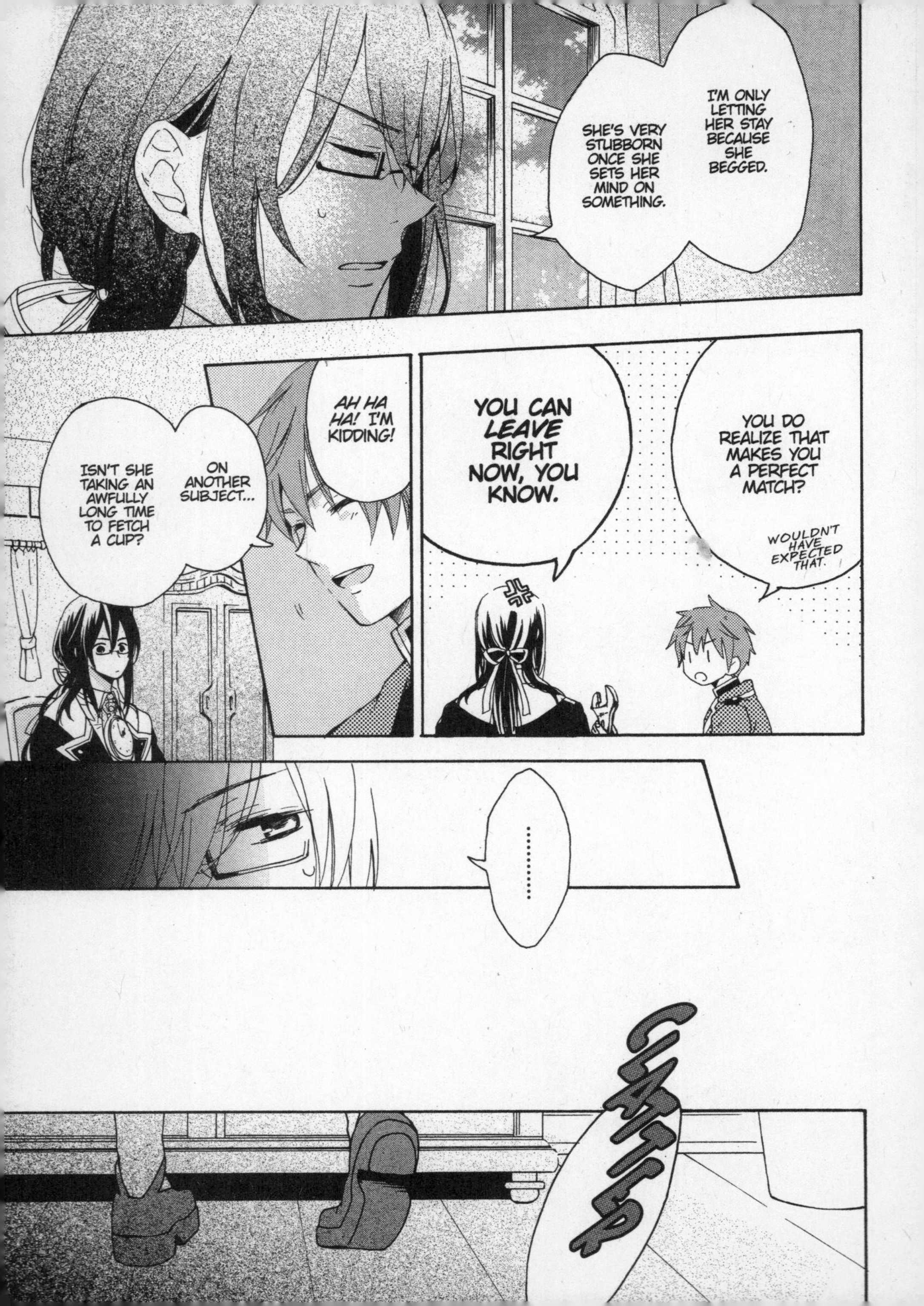
I'M ONLY LETTING HER STAY BECAUSE SHE BEGGED.
SHE'S VERY STUBBORN ONCE SHE SETS HER MIND ON SOMETHING.
YOU DO REALIZE THAT MAKES YOU A PERFECT MATCH?
WOULDN'T HAVE EXPECTED THAT.
YOU CAN *LEAVE* RIGHT NOW, YOU KNOW.
AH HA HA! I'M KIDDING!
ON ANOTHER SUBJECT...
ISN'T SHE TAKING AN AWFULLY LONG TIME TO FETCH A CUP?
......
CLATTER

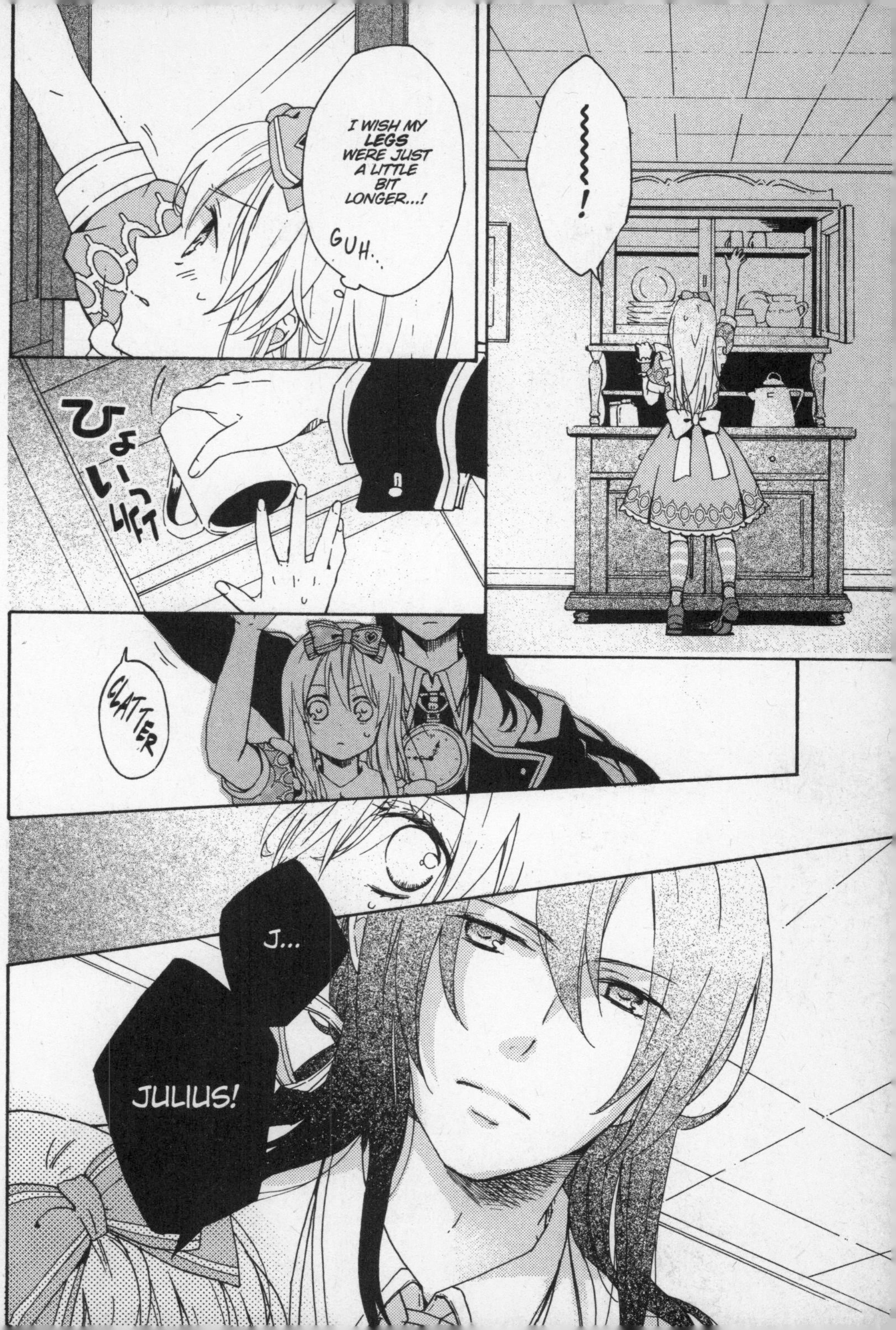

I WISH MY LEGS WERE JUST A LITTLE BIT LONGER...!
GUH...
ひょいっ
LIFT
CLATTER
J...
JULIUS!

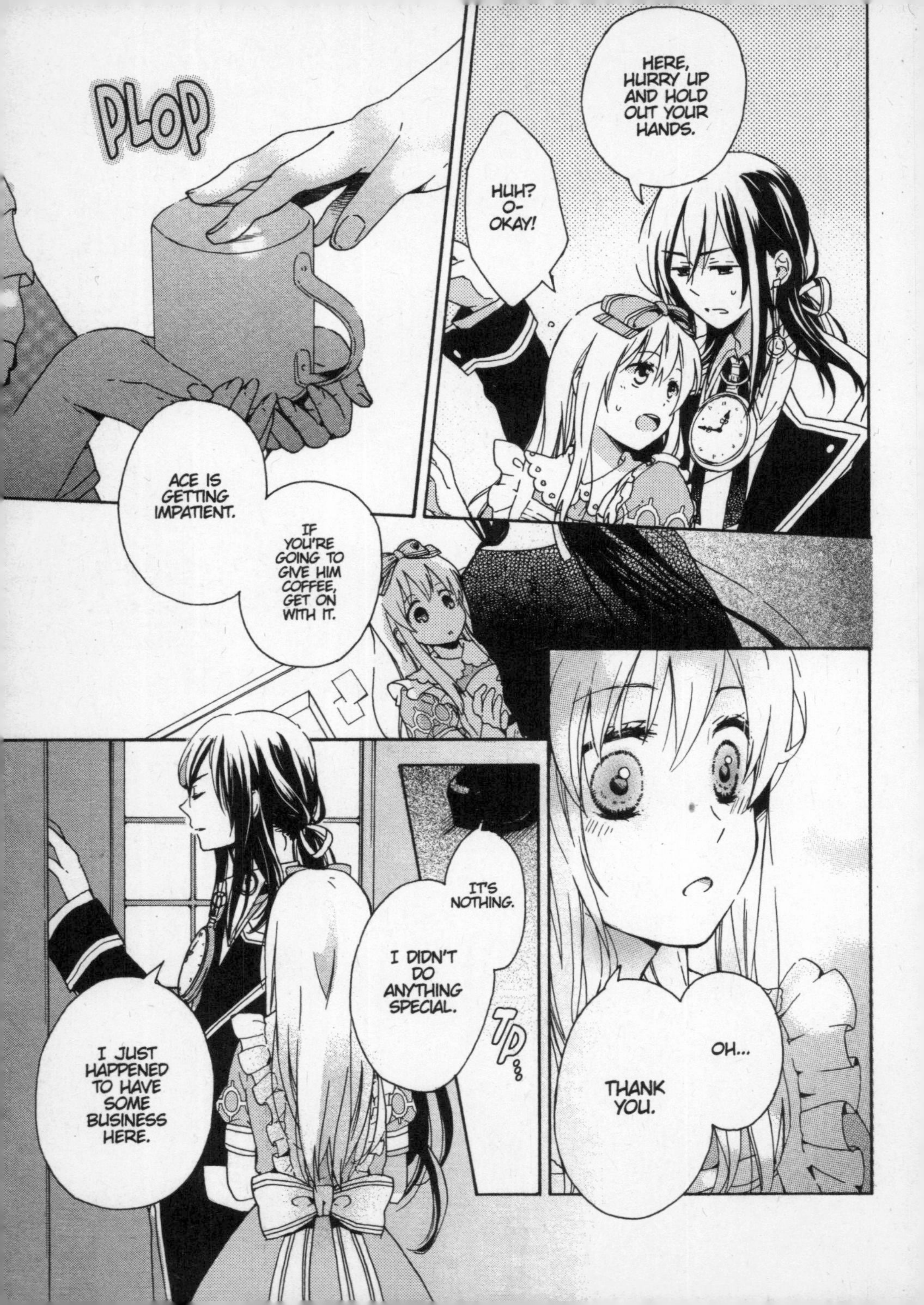
HERE, HURRY UP AND HOLD OUT YOUR HANDS.
HUH? O-OKAY!
PLOP
ACE IS GETTING IMPATIENT.
IF YOU'RE GOING TO GIVE HIM COFFEE, GET ON WITH IT.
OH... THANK YOU.
TP
IT'S NOTHING.
I DIDN'T DO ANYTHING SPECIAL.
I JUST HAPPENED TO HAVE SOME BUSINESS HERE.

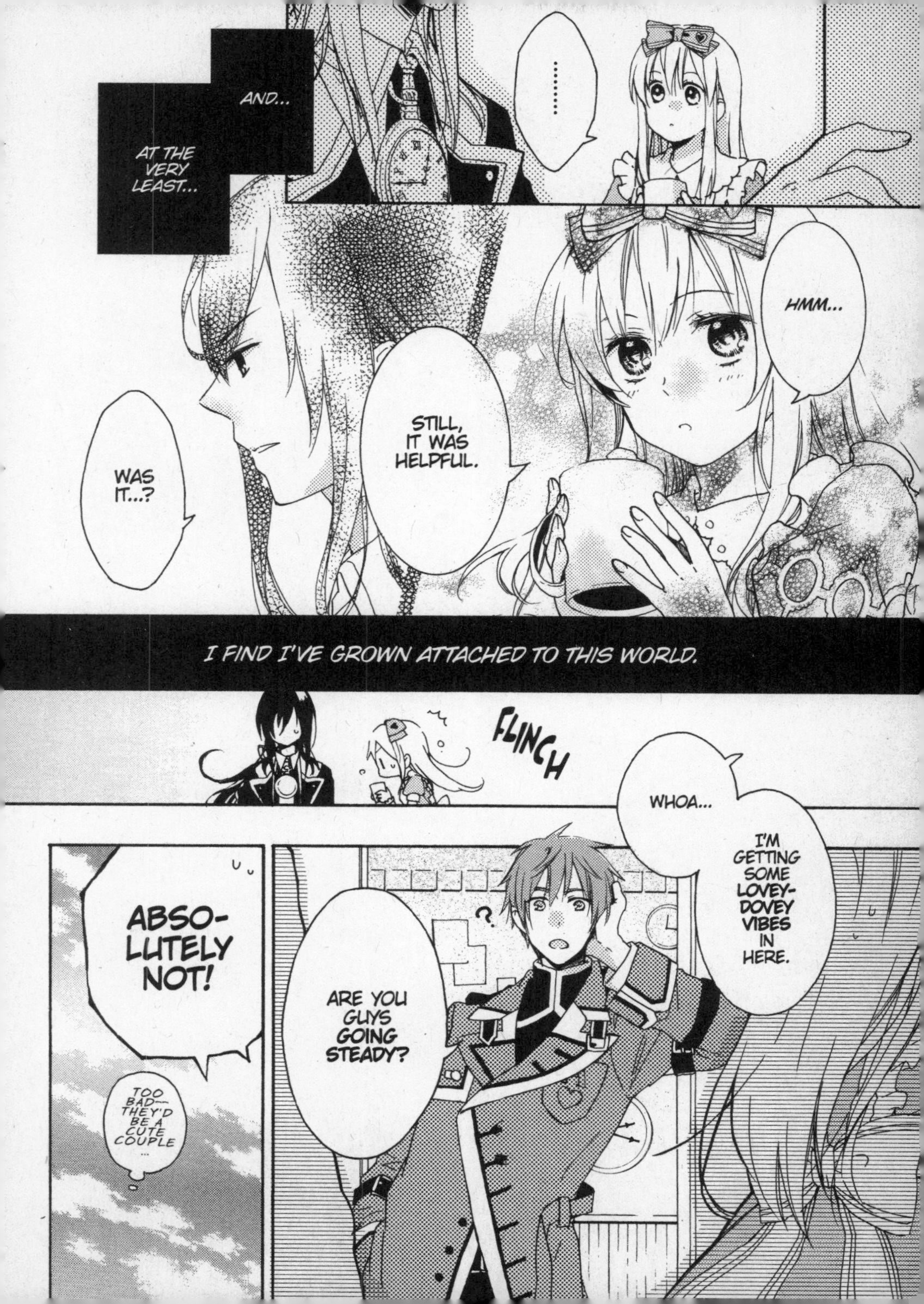
......
AND...
AT THE VERY LEAST...
HMM...
STILL, IT WAS HELPFUL.
WAS IT...?
I FIND I'VE GROWN ATTACHED TO THIS WORLD.
FLINCH
WHOA...
I'M GETTING SOME LOVEY-DOVEY VIBES IN HERE.
ARE YOU GUYS GOING STEADY?
ABSO-LUTELY NOT!
TOO BAD— THEY'D BE A CUTE COUPLE...

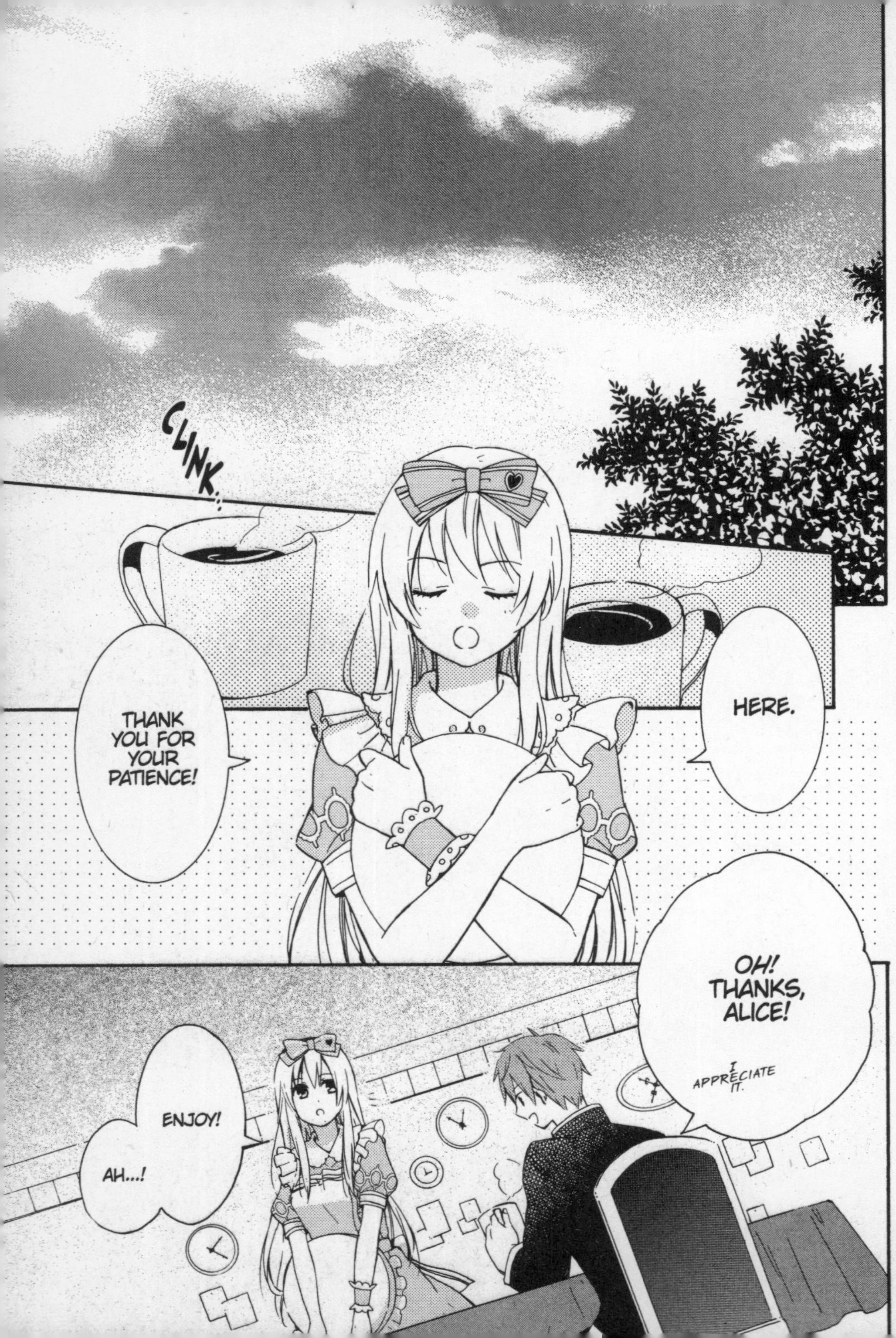
CLINK..
HERE.
THANK YOU FOR YOUR PATIENCE!
OH! THANKS, ALICE!
I APPRECIATE IT.
ENJOY!
AH...!

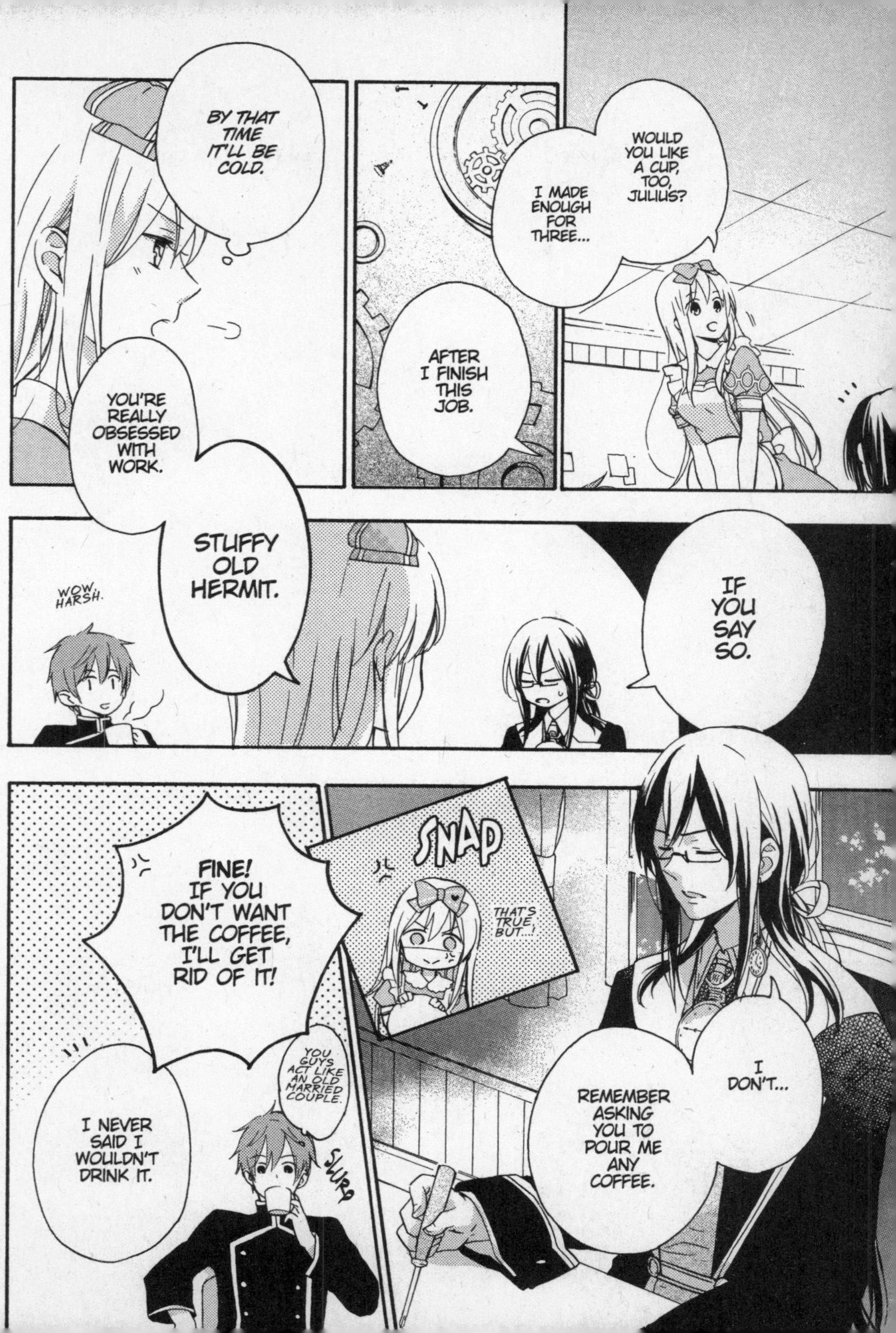
WOULD YOU LIKE A CUP, TOO, JULIUS?
I MADE ENOUGH FOR THREE...
AFTER I FINISH THIS JOB.
BY THAT TIME IT'LL BE COLD.
YOU'RE REALLY OBSESSED WITH WORK.
STUFFY OLD HERMIT.
IF YOU SAY SO.
WOW, HARSH.
I DON'T...
REMEMBER ASKING YOU TO POUR ME ANY COFFEE.
SNAP
THAT'S TRUE, BUT...!
FINE! IF YOU DON'T WANT THE COFFEE, I'LL GET RID OF IT!
YOU GUYS ACT LIKE AN OLD MARRIED COUPLE.
SLURP
I NEVER SAID I WOULDN'T DRINK IT.

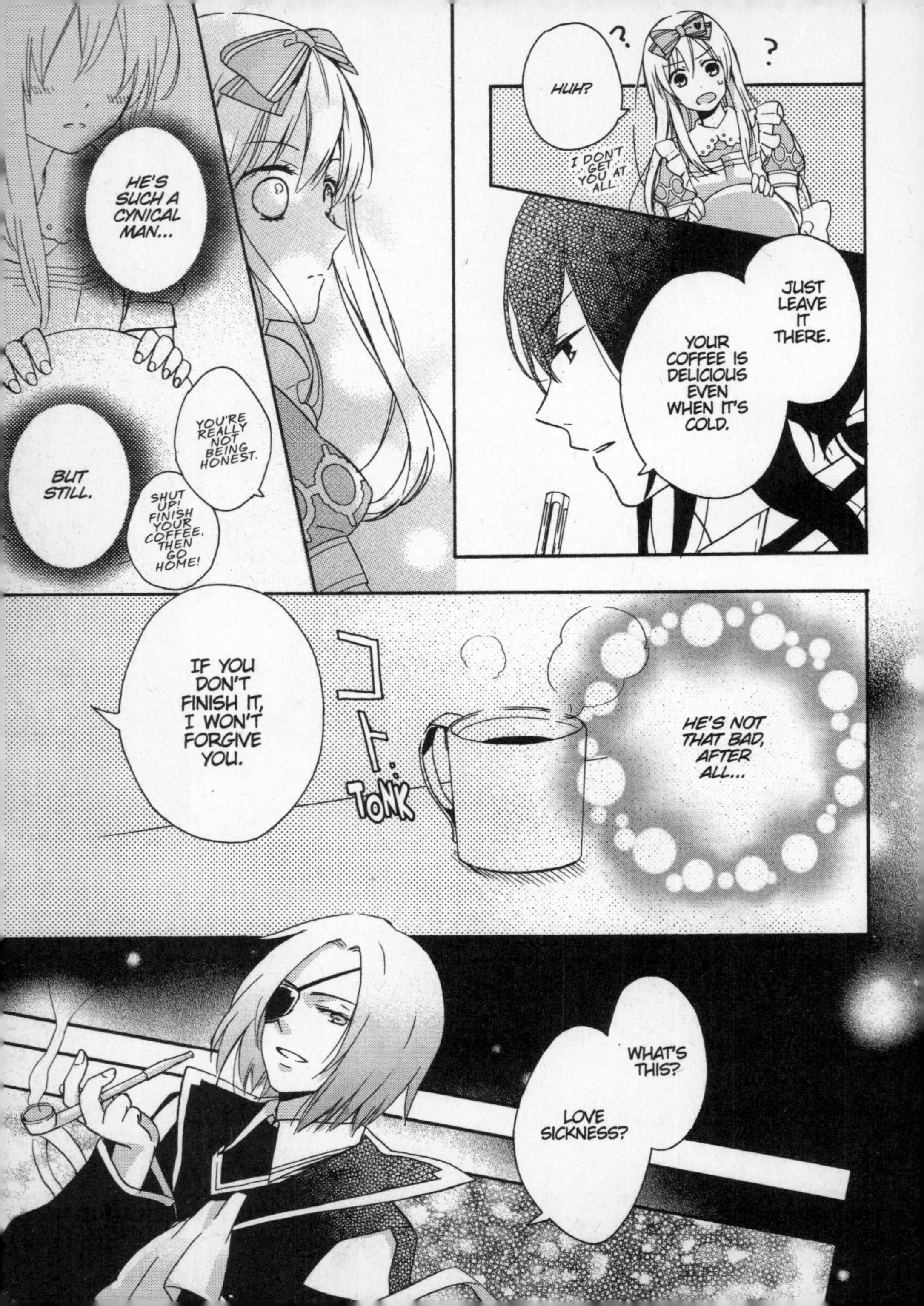
?
?
HUH?
I DON'T GET YOU AT ALL.
JUST LEAVE IT THERE.
YOUR COFFEE IS DELICIOUS EVEN WHEN IT'S COLD.
HE'S SUCH A CYNICAL MAN...
YOU'RE REALLY NOT BEING HONEST.
SHUT UP! FINISH YOUR COFFEE, THEN GO HOME!
BUT STILL.
HE'S NOT THAT BAD, AFTER ALL...
コト
TONK
IF YOU DON'T FINISH IT, I WON'T FORGIVE YOU.
WHAT'S THIS?
LOVE SICKNESS?

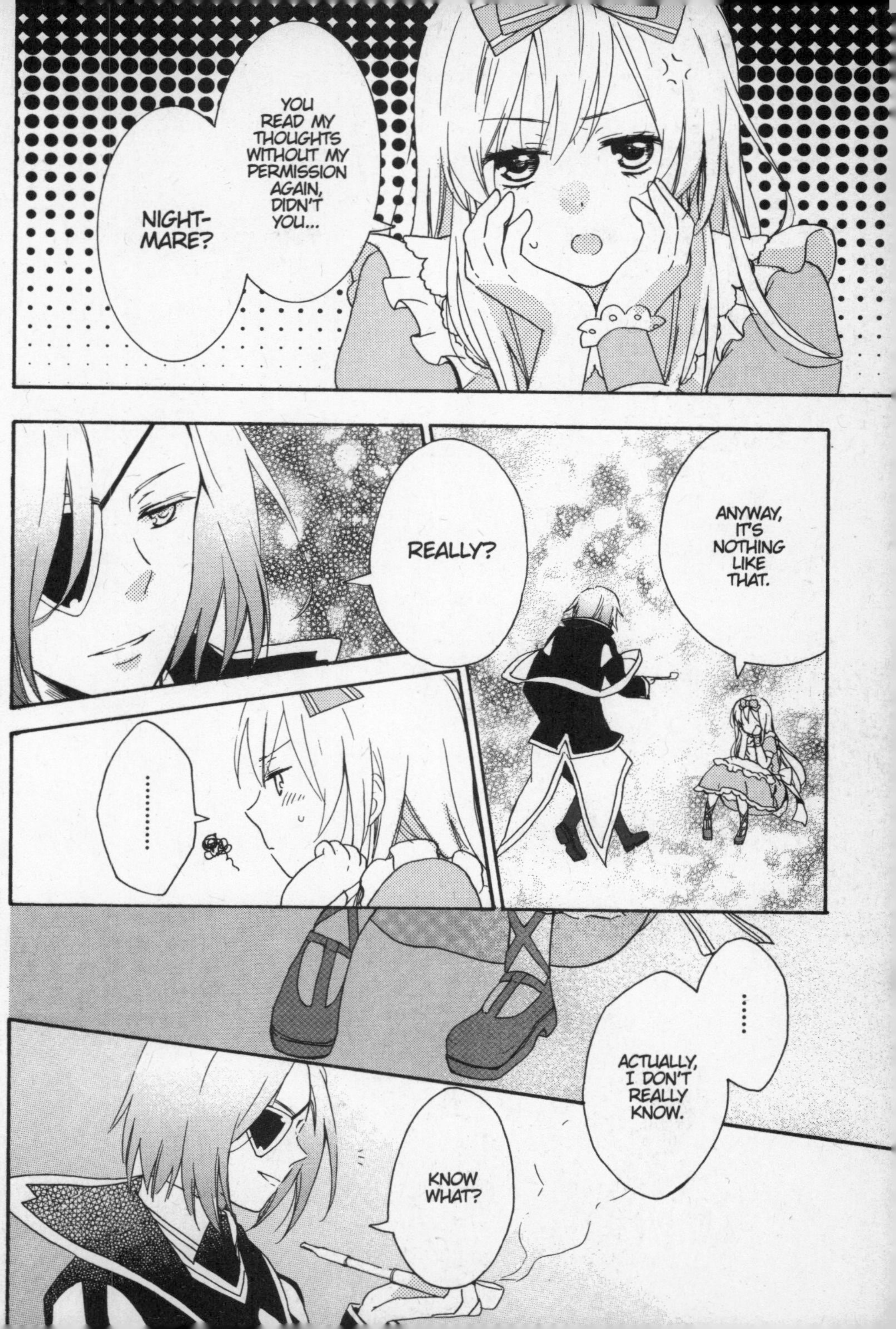
YOU READ MY THOUGHTS WITHOUT MY PERMISSION AGAIN, DIDN'T YOU... NIGHT-MARE?
ANYWAY, IT'S NOTHING LIKE THAT.
REALLY?
......
......
ACTUALLY, I DON'T REALLY KNOW.
KNOW WHAT?

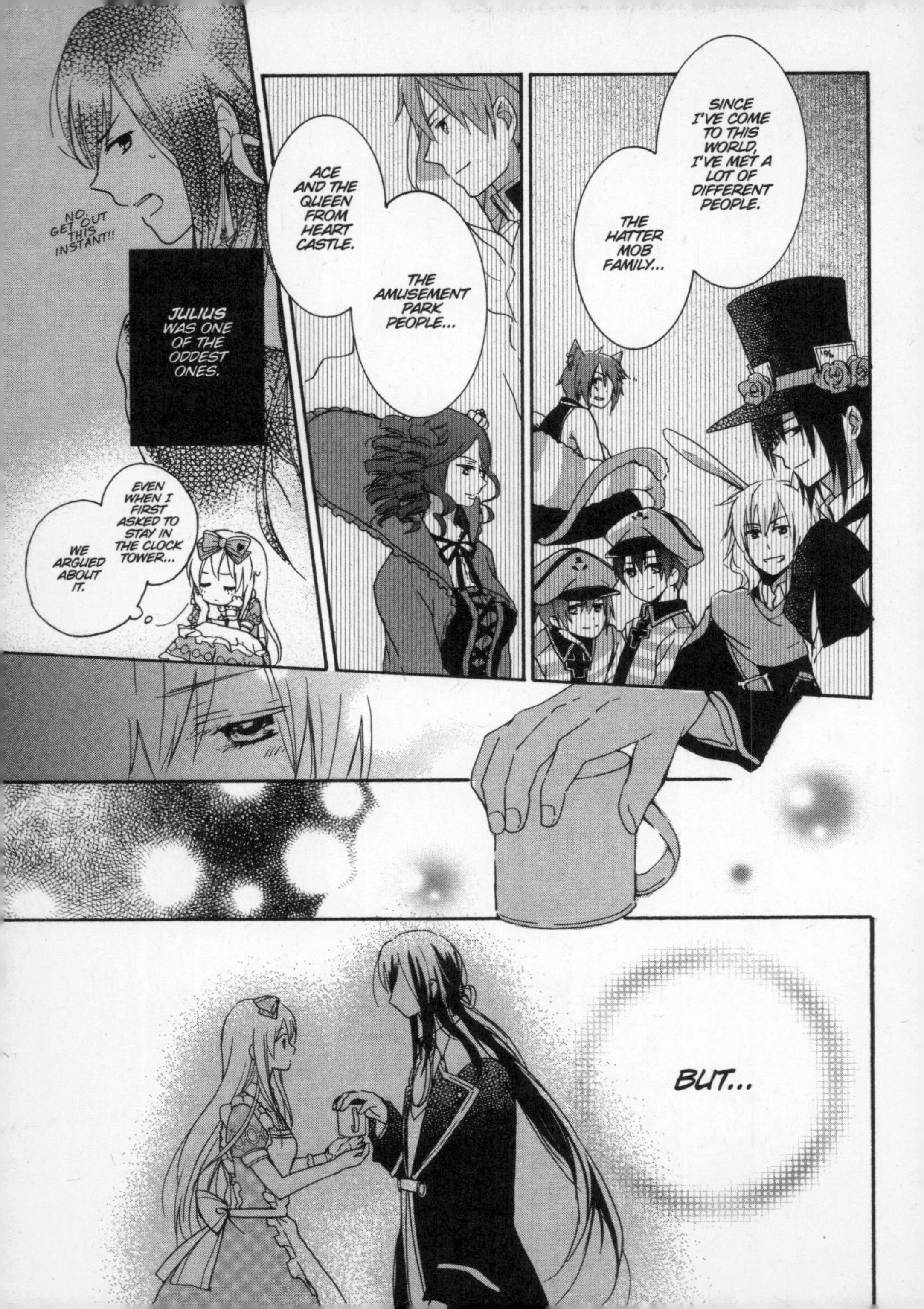
SINCE I'VE COME TO THIS WORLD, I'VE MET A LOT OF DIFFERENT PEOPLE.
THE HATTER MOB FAMILY...
ACE AND THE QUEEN FROM HEART CASTLE.
THE AMUSEMENT PARK PEOPLE...
NO GET OUT THIS INSTANT!!
JULIUS WAS ONE OF THE ODDEST ONES.
EVEN WHEN I FIRST ASKED TO STAY IN THE CLOCK TOWER...
WE ARGUED ABOUT IT.
BUT...

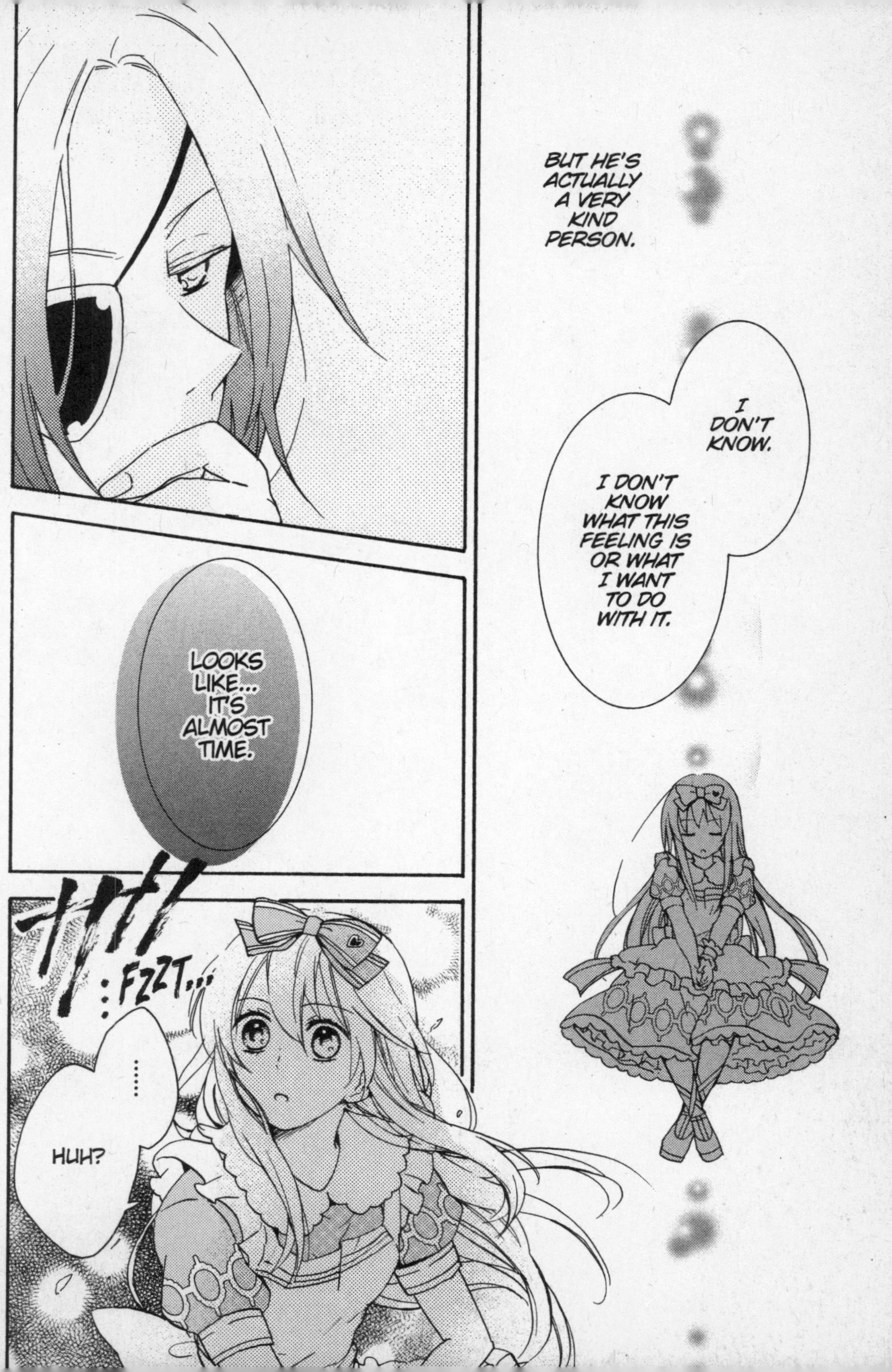
BUT HE'S ACTUALLY A VERY KIND PERSON.
I DON'T KNOW.
I DON'T KNOW WHAT THIS FEELING IS OR WHAT I WANT TO DO WITH IT.
LOOKS LIKE... IT'S ALMOST TIME.
FZZT...
......
HUH?

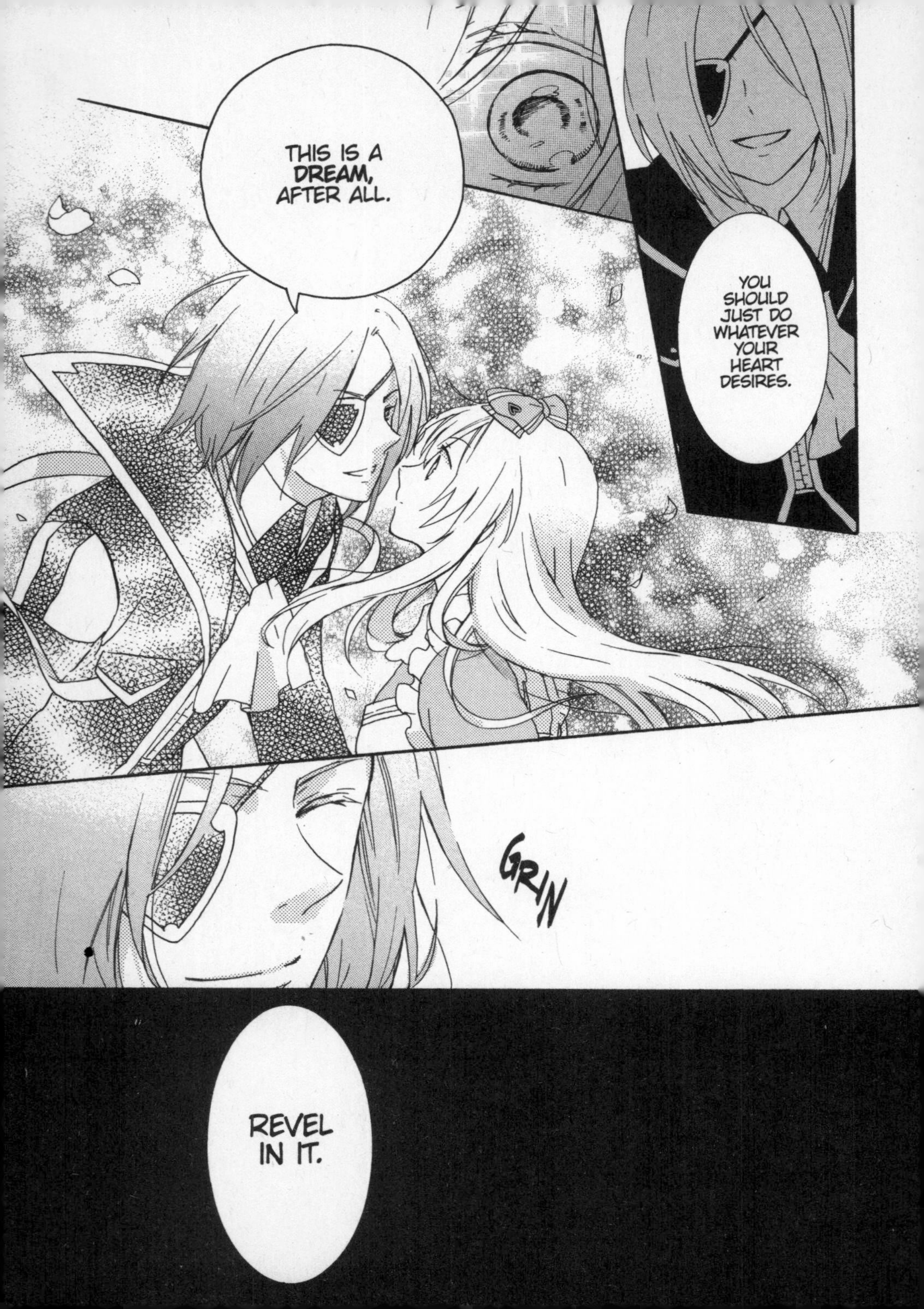
THIS IS A DREAM, AFTER ALL.
YOU SHOULD JUST DO WHATEVER YOUR HEART DESIRES.
GRIN
REVEL IN IT.

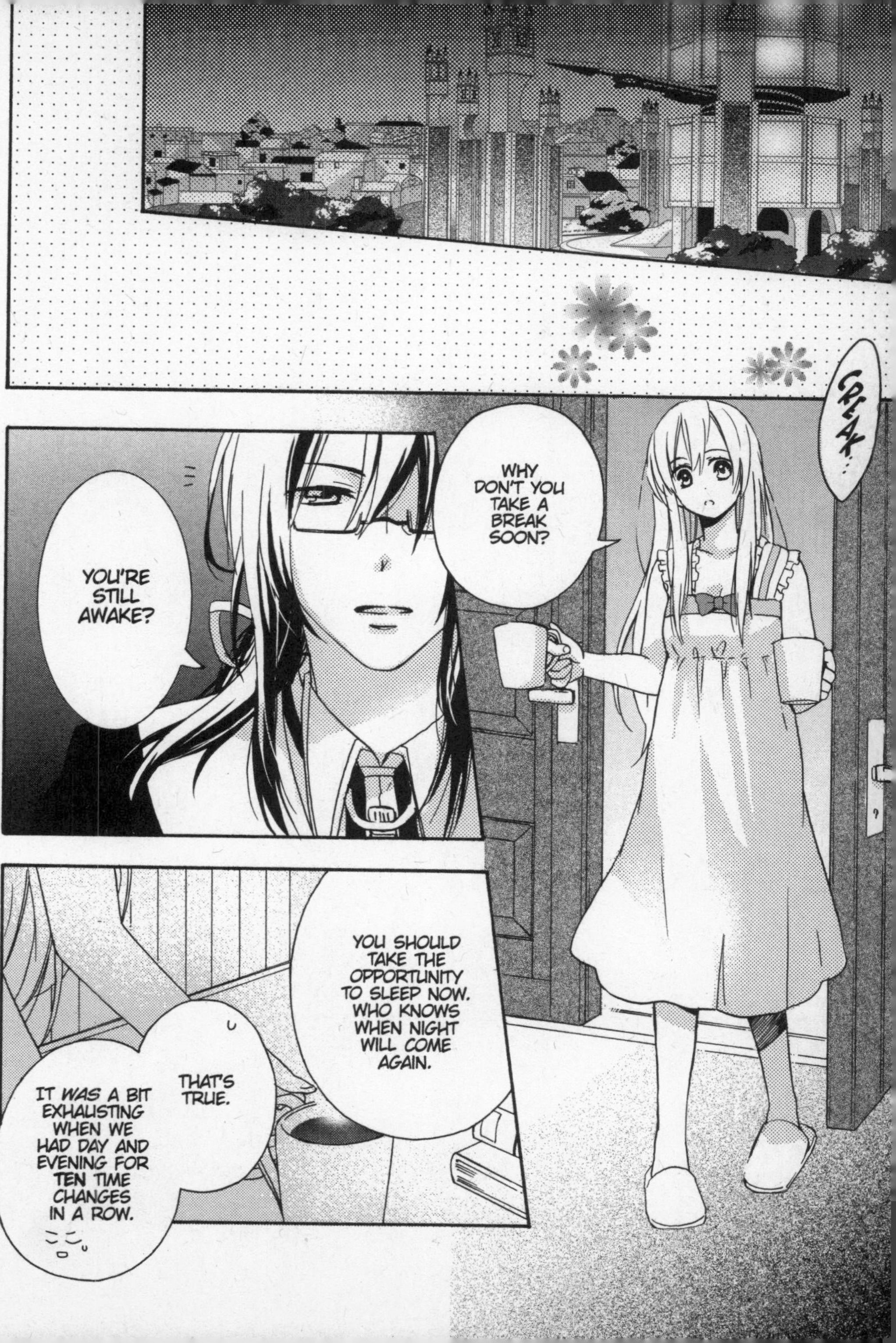
CREAK...
WHY DON'T YOU TAKE A BREAK SOON?
YOU'RE STILL AWAKE?
YOU SHOULD TAKE THE OPPORTUNITY TO SLEEP NOW. WHO KNOWS WHEN NIGHT WILL COME AGAIN.
THAT'S TRUE.
IT *WAS* A BIT EXHAUSTING WHEN WE HAD DAY AND EVENING FOR **TEN** TIME CHANGES IN A ROW.

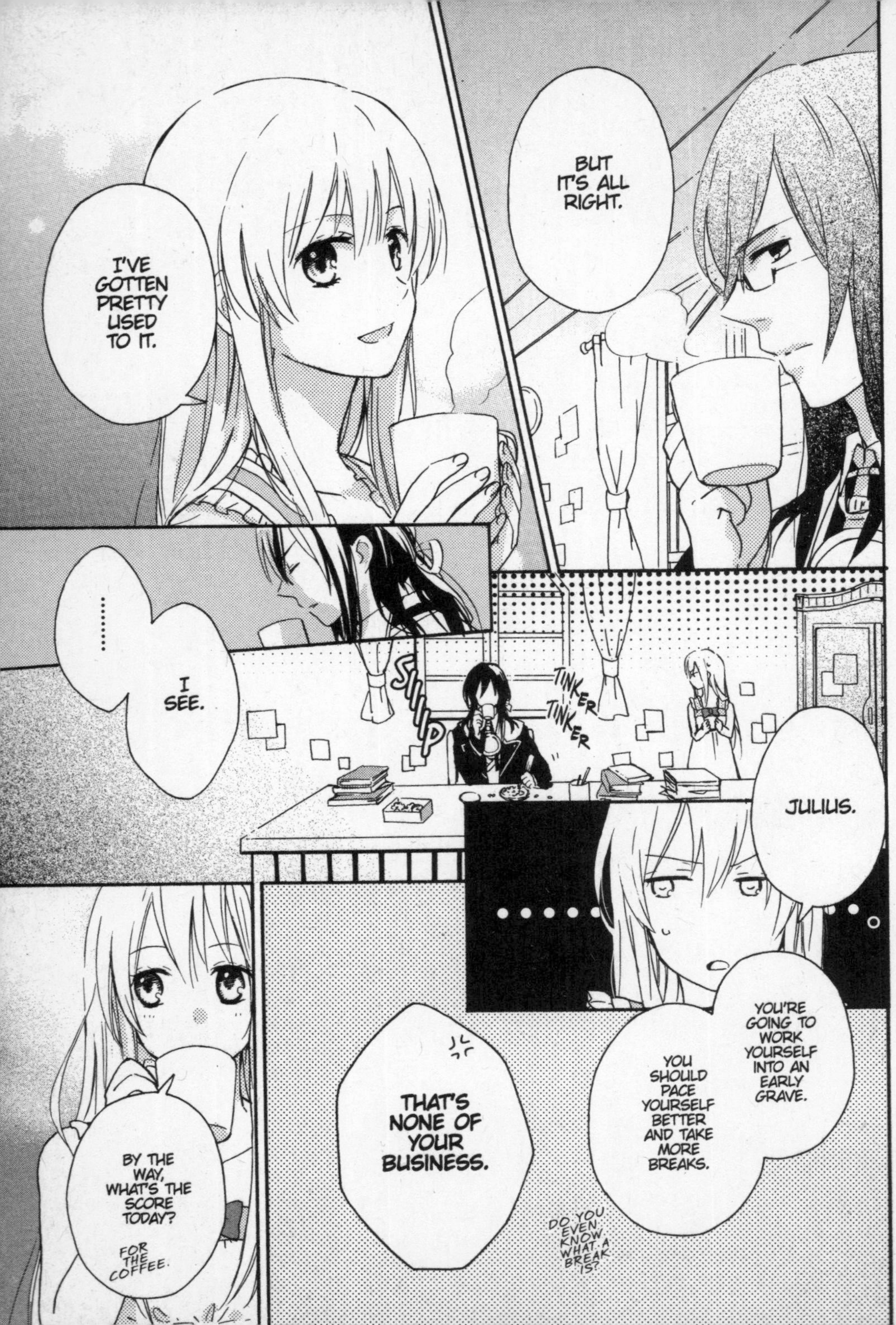
BUT IT'S ALL RIGHT.
I'VE GOTTEN PRETTY USED TO IT.
......
I SEE.
SLURP
TINKER TINKER
JULIUS.
YOU'RE GOING TO WORK YOURSELF INTO AN EARLY GRAVE.
YOU SHOULD PACE YOURSELF BETTER AND TAKE MORE BREAKS.
THAT'S NONE OF YOUR BUSINESS.
DO YOU EVEN KNOW WHAT A BREAK IS?
BY THE WAY, WHAT'S THE SCORE TODAY?
FOR THE COFFEE.

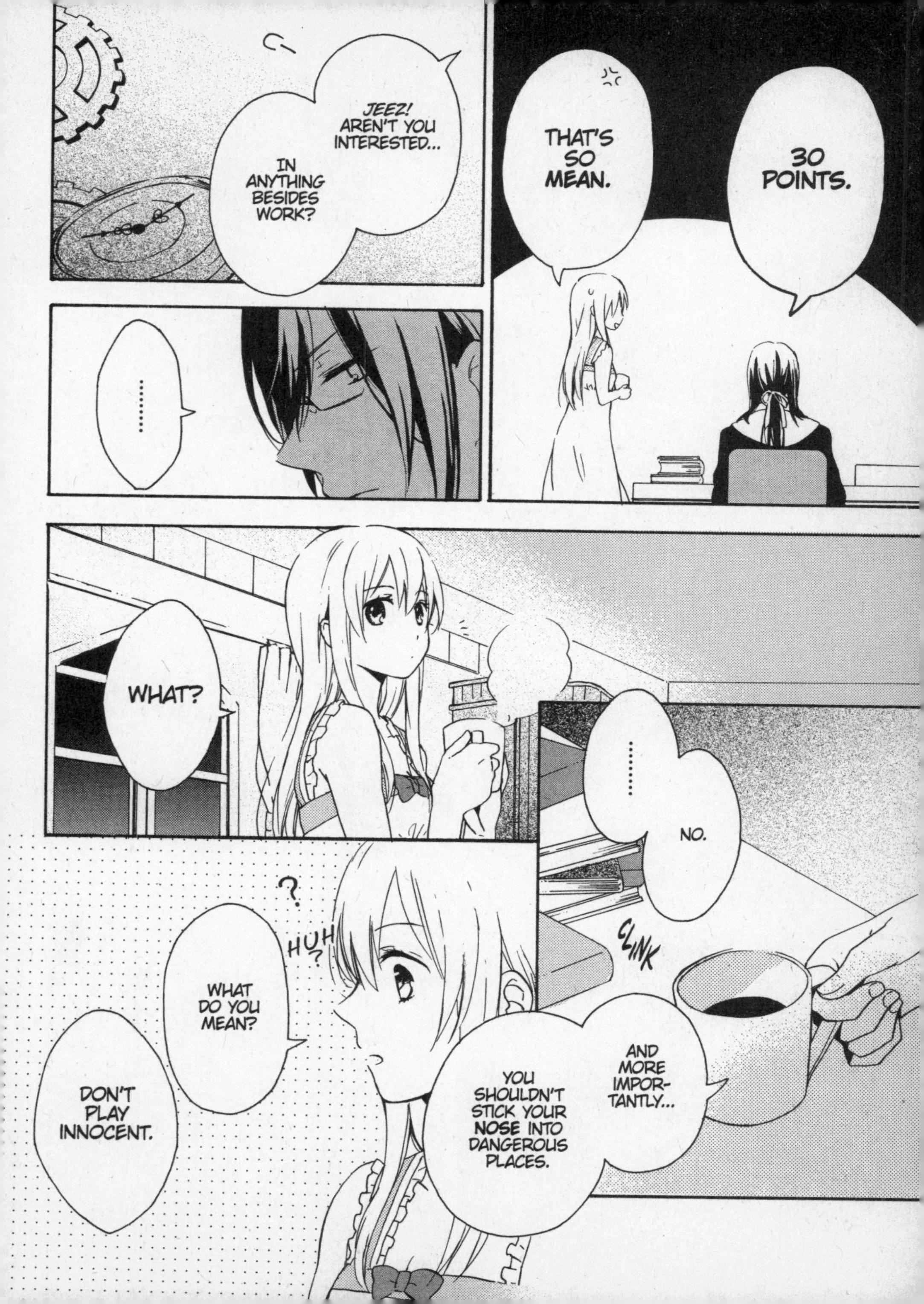
30 POINTS.
THAT'S SO MEAN.
JEEZ! AREN'T YOU INTERESTED...
IN ANYTHING BESIDES WORK?
......
WHAT?
......
NO.
CLINK
HUH?
WHAT DO YOU MEAN?
DON'T PLAY INNOCENT.
AND MORE IMPORTANTLY...
YOU SHOULDN'T STICK YOUR NOSE INTO DANGEROUS PLACES.

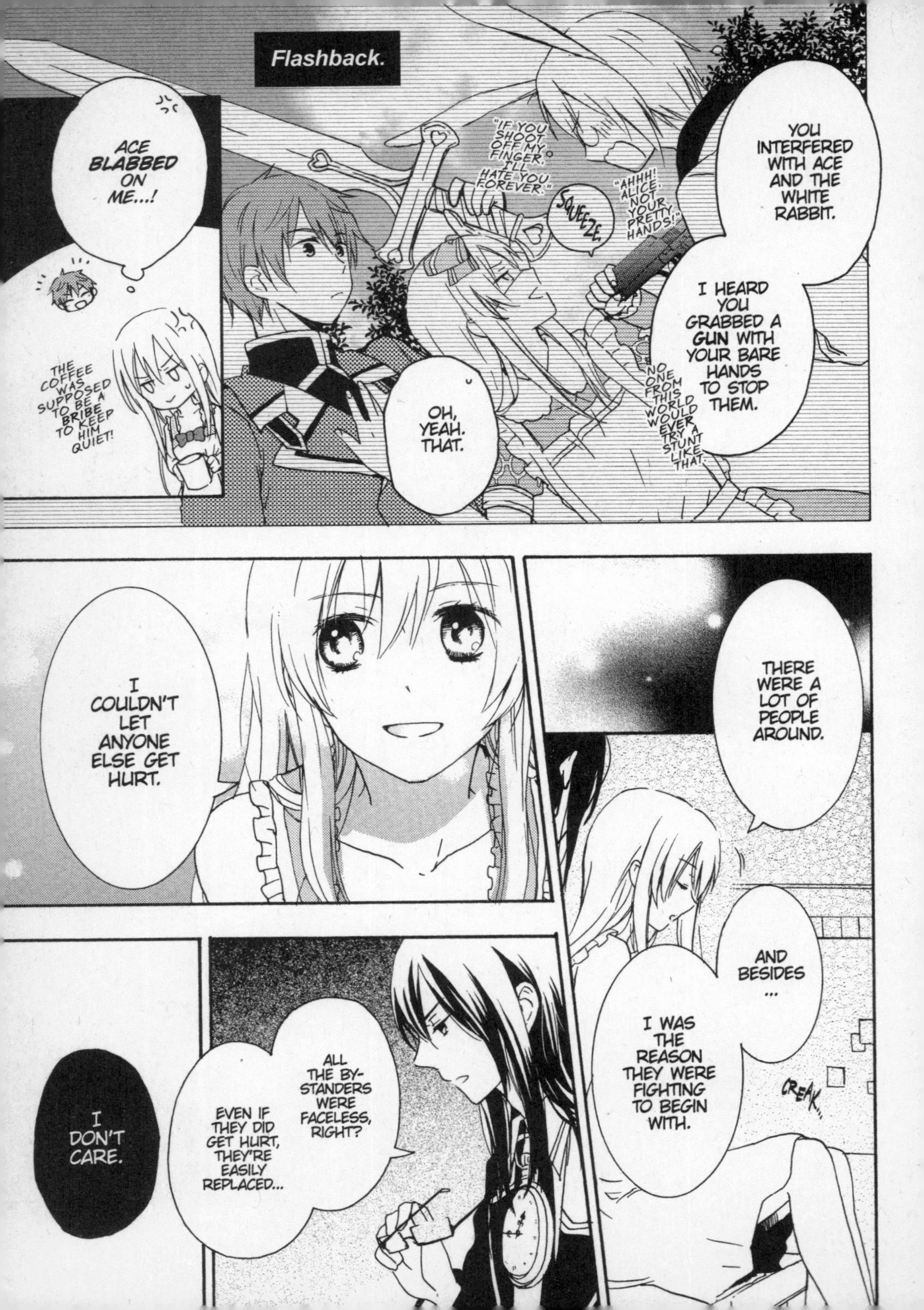
Flashback.
YOU INTERFERED WITH ACE AND THE WHITE RABBIT.
I HEARD YOU GRABBED A GUN WITH YOUR BARE HANDS TO STOP THEM.
NO ONE FROM THIS WORLD WOULD EVER TRY A STUNT LIKE THAT.
"AHHH! ALICE, NOT YOUR PRETTY HANDS!"
SQUEEZE.
"IF YOU SHOOT OFF MY FINGER, I'LL HATE YOU FOREVER."
OH, YEAH. THAT.
ACE BLABBED ON ME...!
THE COFFEE WAS SUPPOSED TO BE A BRIBE TO KEEP HIM QUIET!
THERE WERE A LOT OF PEOPLE AROUND.
AND BESIDES ...
I WAS THE REASON THEY WERE FIGHTING TO BEGIN WITH.
CREAK...
I COULDN'T LET ANYONE ELSE GET HURT.
ALL THE BY-STANDERS WERE FACELESS, RIGHT?
EVEN IF THEY DID GET HURT, THEY'RE EASILY REPLACED...
I DON'T CARE.

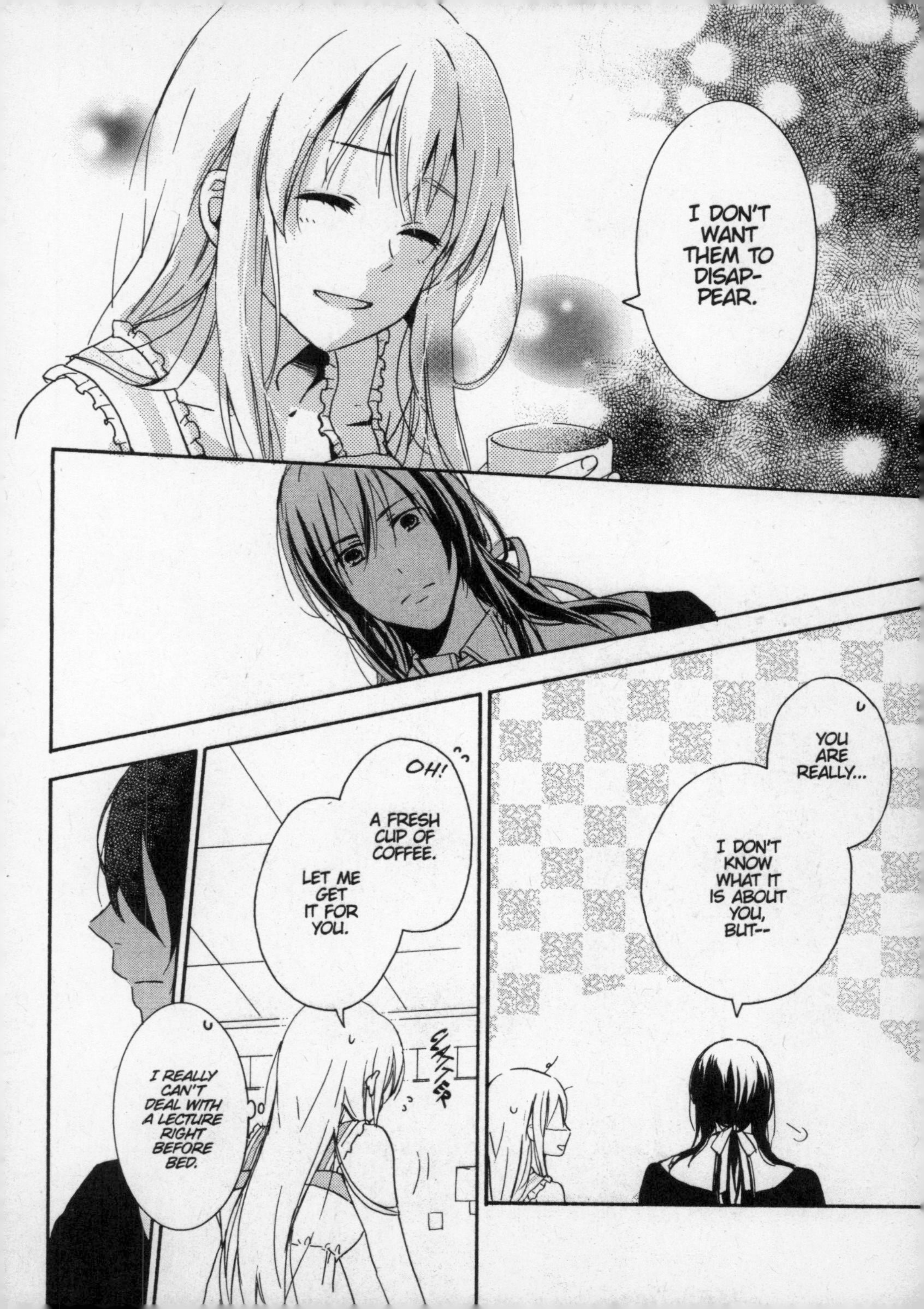
I DON'T WANT THEM TO DISAPPEAR.
YOU ARE REALLY...
I DON'T KNOW WHAT IT IS ABOUT YOU, BUT--
OH!
A FRESH CUP OF COFFEE.
LET ME GET IT FOR YOU.
CLATTER
I REALLY CAN'T DEAL WITH A LECTURE RIGHT BEFORE BED.

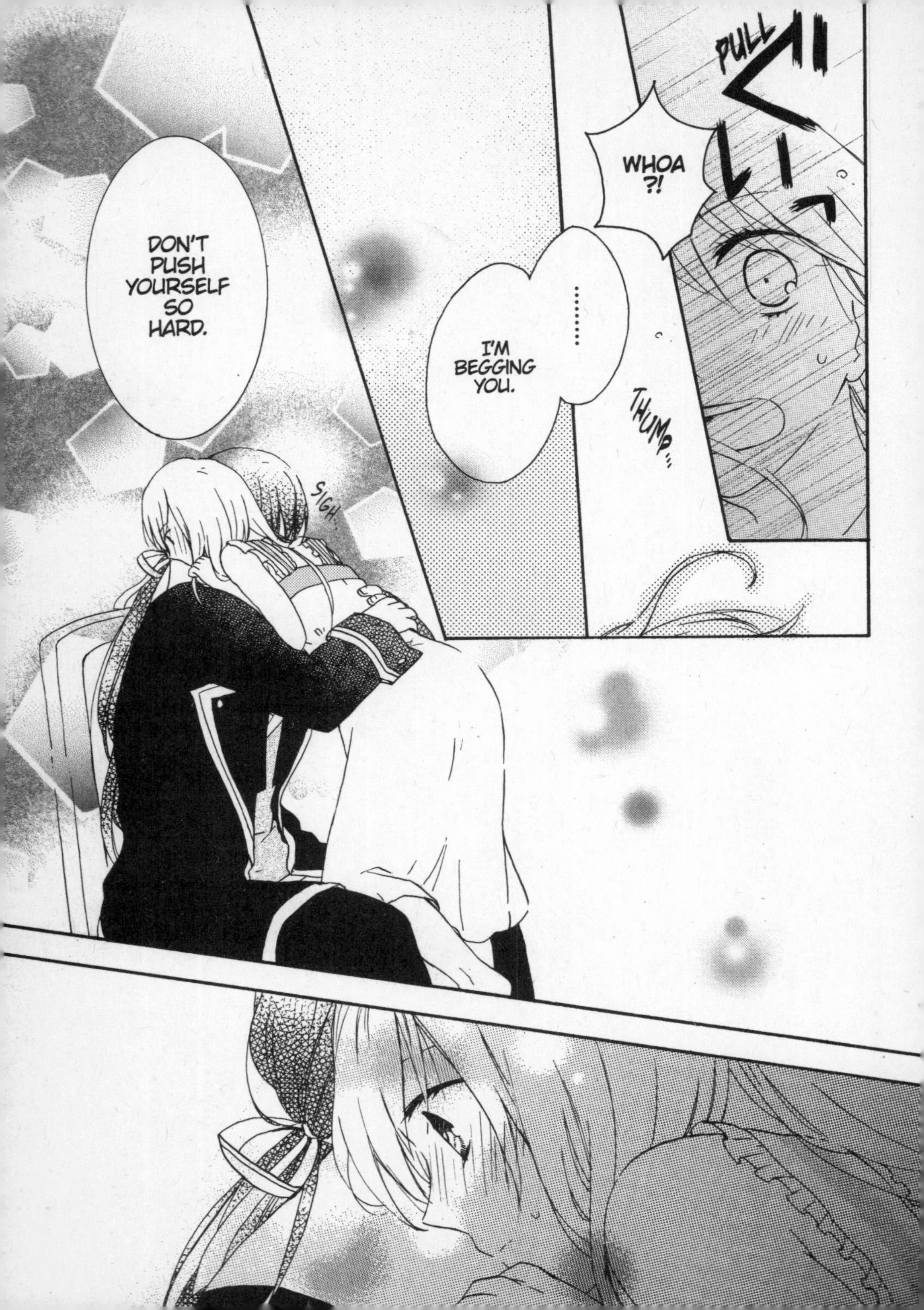
PULL
WHOA ?!
THUMP...
......
I'M BEGGING YOU.
DON'T PUSH YOURSELF SO HARD.
SIGH.

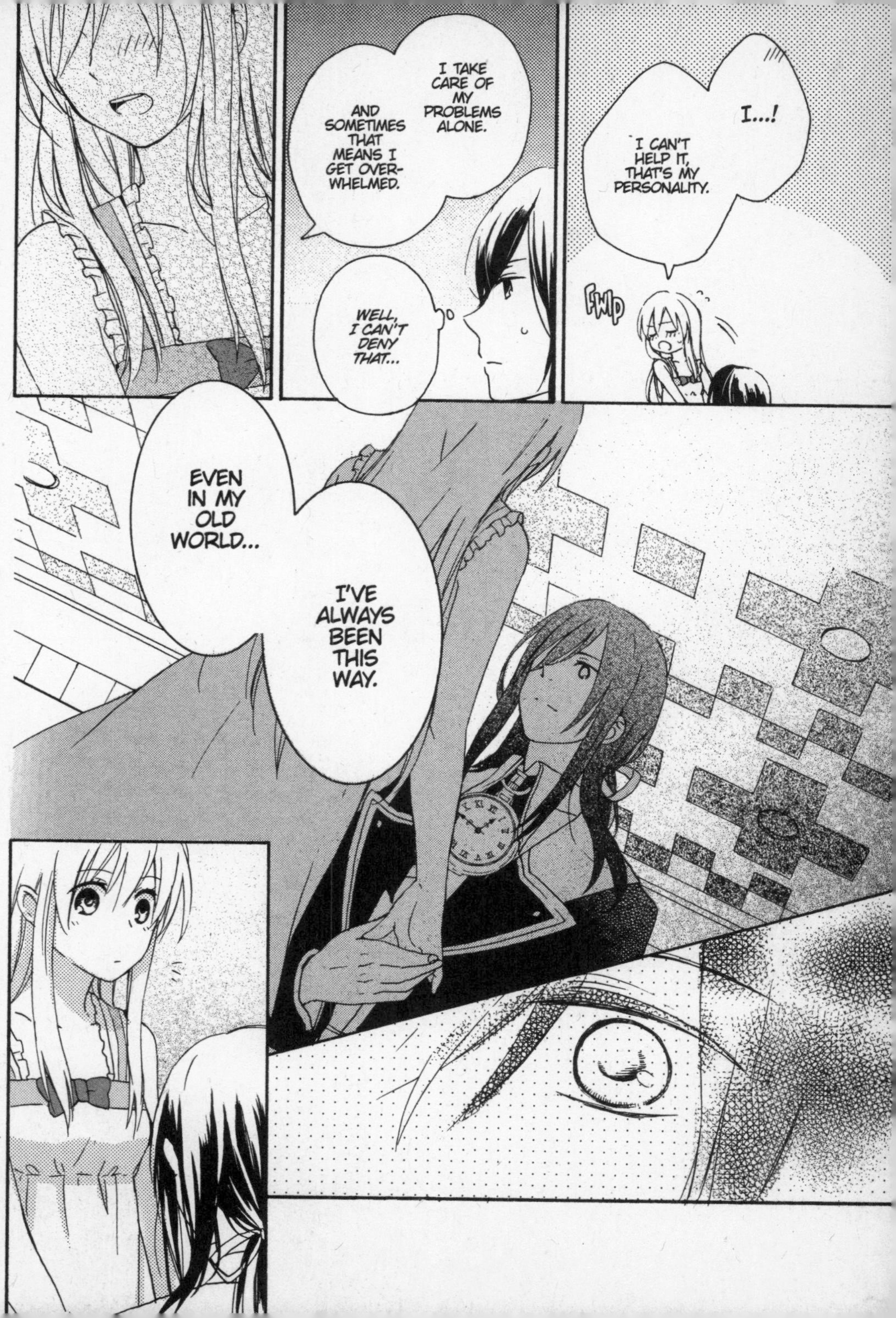
I...!
I CAN'T HELP IT, THAT'S MY PERSONALITY.
FWIP
I TAKE CARE OF MY PROBLEMS ALONE.
AND SOMETIMES THAT MEANS I GET OVER-WHELMED.
WELL, I CAN'T DENY THAT...
EVEN IN MY OLD WORLD...
I'VE ALWAYS BEEN THIS WAY.

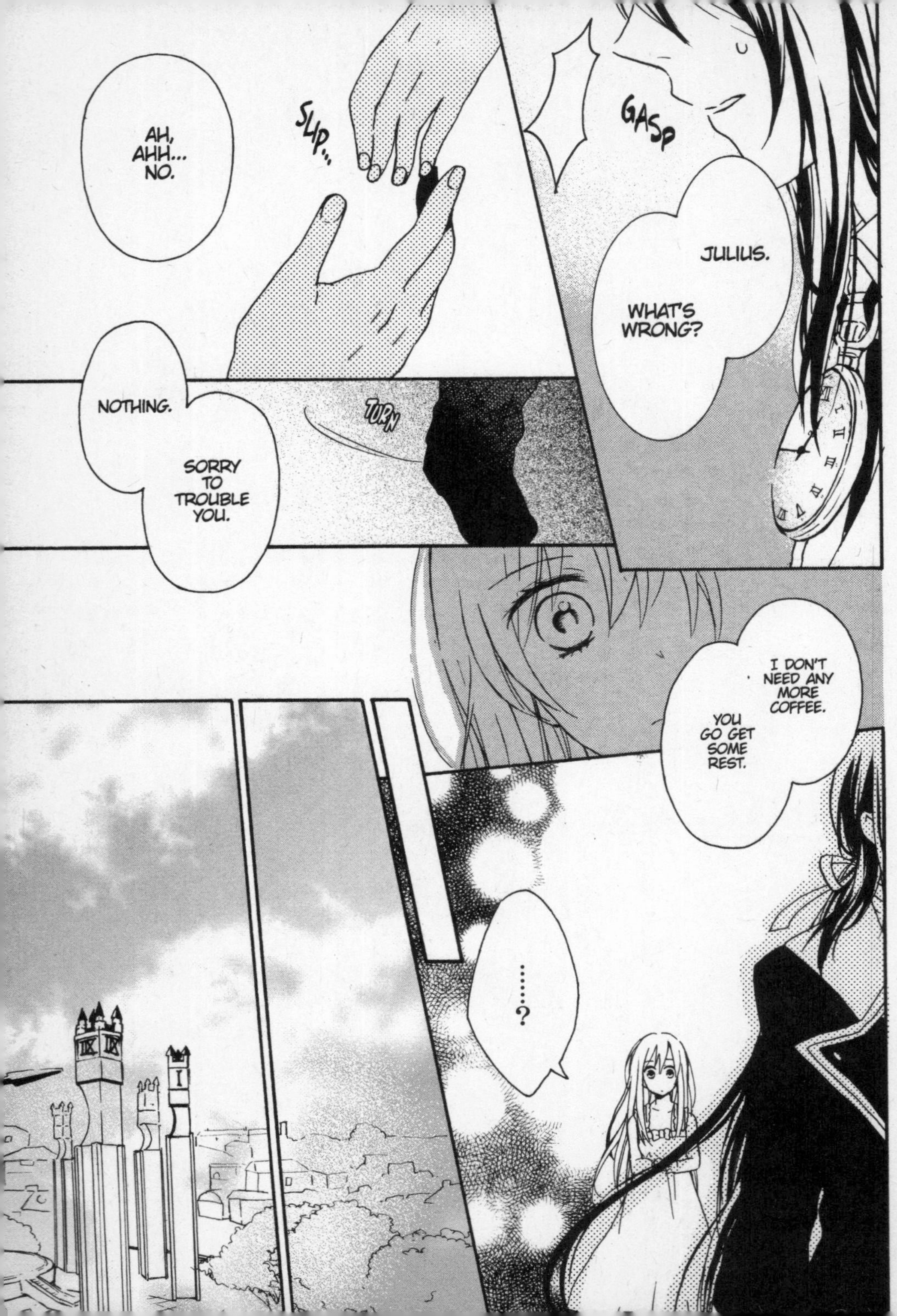
GASP
JULIUS.
WHAT'S WRONG?
SLIP...
AH, AHH... NO.
TURN
NOTHING.
SORRY TO TROUBLE YOU.
I DON'T NEED ANY MORE COFFEE.
YOU GO GET SOME REST.
......?

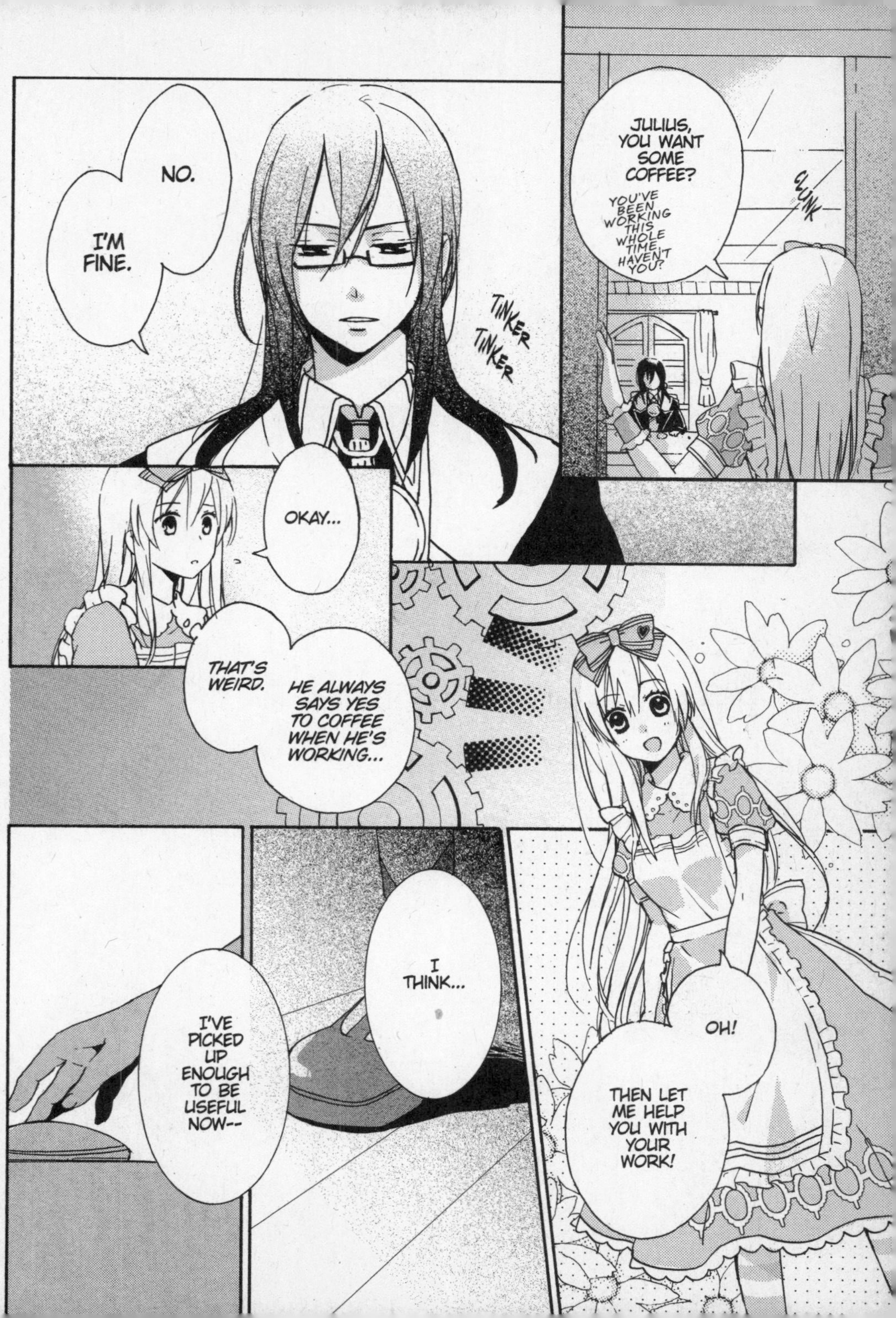
JULIUS, YOU WANT SOME COFFEE?
YOU'VE BEEN WORKING THIS WHOLE TIME, HAVEN'T YOU?
CLUNK
NO.
I'M FINE.
TINKER TINKER
OKAY...
THAT'S WEIRD.
HE ALWAYS SAYS YES TO COFFEE WHEN HE'S WORKING...
I THINK...
I'VE PICKED UP ENOUGH TO BE USEFUL NOW--
OH!
THEN LET ME HELP YOU WITH YOUR WORK!

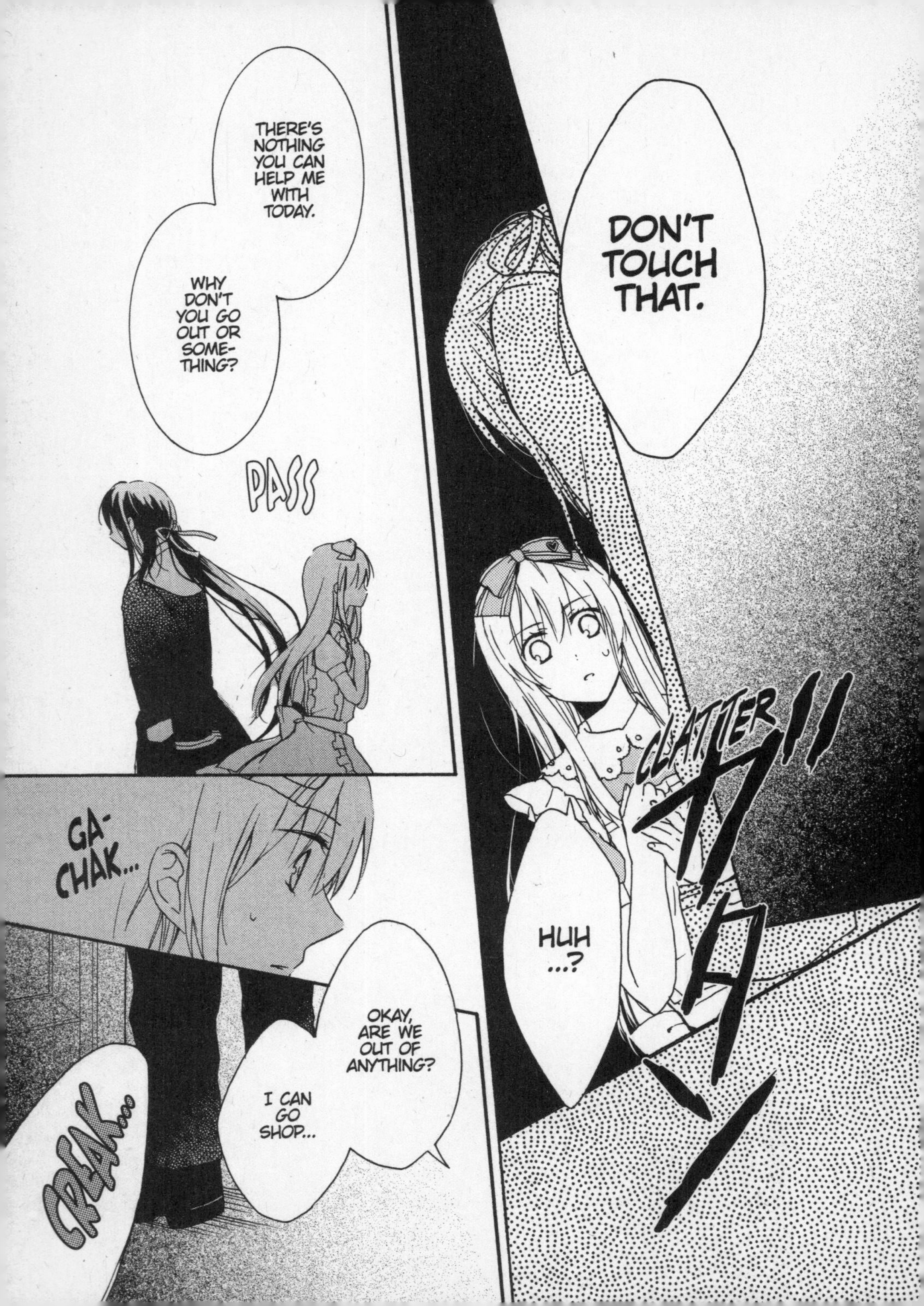
DON'T TOUCH THAT.
CLATTER!!
HUH ...?
THERE'S NOTHING YOU CAN HELP ME WITH TODAY.
WHY DON'T YOU GO OUT OR SOME-THING?
PASS
GA-CHAK...
OKAY, ARE WE OUT OF ANYTHING?
I CAN GO SHOP...
CREAK...

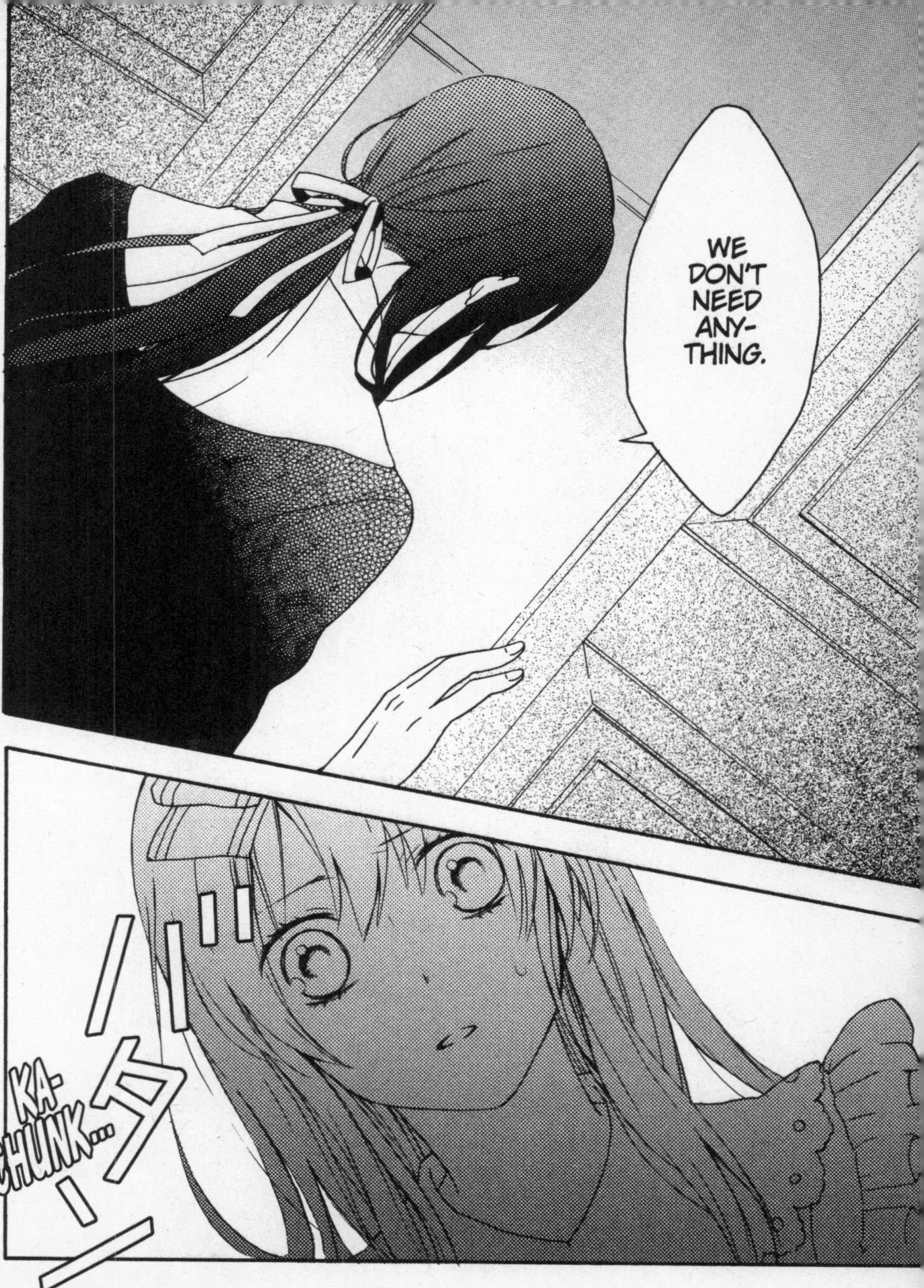
WE DON'T NEED ANY-THING.
KA-CHUNK...

ハートの国のアリス
恋する茨の迷宮

Alice IN THE COUNTRY OF Hearts

Love Labyrinth of Thorns

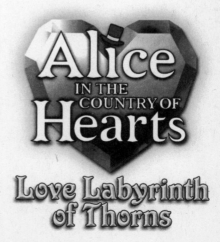

Chapter 2

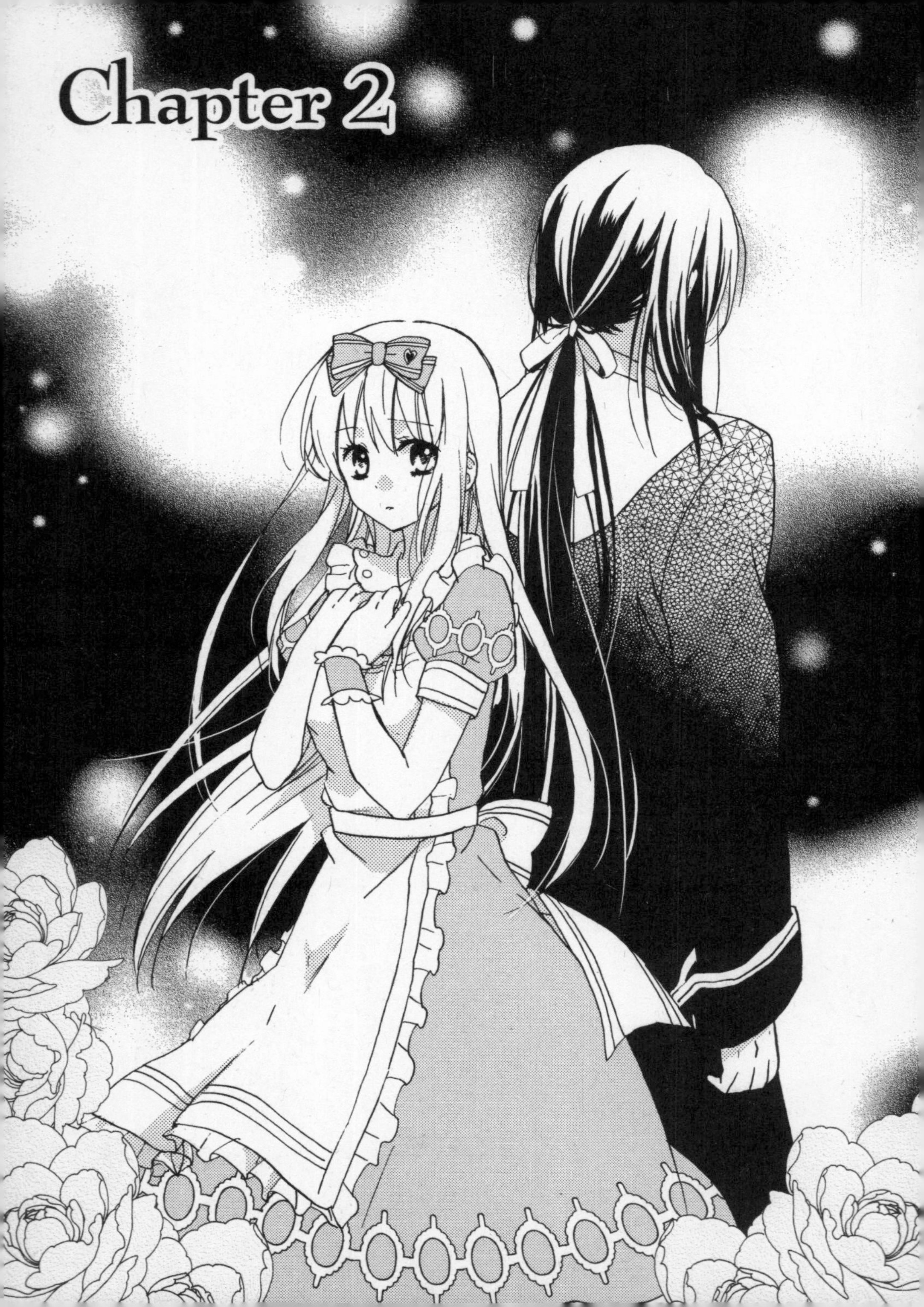

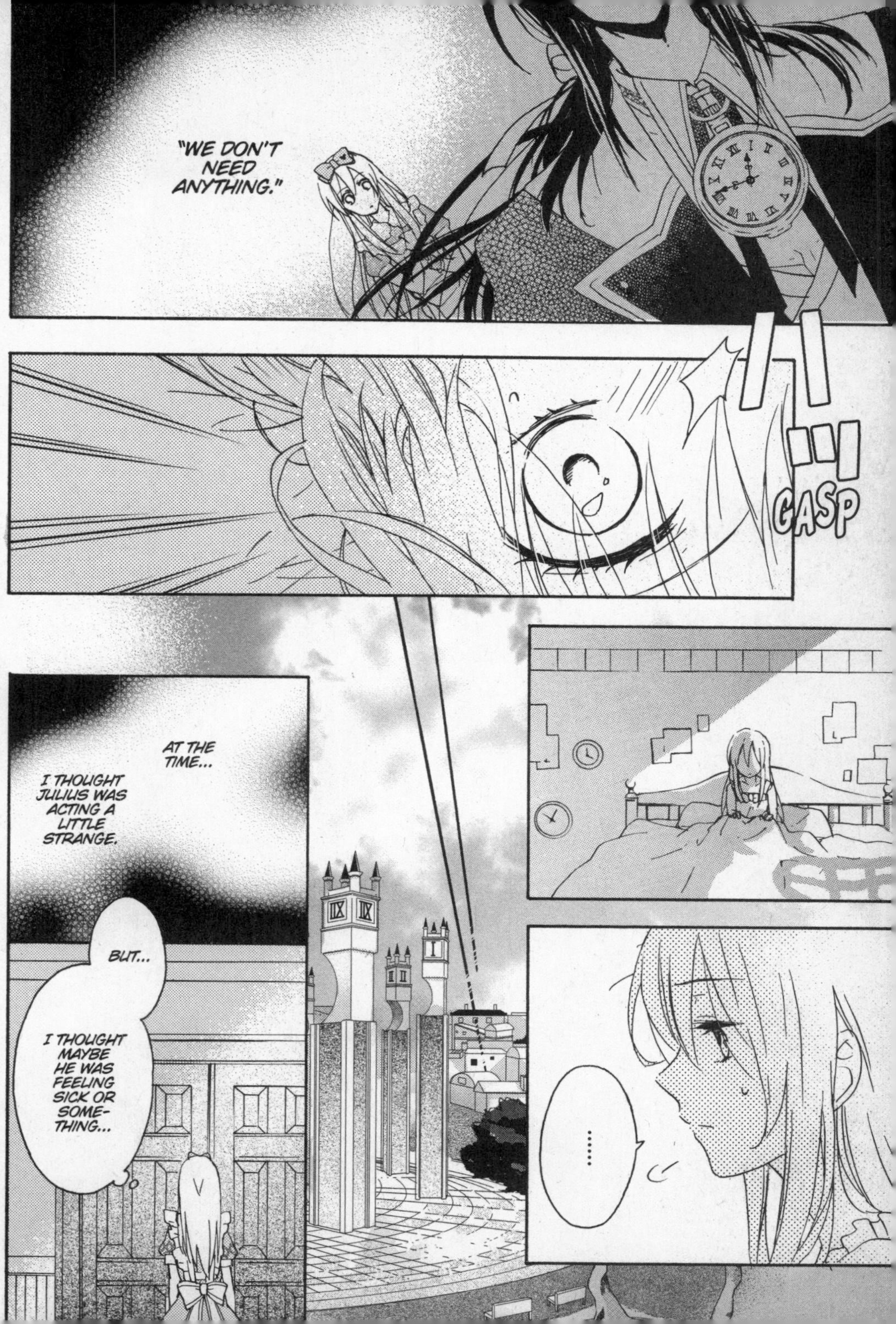
"WE DON'T NEED ANYTHING."
GASP
......
AT THE TIME...
I THOUGHT JULIUS WAS ACTING A LITTLE STRANGE.
BUT...
I THOUGHT MAYBE HE WAS FEELING SICK OR SOME-THING...

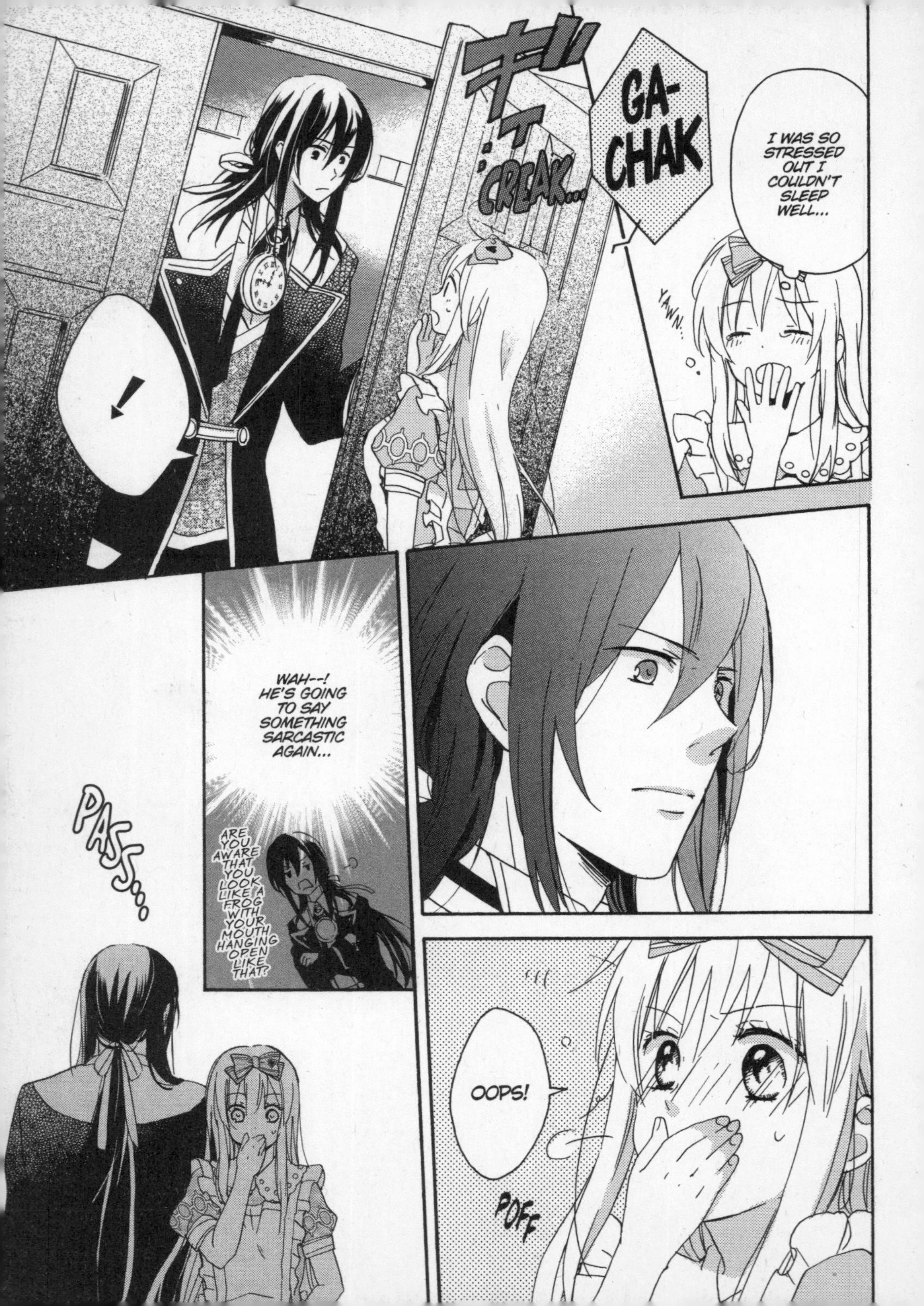
I WAS SO STRESSED OUT I COULDN'T SLEEP WELL...
YAWN...
GA-CHAK
CREAK...
!
WAH--! HE'S GOING TO SAY SOMETHING SARCASTIC AGAIN...
ARE YOU AWARE THAT YOU LOOK LIKE A FROG WITH YOUR MOUTH HANGING OPEN LIKE THAT?
OOPS!
POFF
PASS...

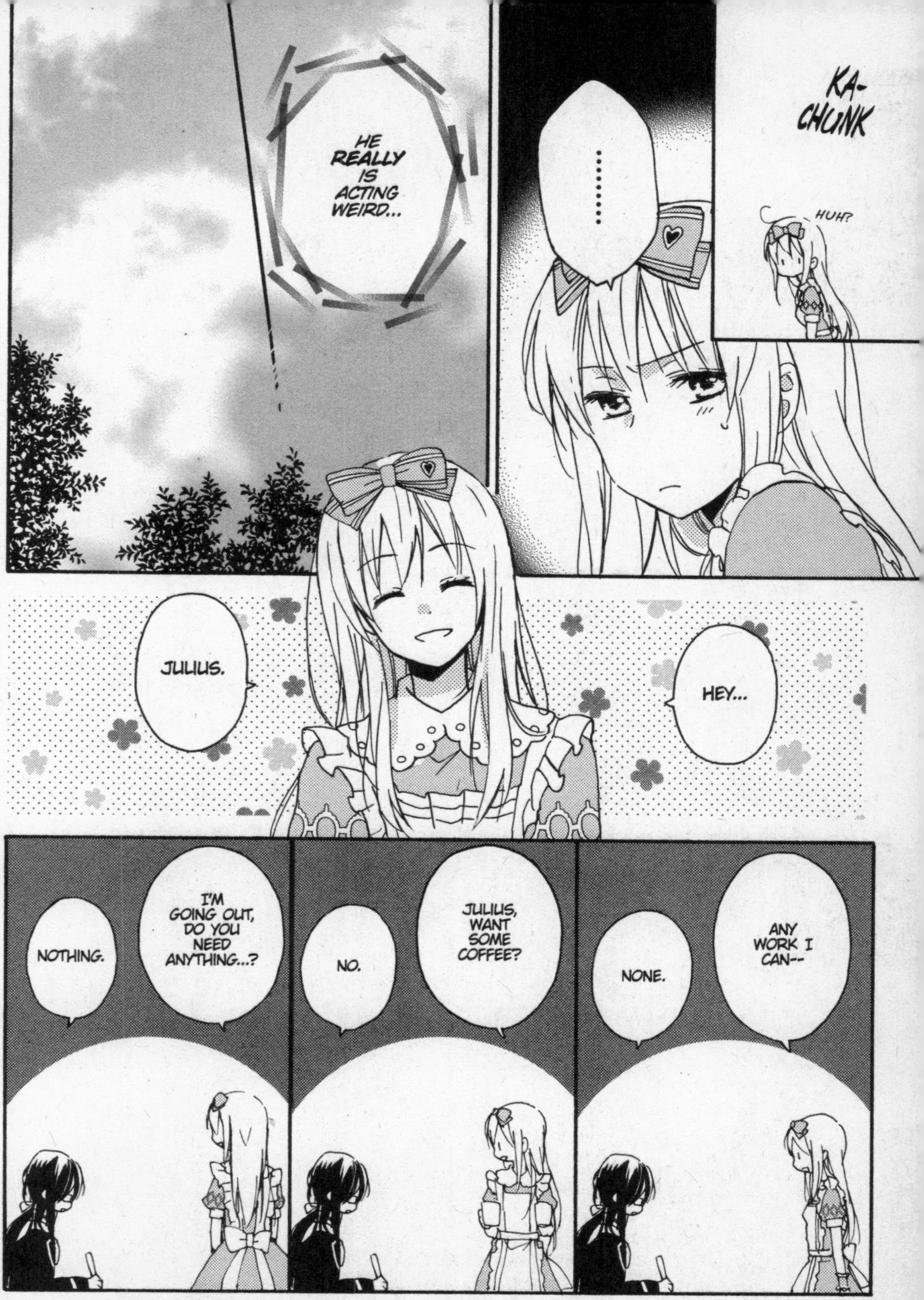
KA-CHUNK
HUH?
......
HE REALLY IS ACTING WEIRD...
HEY...
JULIUS.
ANY WORK I CAN--
NONE.
JULIUS, WANT SOME COFFEE?
NO.
I'M GOING OUT, DO YOU NEED ANYTHING...?
NOTHING.

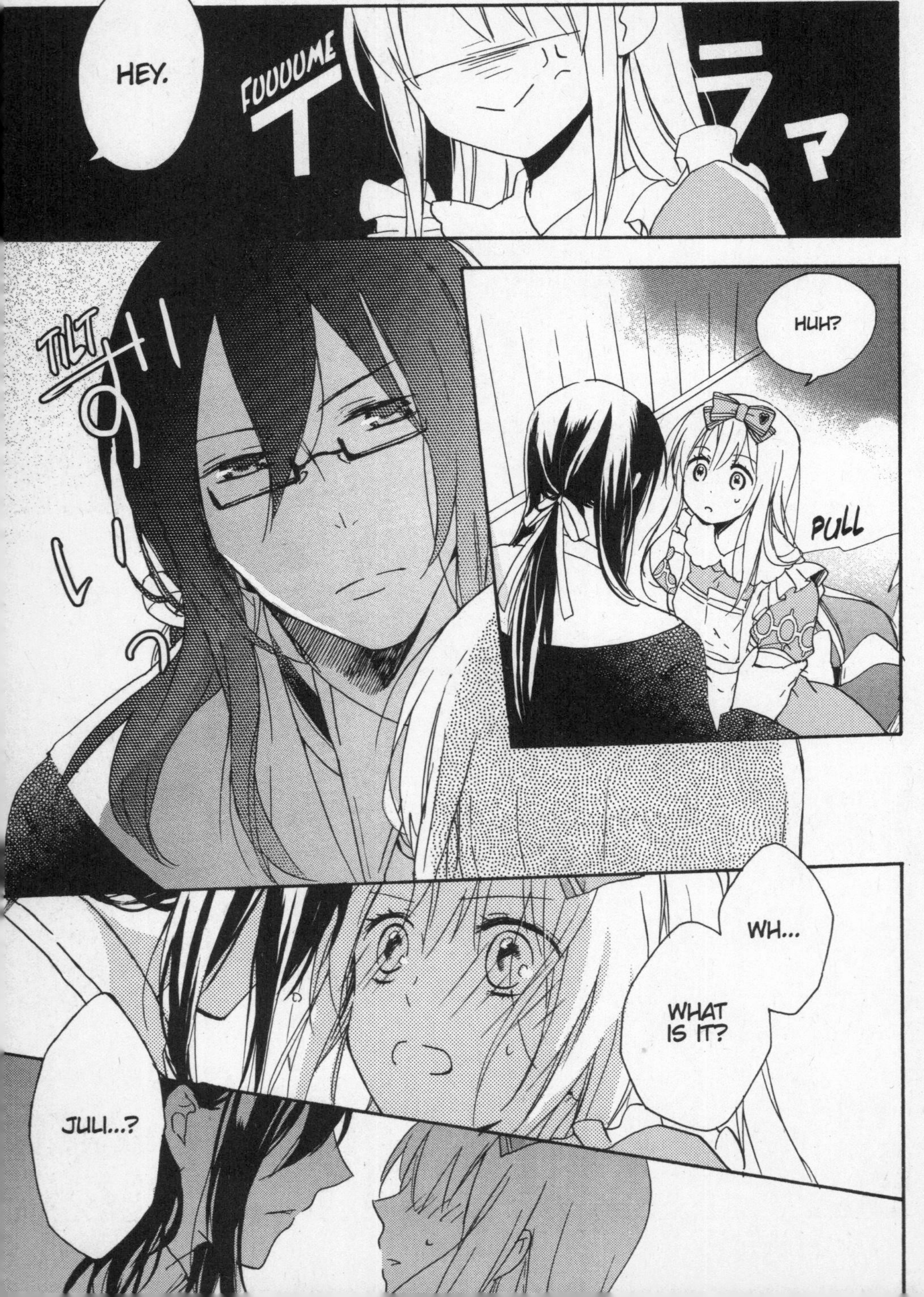
FUUUUME
HEY.
PULL
HUH?
TILT
WH...
WHAT IS IT?
JULI...?

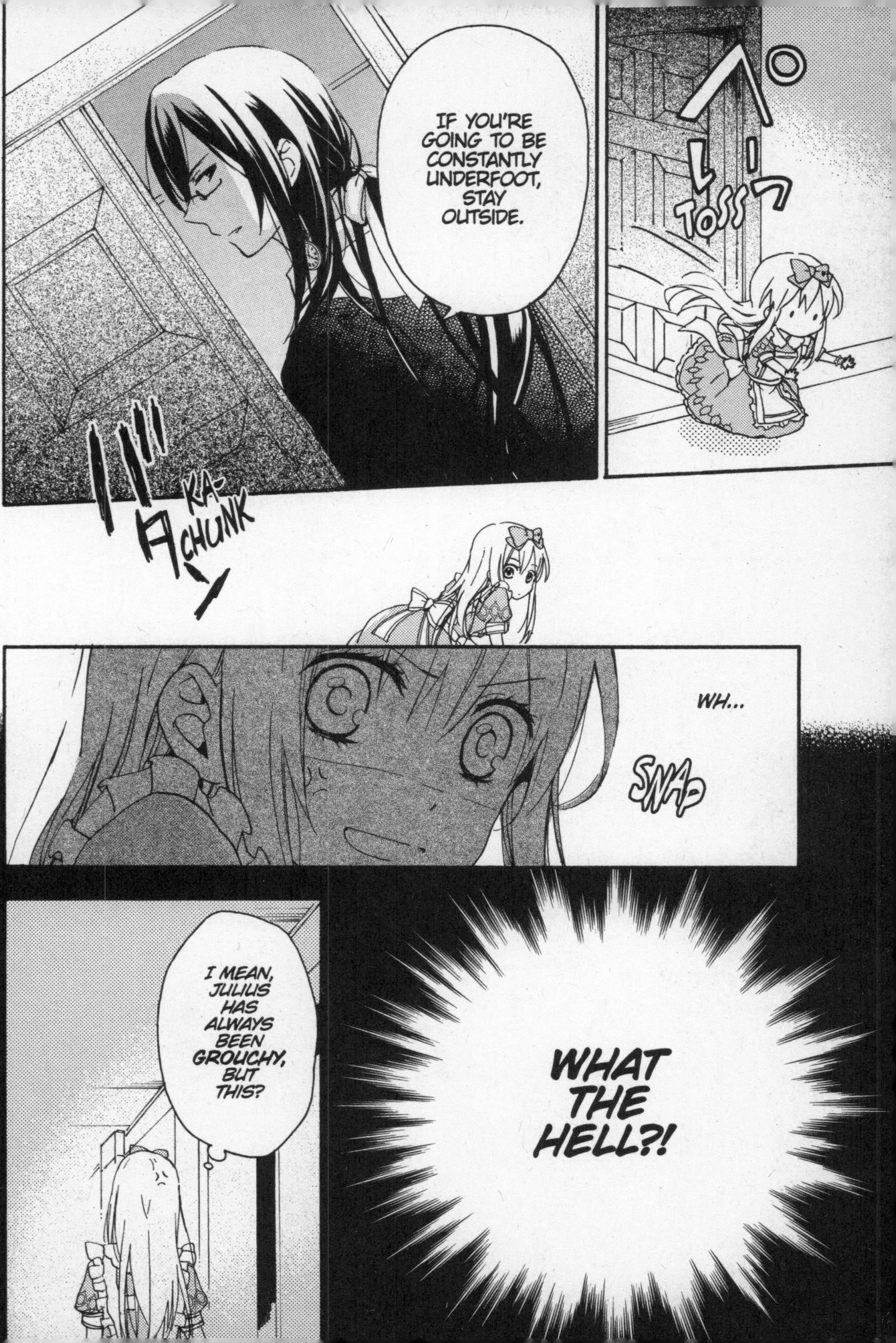
TOSS
IF YOU'RE GOING TO BE CONSTANTLY UNDERFOOT, STAY OUTSIDE.
KA-CHUNK
WH...
SNAP
WHAT THE HELL?!
I MEAN, JULIUS HAS ALWAYS BEEN GROUCHY, BUT THIS?

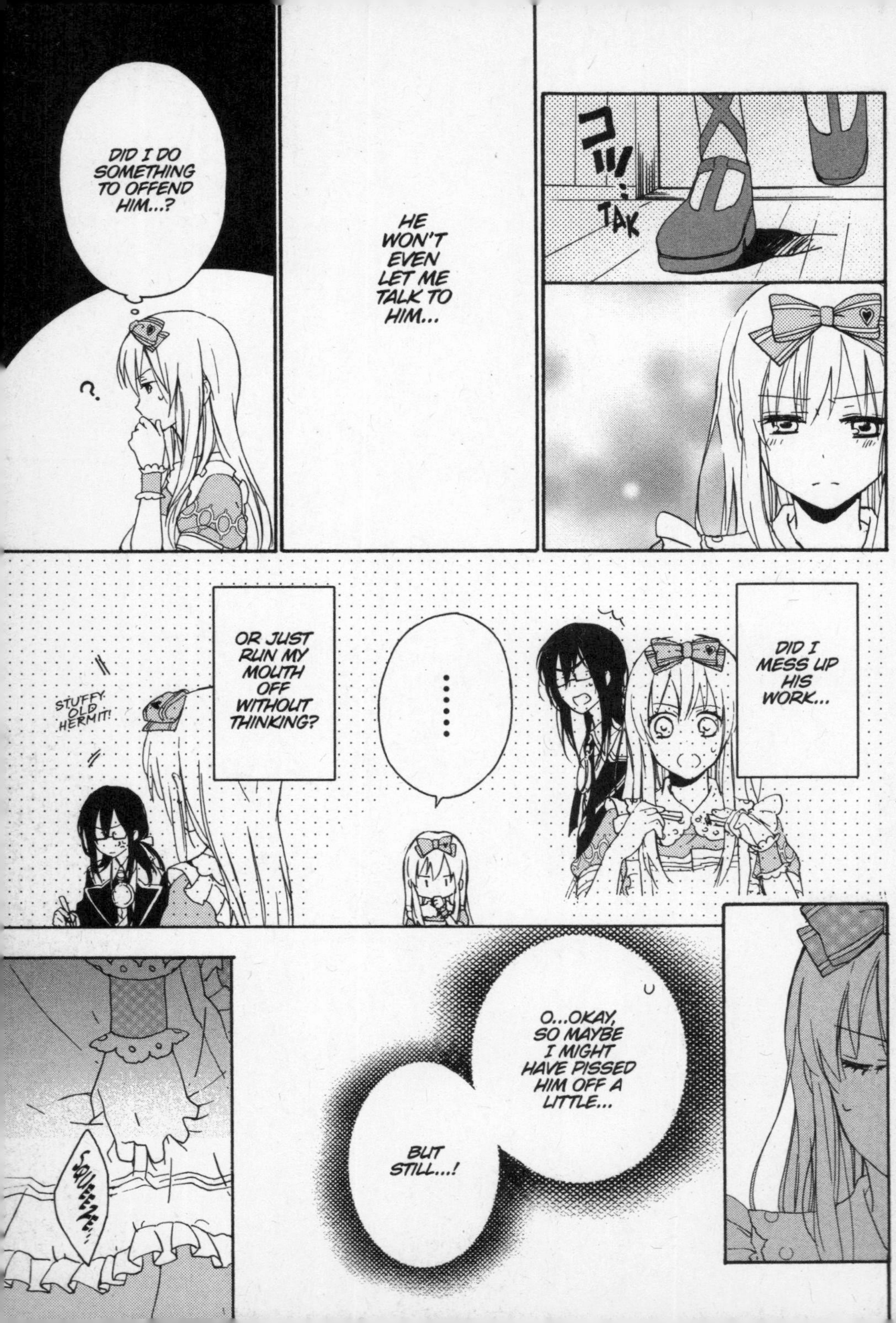
TAK
HE WON'T EVEN LET ME TALK TO HIM...
DID I DO SOMETHING TO OFFEND HIM...?
?
DID I MESS UP HIS WORK...
......
OR JUST RUN MY MOUTH OFF WITHOUT THINKING?
STUFFY OLD HERMIT!
O...OKAY, SO MAYBE I MIGHT HAVE PISSED HIM OFF A LITTLE...
BUT STILL...!
SQUEEEZE...

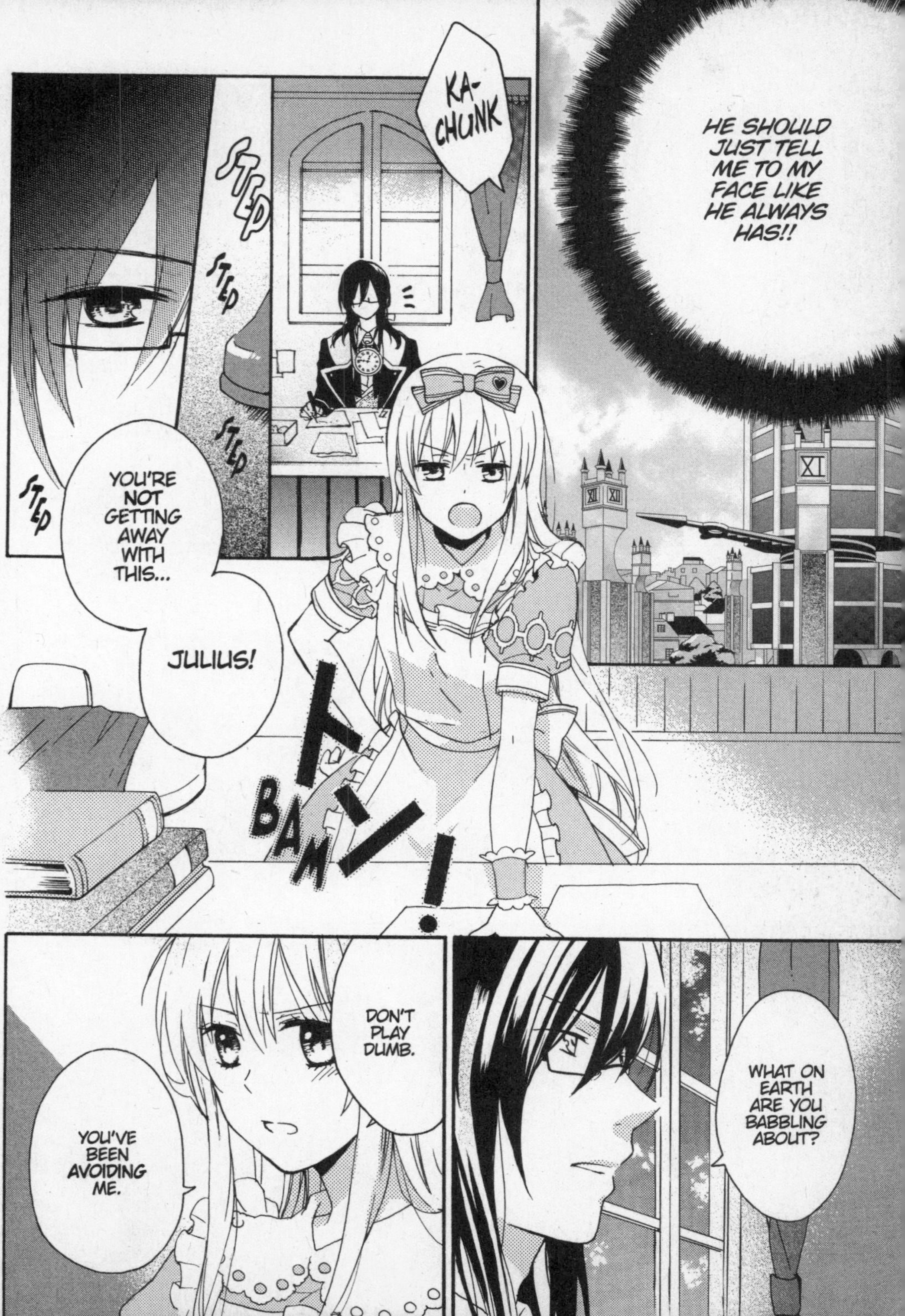
HE SHOULD JUST TELL ME TO MY FACE LIKE HE ALWAYS HAS!!
KA-CHUNK
STEP
STEP
STEP
STEP
YOU'RE NOT GETTING AWAY WITH THIS...
JULIUS!
BAM!
WHAT ON EARTH ARE YOU BABBLING ABOUT?
DON'T PLAY DUMB.
YOU'VE BEEN AVOIDING ME.

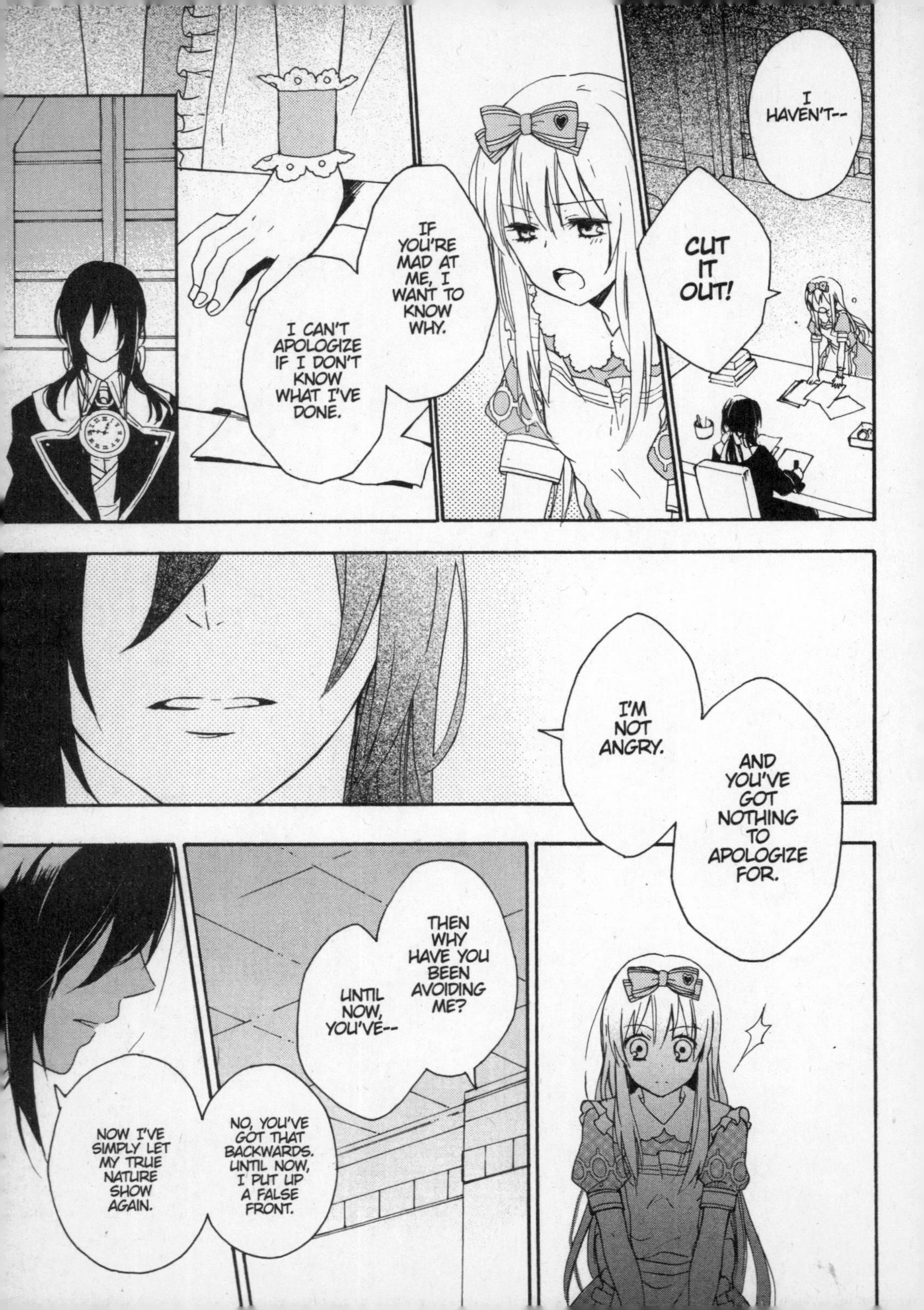
I HAVEN'T--
CUT IT OUT!
IF YOU'RE MAD AT ME, I WANT TO KNOW WHY.
I CAN'T APOLOGIZE IF I DON'T KNOW WHAT I'VE DONE.
I'M NOT ANGRY.
AND YOU'VE GOT NOTHING TO APOLOGIZE FOR.
THEN WHY HAVE YOU BEEN AVOIDING ME?
UNTIL NOW, YOU'VE--
NO, YOU'VE GOT THAT BACKWARDS. UNTIL NOW, I PUT UP A FALSE FRONT.
NOW I'VE SIMPLY LET MY TRUE NATURE SHOW AGAIN.

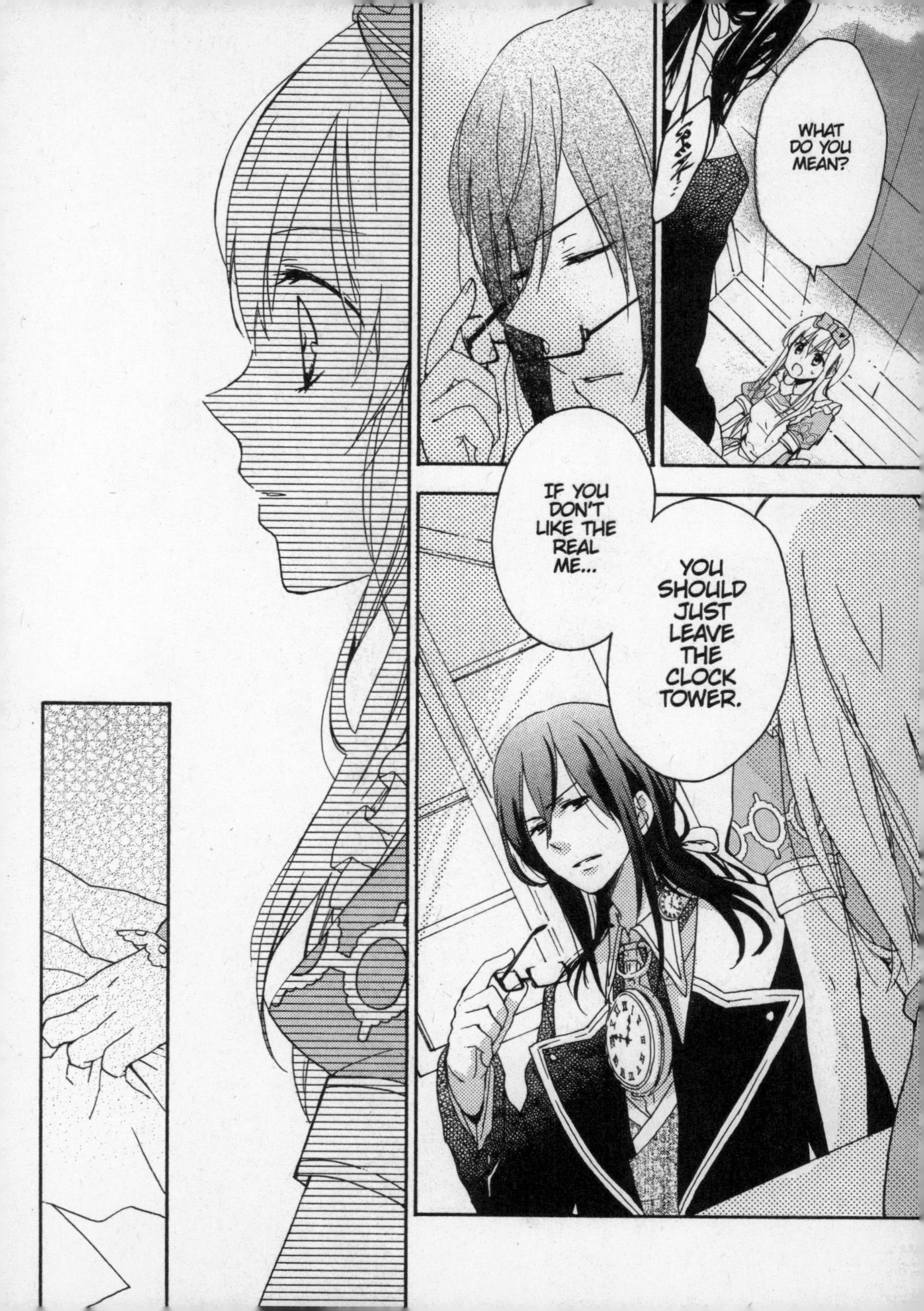
WHAT DO YOU MEAN?
CREAK...
IF YOU DON'T LIKE THE REAL ME...
YOU SHOULD JUST LEAVE THE CLOCK TOWER.

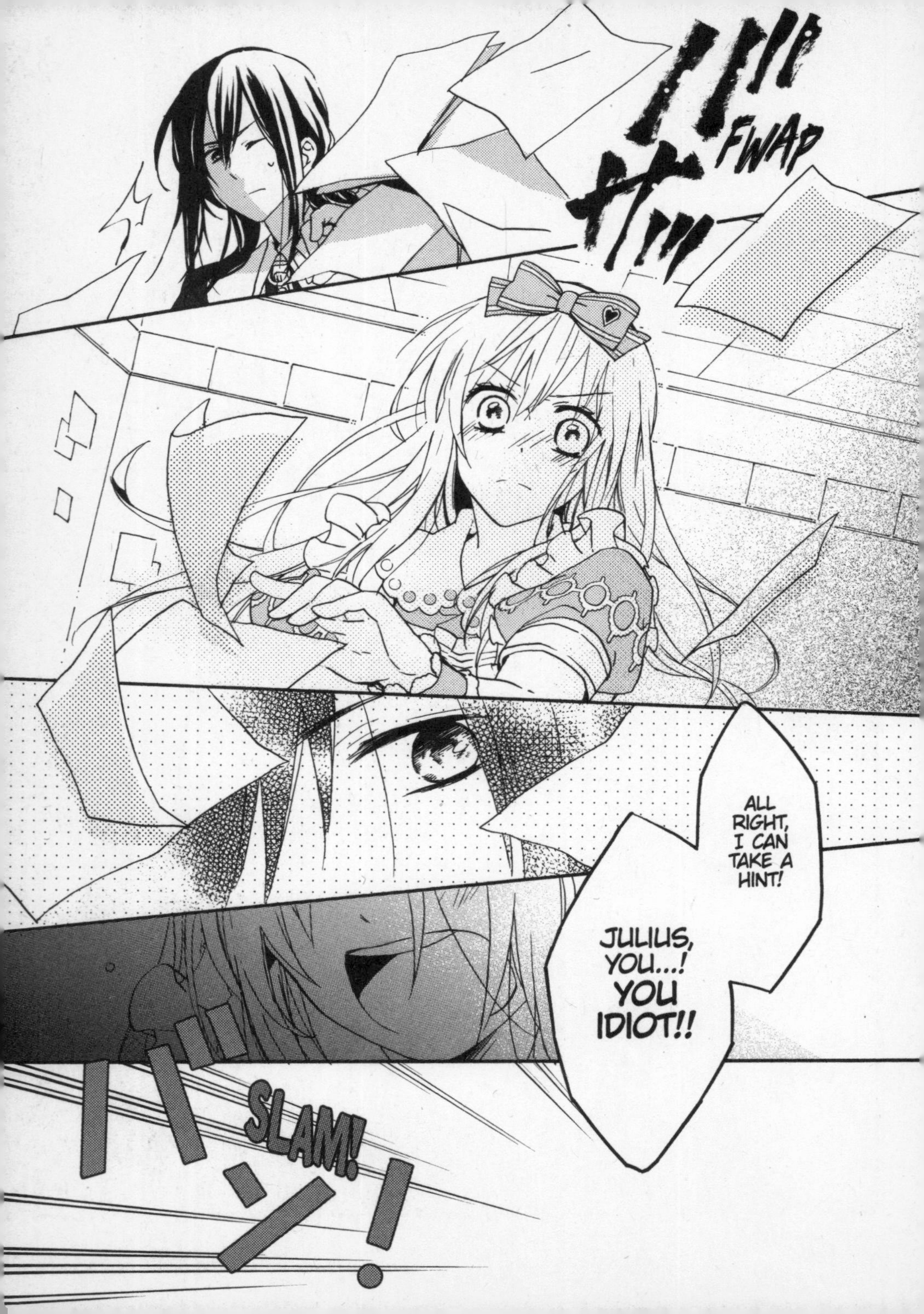
FWAP
ALL RIGHT, I CAN TAKE A HINT!
JULIUS, YOU...! YOU IDIOT!!
SLAM!

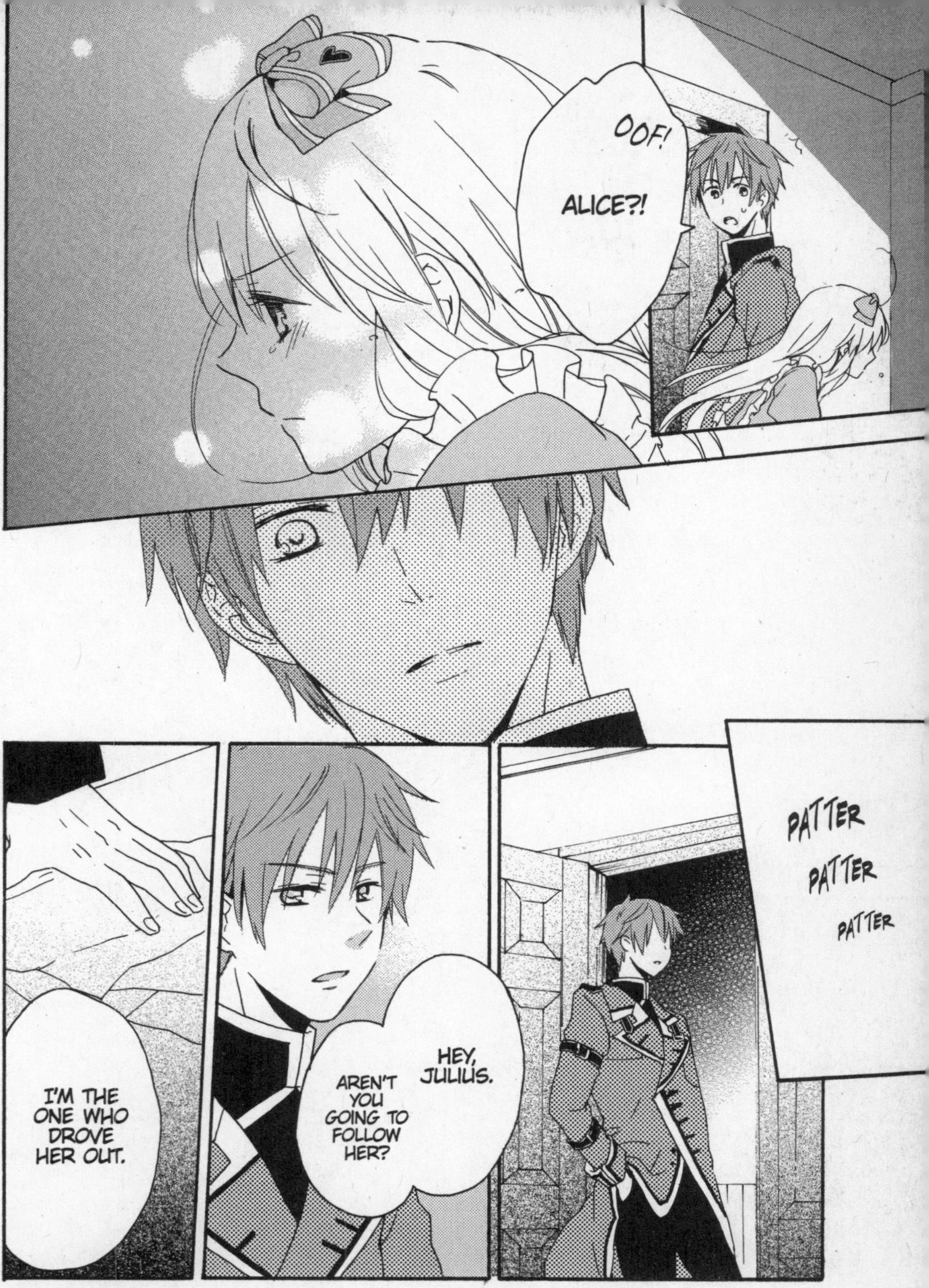
OOF!
ALICE?!
PATTER
PATTER
PATTER
HEY, JULIUS.
AREN'T YOU GOING TO FOLLOW HER?
I'M THE ONE WHO DROVE HER OUT.

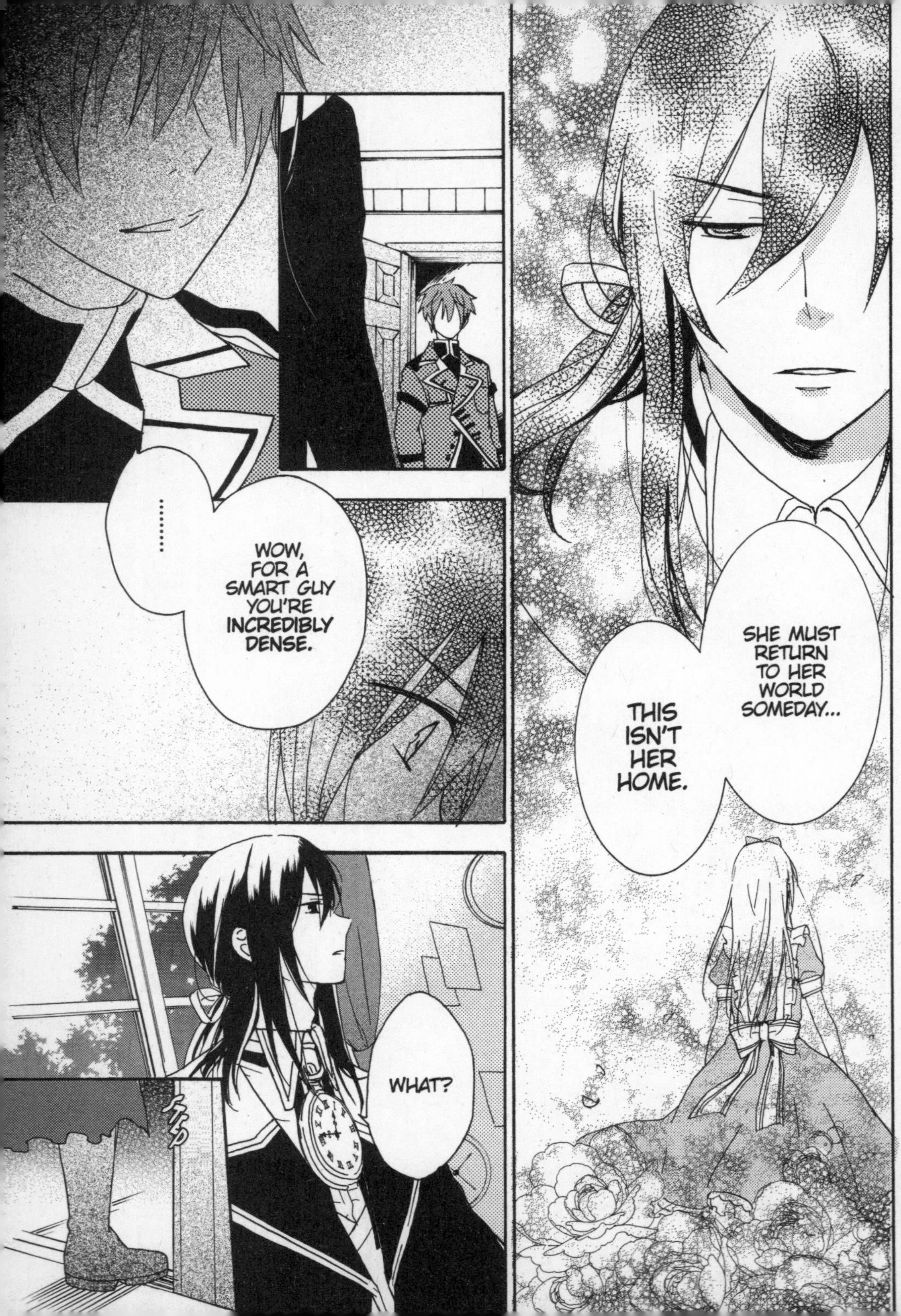
SHE MUST RETURN TO HER WORLD SOMEDAY...
THIS ISN'T HER HOME.
......
WOW, FOR A SMART GUY YOU'RE INCREDIBLY DENSE.
WHAT?

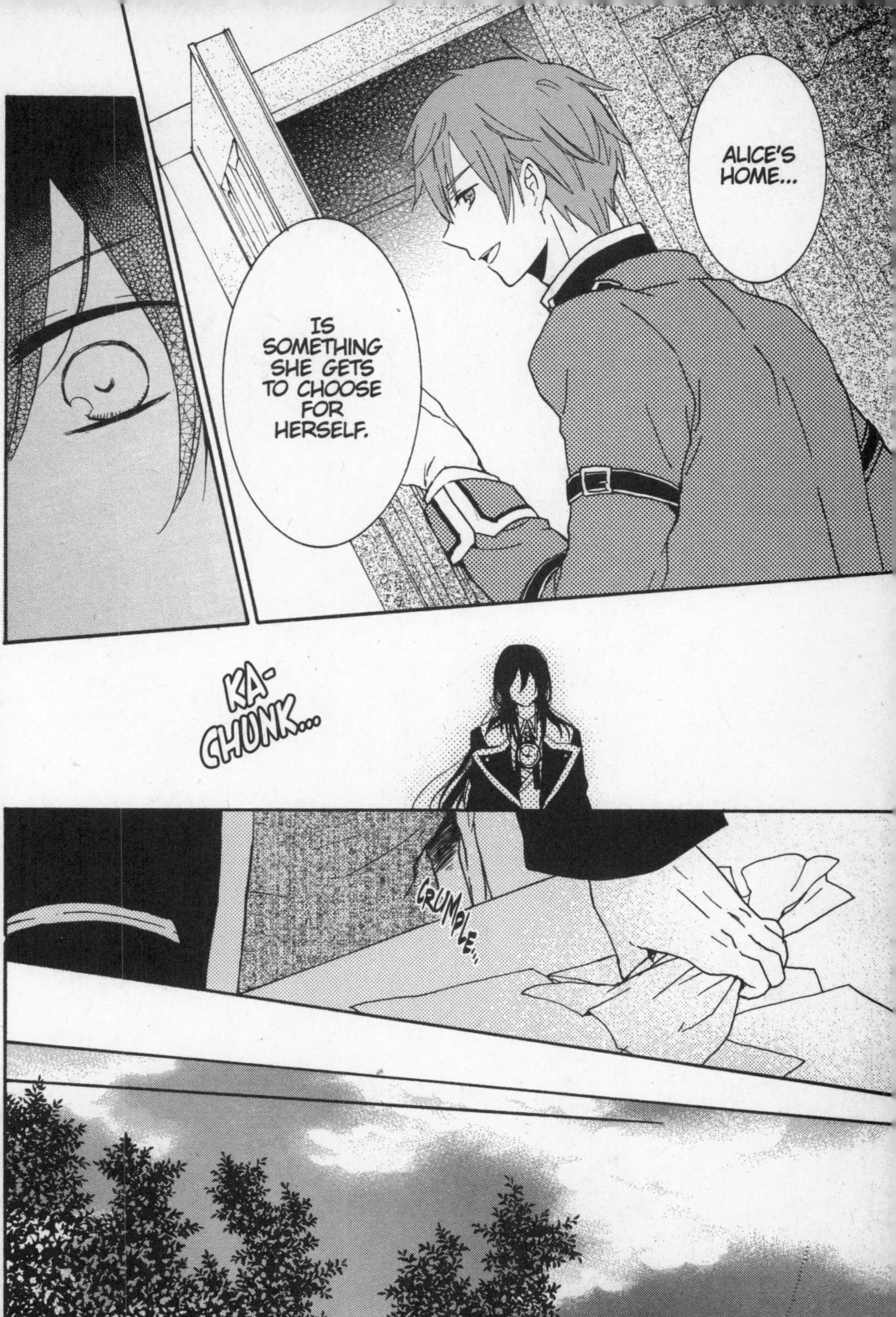
ALICE'S HOME...
IS SOMETHING SHE GETS TO CHOOSE FOR HERSELF.
KA-CHUNK...
CRUMPLE...

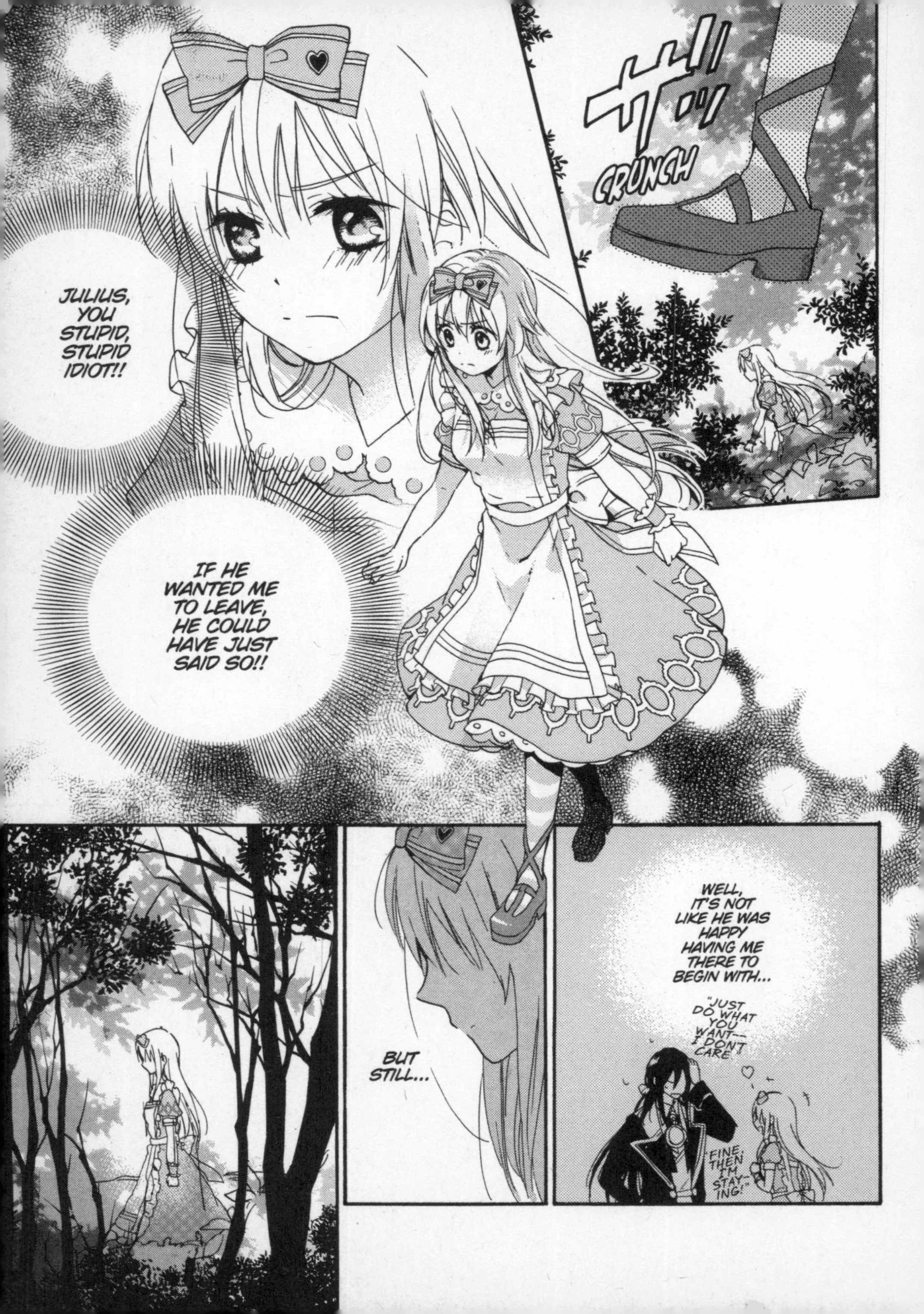
CRUNCH
JULIUS, YOU STUPID, STUPID IDIOT!!
IF HE WANTED ME TO LEAVE, HE COULD HAVE JUST SAID SO!!
WELL, IT'S NOT LIKE HE WAS HAPPY HAVING ME THERE TO BEGIN WITH...
"JUST DO WHAT YOU WANT— I DON'T CARE."
"FINE, THEN I'M STAYING!"
BUT STILL...

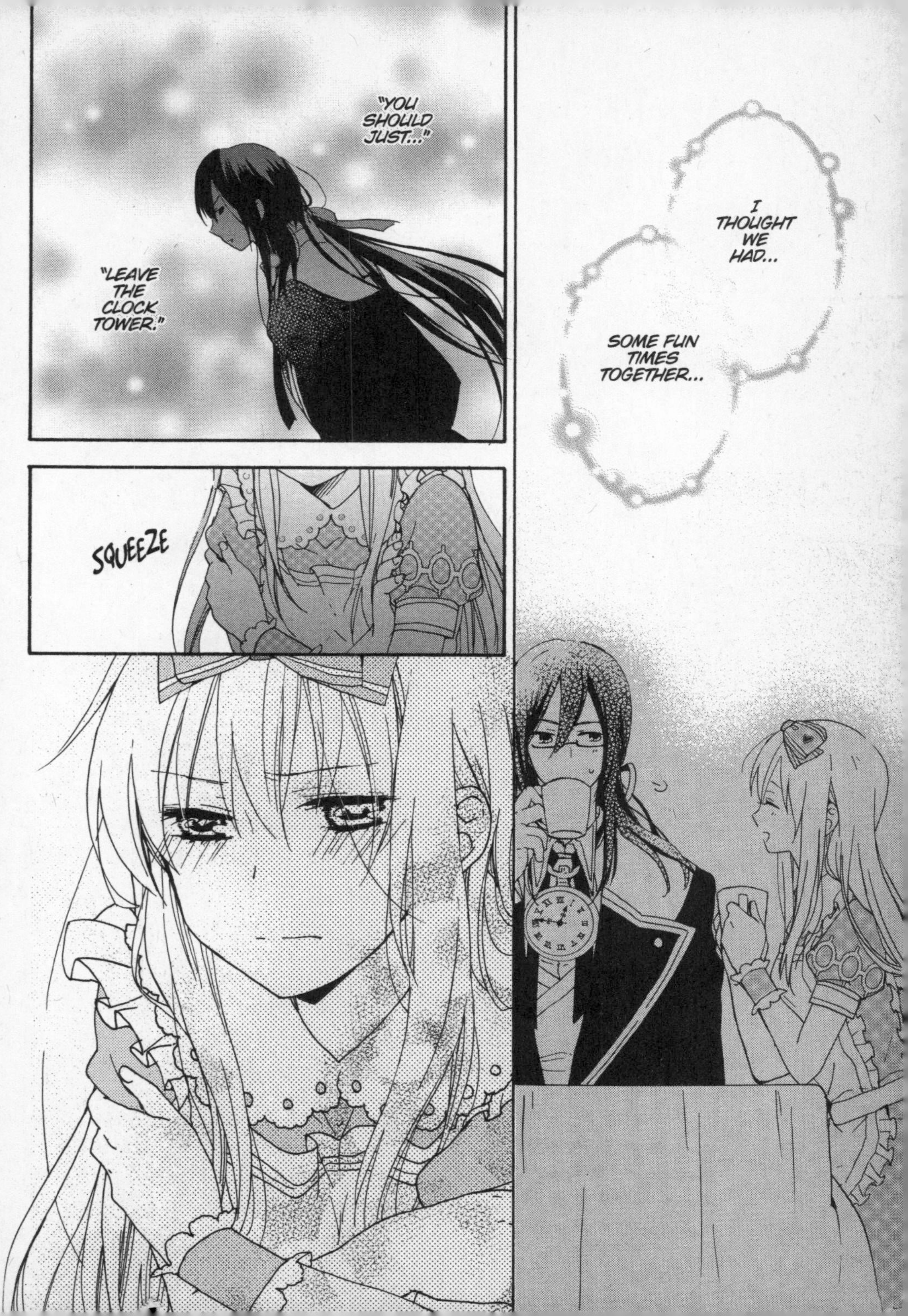
I THOUGHT WE HAD...
SOME FUN TIMES TOGETHER...
"YOU SHOULD JUST..."
"LEAVE THE CLOCK TOWER."
SQUEEZE

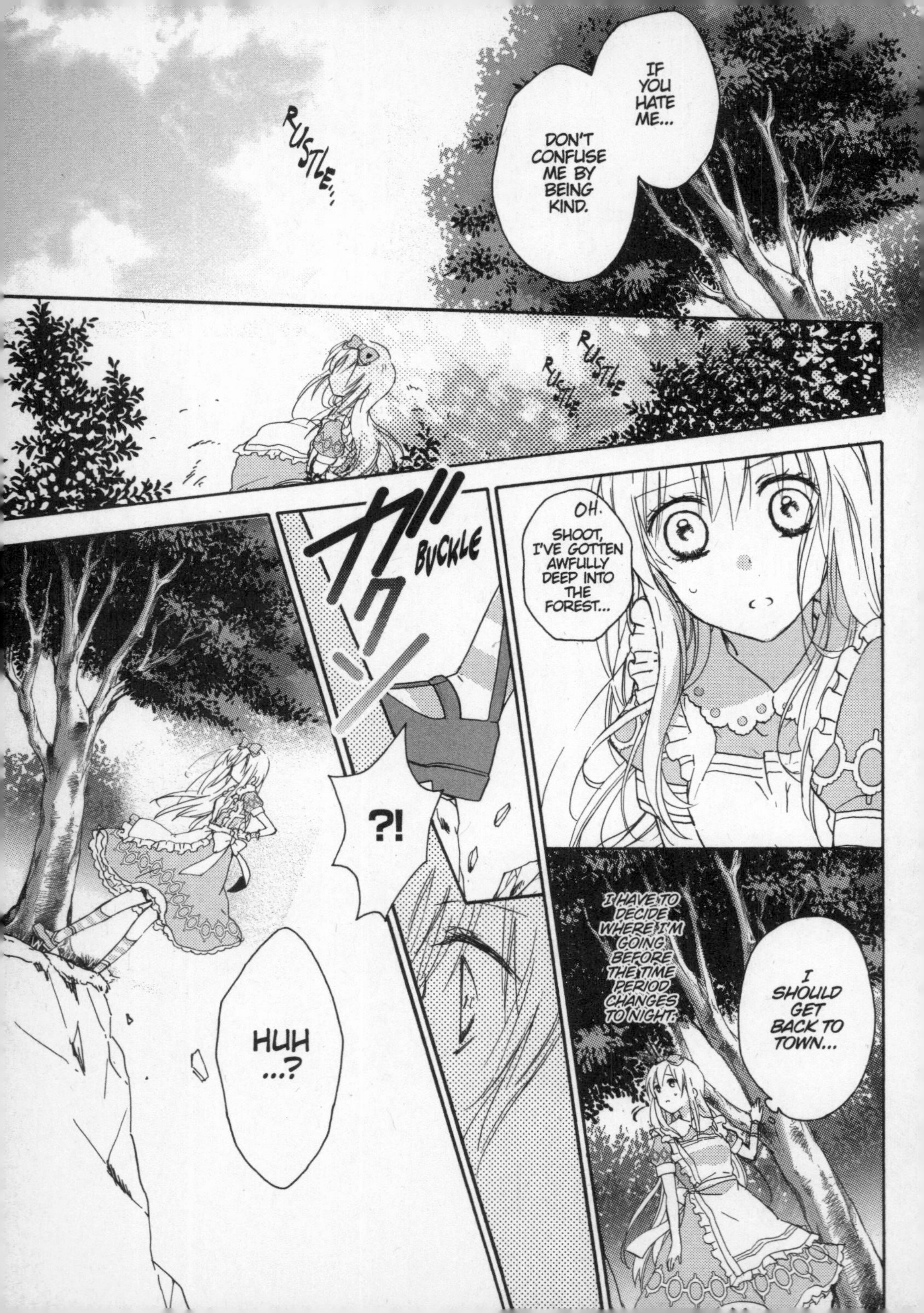
IF YOU HATE ME...
DON'T CONFUSE ME BY BEING KIND.
RUSTLE...
RUSTLE
RUSTLE
OH.
SHOOT, I'VE GOTTEN AWFULLY DEEP INTO THE FOREST...
I SHOULD GET BACK TO TOWN...
I HAVE TO DECIDE WHERE I'M GOING BEFORE THE TIME PERIOD CHANGES TO NIGHT.
BUCKLE
?!
HUH ...?

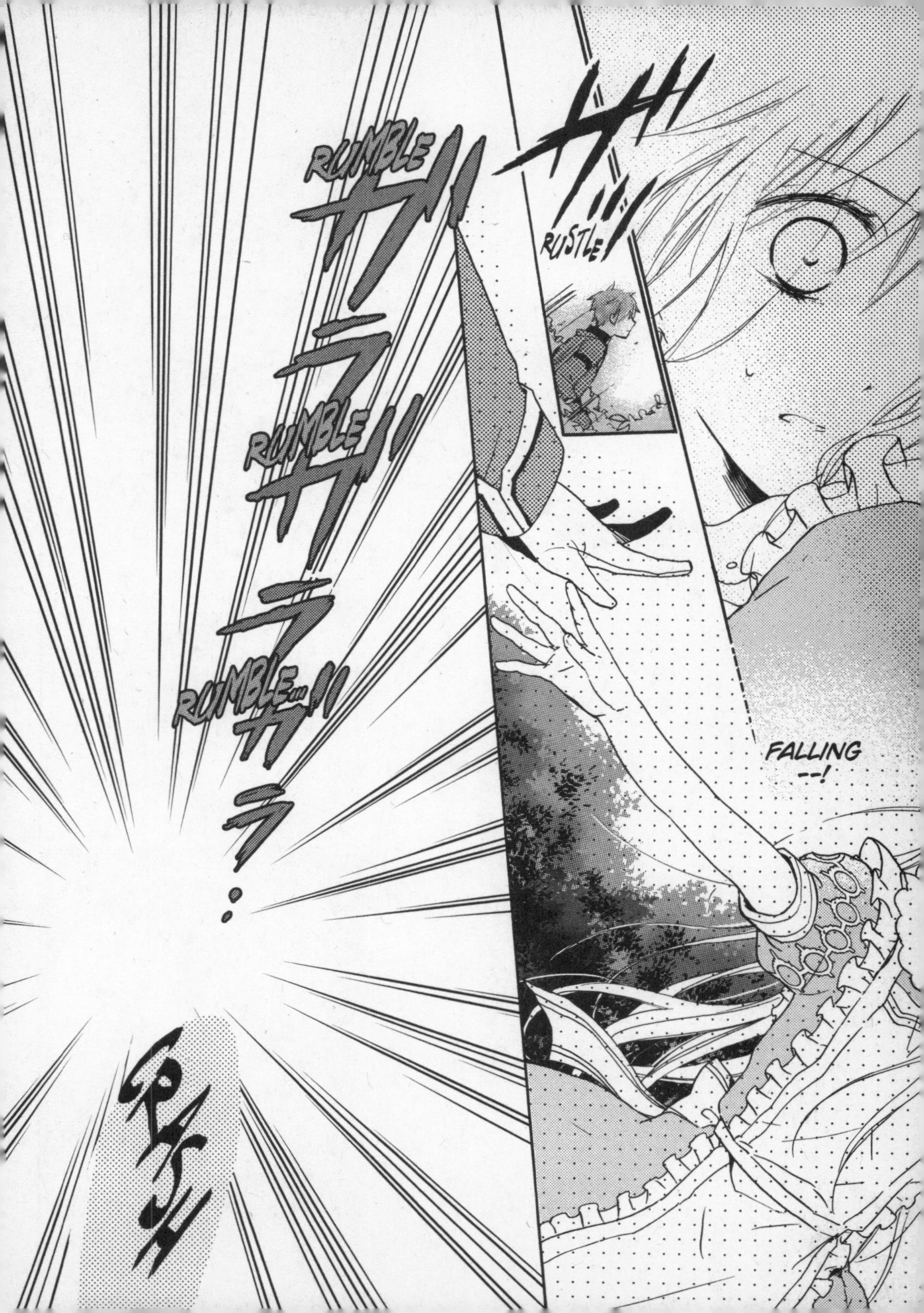
RUSTLE
FALLING --!
RUMBLE
RUMBLE
RUMBLE...!!
CRASH

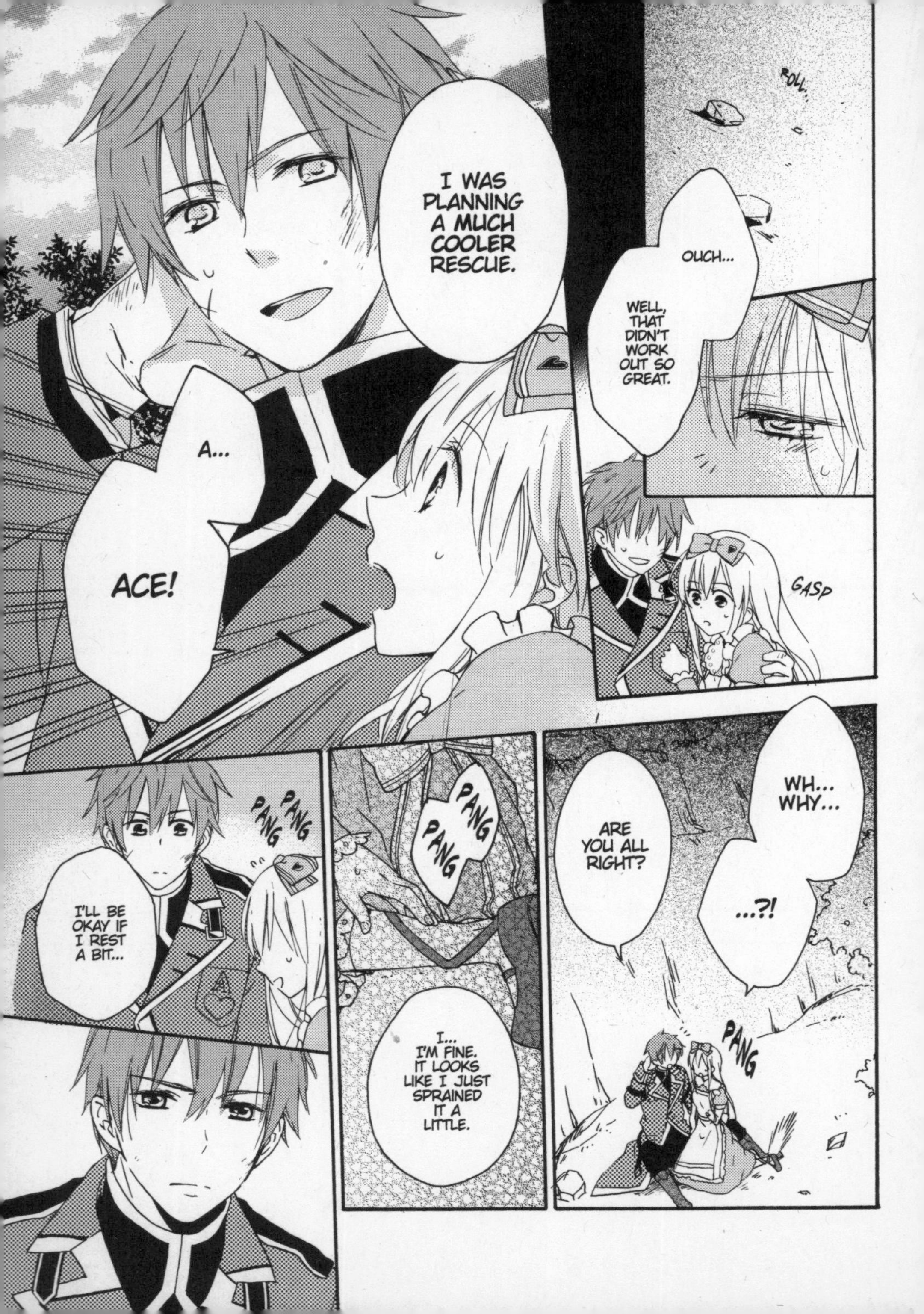
ROLL
OUCH...
WELL, THAT DIDN'T WORK OUT SO GREAT.
GASP
I WAS PLANNING A MUCH COOLER RESCUE.
A...
ACE!
WH... WHY...
...?!
ARE YOU ALL RIGHT?
PANG
PANG PANG
I... I'M FINE. IT LOOKS LIKE I JUST SPRAINED IT A LITTLE.
PANG PANG
I'LL BE OKAY IF I REST A BIT...

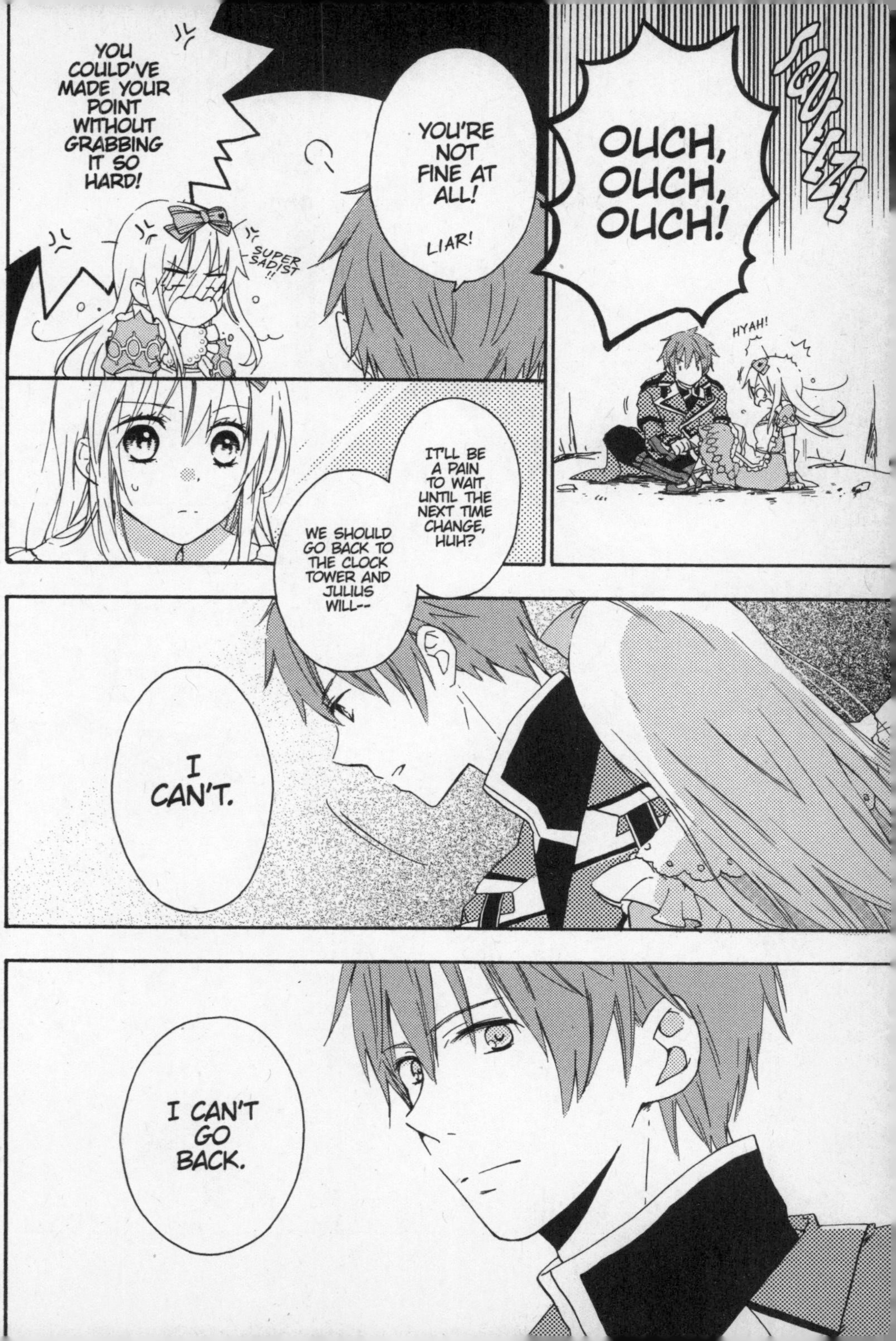
SQUEEZE
OUCH, OUCH, OUCH!
HYAH!
YOU'RE NOT FINE AT ALL!
LIAR!
YOU COULD'VE MADE YOUR POINT WITHOUT GRABBING IT SO HARD!
SUPER SADIST!!
IT'LL BE A PAIN TO WAIT UNTIL THE NEXT TIME CHANGE, HUH?
WE SHOULD GO BACK TO THE CLOCK TOWER AND JULIUS WILL--
I CAN'T.
I CAN'T GO BACK.

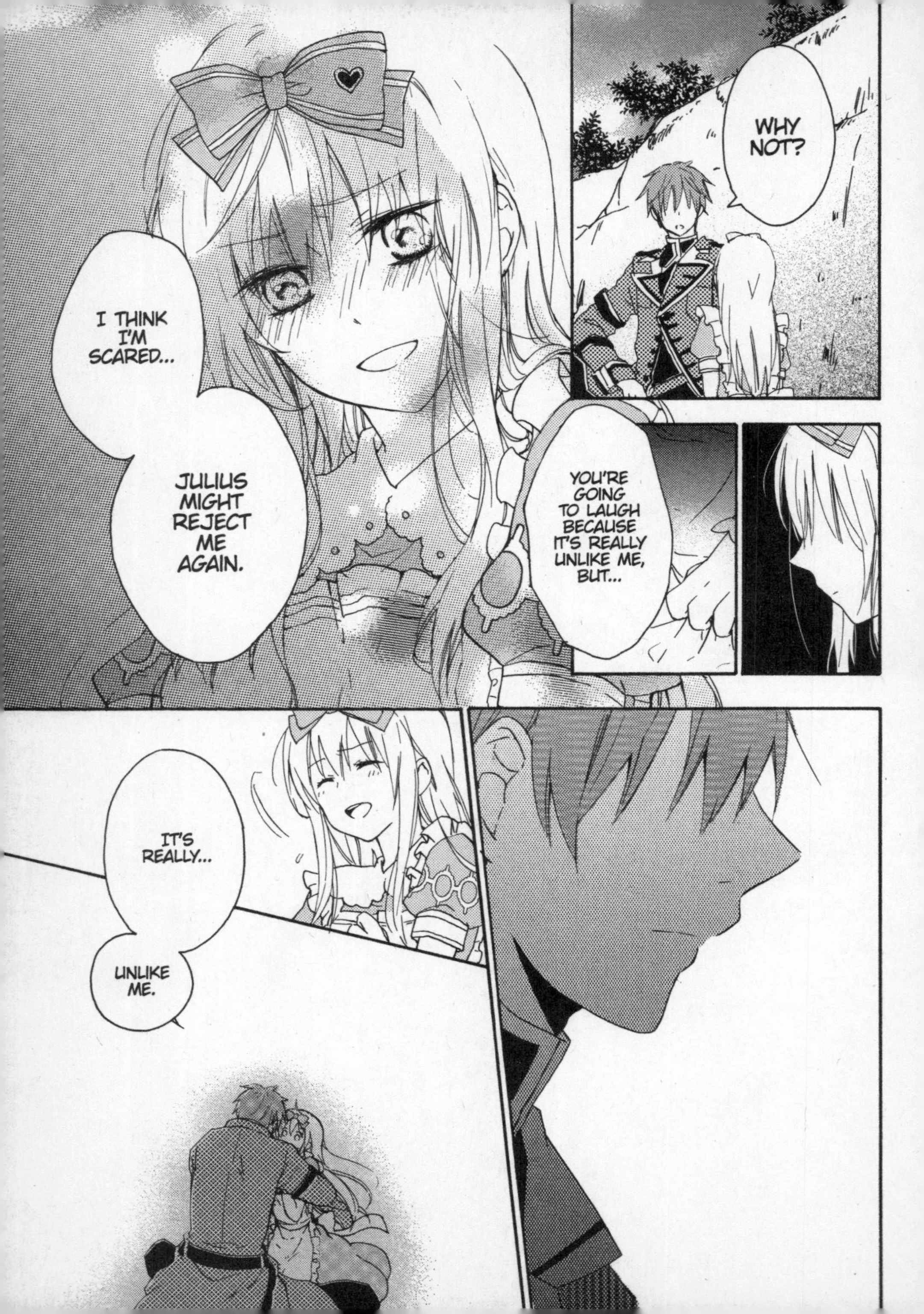
WHY NOT?
YOU'RE GOING TO LAUGH BECAUSE IT'S REALLY UNLIKE ME, BUT...
I THINK I'M SCARED...
JULIUS MIGHT REJECT ME AGAIN.
IT'S REALLY...
UNLIKE ME.

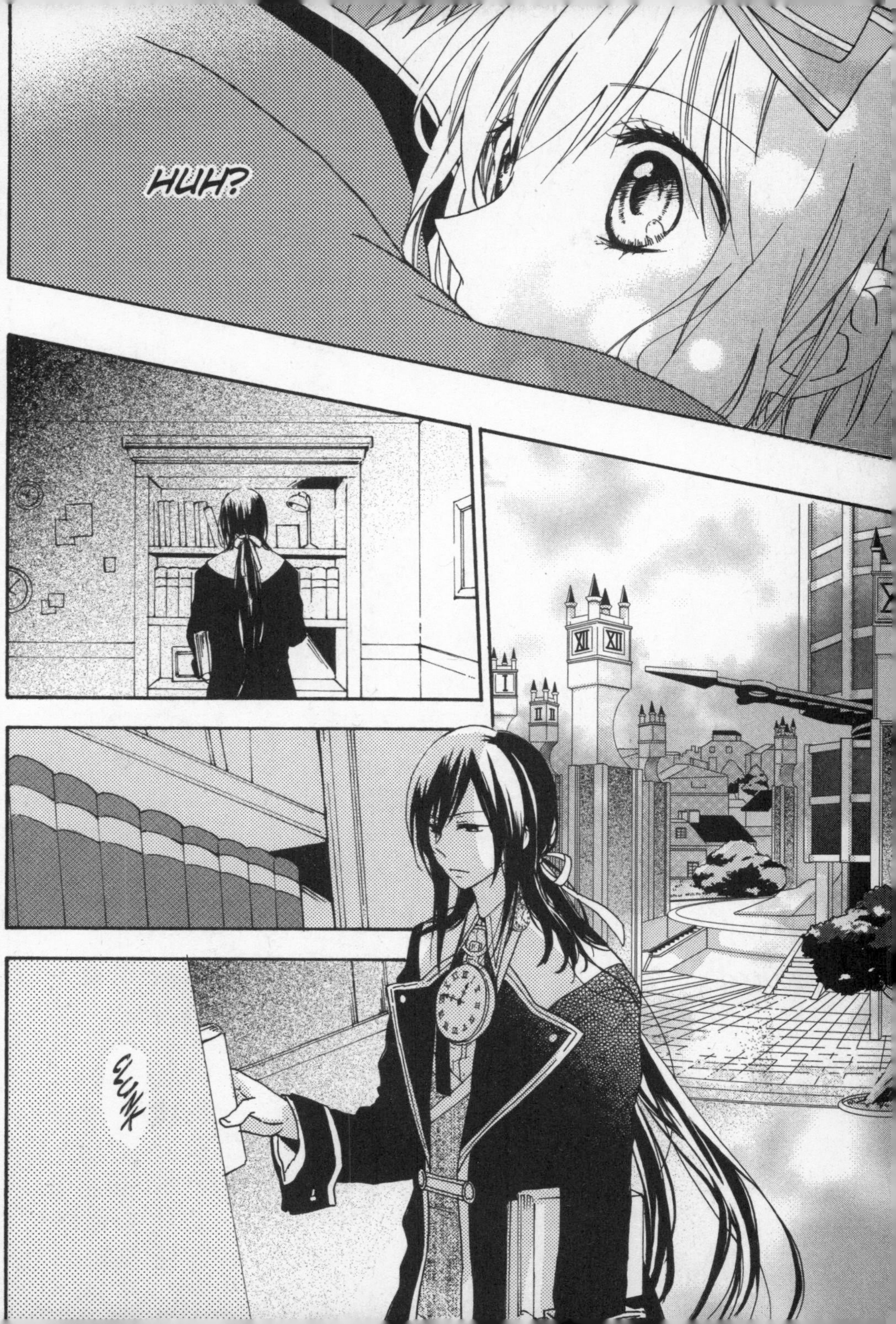
HUH?
CLUNK

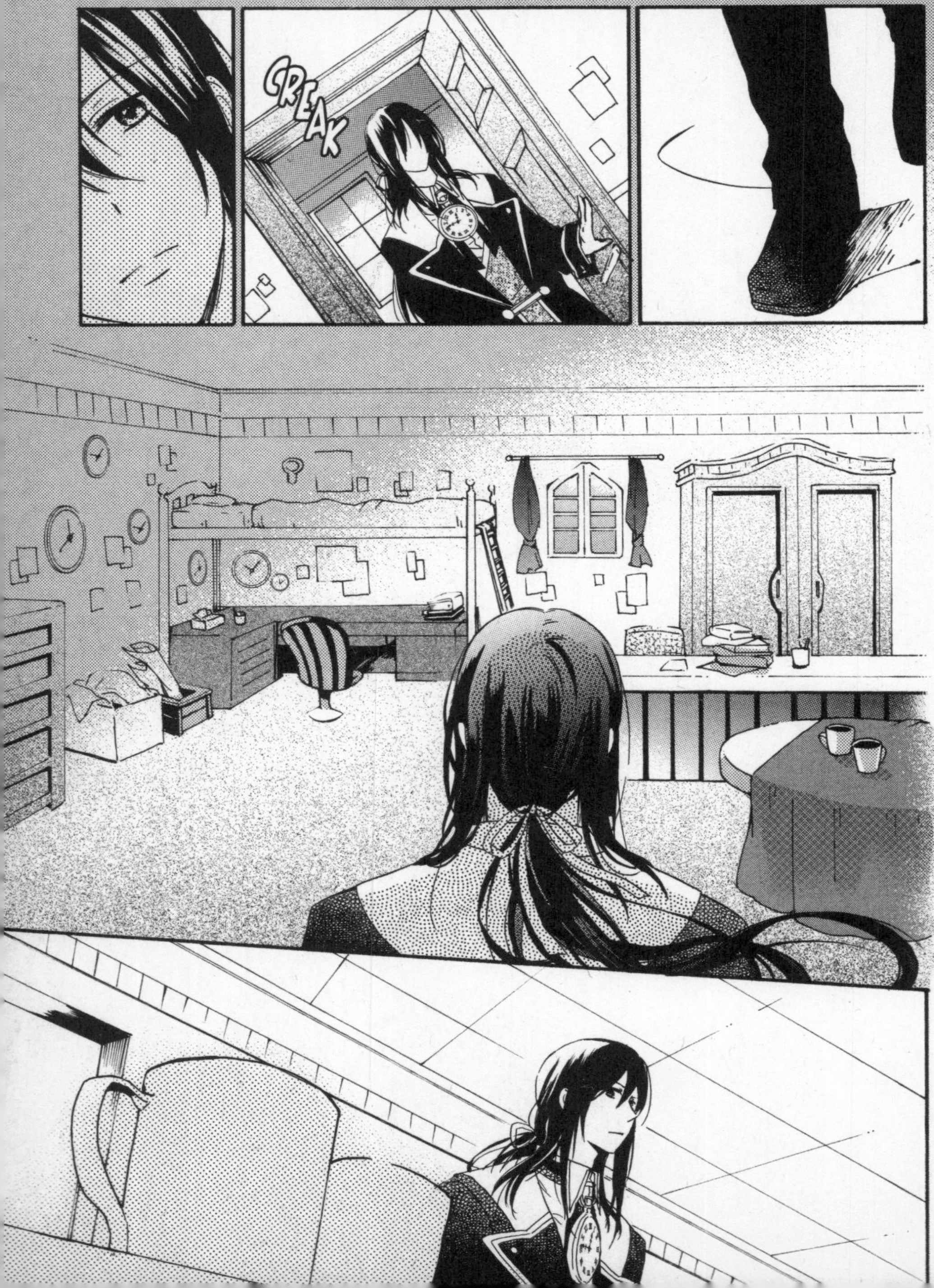
CREAK

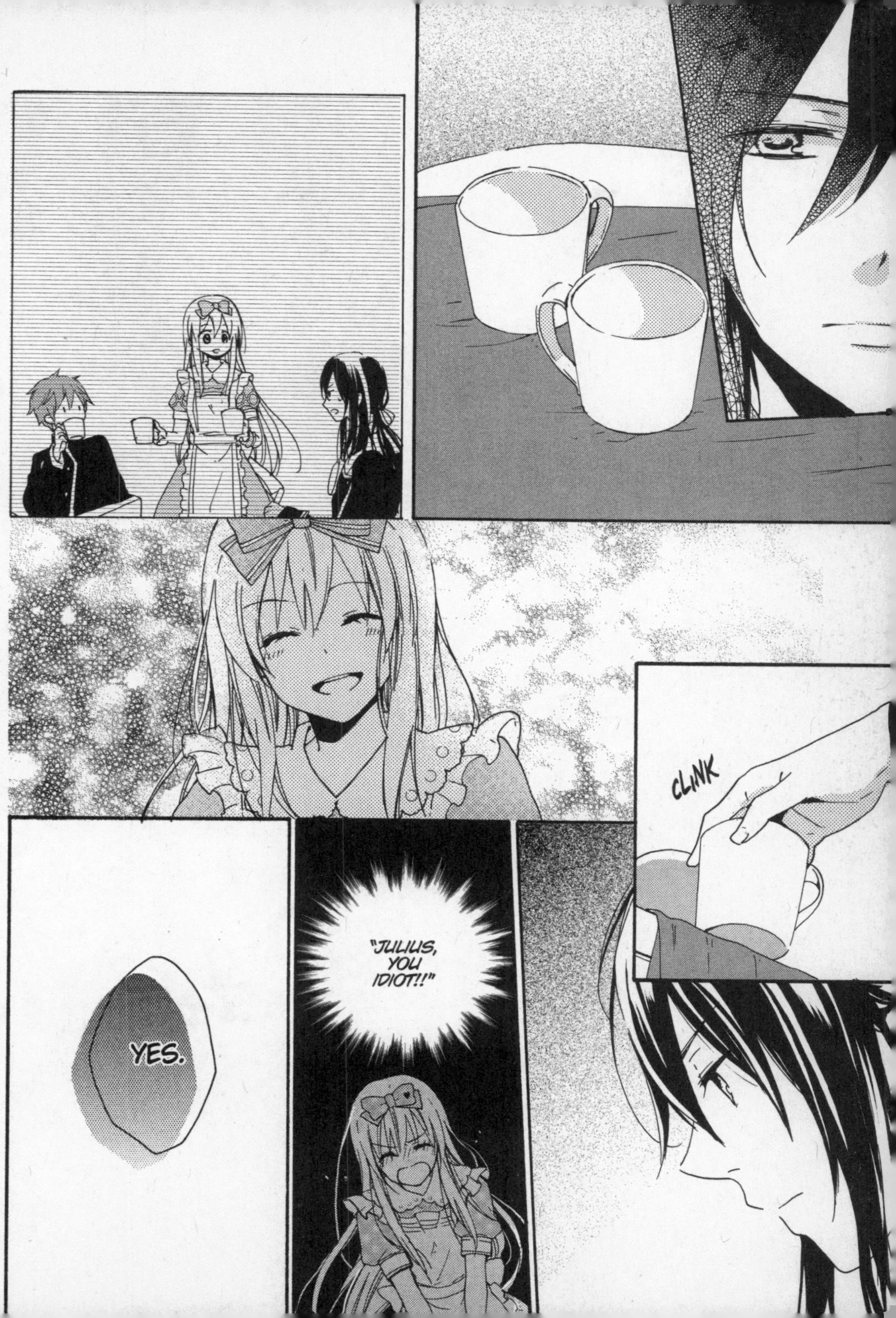
CLINK
"JULIUS, YOU IDIOT!!"
YES.

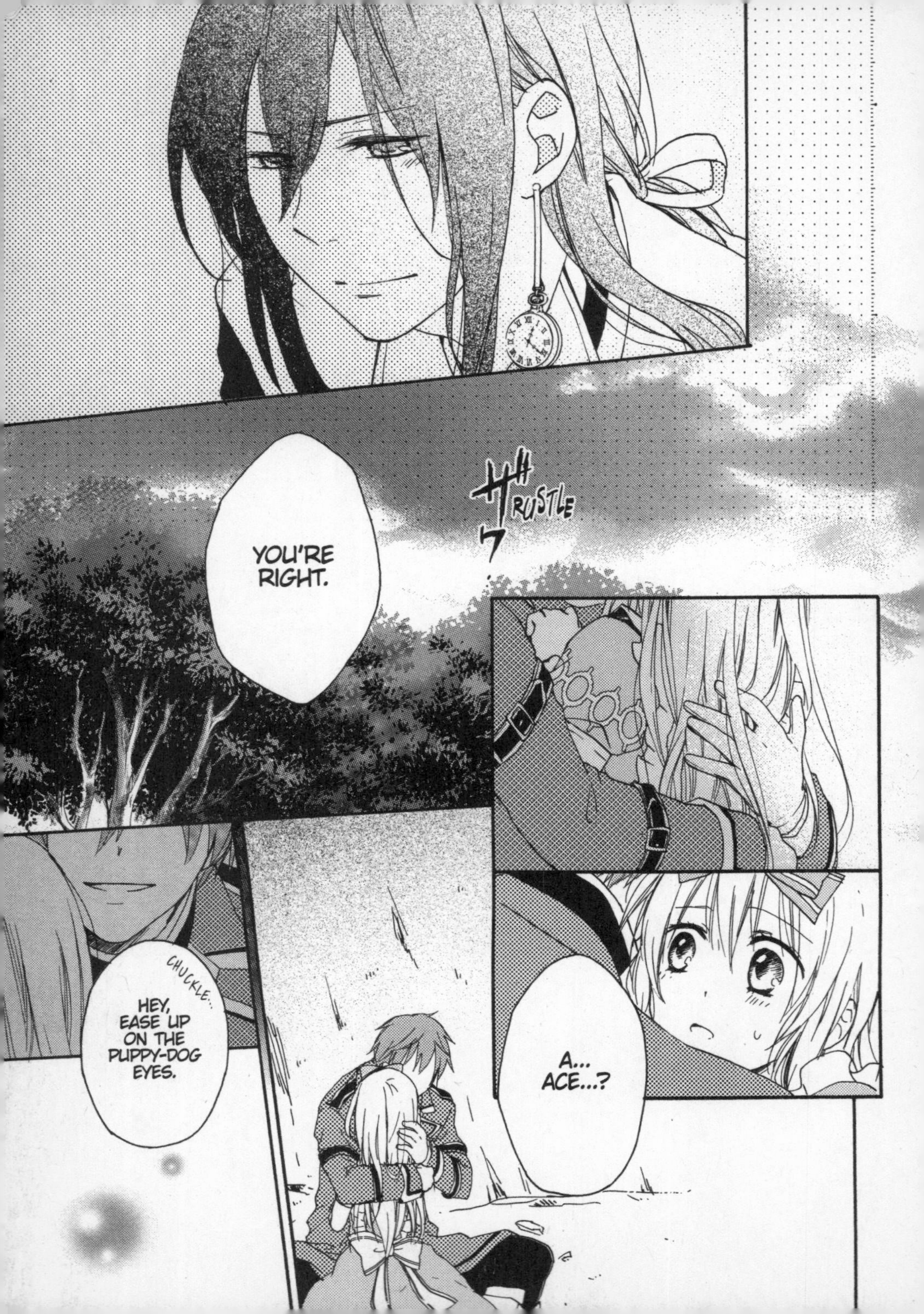
RUSTLE
YOU'RE RIGHT.
A... ACE...?
CHUCKLE...
HEY, EASE UP ON THE PUPPY-DOG EYES.

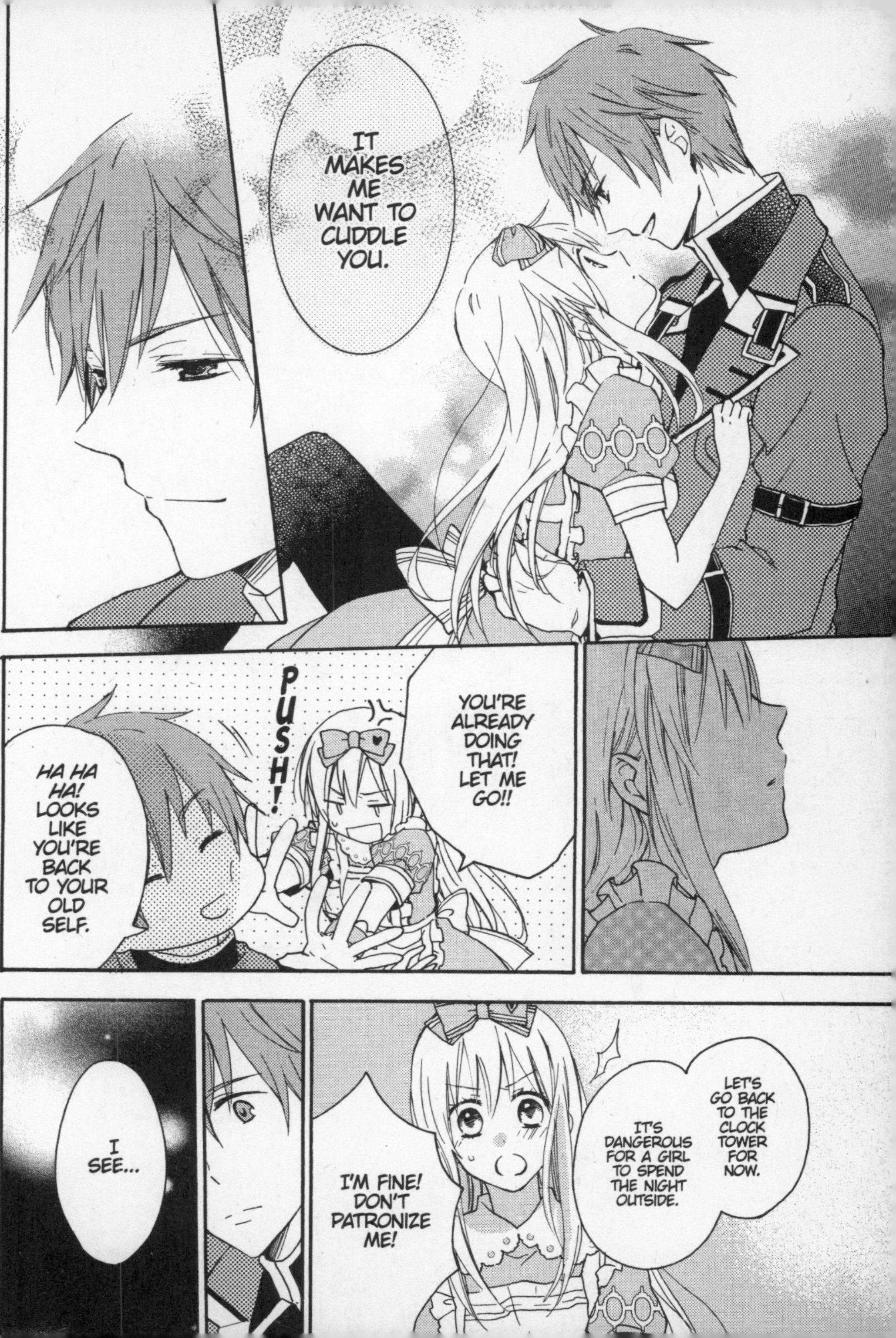
IT MAKES ME WANT TO CUDDLE YOU.
YOU'RE ALREADY DOING THAT! LET ME GO!!
PUSH!
HA HA HA! LOOKS LIKE YOU'RE BACK TO YOUR OLD SELF.
LET'S GO BACK TO THE CLOCK TOWER FOR NOW.
IT'S DANGEROUS FOR A GIRL TO SPEND THE NIGHT OUTSIDE.
I'M FINE! DON'T PATRONIZE ME!
I SEE...

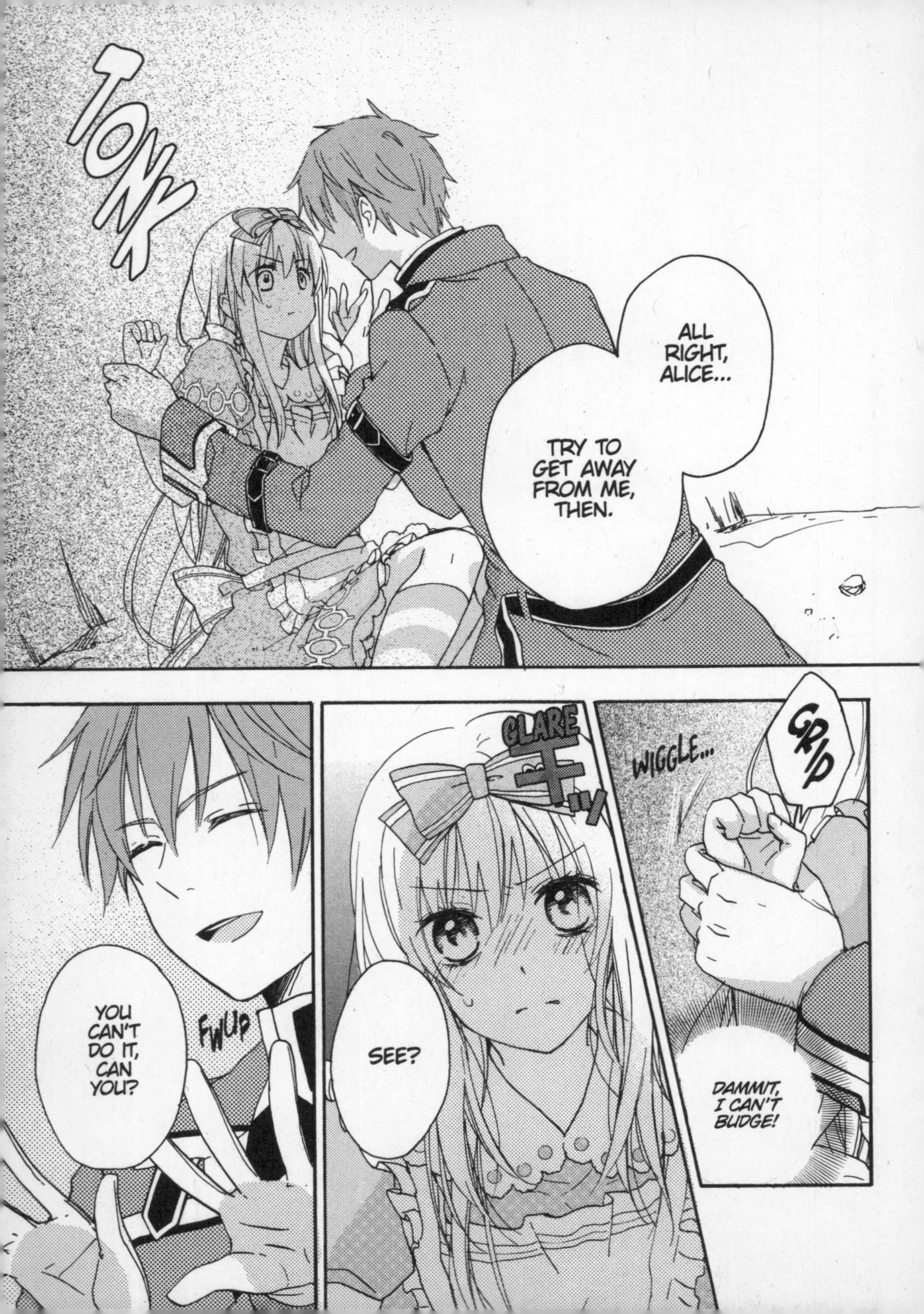
ALL RIGHT, ALICE...
TRY TO GET AWAY FROM ME, THEN.
TONK
GRIP
WIGGLE...
DAMMIT, I CAN'T BUDGE!
GLARE
SEE?
FWUP
YOU CAN'T DO IT, CAN YOU?

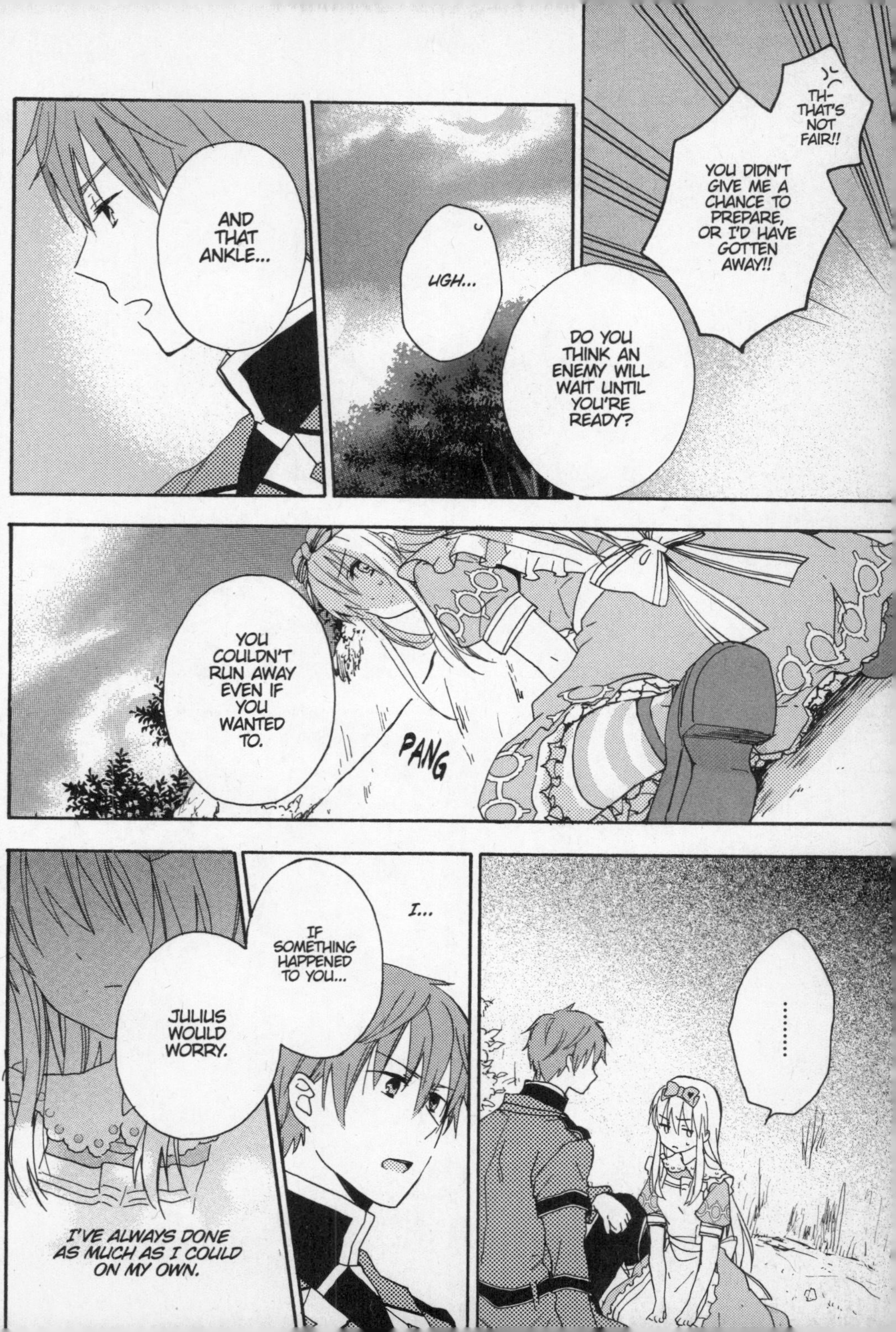
TH-THAT'S NOT FAIR!!
YOU DIDN'T GIVE ME A CHANCE TO PREPARE, OR I'D HAVE GOTTEN AWAY!!
DO YOU THINK AN ENEMY WILL WAIT UNTIL YOU'RE READY?
UGH...
AND THAT ANKLE...
YOU COULDN'T RUN AWAY EVEN IF YOU WANTED TO.
PANG
......
I...
IF SOMETHING HAPPENED TO YOU...
JULIUS WOULD WORRY.
I'VE ALWAYS DONE AS MUCH AS I COULD ON MY OWN.

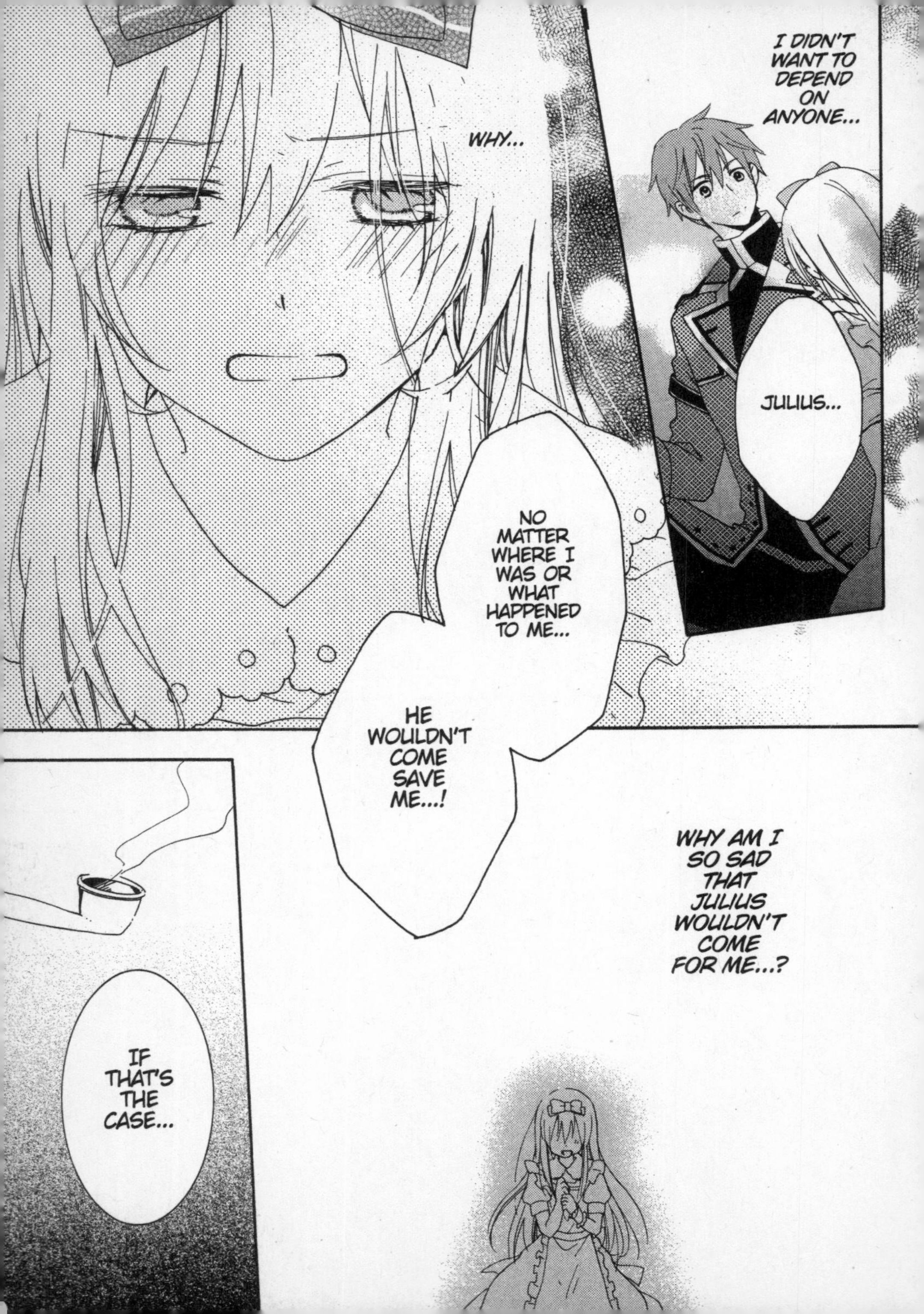
I DIDN'T WANT TO DEPEND ON ANYONE...
JULIUS...
WHY...
NO MATTER WHERE I WAS OR WHAT HAPPENED TO ME...
HE WOULDN'T COME SAVE ME...!
WHY AM I SO SAD THAT JULIUS WOULDN'T COME FOR ME...?
IF THAT'S THE CASE...

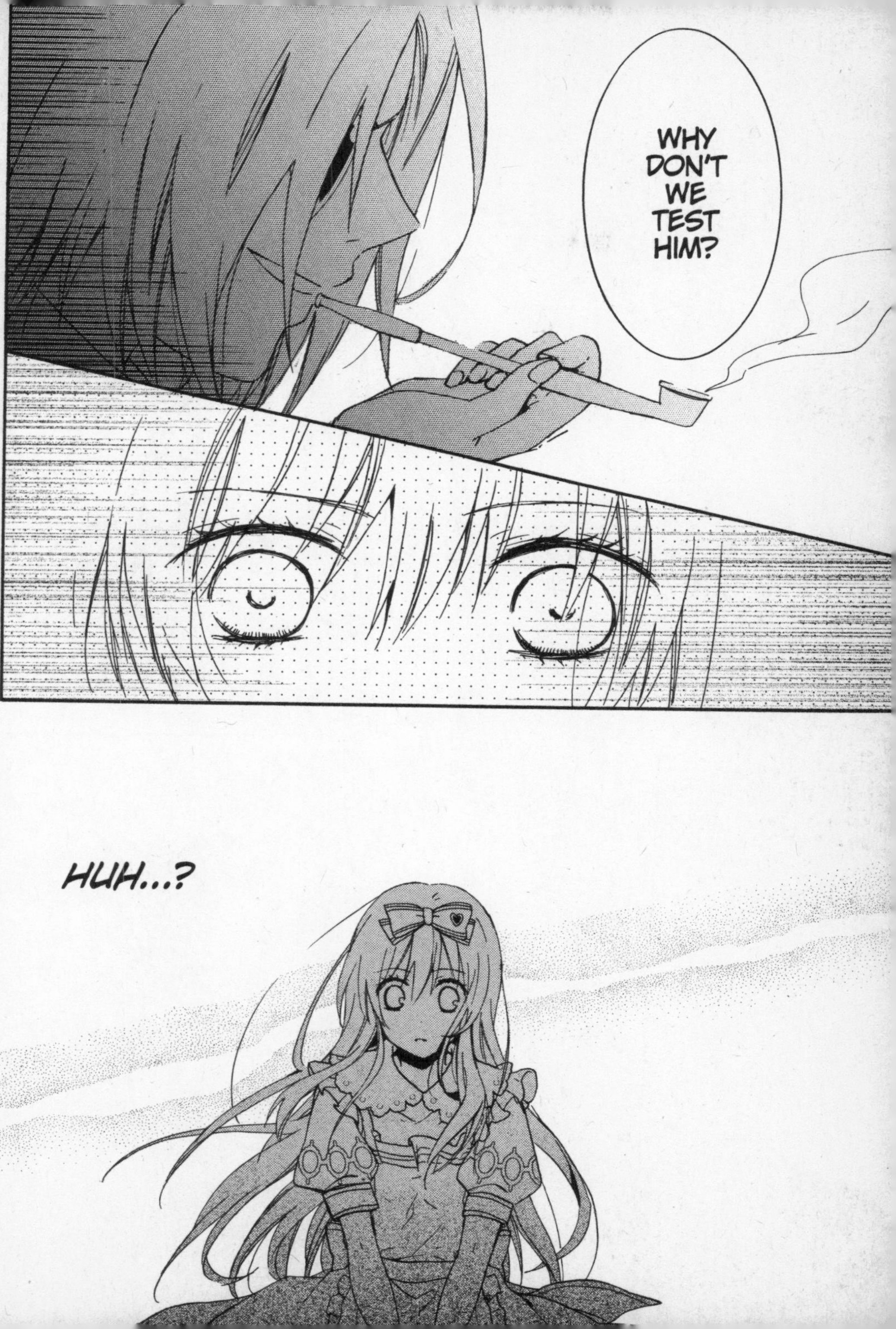
WHY DON'T WE TEST HIM?
HUH...?

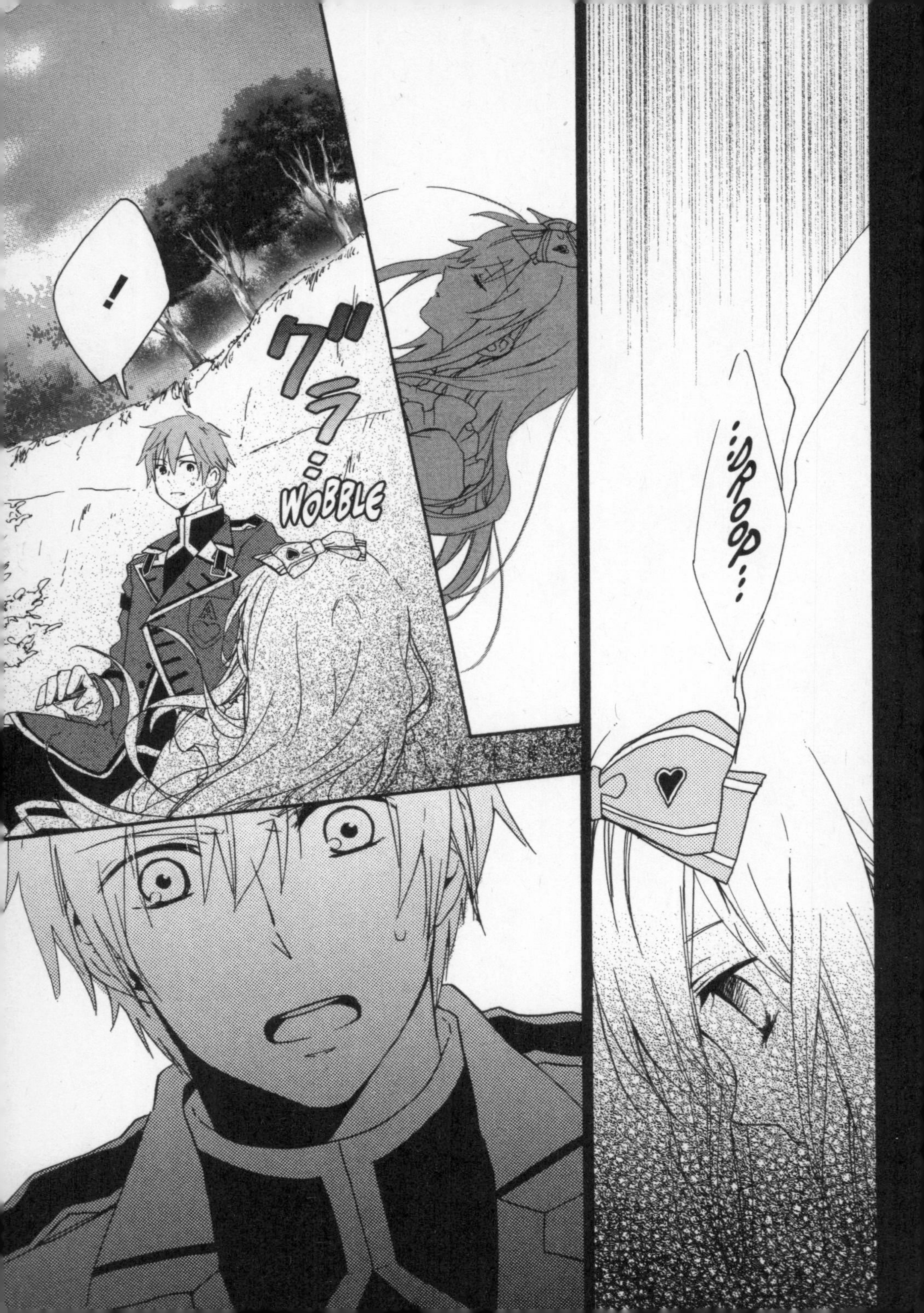
...DROOP...
!
グラ...
WOBBLE

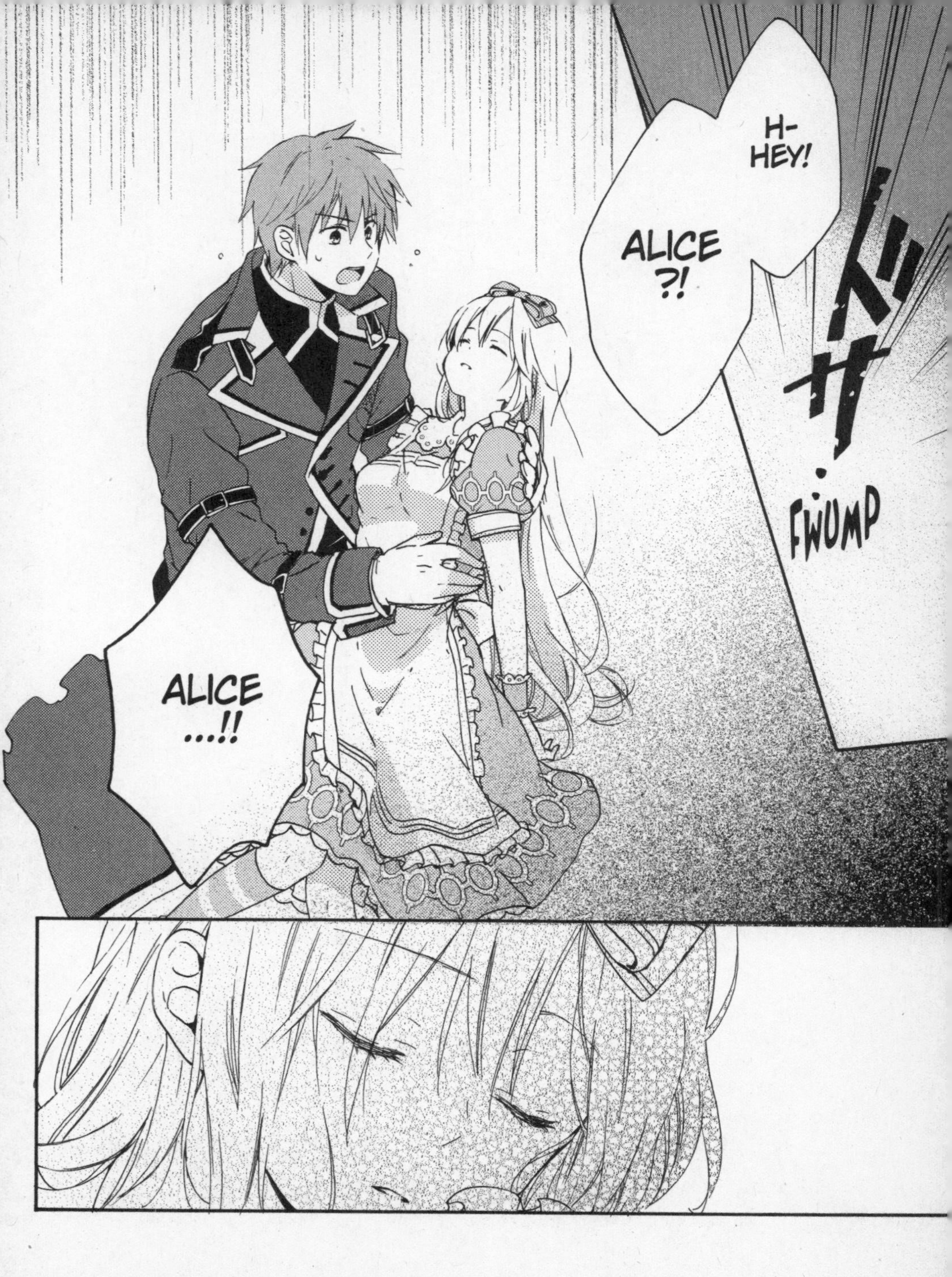
H-HEY! ALICE?!
FWUMP
ALICE ...!!

ハートの国のアリス
恋する茨の迷宮

Alice
IN THE
COUNTRY OF
Hearts

Love Labyrinth of Thorns

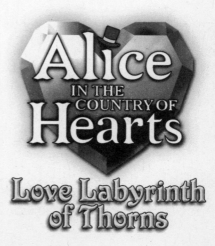

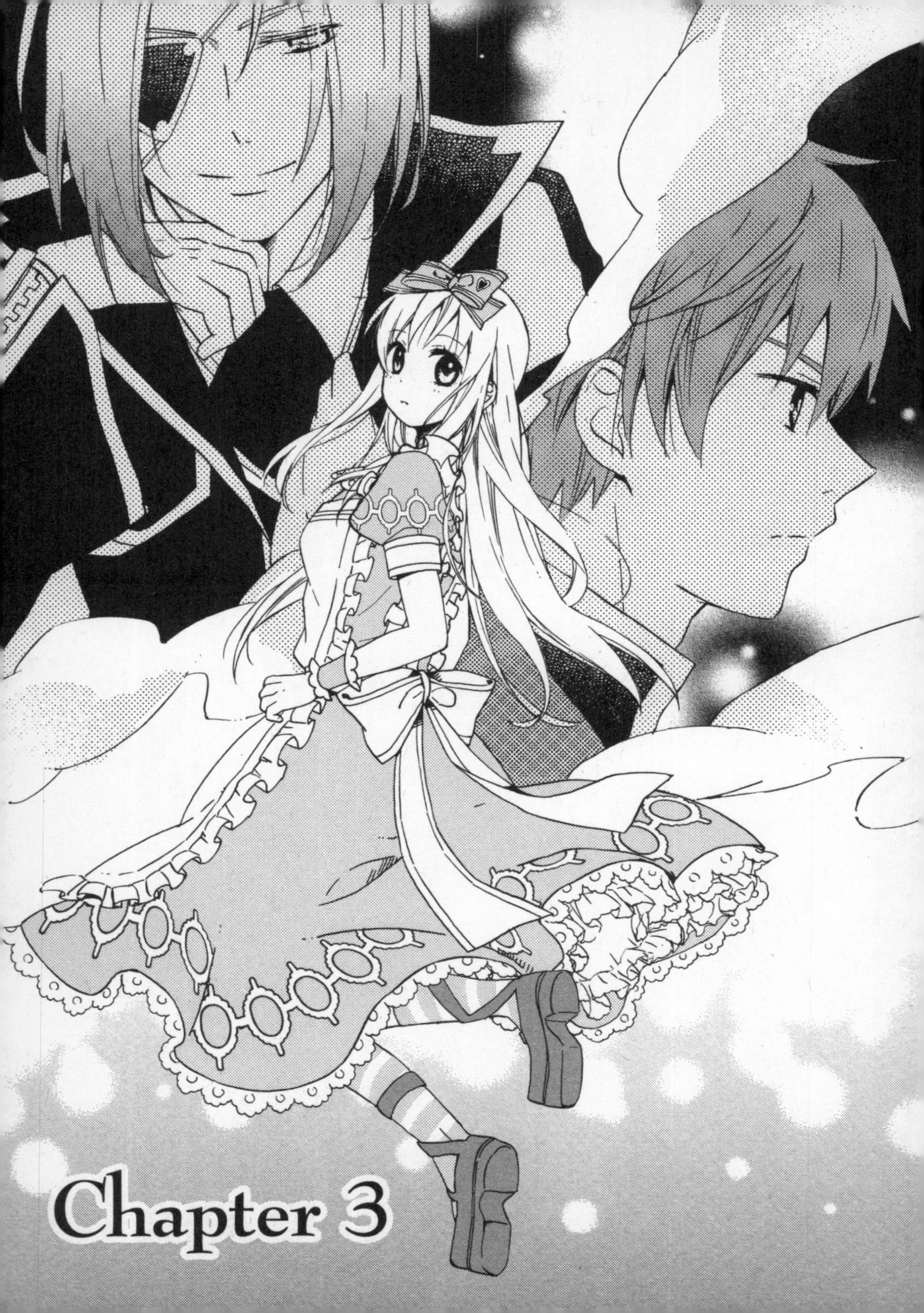
Chapter 3

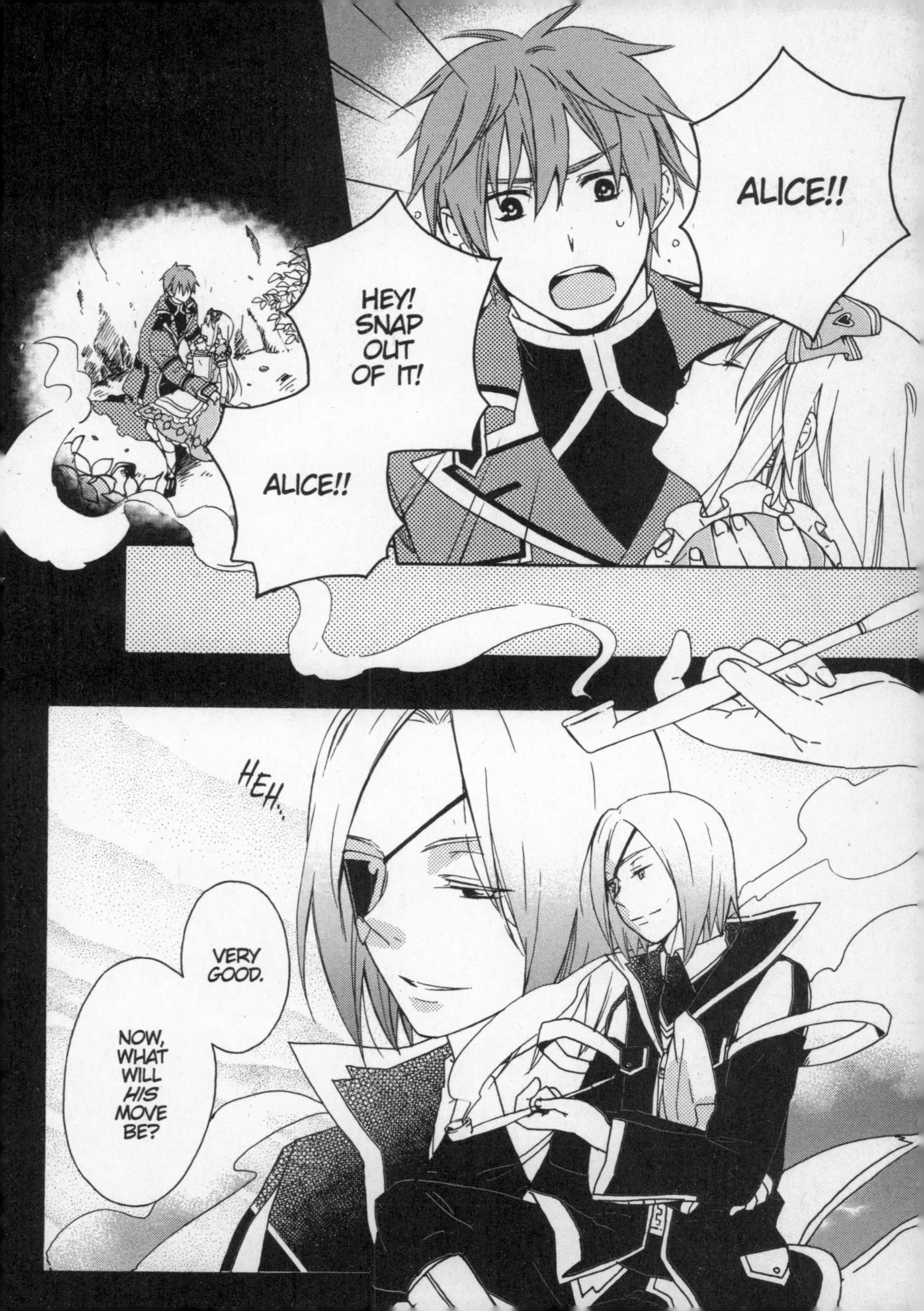
ALICE!!
HEY! SNAP OUT OF IT!
ALICE!!
HEH...
VERY GOOD.
NOW, WHAT WILL *HIS* MOVE BE?

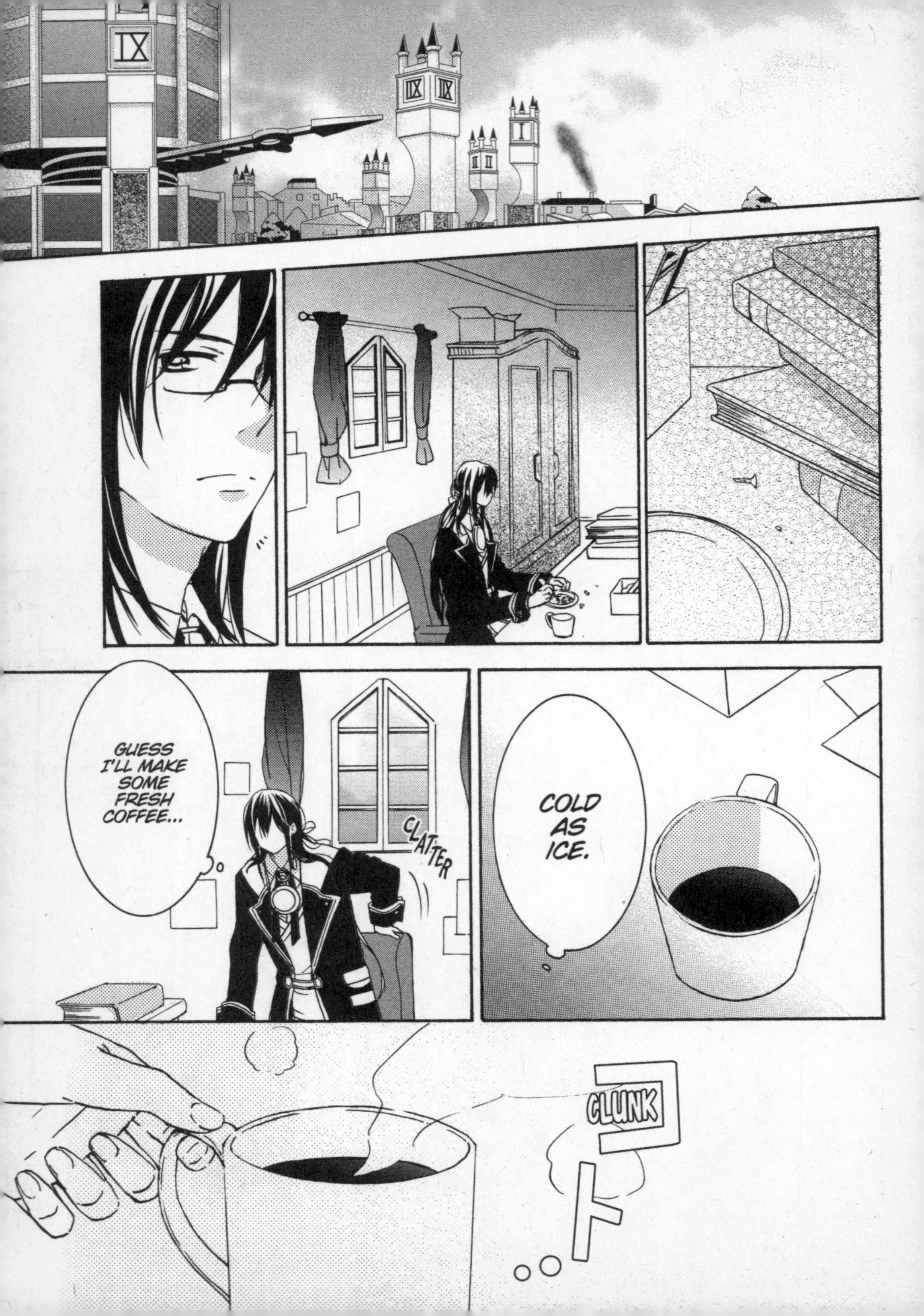
COLD AS ICE.
GUESS I'LL MAKE SOME FRESH COFFEE...
CLATTER
CLUNK

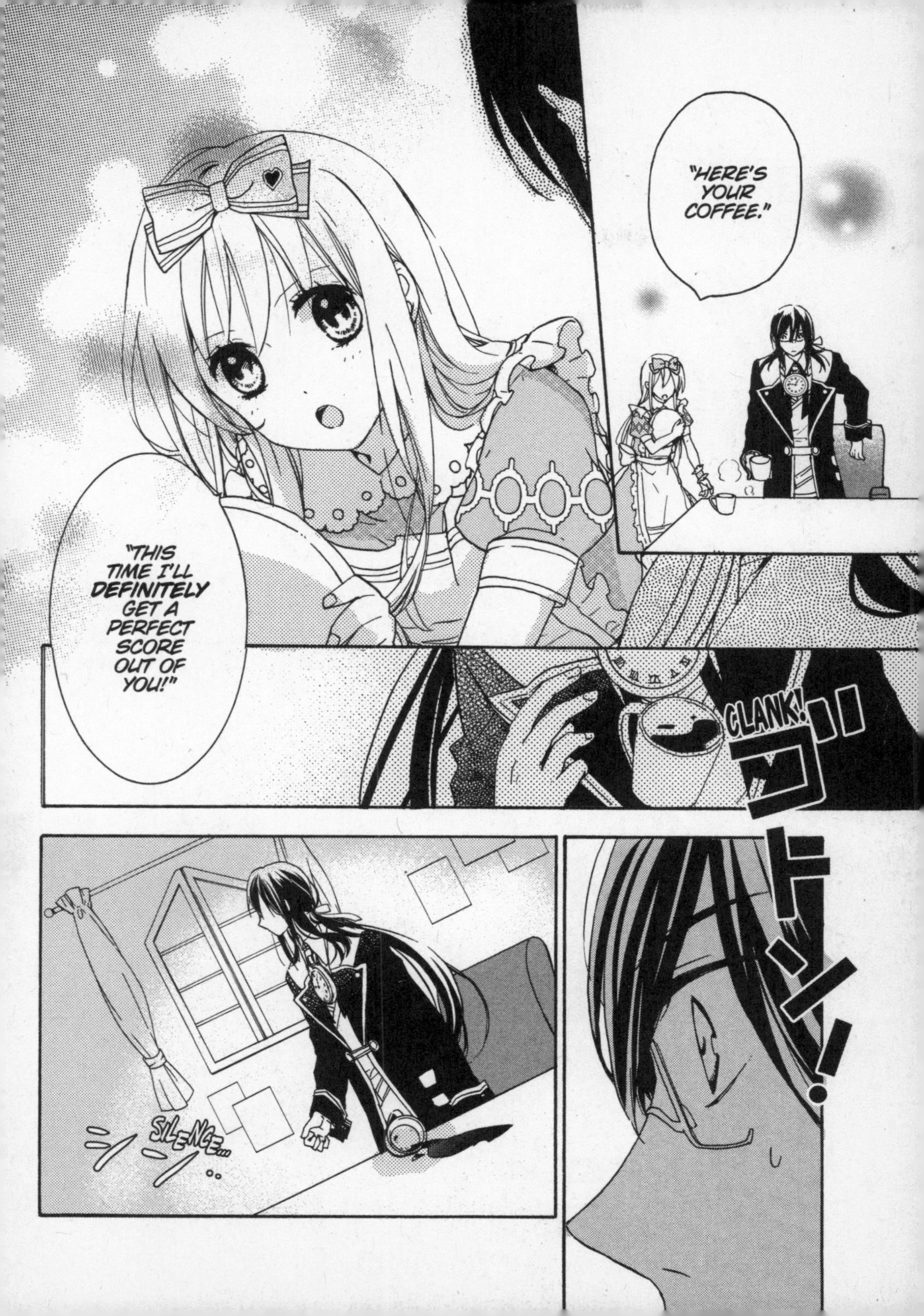
"HERE'S YOUR COFFEE."
"THIS TIME I'LL **DEFINITELY** GET A PERFECT SCORE OUT OF YOU!"
CLANK!
SILENCE...

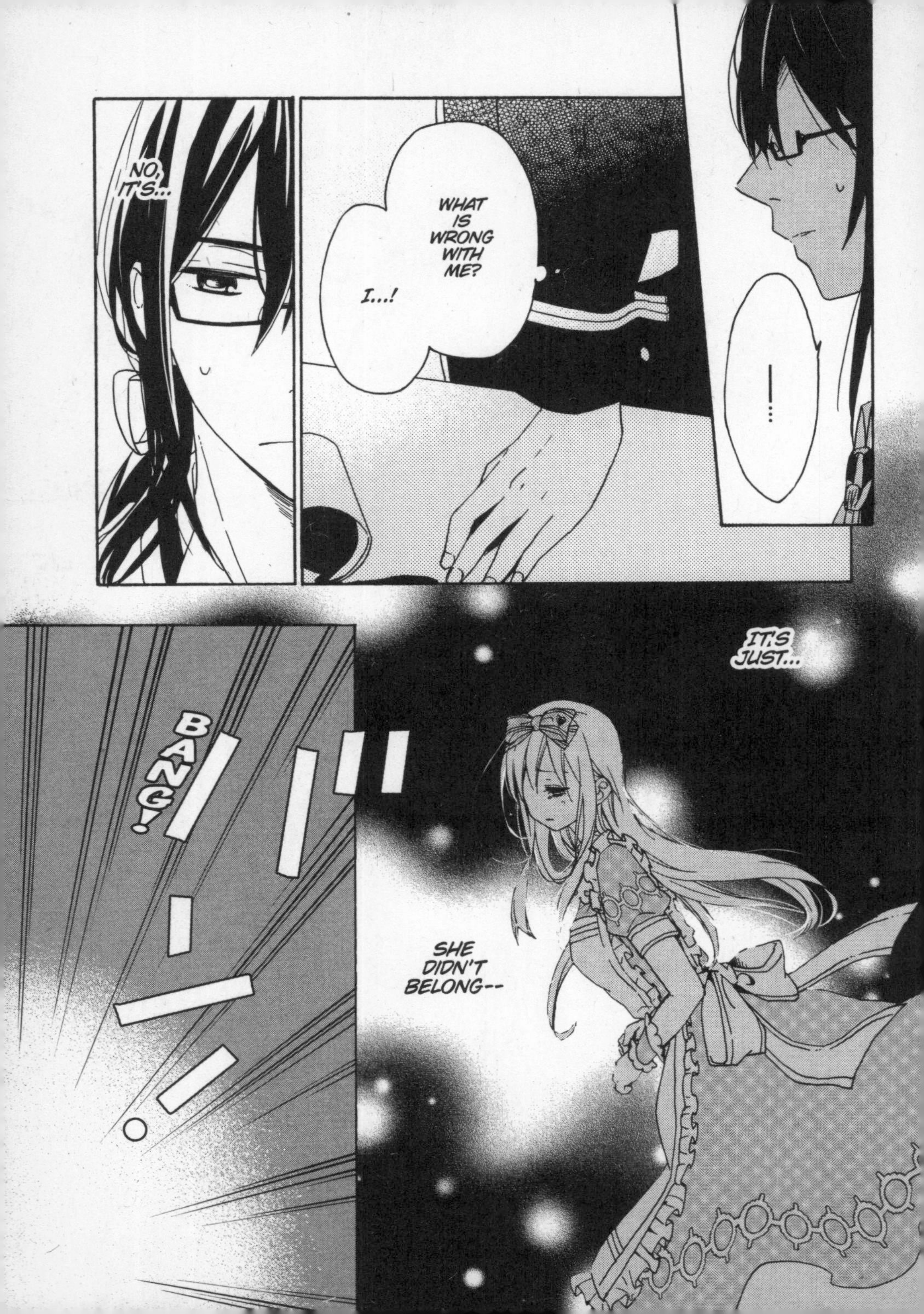

...
WHAT IS WRONG WITH ME?
I...!
NO, IT'S...
IT'S JUST...
SHE DIDN'T BELONG--
BANG!

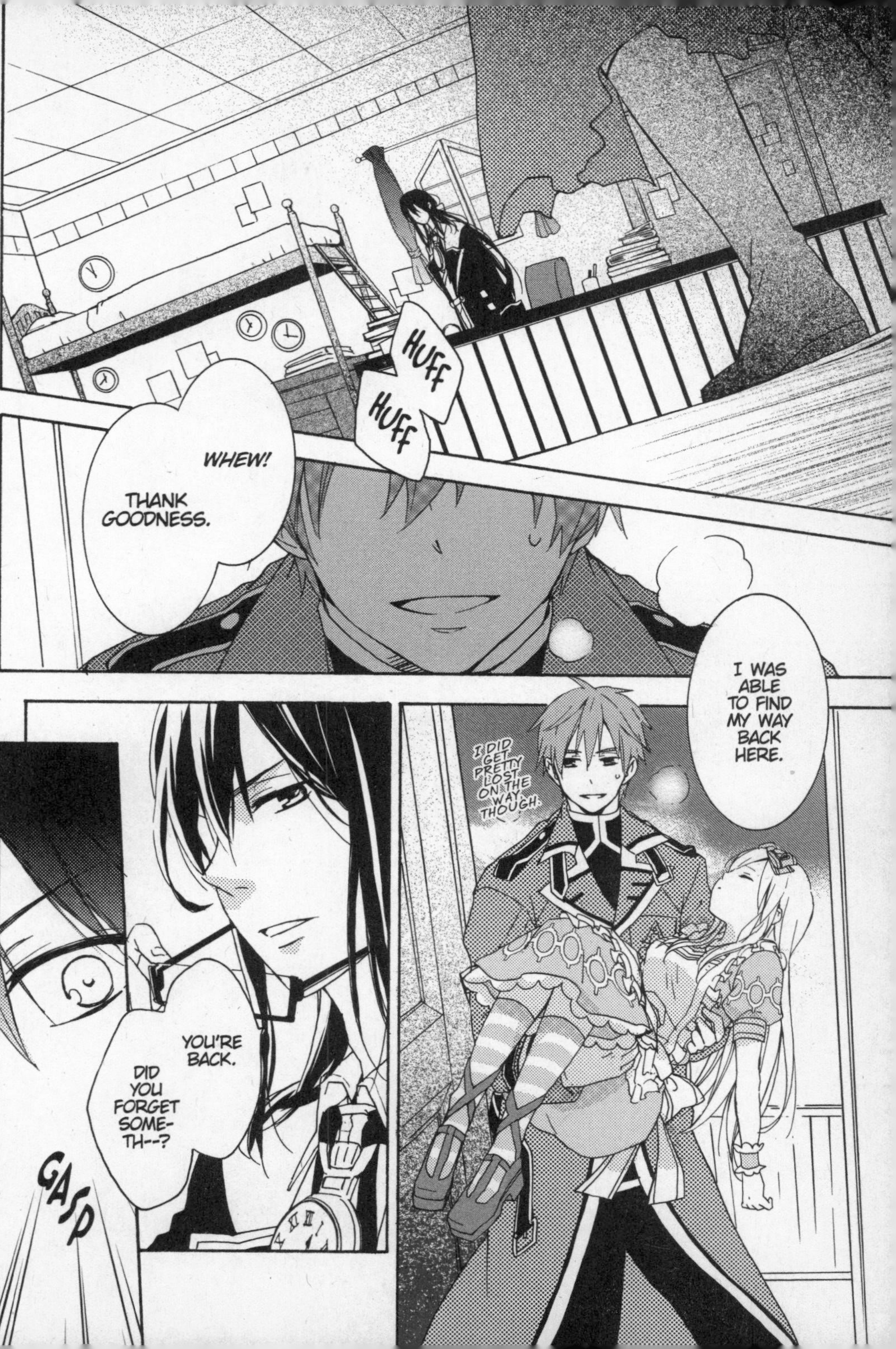
HUFF HUFF
WHEW!
THANK GOODNESS.
I WAS ABLE TO FIND MY WAY BACK HERE.
I DID GET PRETTY LOST ON THE WAY THOUGH.
YOU'RE BACK.
DID YOU FORGET SOME-TH--?
GASP

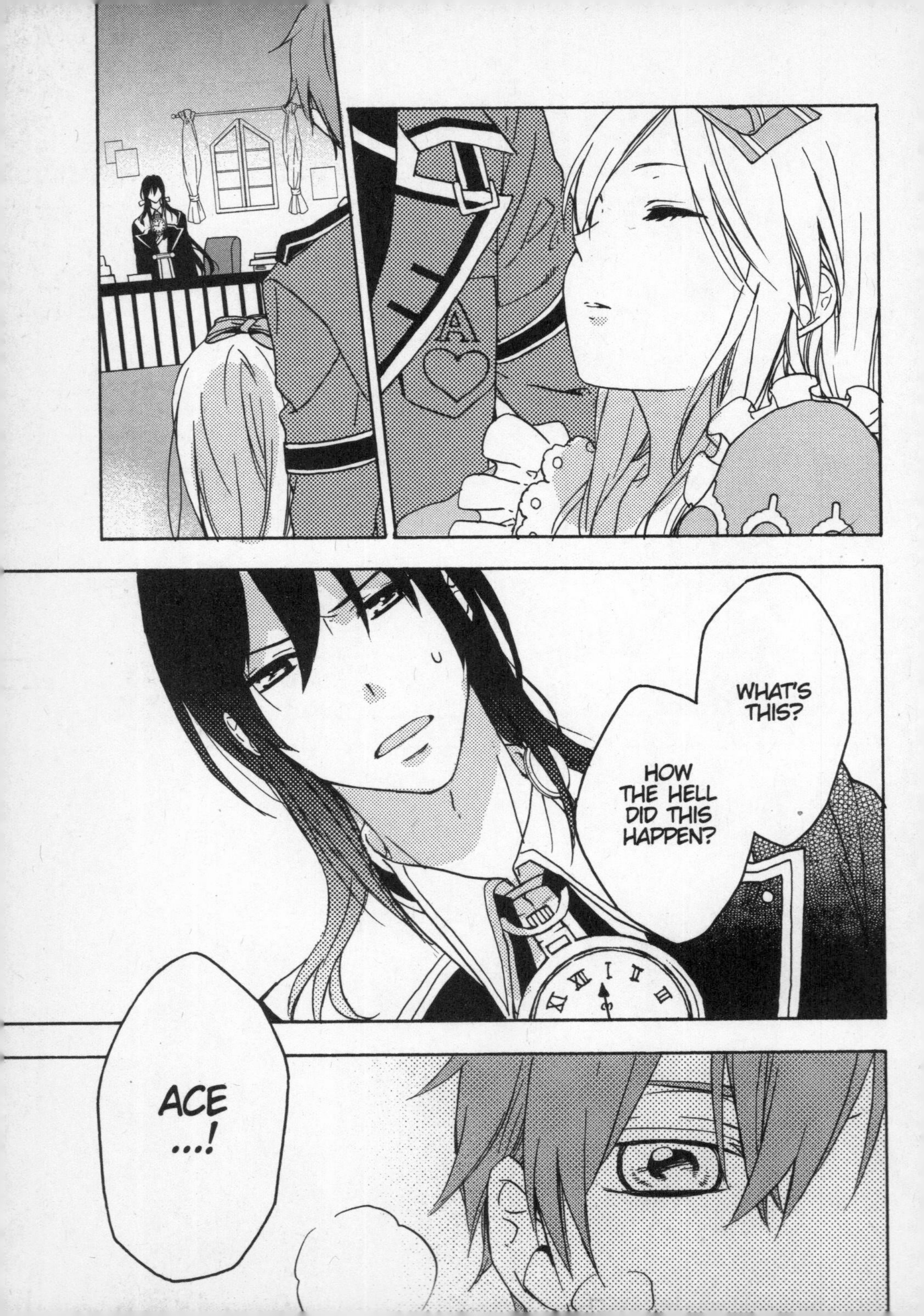
WHAT'S THIS?
HOW THE HELL DID THIS HAPPEN?
ACE ...!

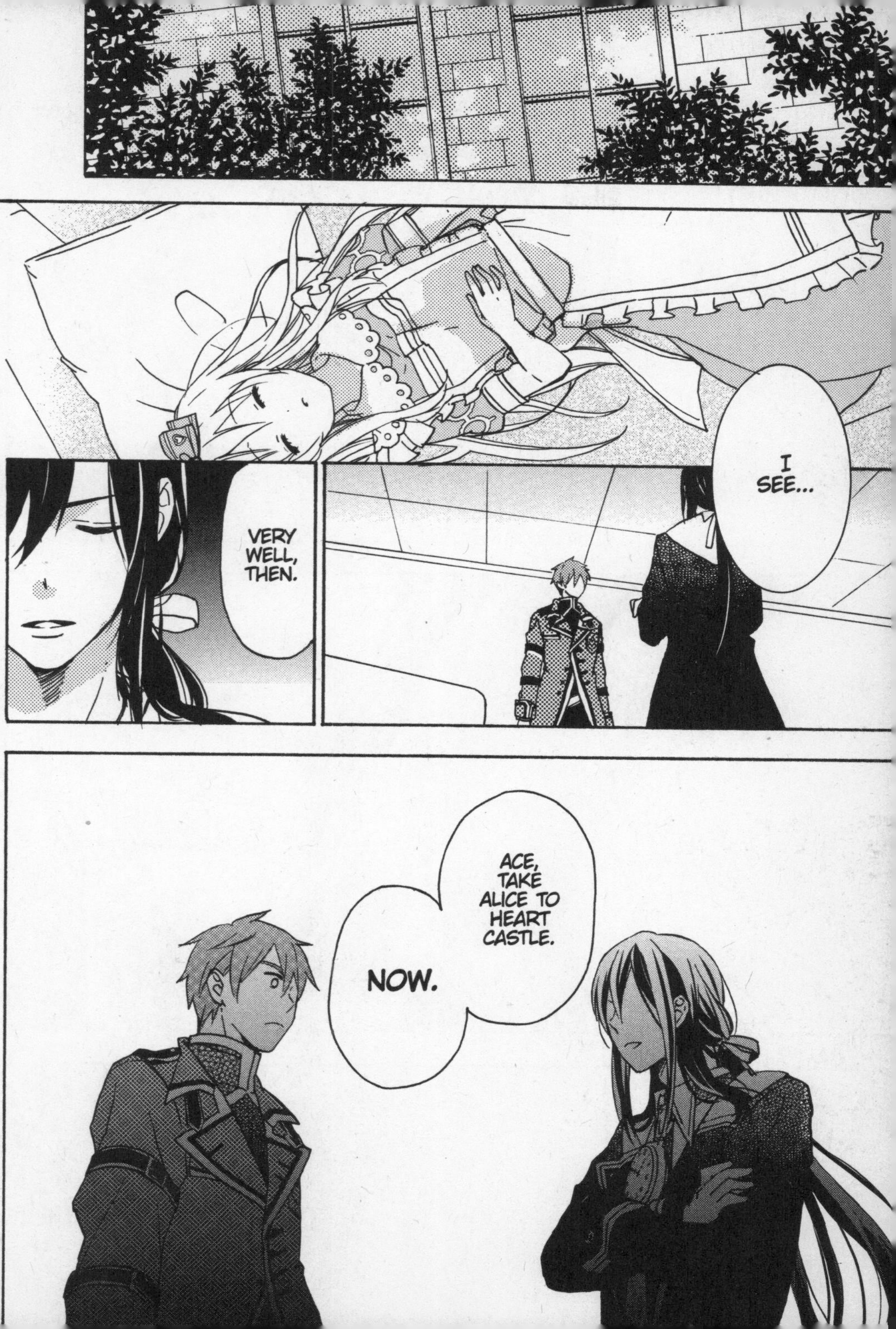
I SEE...
VERY WELL, THEN.
ACE, TAKE ALICE TO HEART CASTLE.
NOW.

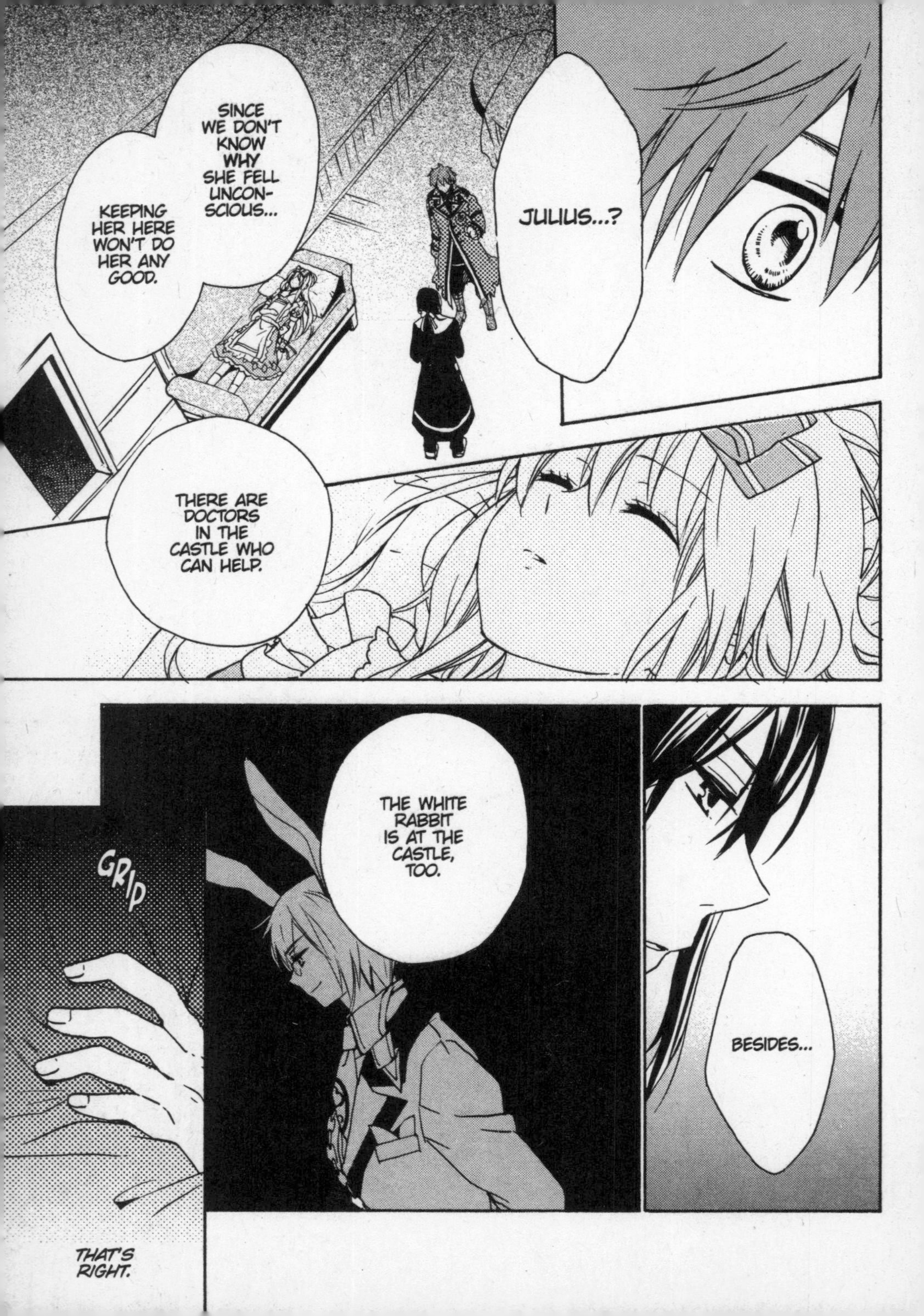
JULIUS...?
SINCE WE DON'T KNOW WHY SHE FELL UNCONSCIOUS...
KEEPING HER HERE WON'T DO HER ANY GOOD.
THERE ARE DOCTORS IN THE CASTLE WHO CAN HELP.
BESIDES...
THE WHITE RABBIT IS AT THE CASTLE, TOO.
GRIP
THAT'S RIGHT.

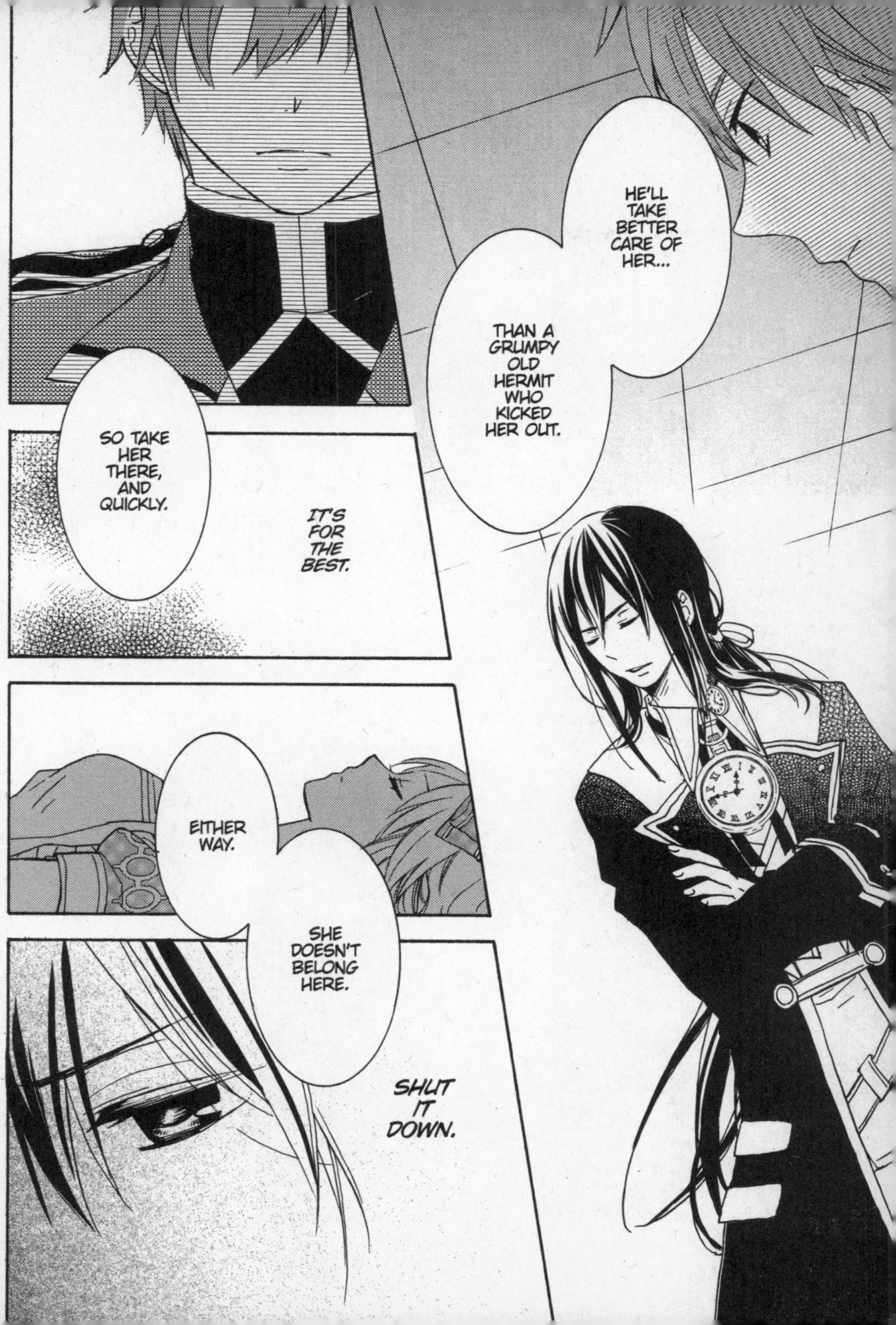
HE'LL TAKE BETTER CARE OF HER...
THAN A GRUMPY OLD HERMIT WHO KICKED HER OUT.
SO TAKE HER THERE, AND QUICKLY.
IT'S FOR THE BEST.
EITHER WAY.
SHE DOESN'T BELONG HERE.
SHUT IT DOWN.

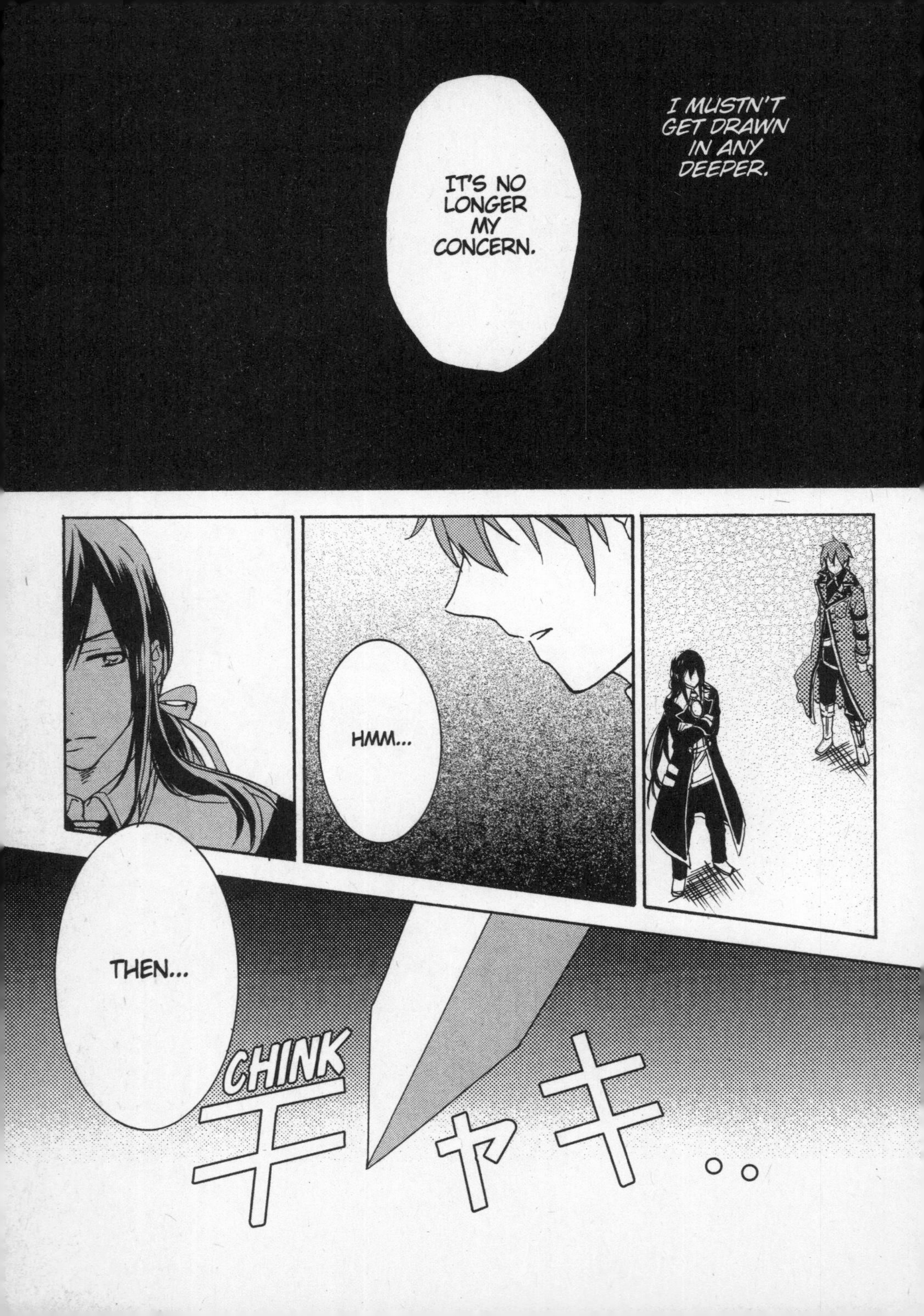
I MUSTN'T GET DRAWN IN ANY DEEPER.
IT'S NO LONGER MY CONCERN.
HMM...
THEN...
CHINK
チャキ。。

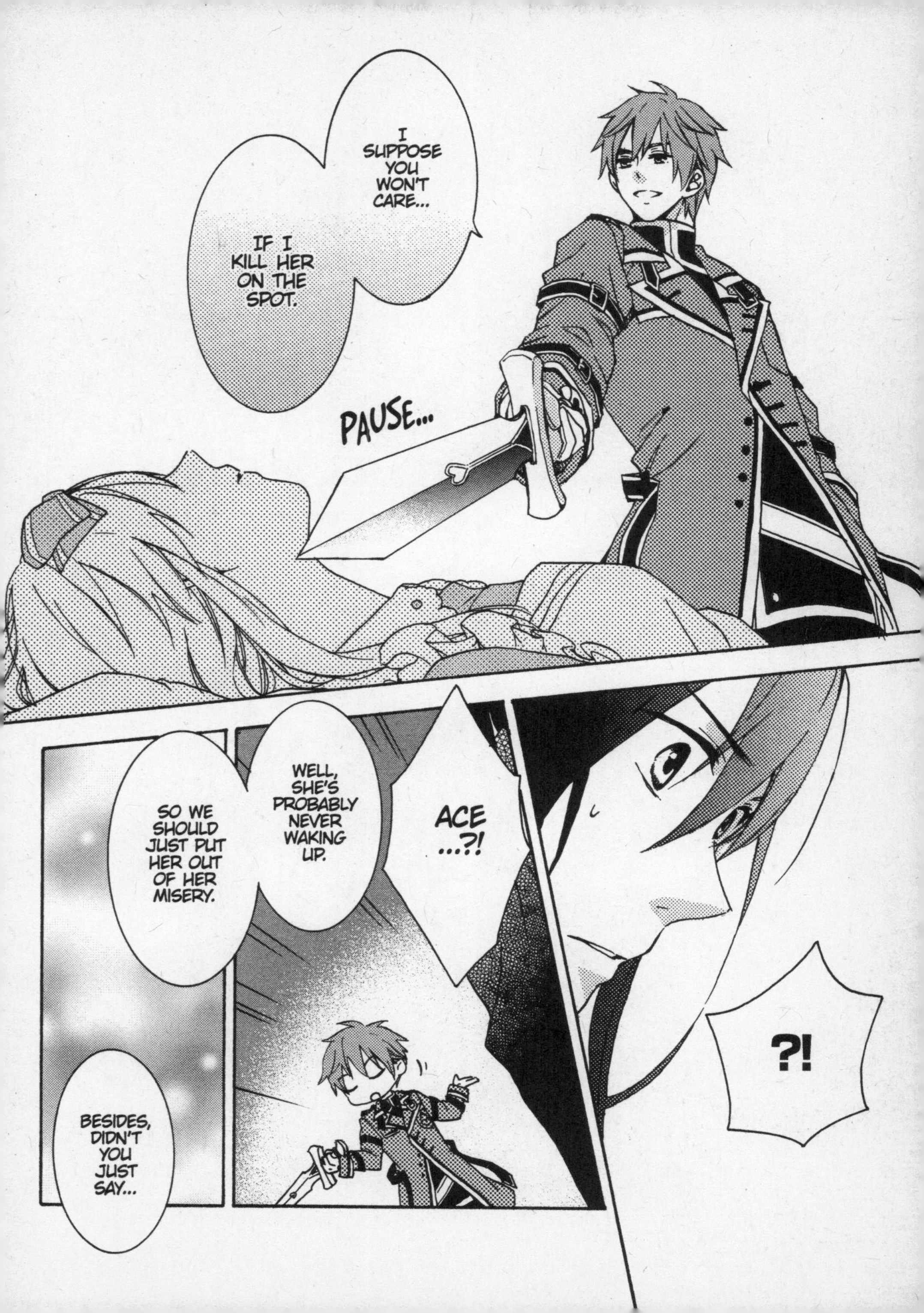
I SUPPOSE YOU WON'T CARE...
IF I KILL HER ON THE SPOT.
PAUSE...
ACE ...?!
?!
WELL, SHE'S PROBABLY NEVER WAKING UP.
SO WE SHOULD JUST PUT HER OUT OF HER MISERY.
BESIDES, DIDN'T YOU JUST SAY...

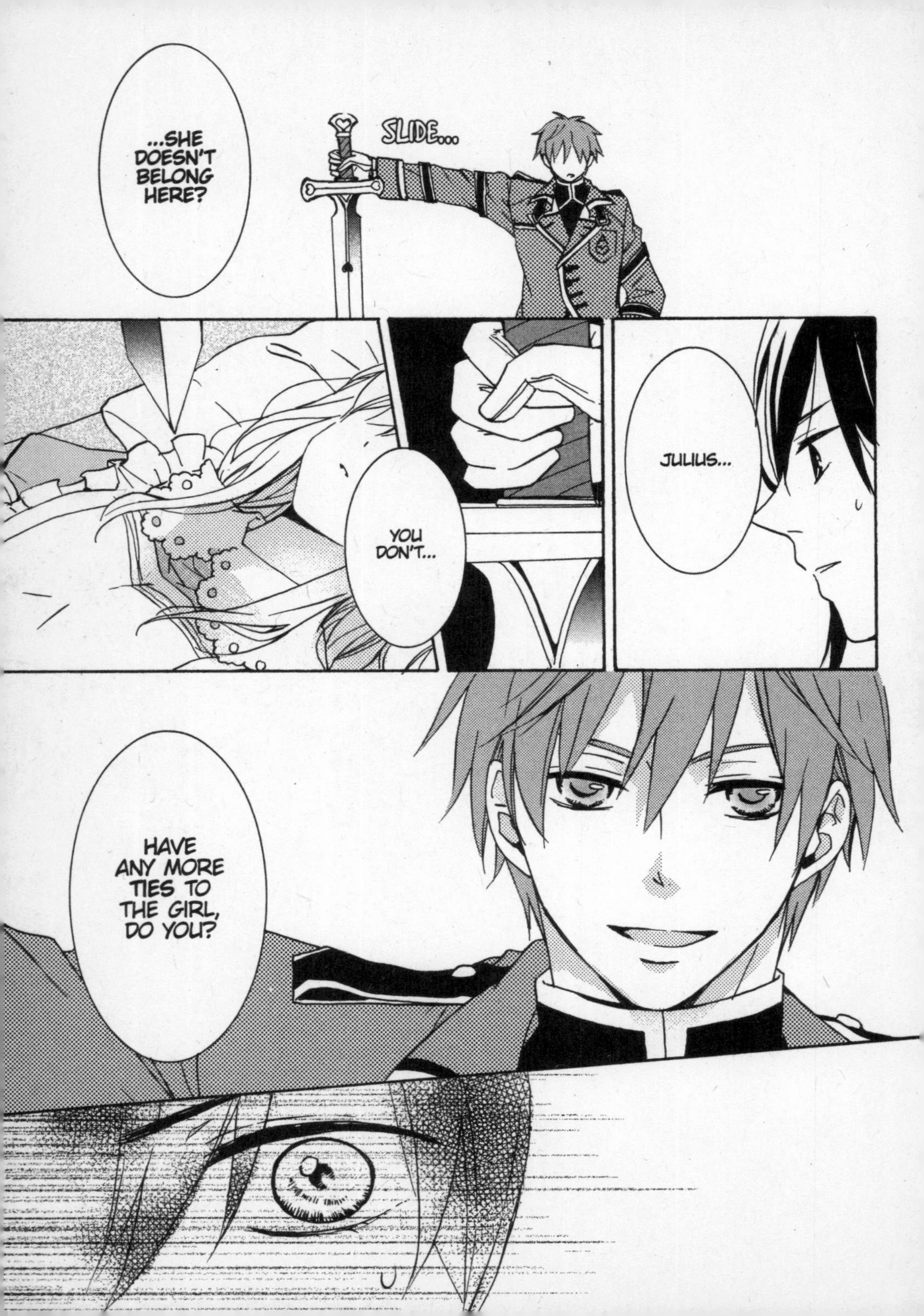
SLIDE...
...SHE DOESN'T BELONG HERE?
JULIUS...
YOU DON'T...
HAVE ANY MORE TIES TO THE GIRL, DO YOU?

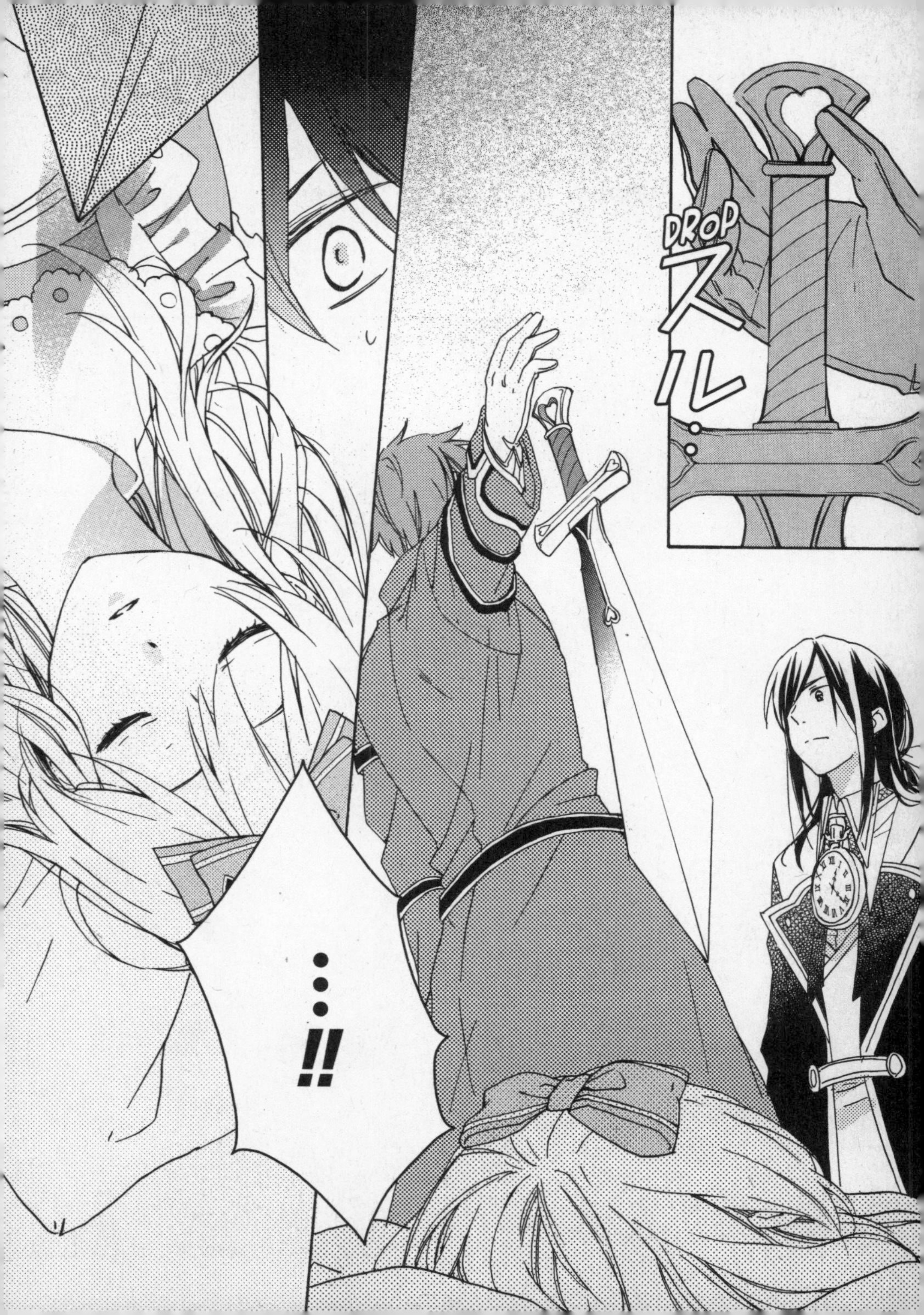
DROP
スル
...!!

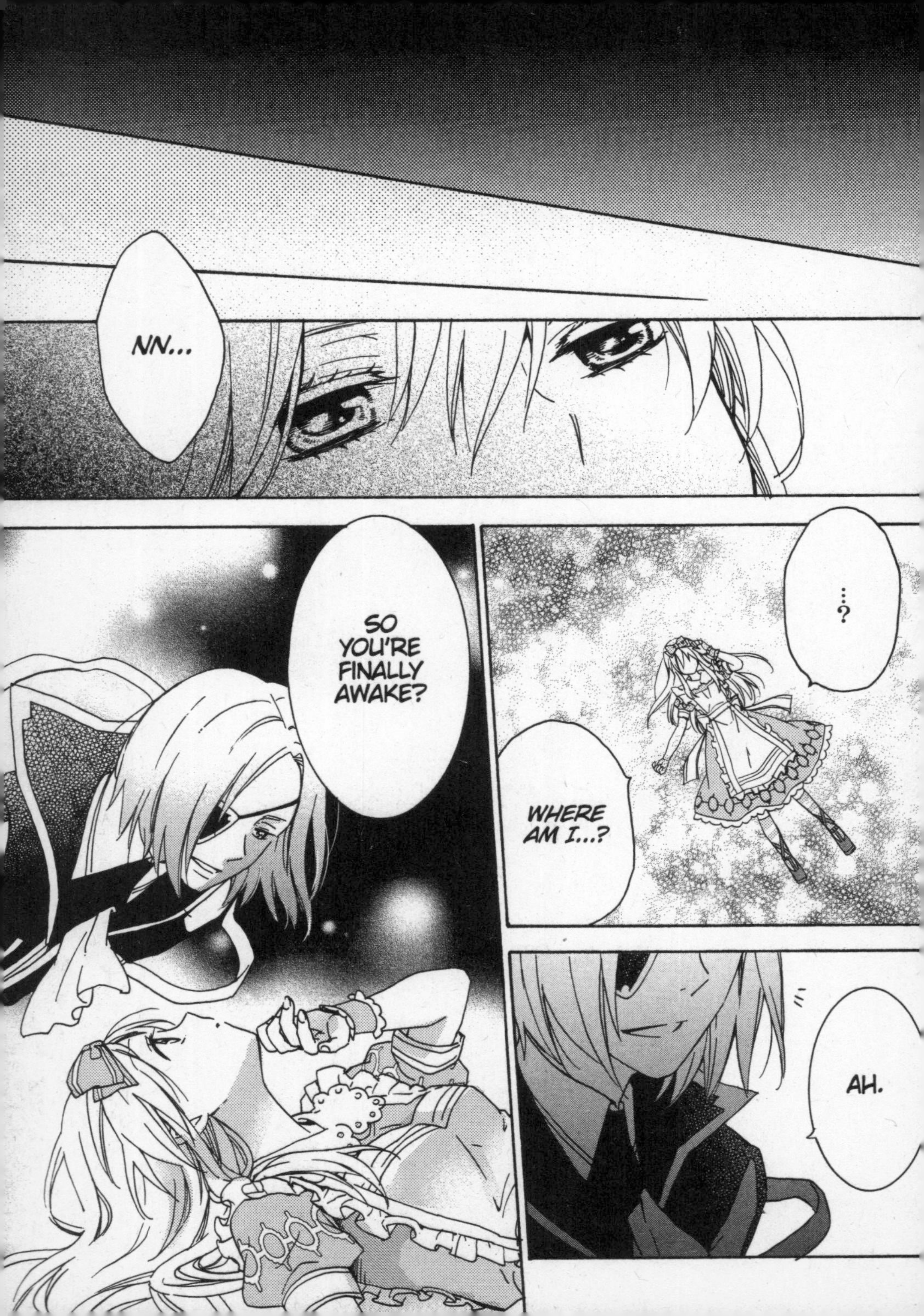
NN...
...?
WHERE AM I...?
AH.
SO YOU'RE FINALLY AWAKE?

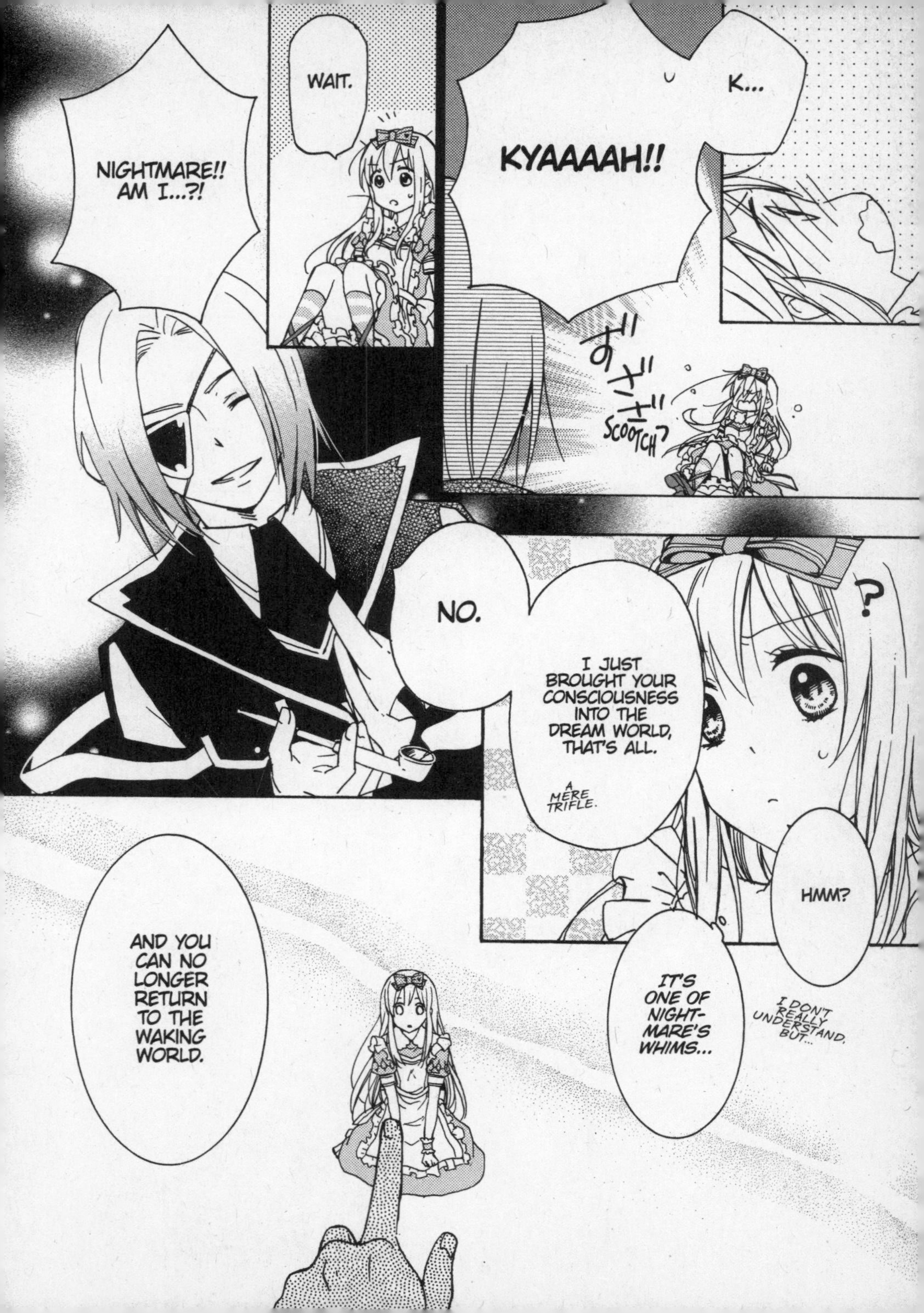
K...
KYAAAAH!!
SCOOTCH
WAIT.
NIGHTMARE!! AM I...?!
?
NO.
I JUST BROUGHT YOUR CONSCIOUSNESS INTO THE DREAM WORLD, THAT'S ALL.
A MERE TRIFLE.
HMM?
IT'S ONE OF NIGHT-MARE'S WHIMS...
I DON'T REALLY UNDERSTAND, BUT...
AND YOU CAN NO LONGER RETURN TO THE WAKING WORLD.

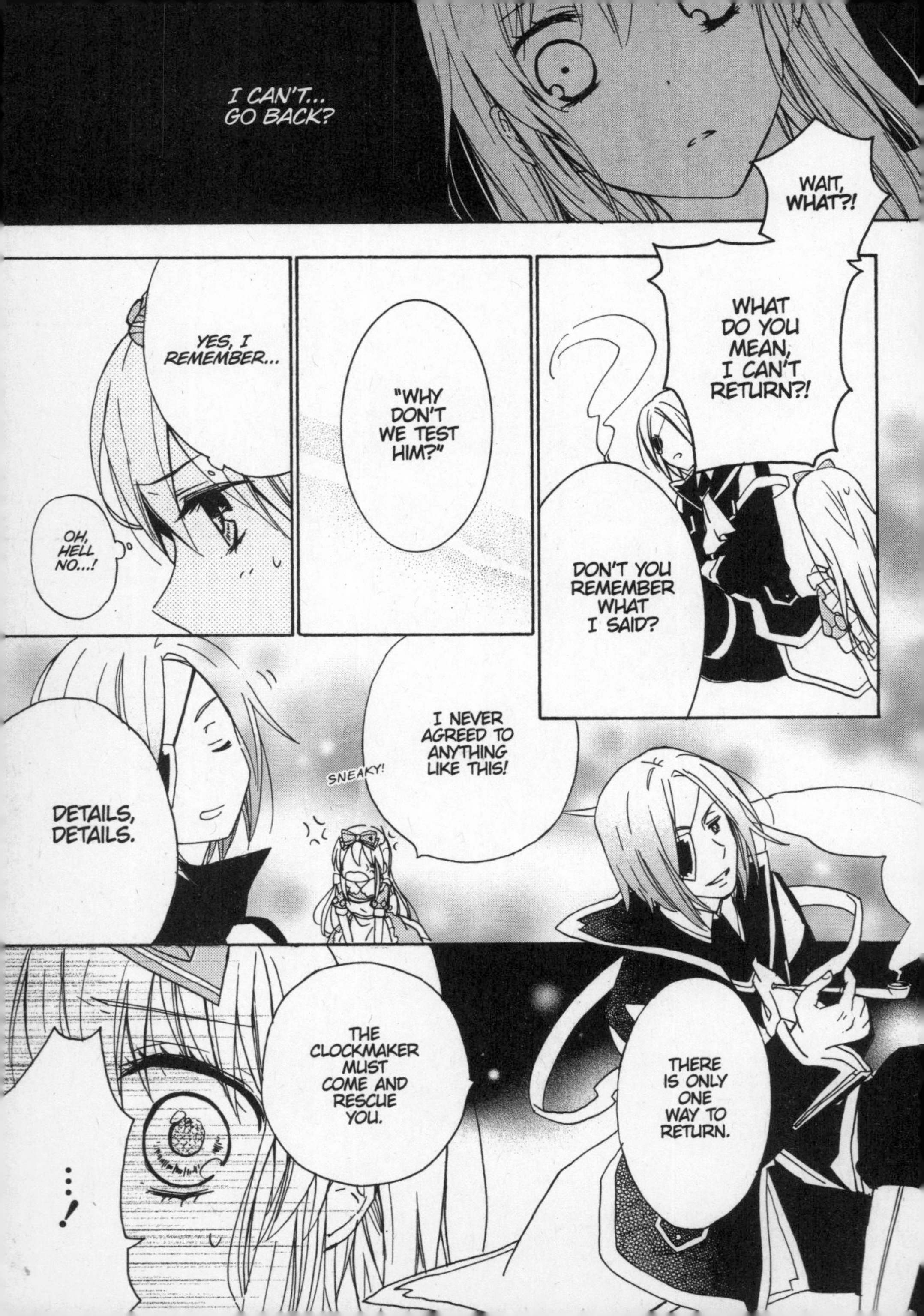
I CAN'T... GO BACK?
WAIT, WHAT?!
WHAT DO YOU MEAN, I CAN'T RETURN?!
DON'T YOU REMEMBER WHAT I SAID?
"WHY DON'T WE TEST HIM?"
YES, I REMEMBER...
OH, HELL NO...!
I NEVER AGREED TO ANYTHING LIKE THIS!
SNEAKY!
DETAILS, DETAILS.
THERE IS ONLY ONE WAY TO RETURN.
THE CLOCKMAKER MUST COME AND RESCUE YOU.
...!

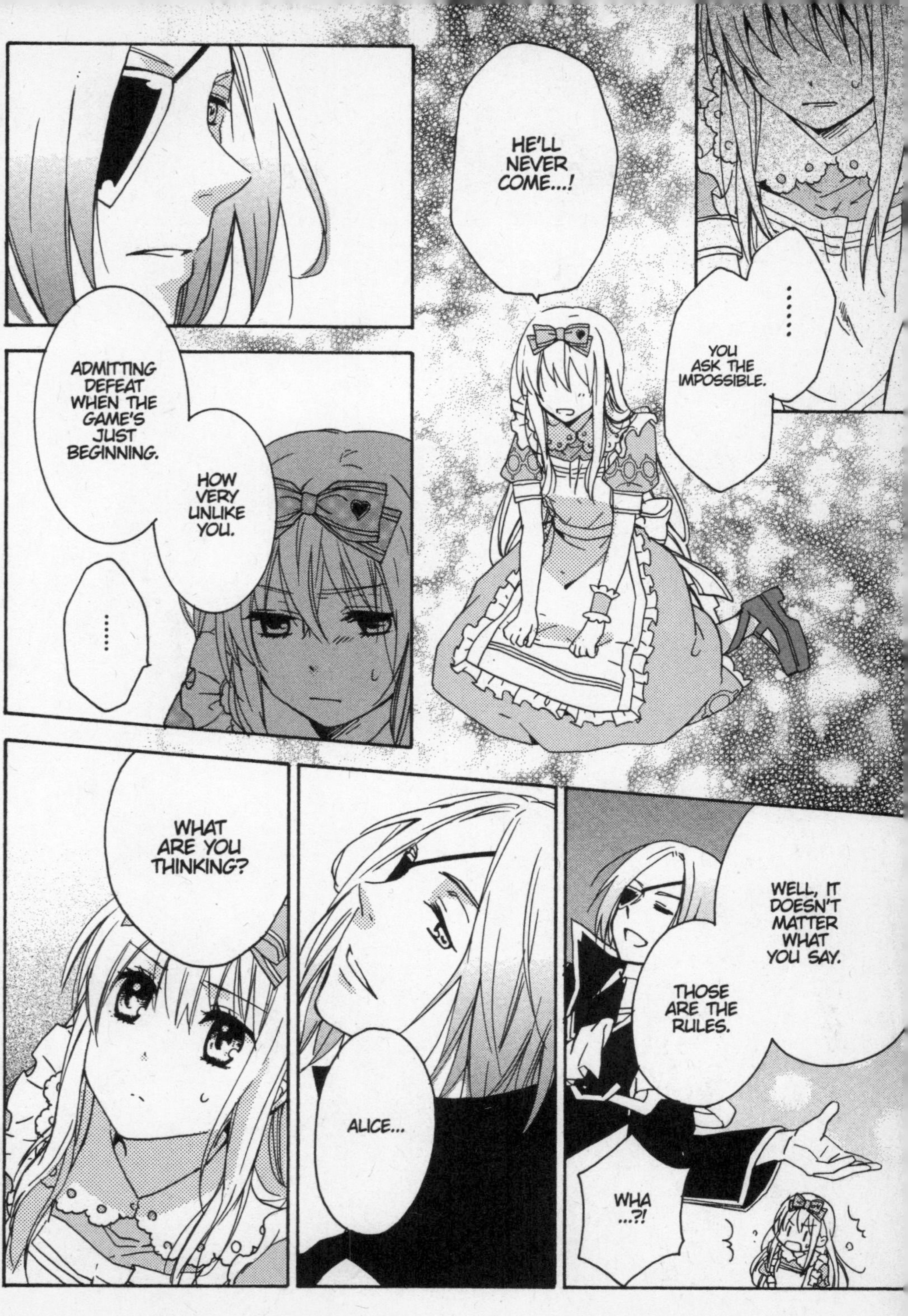
......
YOU ASK THE IMPOSSIBLE.
HE'LL NEVER COME...!
ADMITTING DEFEAT WHEN THE GAME'S JUST BEGINNING.
HOW VERY UNLIKE YOU.
......
WELL, IT DOESN'T MATTER WHAT YOU SAY.
THOSE ARE THE RULES.
WHA ...?!
ALICE...
WHAT ARE YOU THINKING?

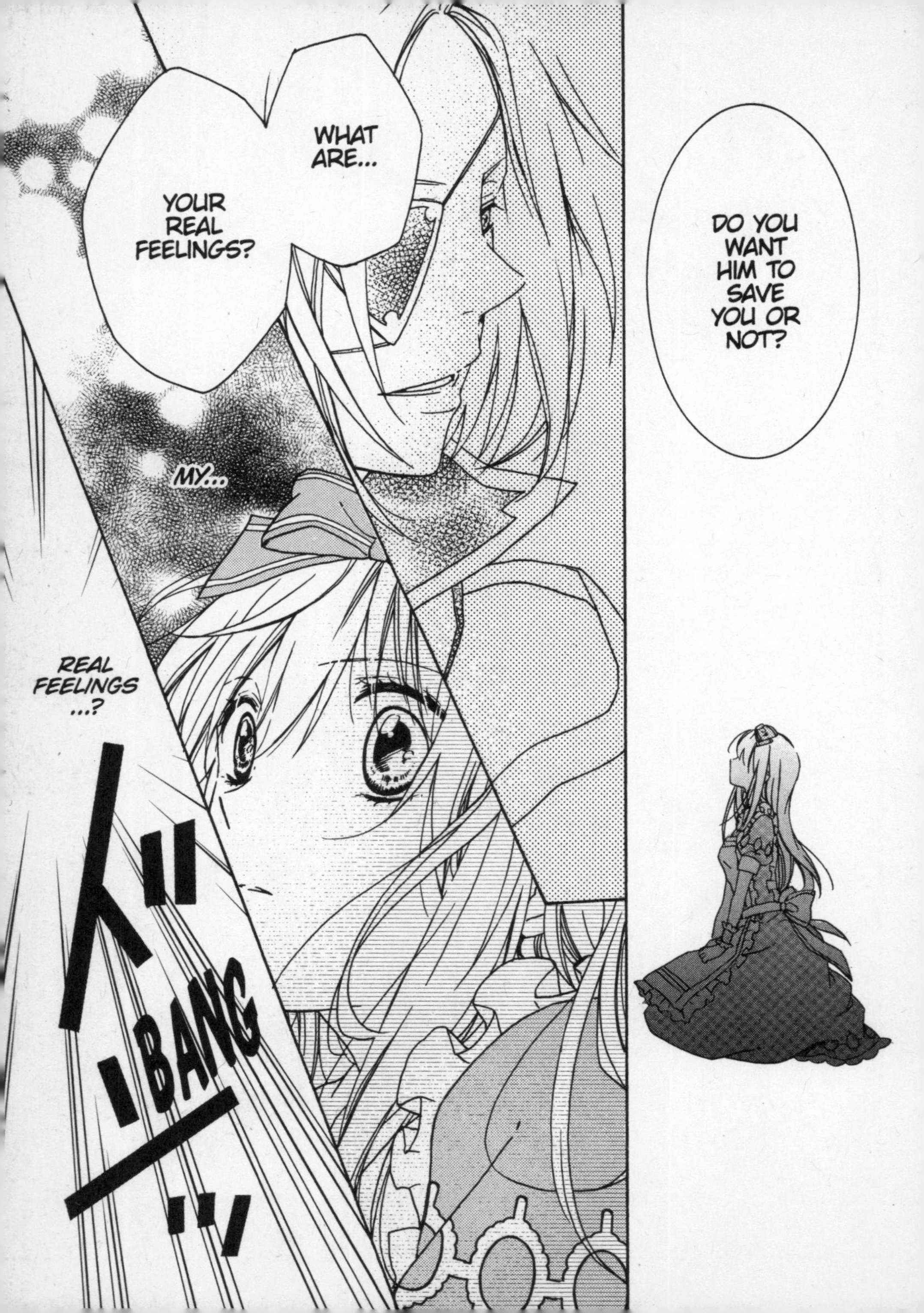
DO YOU WANT HIM TO SAVE YOU OR NOT?
WHAT ARE...
YOUR REAL FEELINGS?
MY...
REAL FEELINGS ...?
BANG

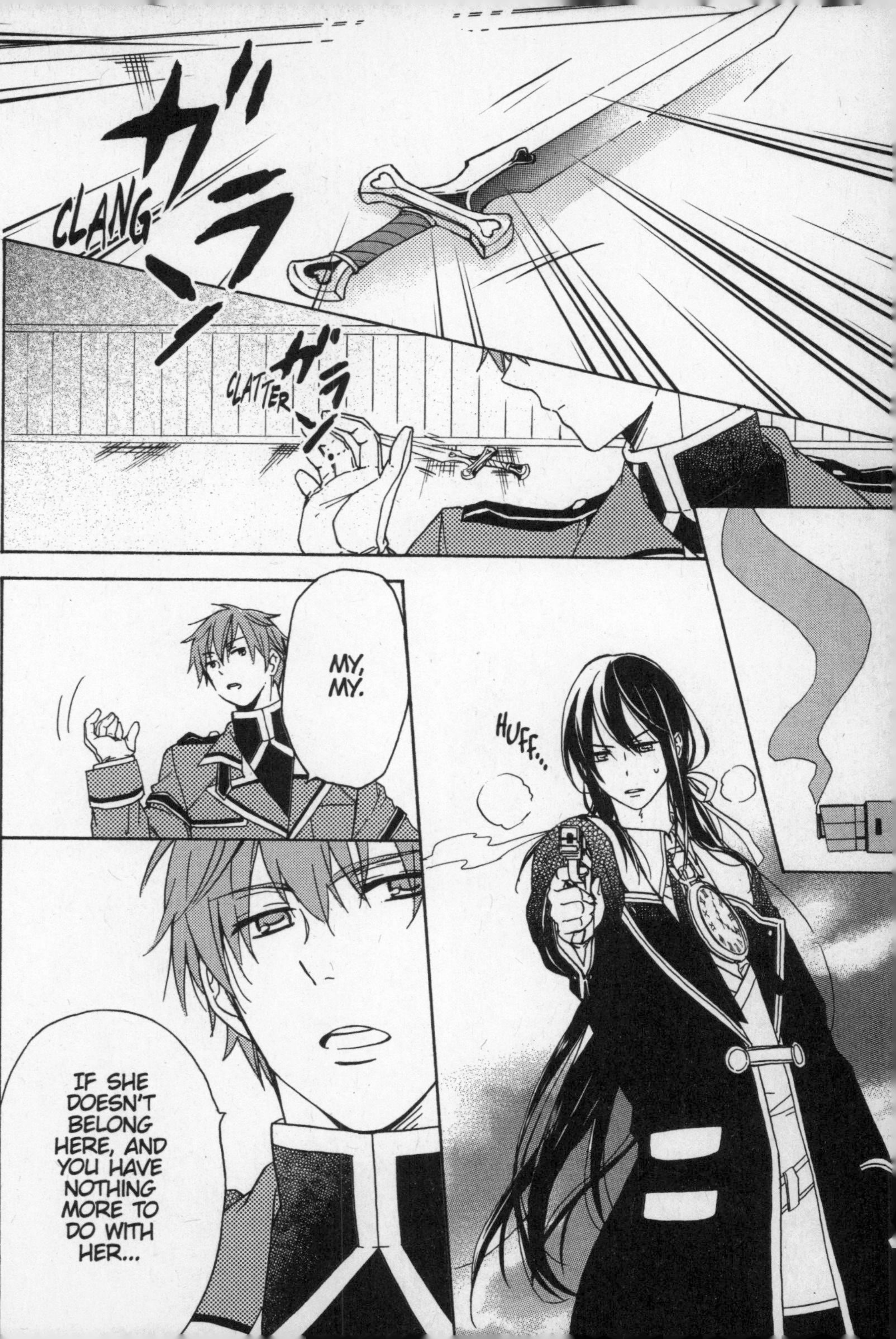
ガラーン
CLANG
ガラーン
CLATTER
HUFF...
MY, MY.
IF SHE DOESN'T BELONG HERE, AND YOU HAVE NOTHING MORE TO DO WITH HER...

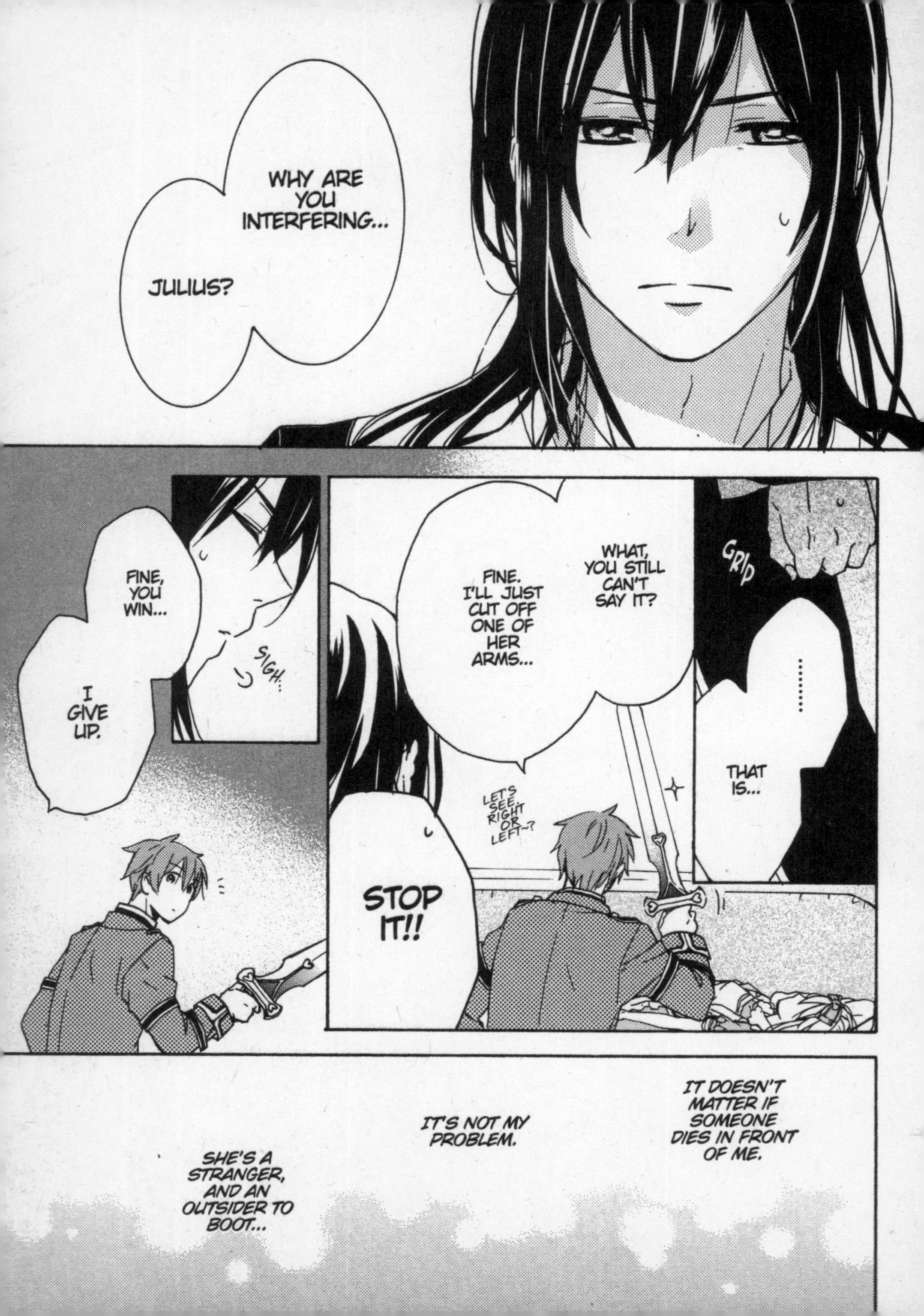
WHY ARE YOU INTERFERING...
JULIUS?
GRIP
......
THAT IS...
WHAT, YOU STILL CAN'T SAY IT?
FINE. I'LL JUST CUT OFF ONE OF HER ARMS...
LET'S SEE, RIGHT OR LEFT~?
STOP IT!!
FINE, YOU WIN...
SIGH...
I GIVE UP.
IT DOESN'T MATTER IF SOMEONE DIES IN FRONT OF ME.
IT'S NOT MY PROBLEM.
SHE'S A STRANGER, AND AN OUTSIDER TO BOOT...

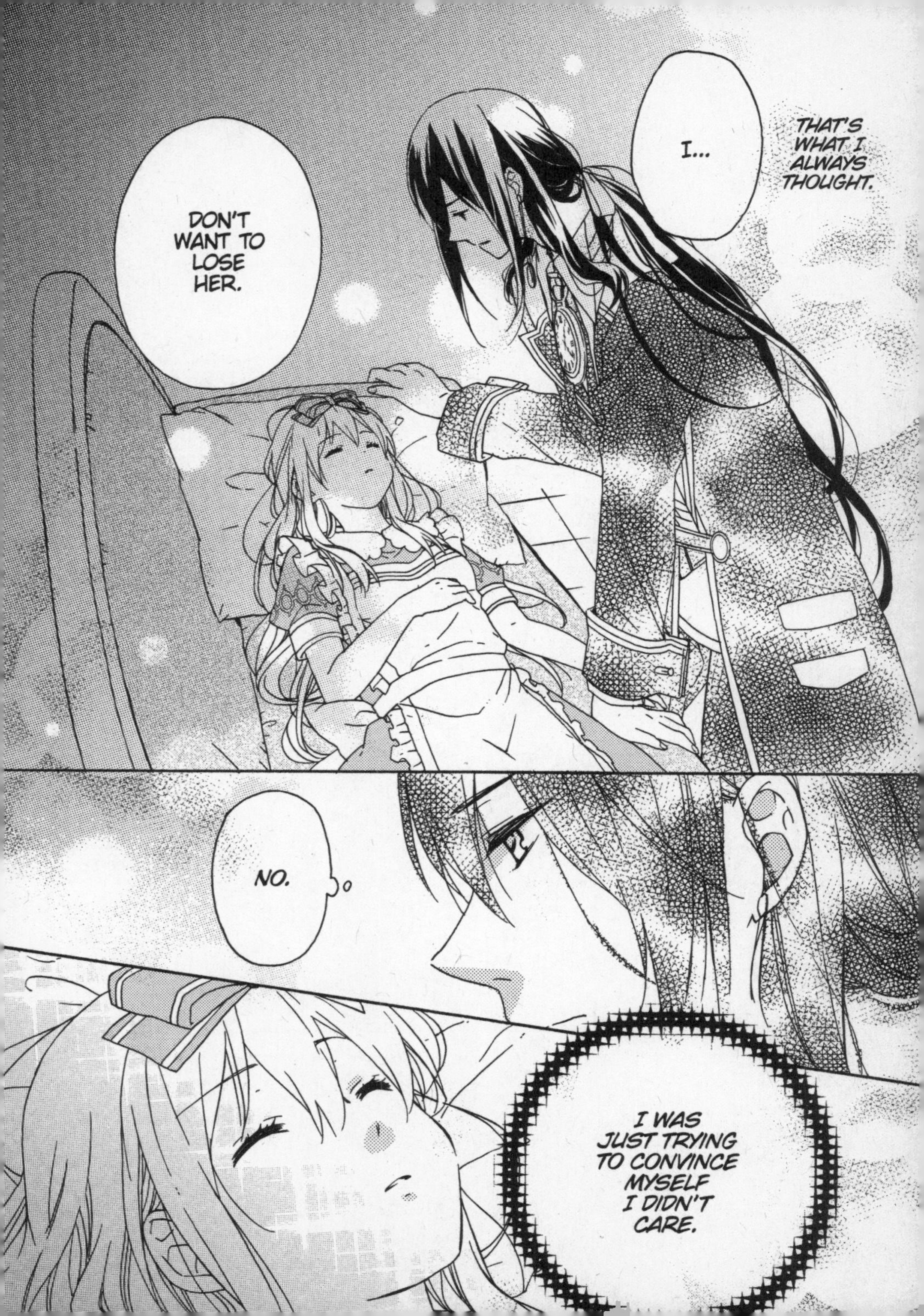
THAT'S WHAT I ALWAYS THOUGHT.
I...
DON'T WANT TO LOSE HER.
NO.
I WAS JUST TRYING TO CONVINCE MYSELF I DIDN'T CARE.

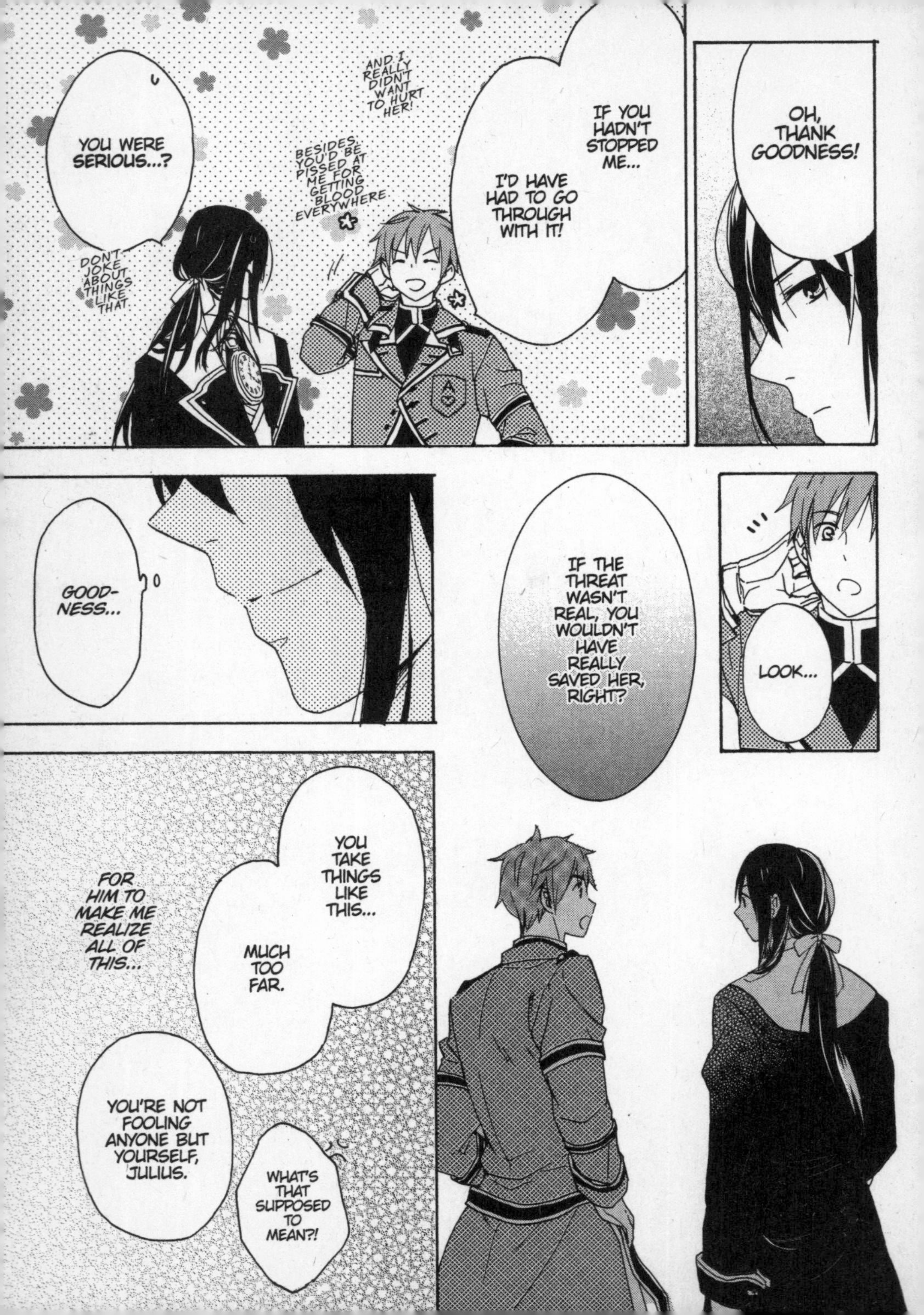
OH, THANK GOODNESS!
IF YOU HADN'T STOPPED ME...
I'D HAVE HAD TO GO THROUGH WITH IT!
AND I REALLY DIDN'T WANT TO HURT HER!
BESIDES, YOU'D BE PISSED AT ME FOR GETTING BLOOD EVERYWHERE.
YOU WERE SERIOUS...?
DON'T JOKE ABOUT THINGS LIKE THAT.
LOOK...
IF THE THREAT WASN'T REAL, YOU WOULDN'T HAVE REALLY SAVED HER, RIGHT?
GOODNESS...
YOU TAKE THINGS LIKE THIS...
MUCH TOO FAR.
FOR HIM TO MAKE ME REALIZE ALL OF THIS...
YOU'RE NOT FOOLING ANYONE BUT YOURSELF, JULIUS.
WHAT'S THAT SUPPOSED TO MEAN?!

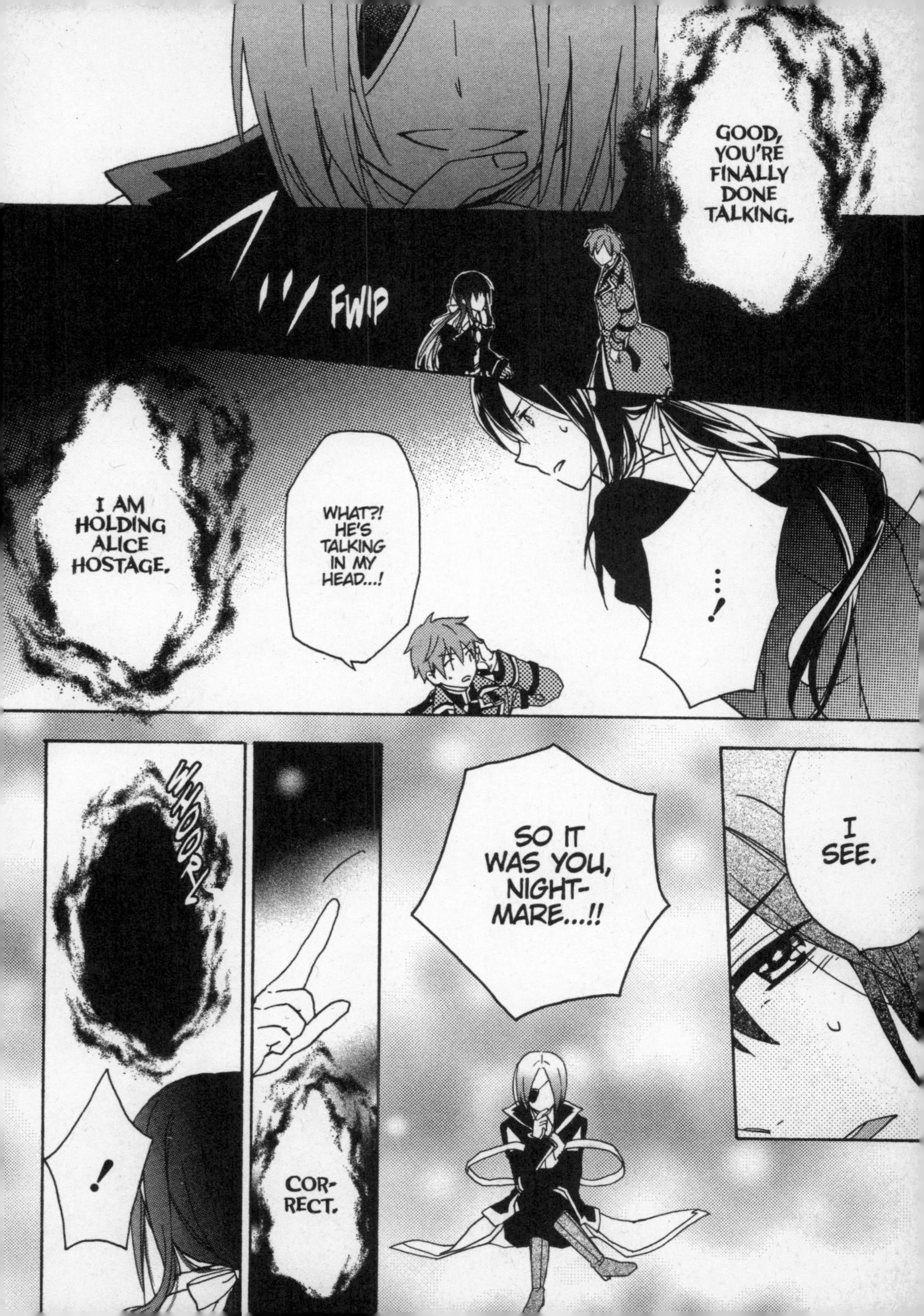
GOOD, YOU'RE FINALLY DONE TALKING.
FWIP
...!
WHAT?! HE'S TALKING IN MY HEAD...!
I AM HOLDING ALICE HOSTAGE.
I SEE.
SO IT WAS YOU, NIGHT-MARE...!!
COR-RECT.
WHOOORL
!

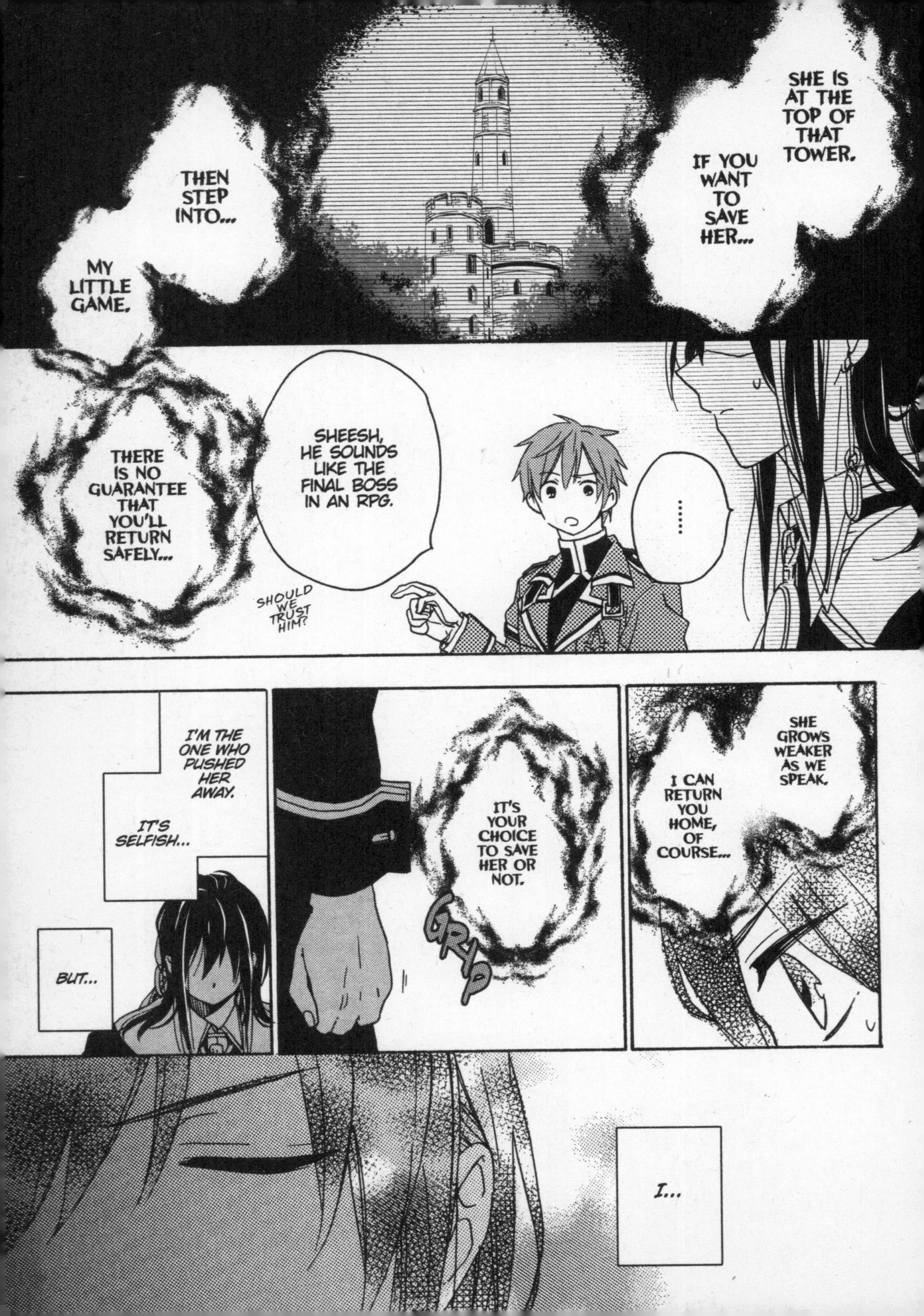
SHE IS AT THE TOP OF THAT TOWER.
IF YOU WANT TO SAVE HER...
THEN STEP INTO...
MY LITTLE GAME.
......
SHEESH, HE SOUNDS LIKE THE FINAL BOSS IN AN RPG.
SHOULD WE TRUST HIM?
THERE IS NO GUARANTEE THAT YOU'LL RETURN SAFELY...
SHE GROWS WEAKER AS WE SPEAK.
I CAN RETURN YOU HOME, OF COURSE...
IT'S YOUR CHOICE TO SAVE HER OR NOT.
GRIP
I'M THE ONE WHO PUSHED HER AWAY.
IT'S SELFISH...
BUT...
I...

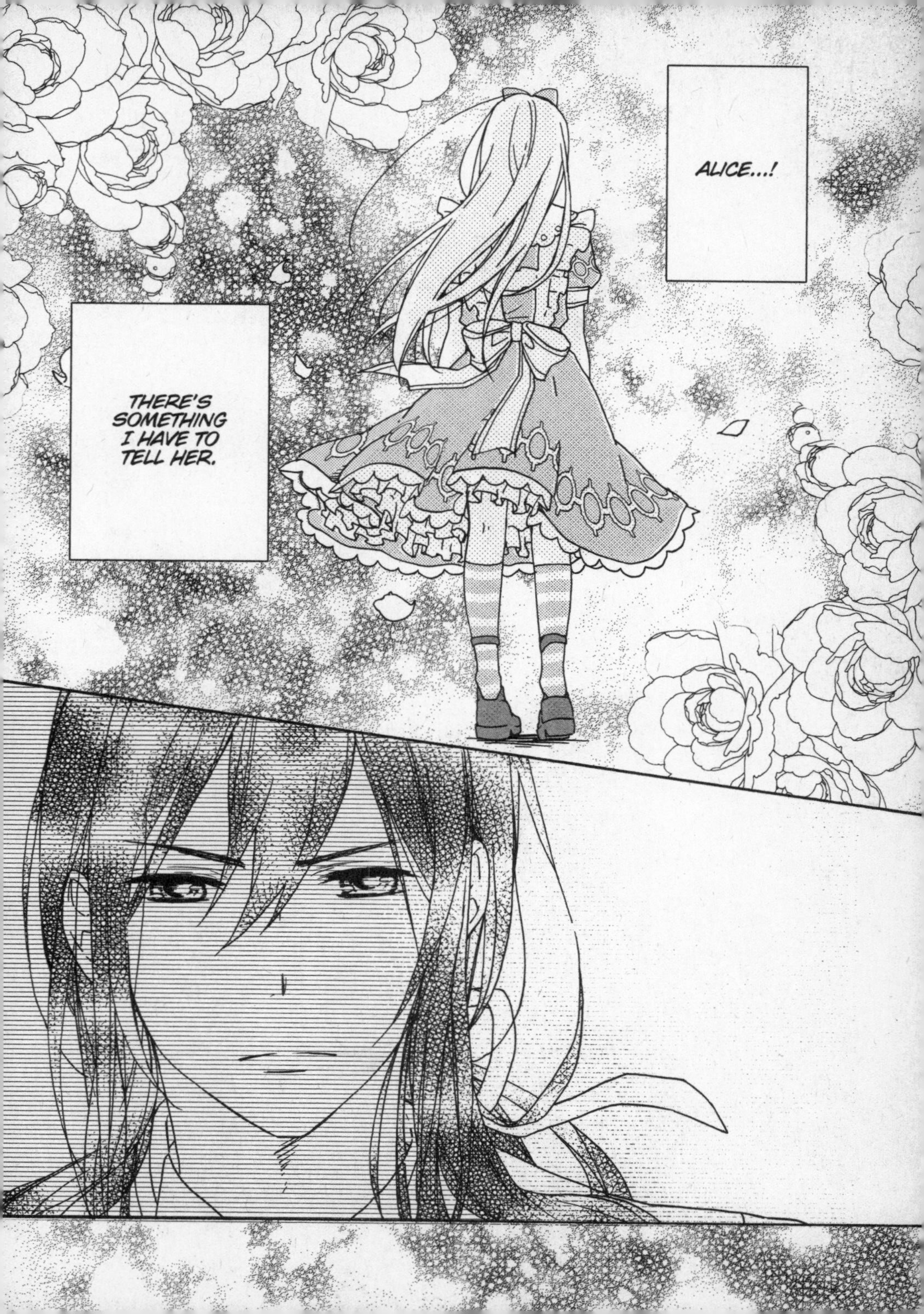
ALICE...!
THERE'S SOMETHING I HAVE TO TELL HER.

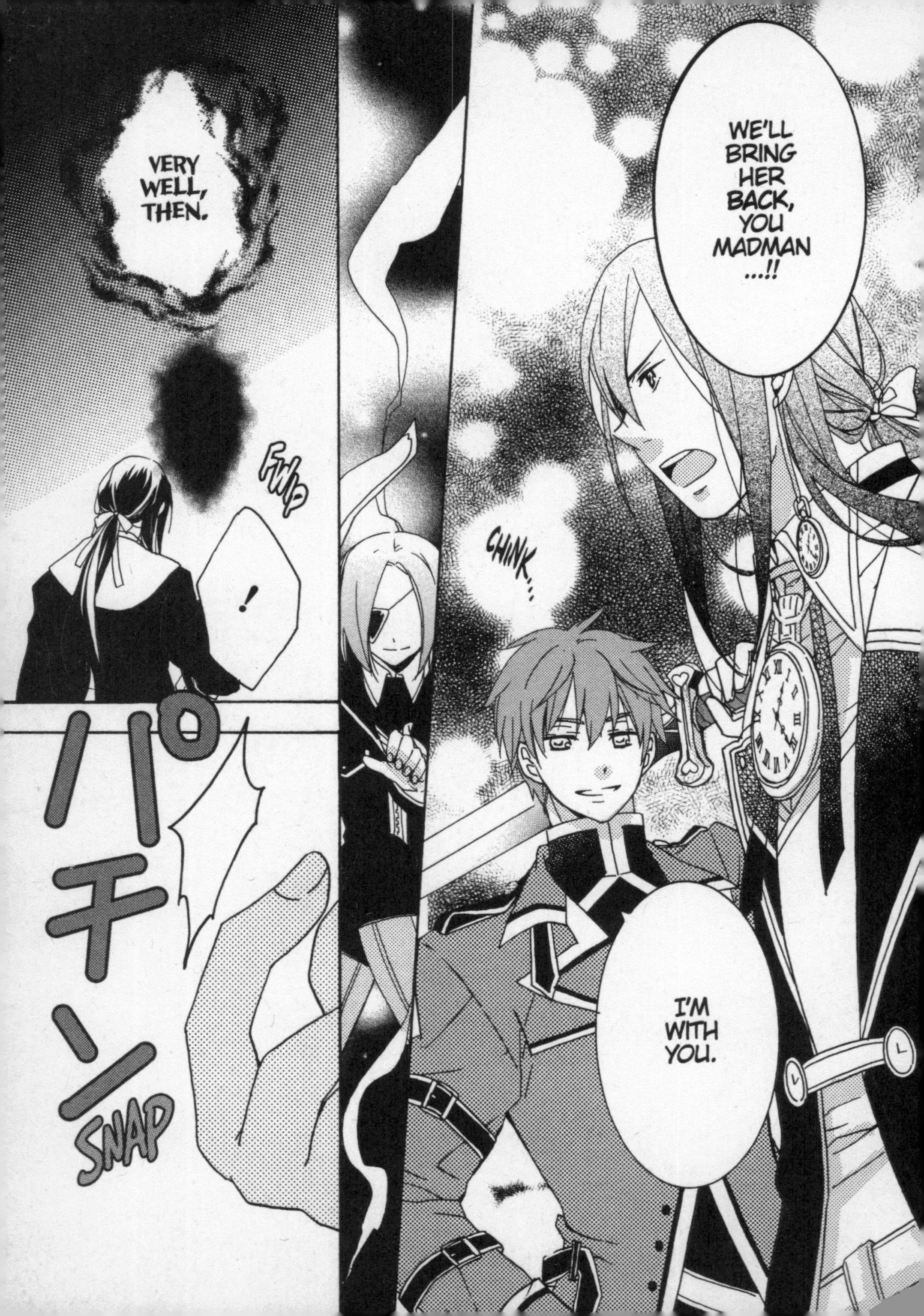
WE'LL BRING HER BACK, YOU MADMAN ...!!
CHINK...
I'M WITH YOU.
VERY WELL, THEN.
FWIP
!
パチン
SNAP

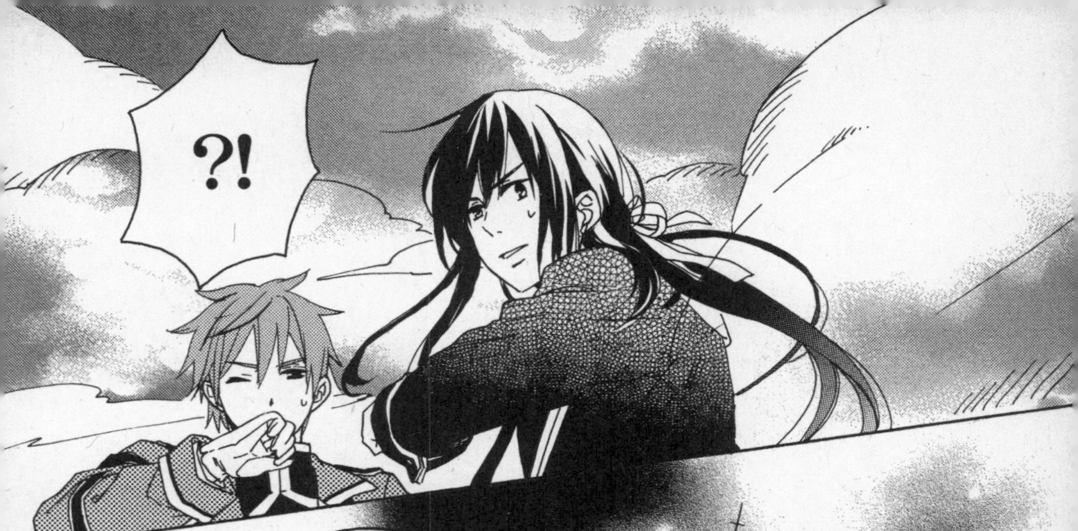
?!

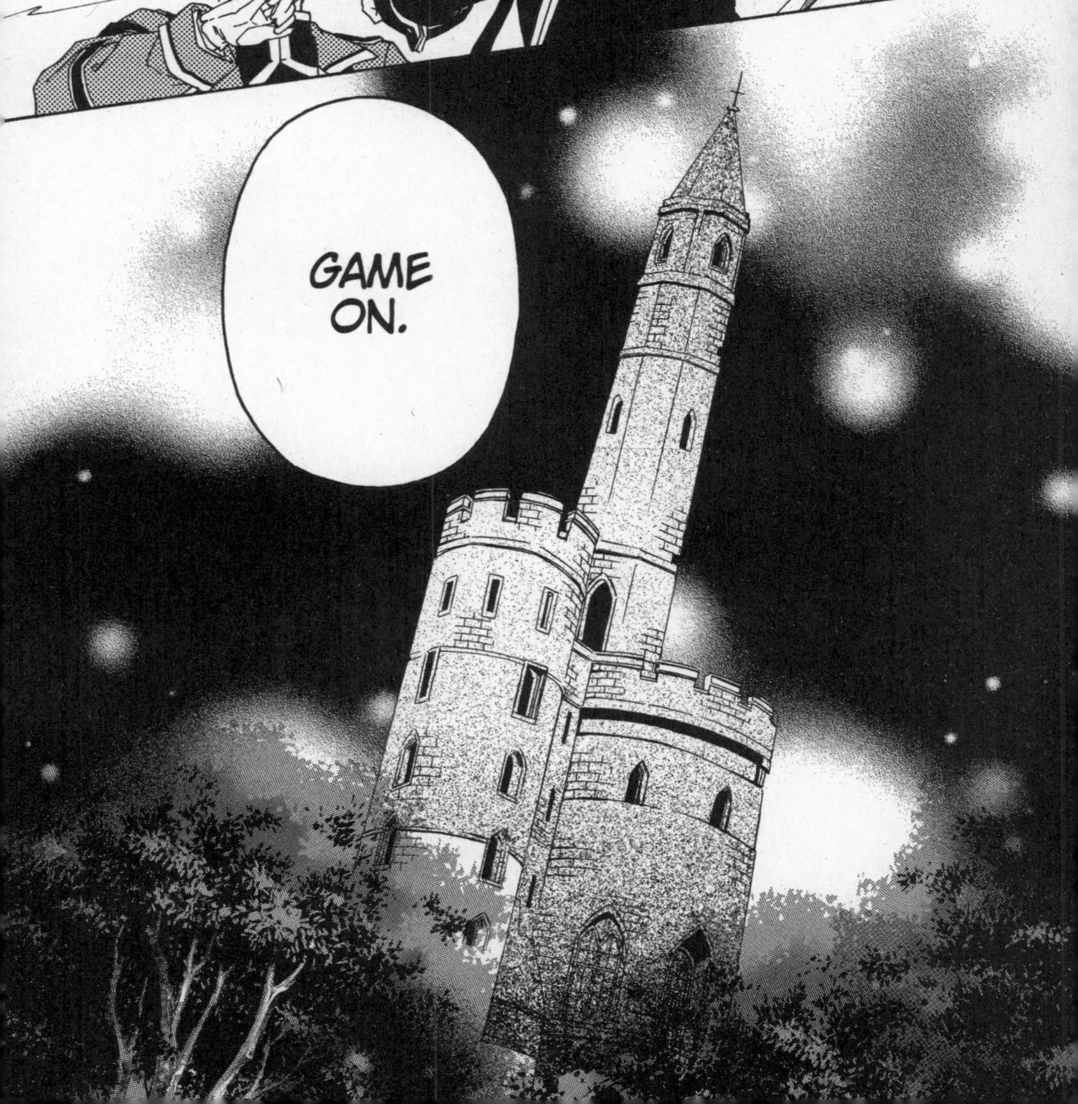
GAME ON.

ハートの国のアリス

恋(こい)する茨(いばら)の迷宮(ラビリンス)

Alice
IN THE
COUNTRY OF
Hearts

Love Labyrinth
of Thorns

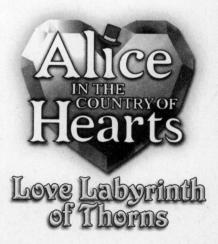

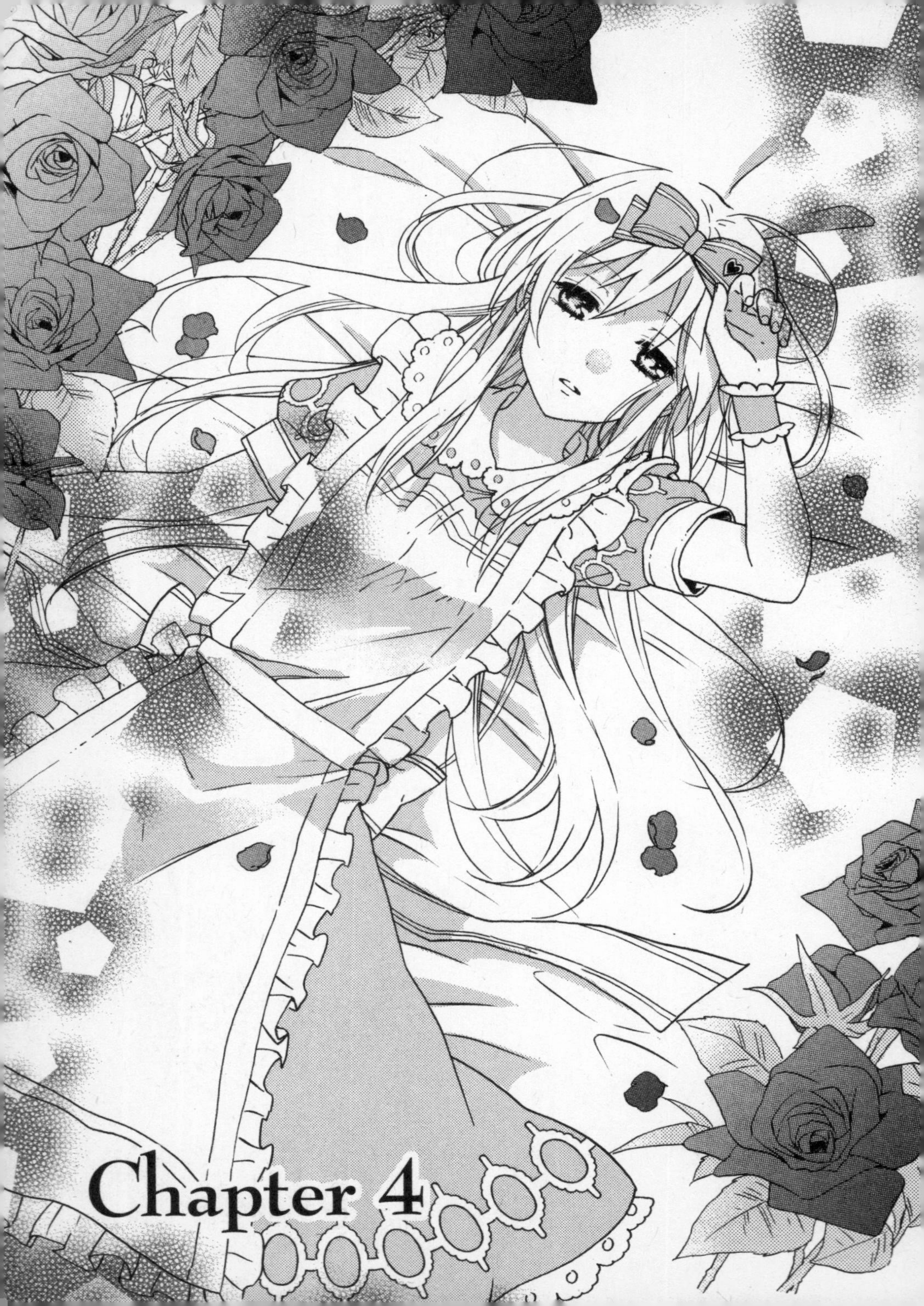
Chapter 4

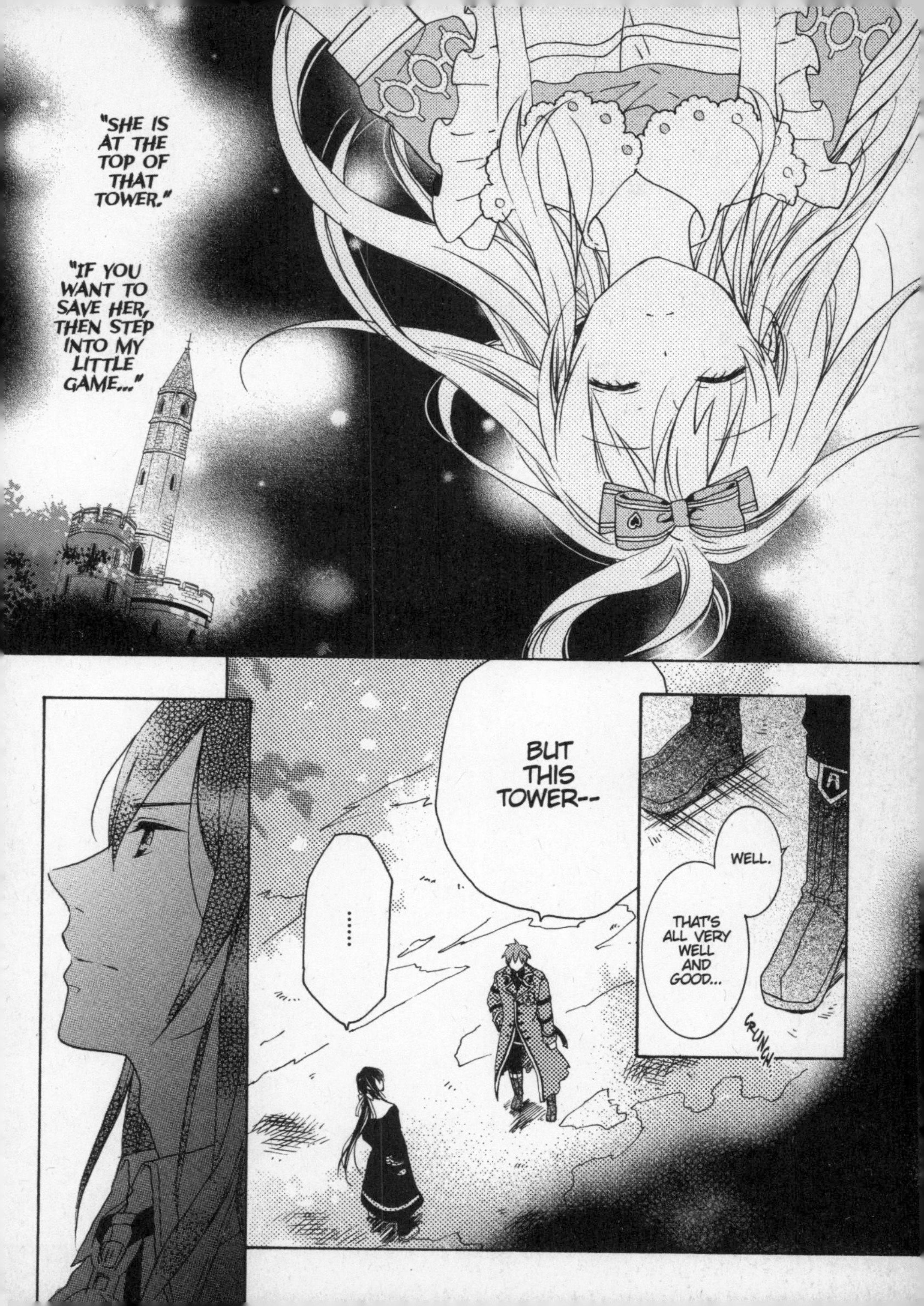
"SHE IS AT THE TOP OF THAT TOWER."
"IF YOU WANT TO SAVE HER, THEN STEP INTO MY LITTLE GAME..."
WELL.
THAT'S ALL VERY WELL AND GOOD...
CRUNCH
BUT THIS TOWER--
......

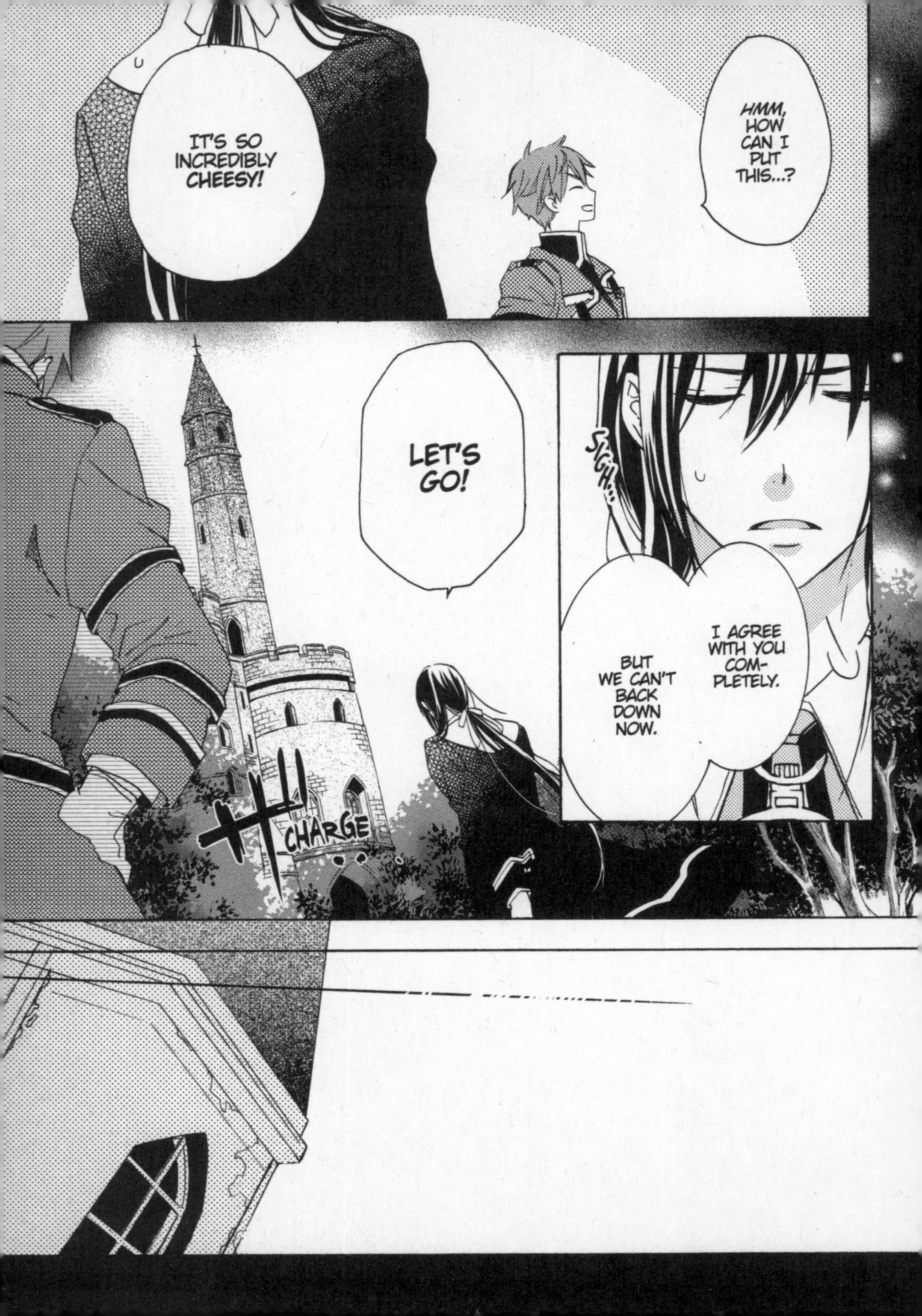
HMM, HOW CAN I PUT THIS...?
IT'S SO INCREDIBLY CHEESY!
SIGH...
I AGREE WITH YOU COM-PLETELY.
BUT WE CAN'T BACK DOWN NOW.
LET'S GO!
CHARGE

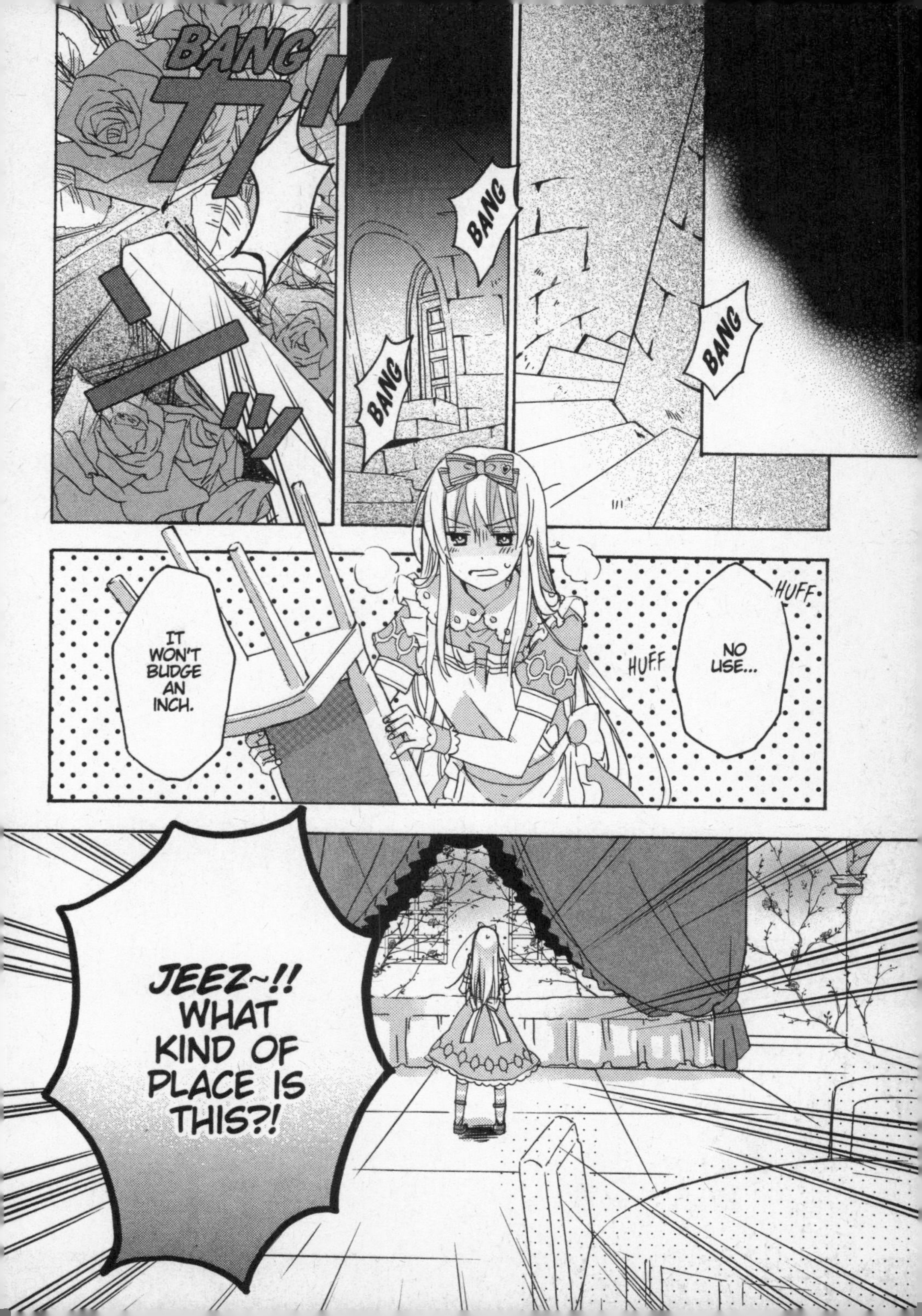
BANG
BANG
BANG
BANG
HUFF
NO USE...
HUFF
IT WON'T BUDGE AN INCH.
JEEZ~!! WHAT KIND OF PLACE IS THIS?!

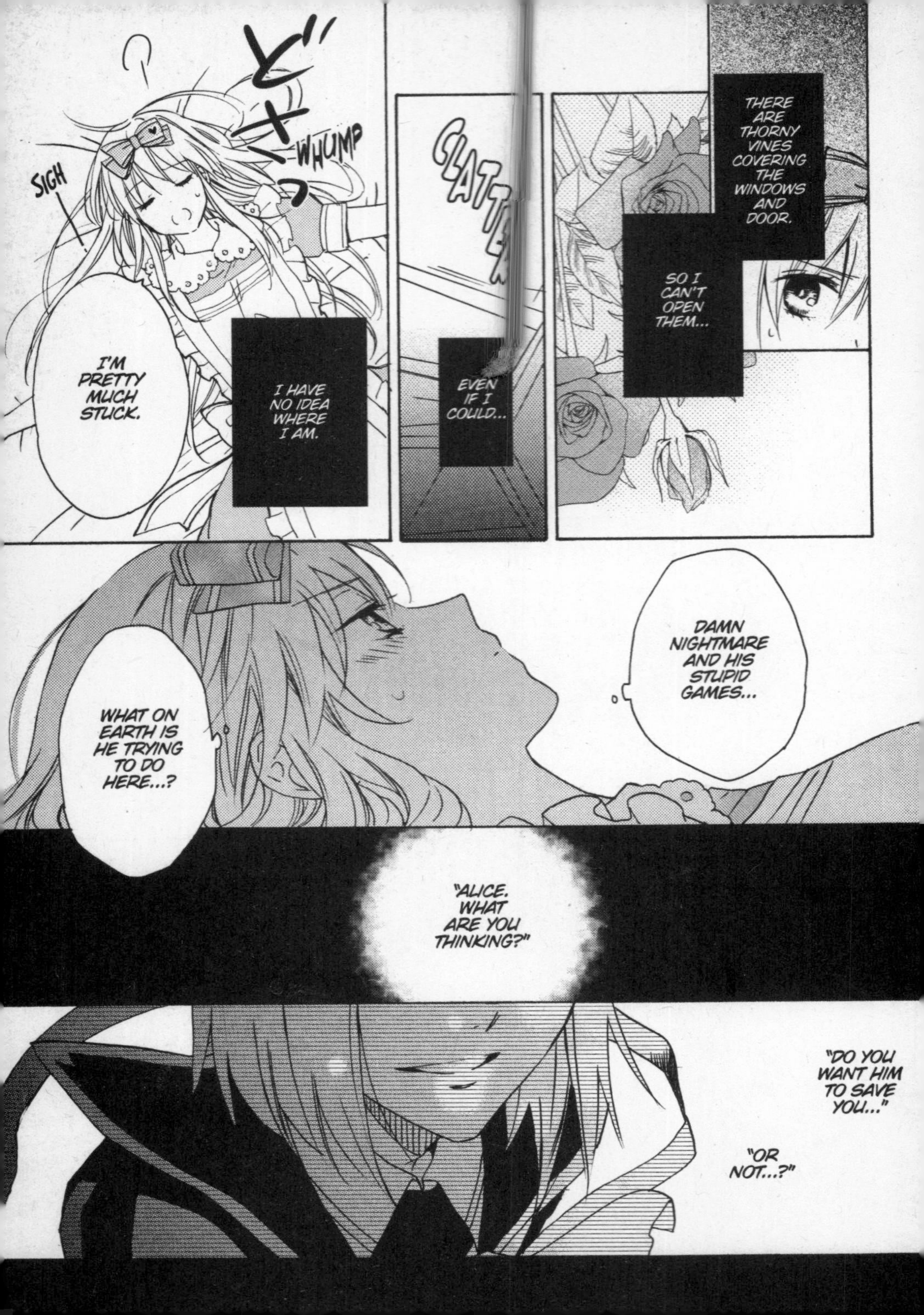
THERE ARE THORNY VINES COVERING THE WINDOWS AND DOOR.
SO I CAN'T OPEN THEM...
CLATTER
EVEN IF I COULD...
I HAVE NO IDEA WHERE I AM.
WHUMP
SIGH
I'M PRETTY MUCH STUCK.
DAMN NIGHTMARE AND HIS STUPID GAMES...
WHAT ON EARTH IS HE TRYING TO DO HERE...?
"ALICE. WHAT ARE YOU THINKING?"
"DO YOU WANT HIM TO SAVE YOU..."
"OR NOT...?"

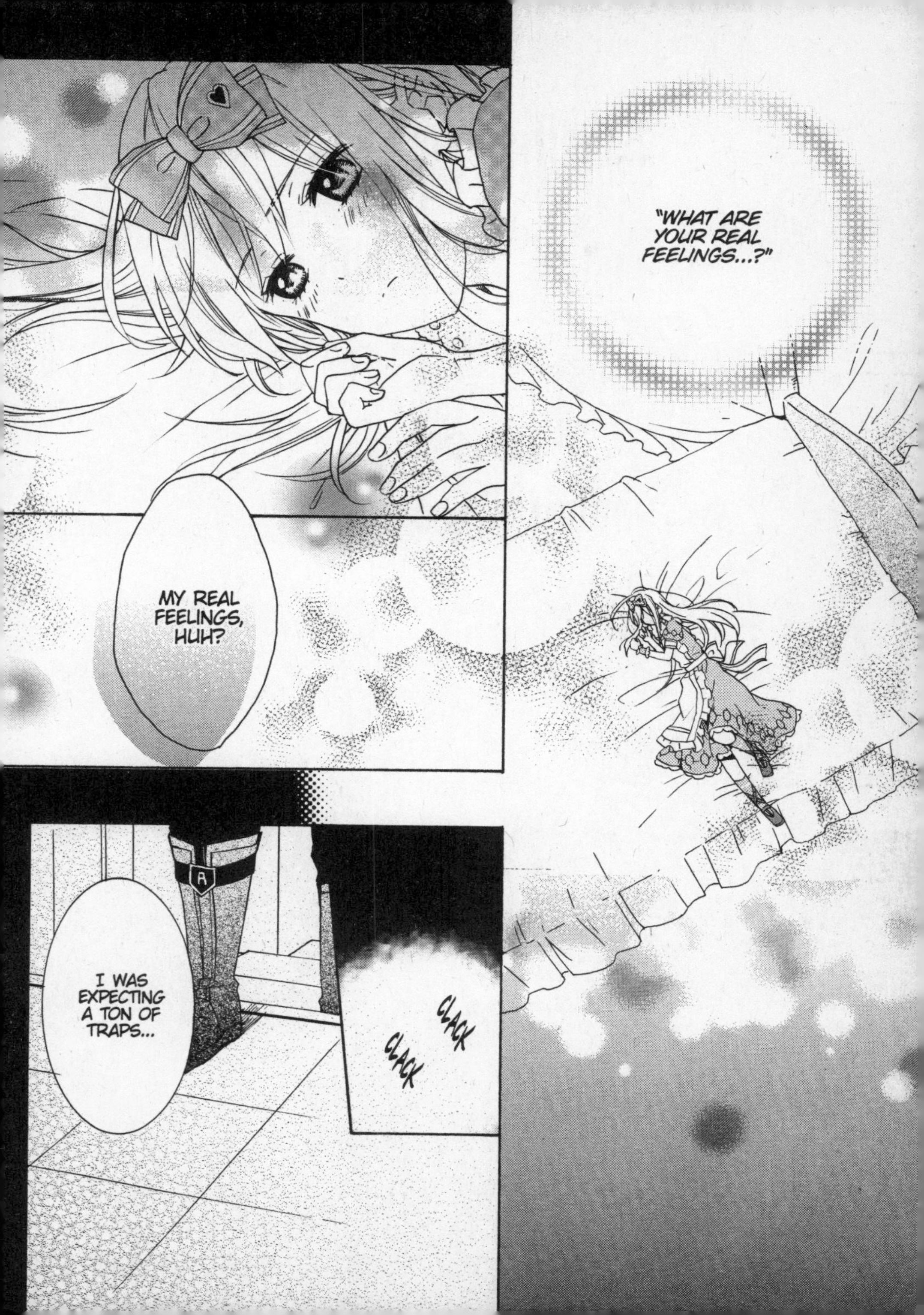
"WHAT ARE YOUR REAL FEELINGS...?"
MY REAL FEELINGS, HUH?
CLACK
CLACK
I WAS EXPECTING A TON OF TRAPS...

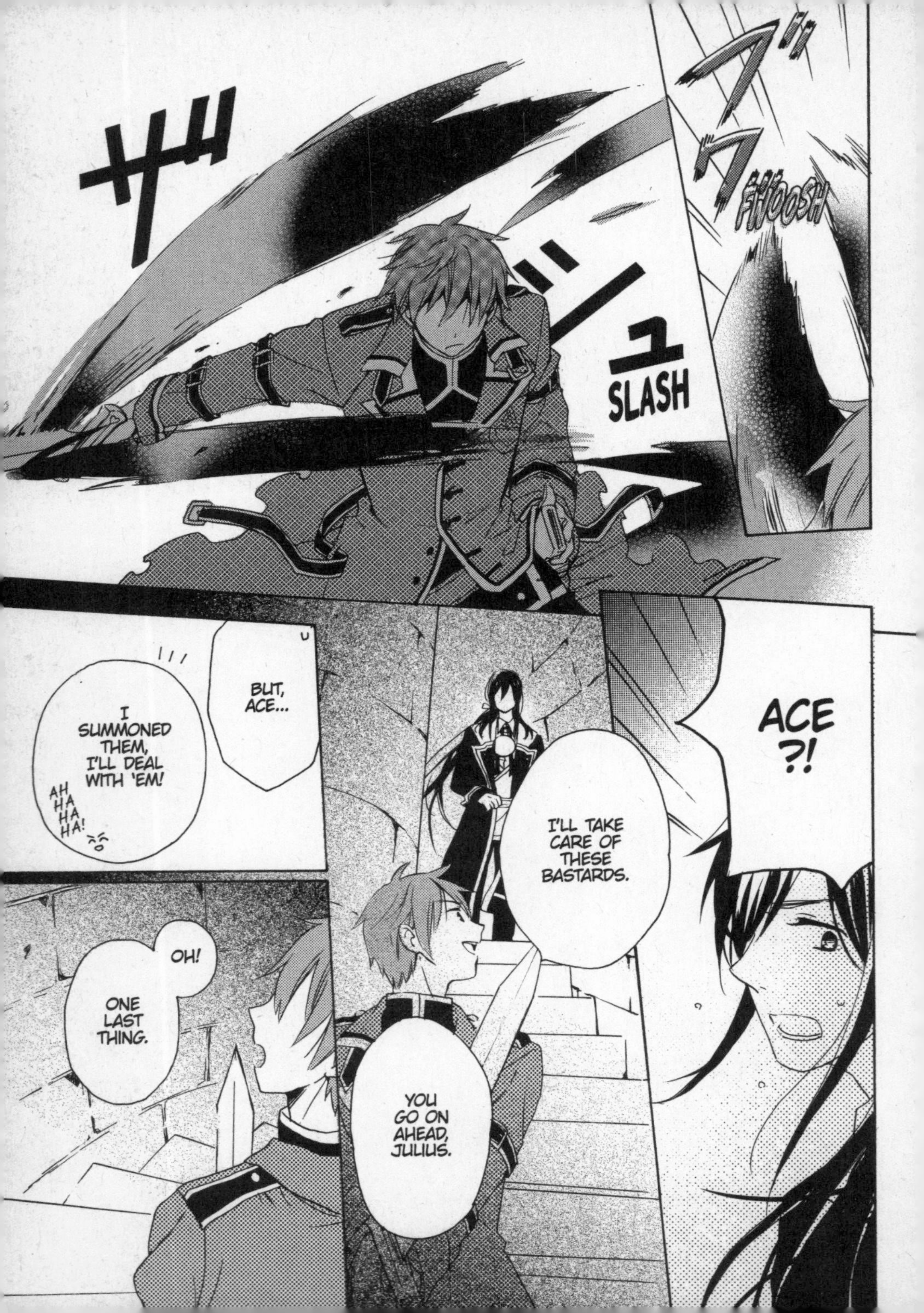
ブワ
FWOOSH
ザッ
ジュ
SLASH
ACE ?!
I'LL TAKE CARE OF THESE BASTARDS.
YOU GO ON AHEAD, JULIUS.
BUT, ACE...
I SUMMONED THEM, I'LL DEAL WITH 'EM!
AH HA HA HA!
OH!
ONE LAST THING.

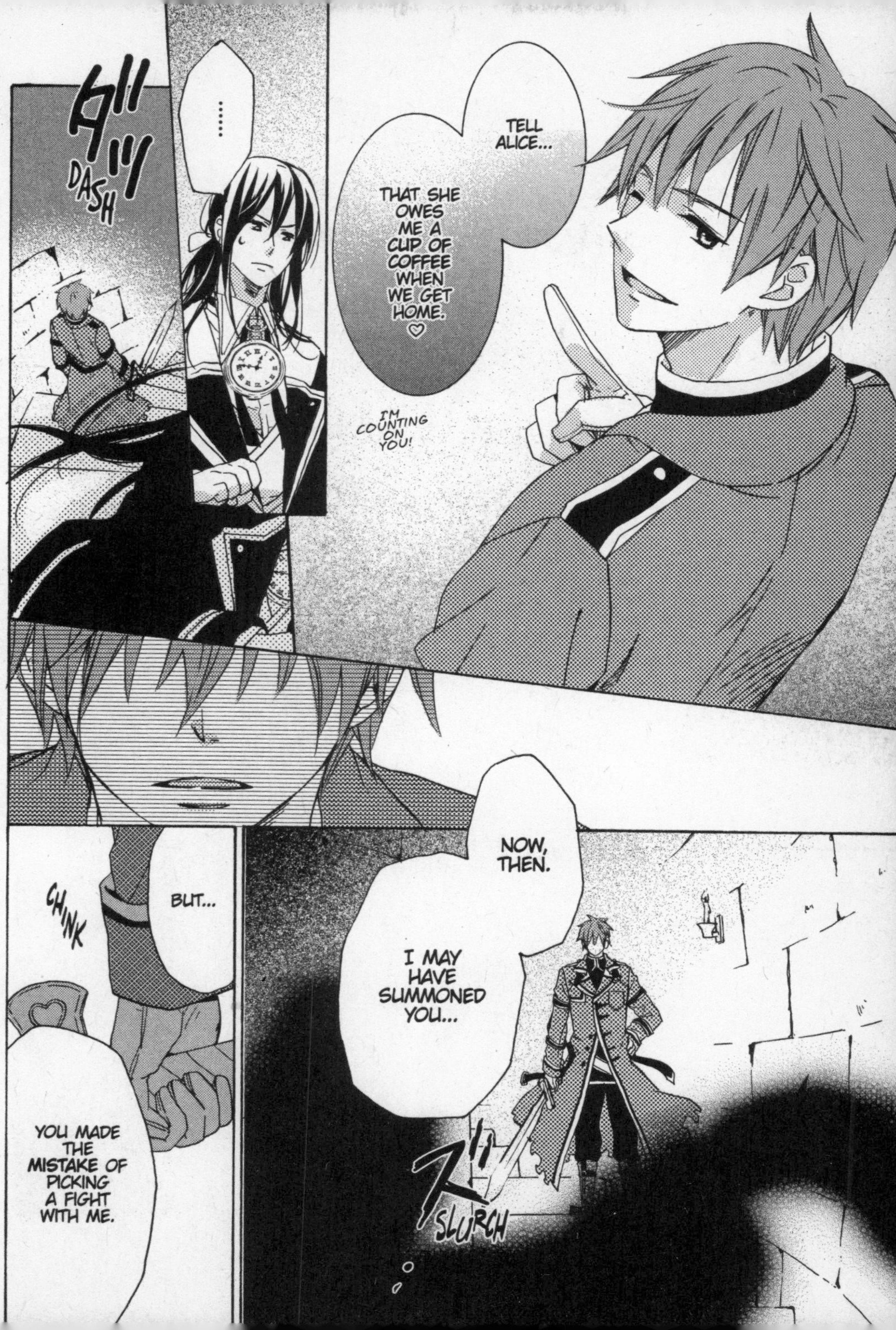
TELL ALICE...
THAT SHE OWES ME A CUP OF COFFEE WHEN WE GET HOME. ♡
I'M COUNTING ON YOU!
......
DASH
NOW, THEN.
I MAY HAVE SUMMONED YOU...
SLURCH
CHINK
BUT...
YOU MADE THE MISTAKE OF PICKING A FIGHT WITH ME.

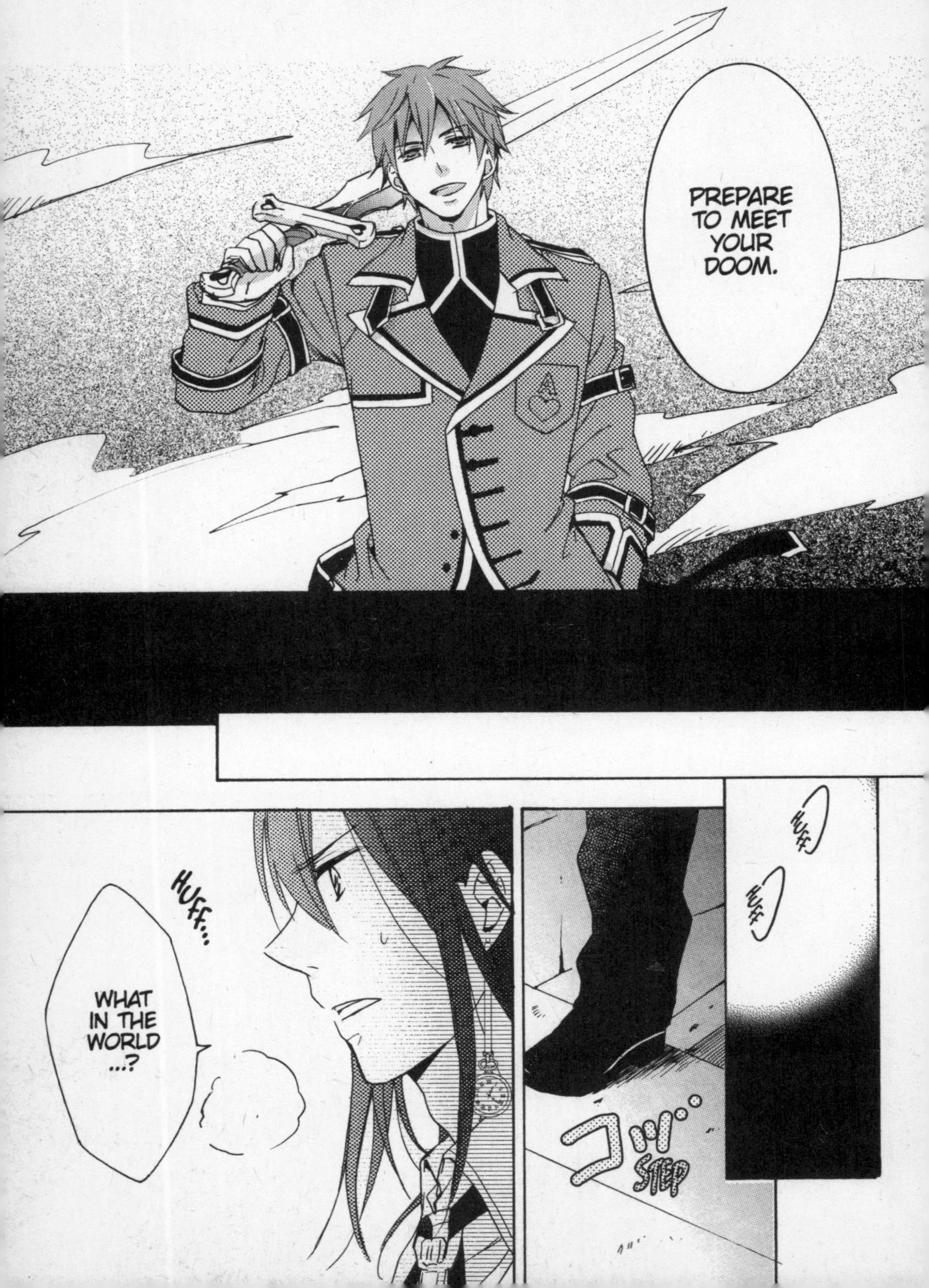
PREPARE TO MEET YOUR DOOM.
HUFF
HUFF
STEP
HUFF...
WHAT IN THE WORLD ...?

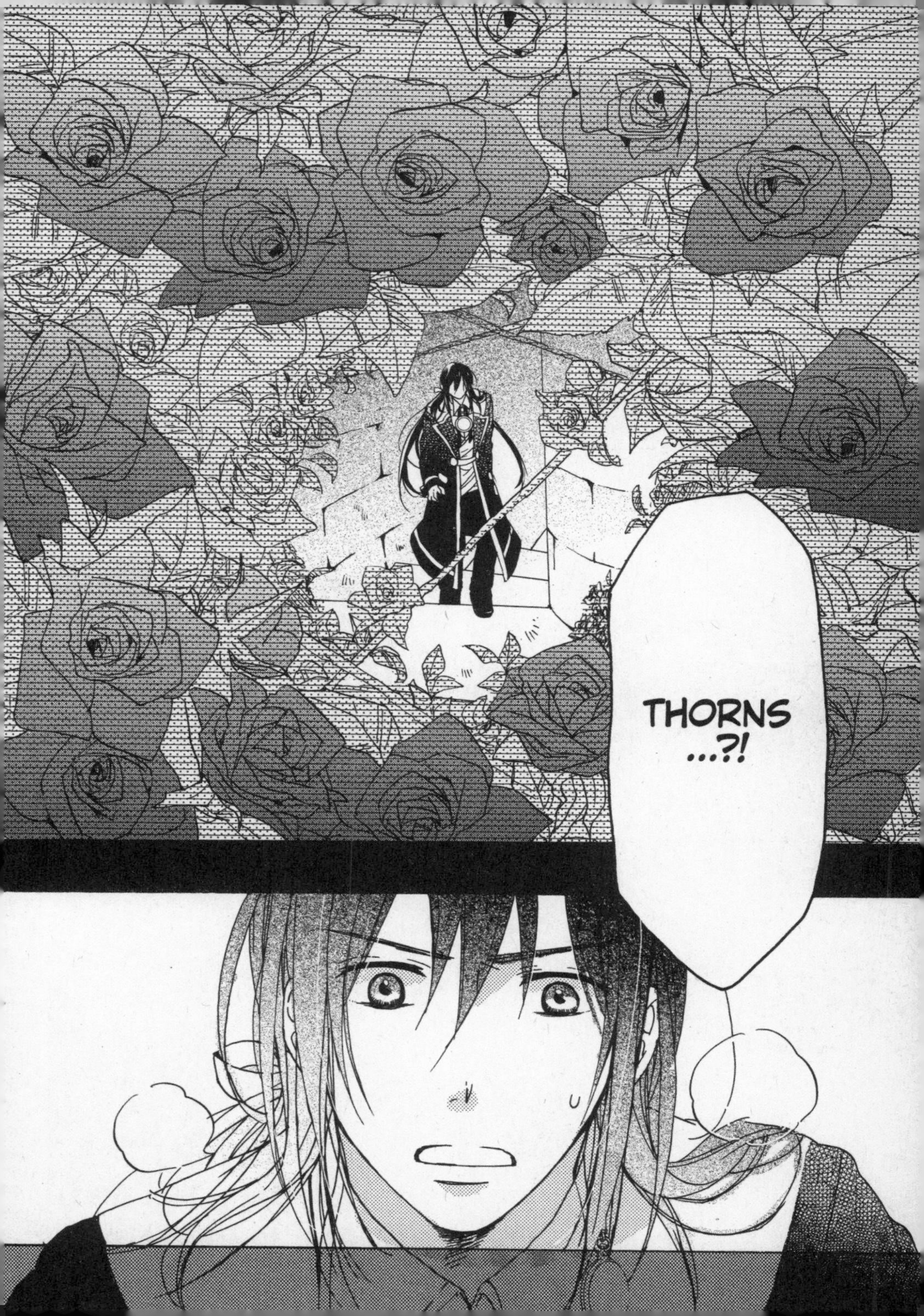
THORNS ...?!

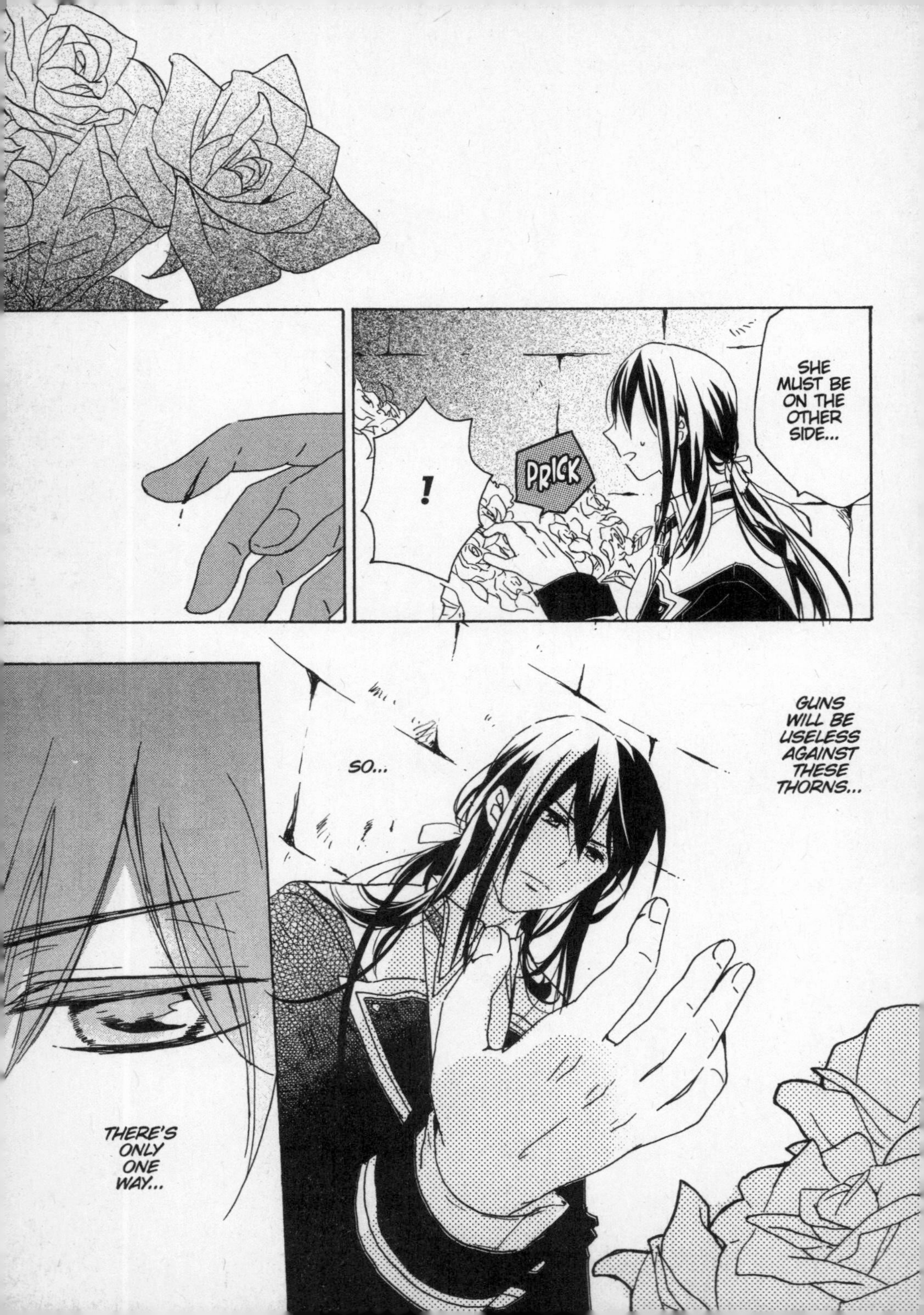
SHE MUST BE ON THE OTHER SIDE...
PRICK
!
GUNS WILL BE USELESS AGAINST THESE THORNS...
SO...
THERE'S ONLY ONE WAY...

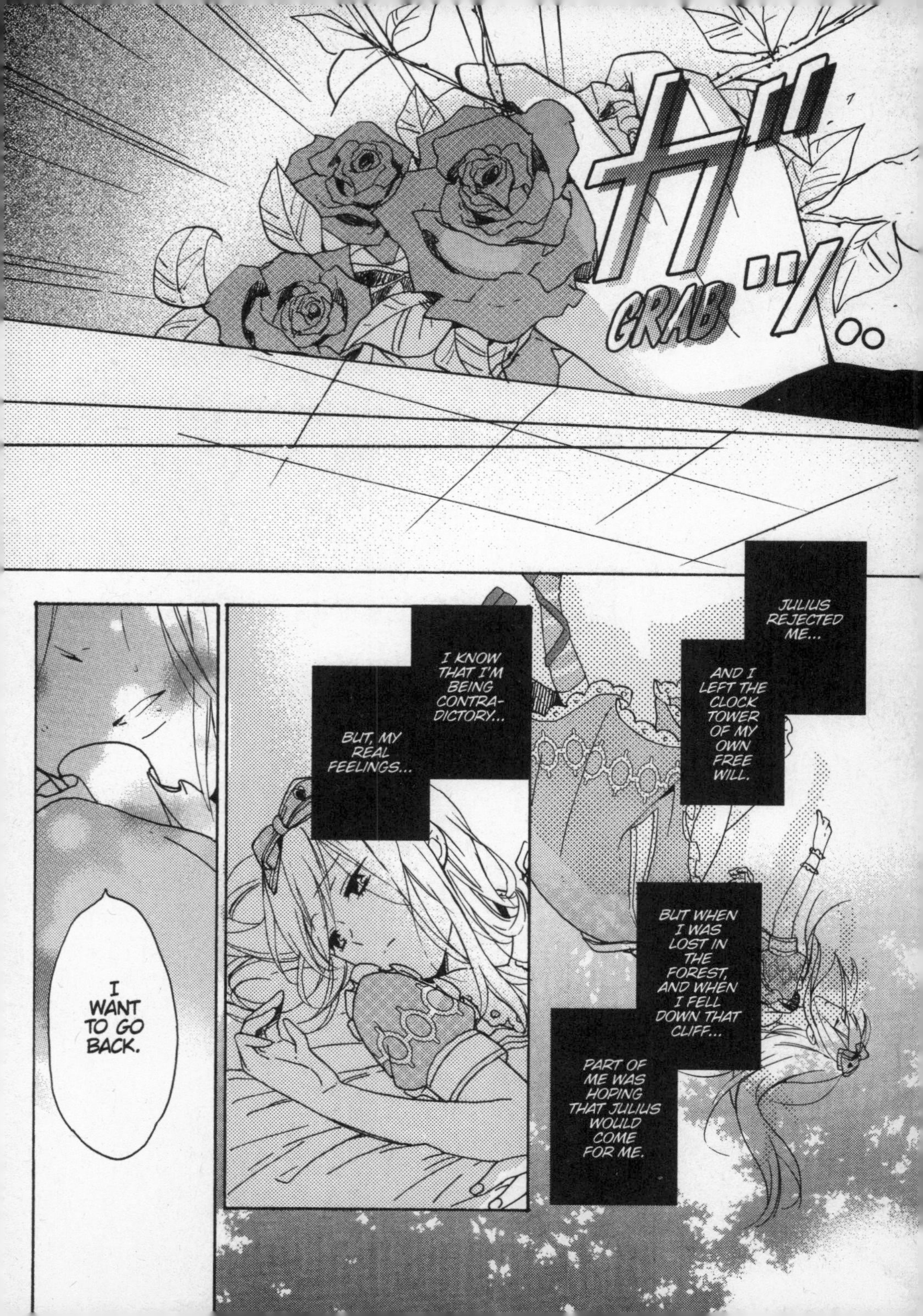
ガッ
GRAB
JULIUS REJECTED ME...
AND I LEFT THE CLOCK TOWER OF MY OWN FREE WILL.
BUT WHEN I WAS LOST IN THE FOREST, AND WHEN I FELL DOWN THAT CLIFF...
PART OF ME WAS HOPING THAT JULIUS WOULD COME FOR ME.
I KNOW THAT I'M BEING CONTRA-DICTORY...
BUT, MY REAL FEELINGS...
I WANT TO GO BACK.

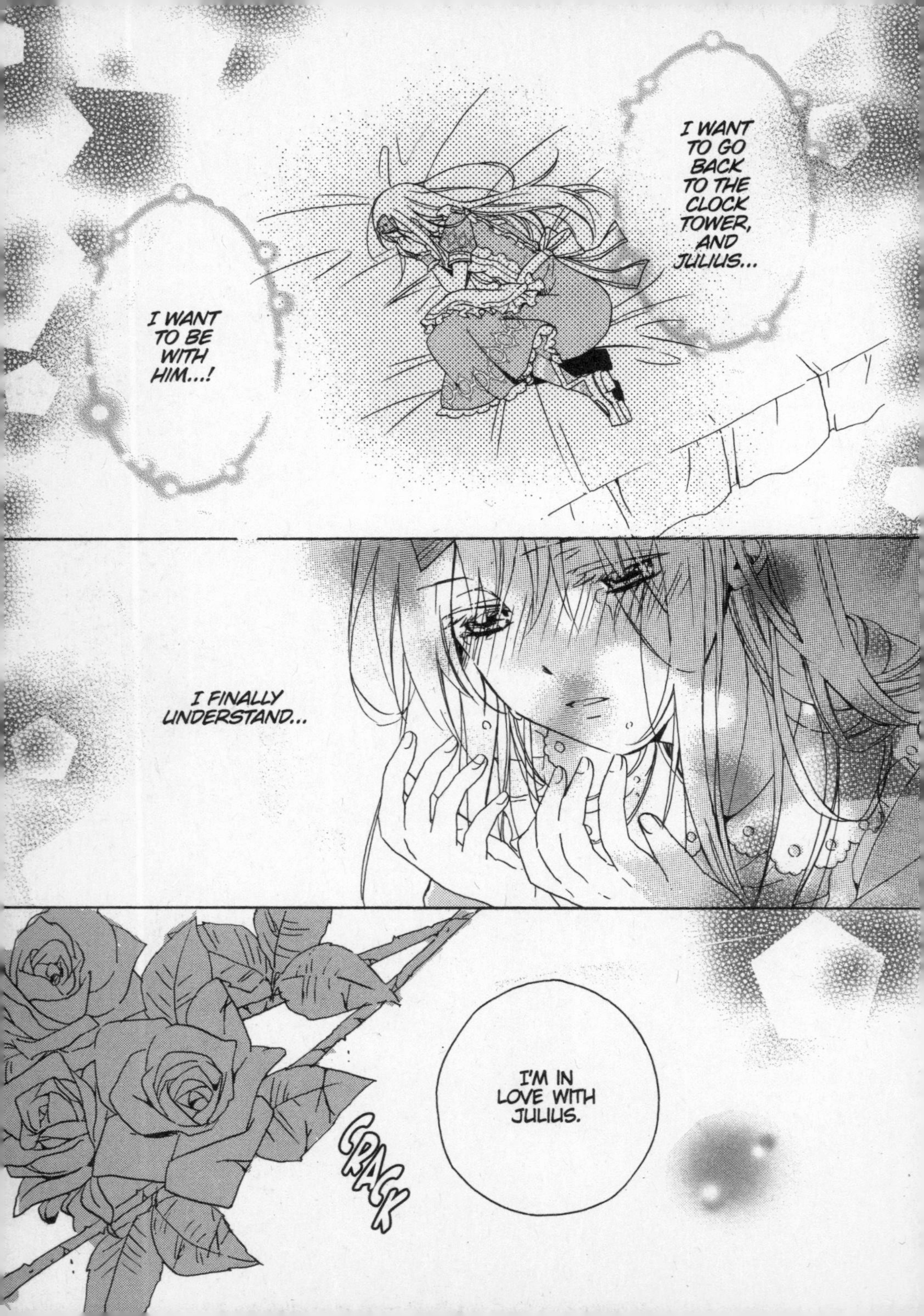
I WANT TO GO BACK TO THE CLOCK TOWER, AND JULIUS...
I WANT TO BE WITH HIM...!
I FINALLY UNDERSTAND...
I'M IN LOVE WITH JULIUS.
CRACK

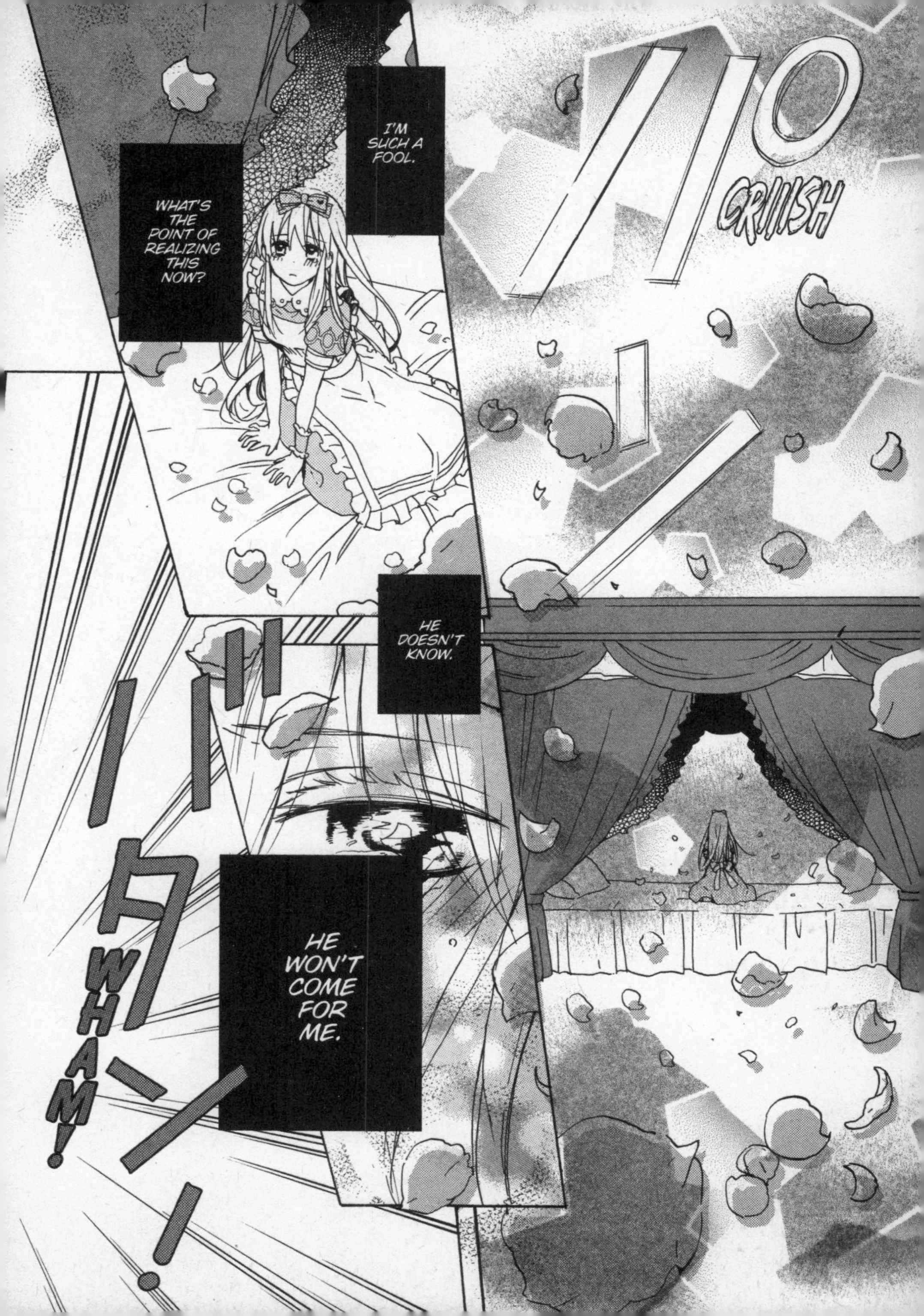
CRIIISH
I'M SUCH A FOOL.
WHAT'S THE POINT OF REALIZING THIS NOW?
HE DOESN'T KNOW.
HE WON'T COME FOR ME.
WHAM!

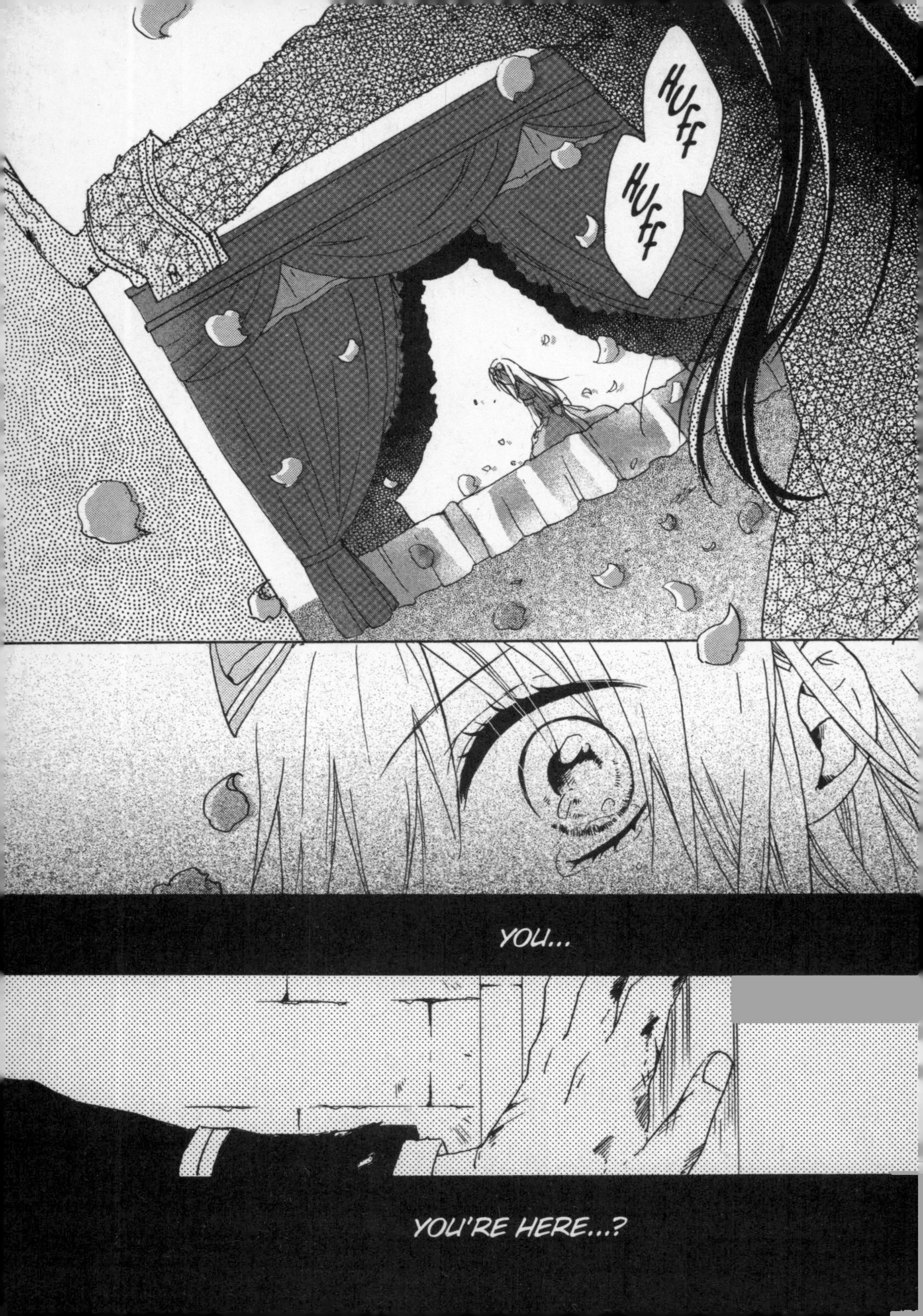
HUFF HUFF
YOU...
YOU'RE HERE...?

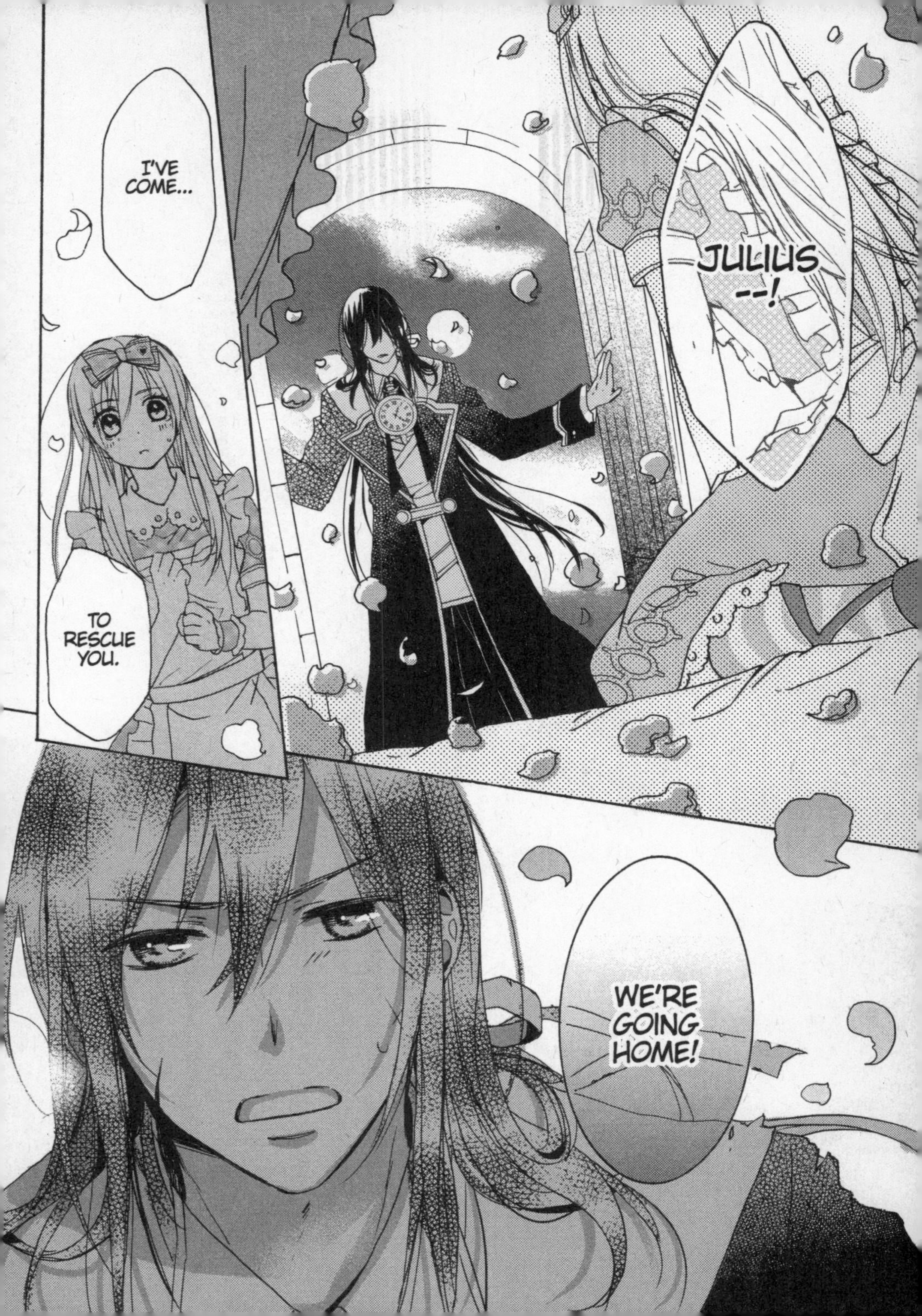
JULIUS --!
I'VE COME...
TO RESCUE YOU.
WE'RE GOING HOME!

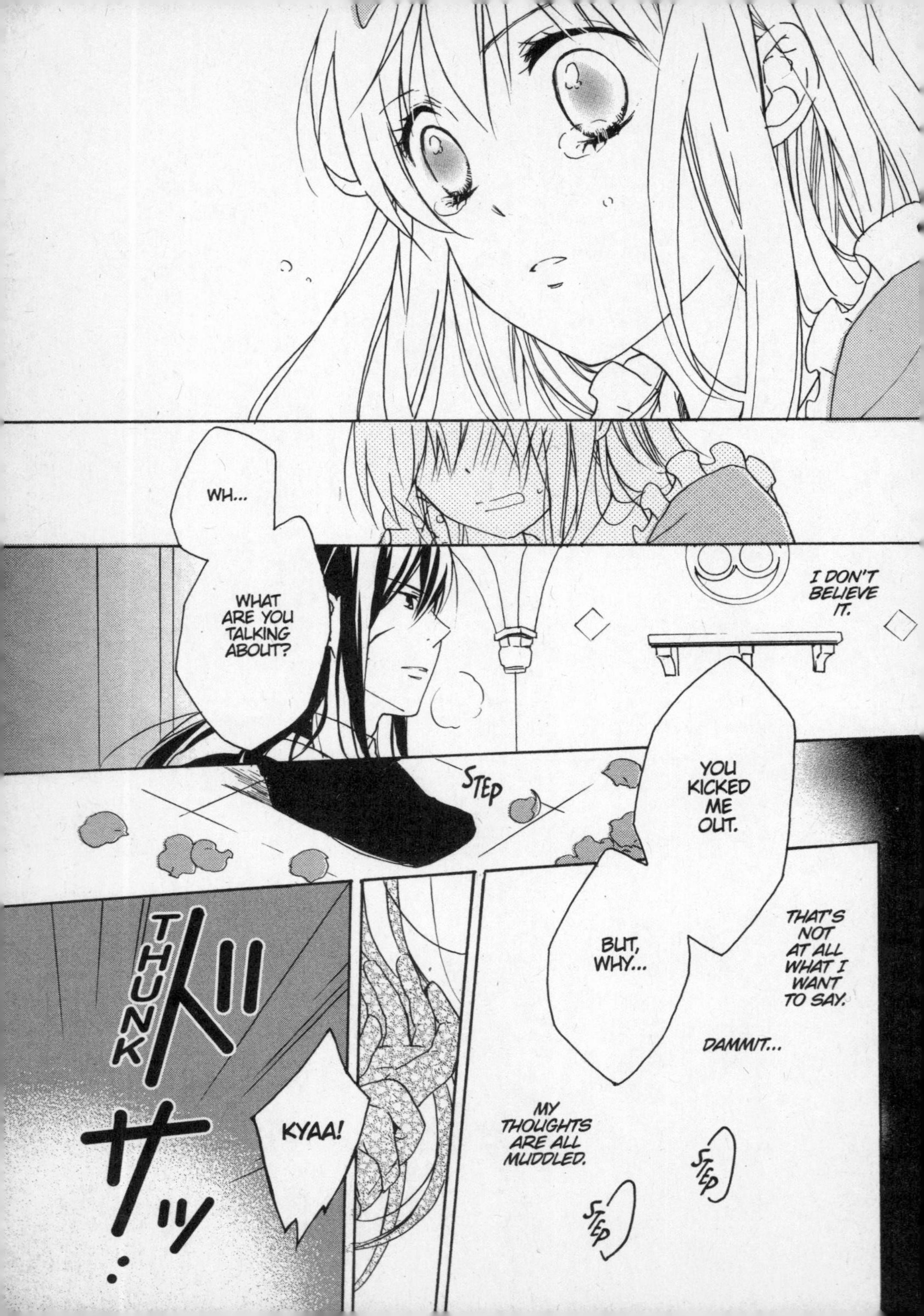
WH...
I DON'T BELIEVE IT.
WHAT ARE YOU TALKING ABOUT?
YOU KICKED ME OUT.
STEP
THAT'S NOT AT ALL WHAT I WANT TO SAY.
BUT, WHY...
DAMMIT...
MY THOUGHTS ARE ALL MUDDLED.
STEP
STEP
THUNK
KYAA!

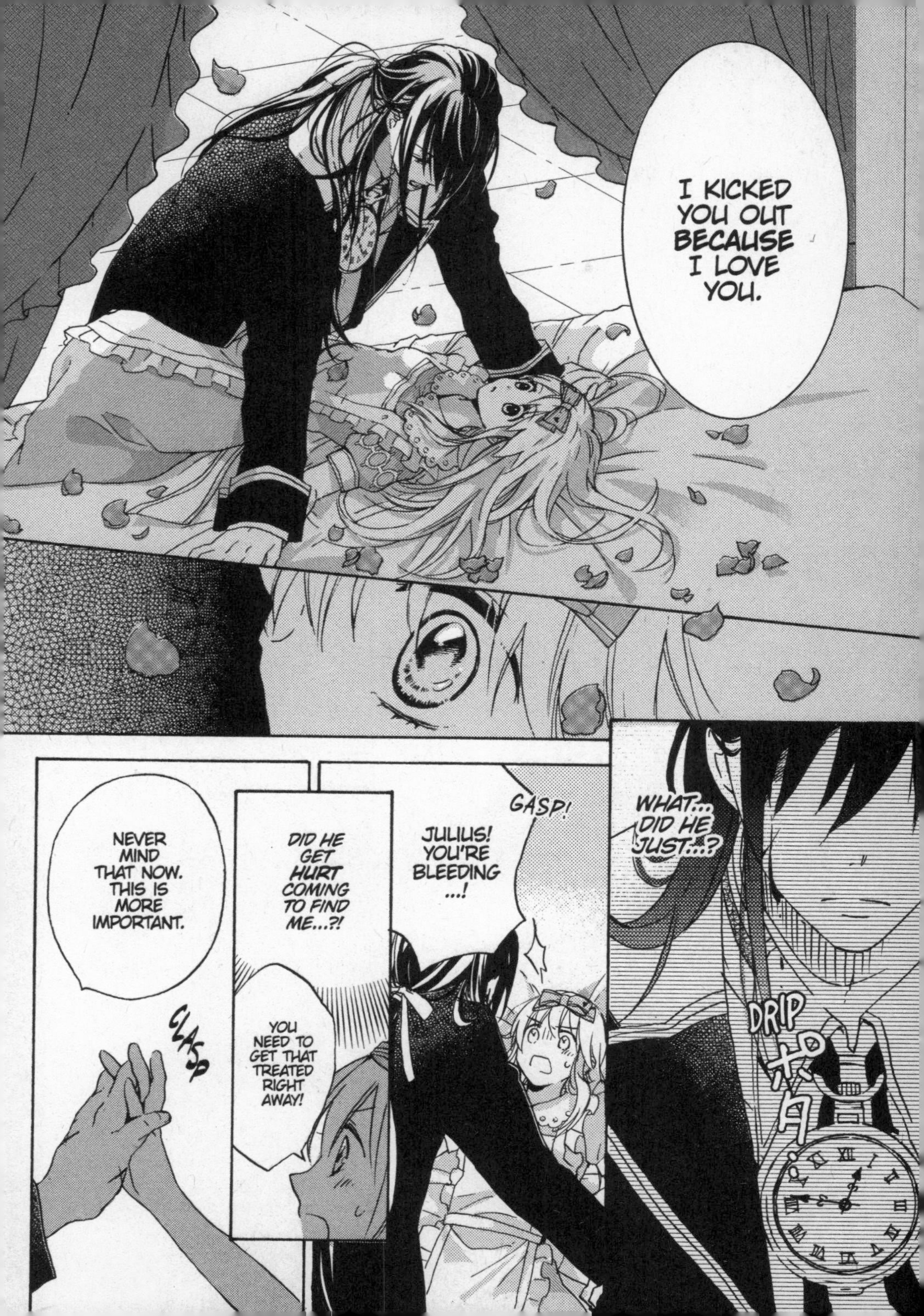
I KICKED YOU OUT BECAUSE I LOVE YOU.
WHAT... DID HE JUST...?
DRIP
ポタ
GASP!
JULIUS! YOU'RE BLEEDING...!
DID HE GET HURT COMING TO FIND ME...?!
YOU NEED TO GET THAT TREATED RIGHT AWAY!
NEVER MIND THAT NOW. THIS IS MORE IMPORTANT.
CLASP

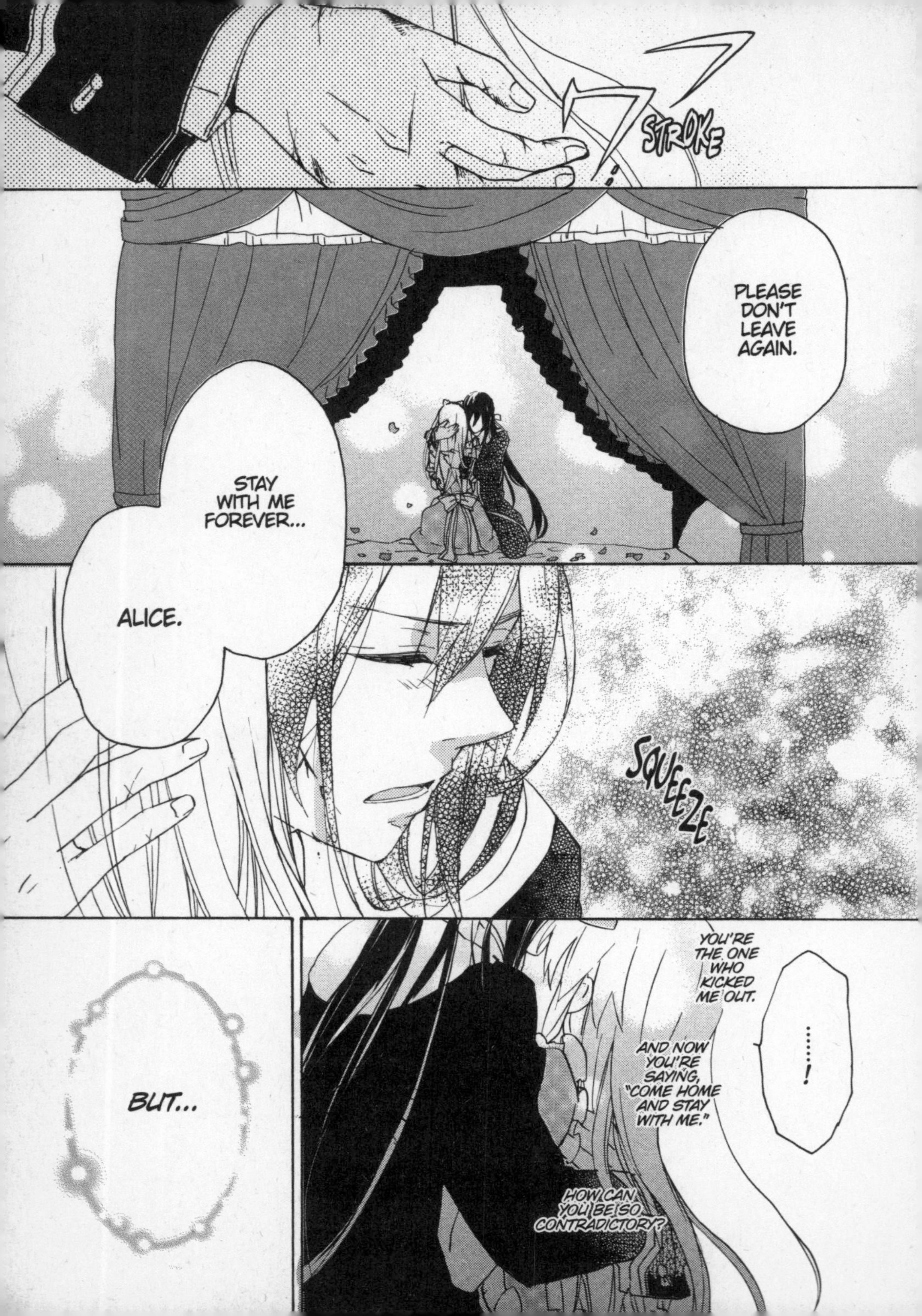
STROKE
PLEASE DON'T LEAVE AGAIN.
STAY WITH ME FOREVER...
ALICE.
SQUEEZE
YOU'RE THE ONE WHO KICKED ME OUT.
......!
AND NOW YOU'RE SAYING, "COME HOME AND STAY WITH ME."
HOW CAN YOU BE SO CONTRADICTORY?
BUT...

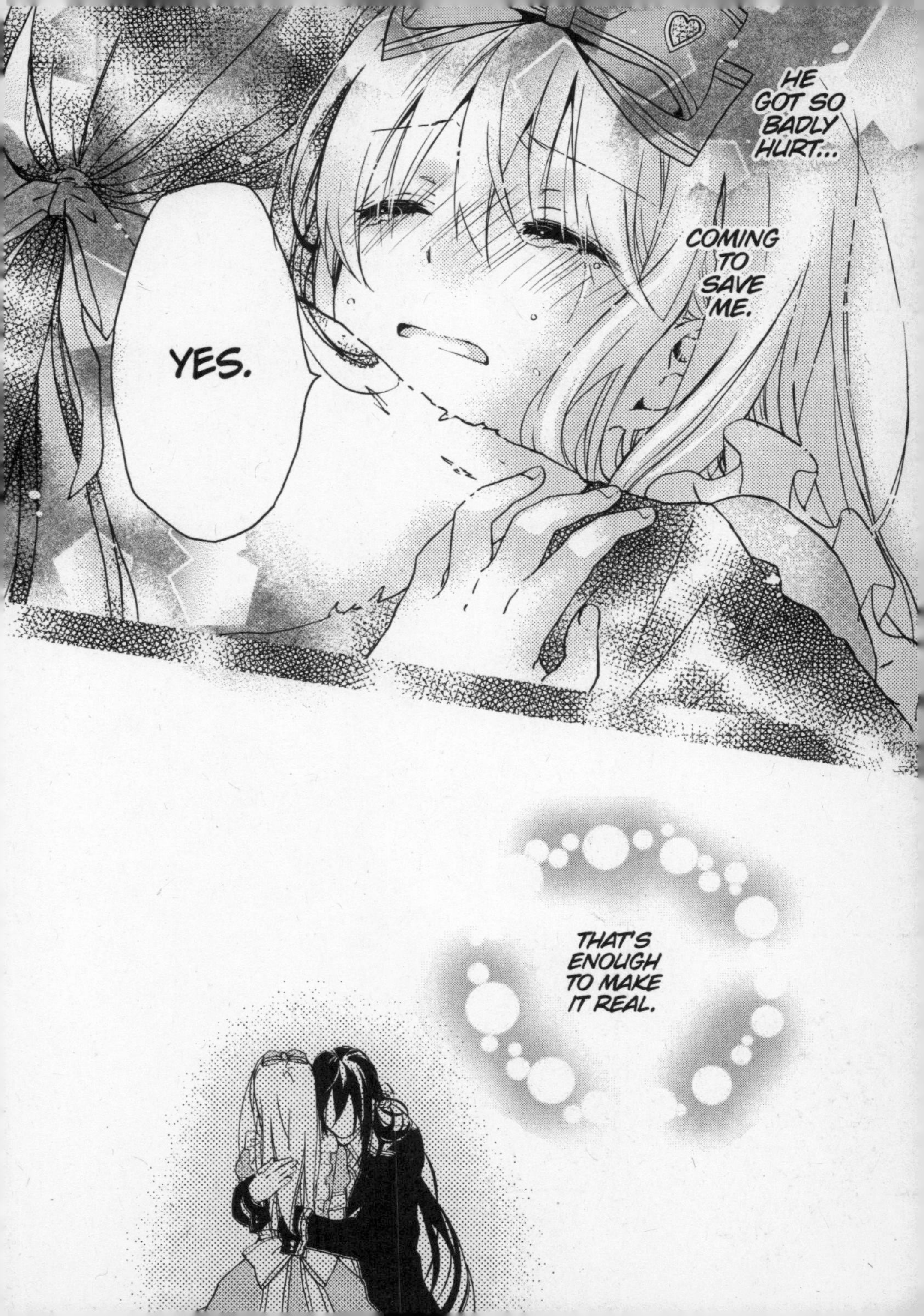
HE GOT SO BADLY HURT...
COMING TO SAVE ME.
YES.
THAT'S ENOUGH TO MAKE IT REAL.

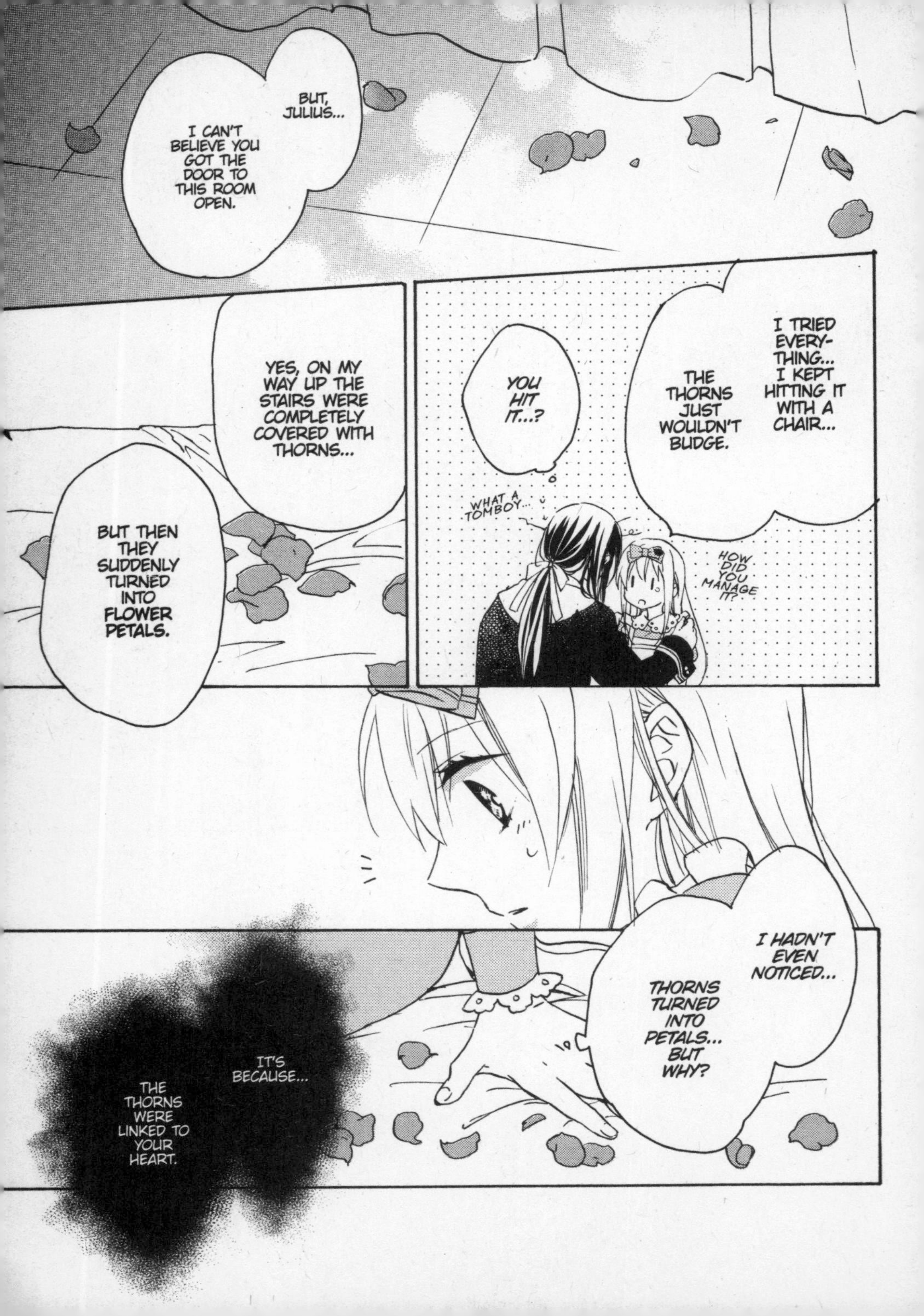

BUT, JULIUS...
I CAN'T BELIEVE YOU GOT THE DOOR TO THIS ROOM OPEN.
I TRIED EVERYTHING... I KEPT HITTING IT WITH A CHAIR...
THE THORNS JUST WOULDN'T BUDGE.
YOU HIT IT...?
WHAT A TOMBOY...
HOW DID YOU MANAGE IT?
YES, ON MY WAY UP THE STAIRS WERE COMPLETELY COVERED WITH THORNS...
BUT THEN THEY SUDDENLY TURNED INTO FLOWER PETALS.
I HADN'T EVEN NOTICED...
THORNS TURNED INTO PETALS... BUT WHY?
IT'S BECAUSE...
THE THORNS WERE LINKED TO YOUR HEART.

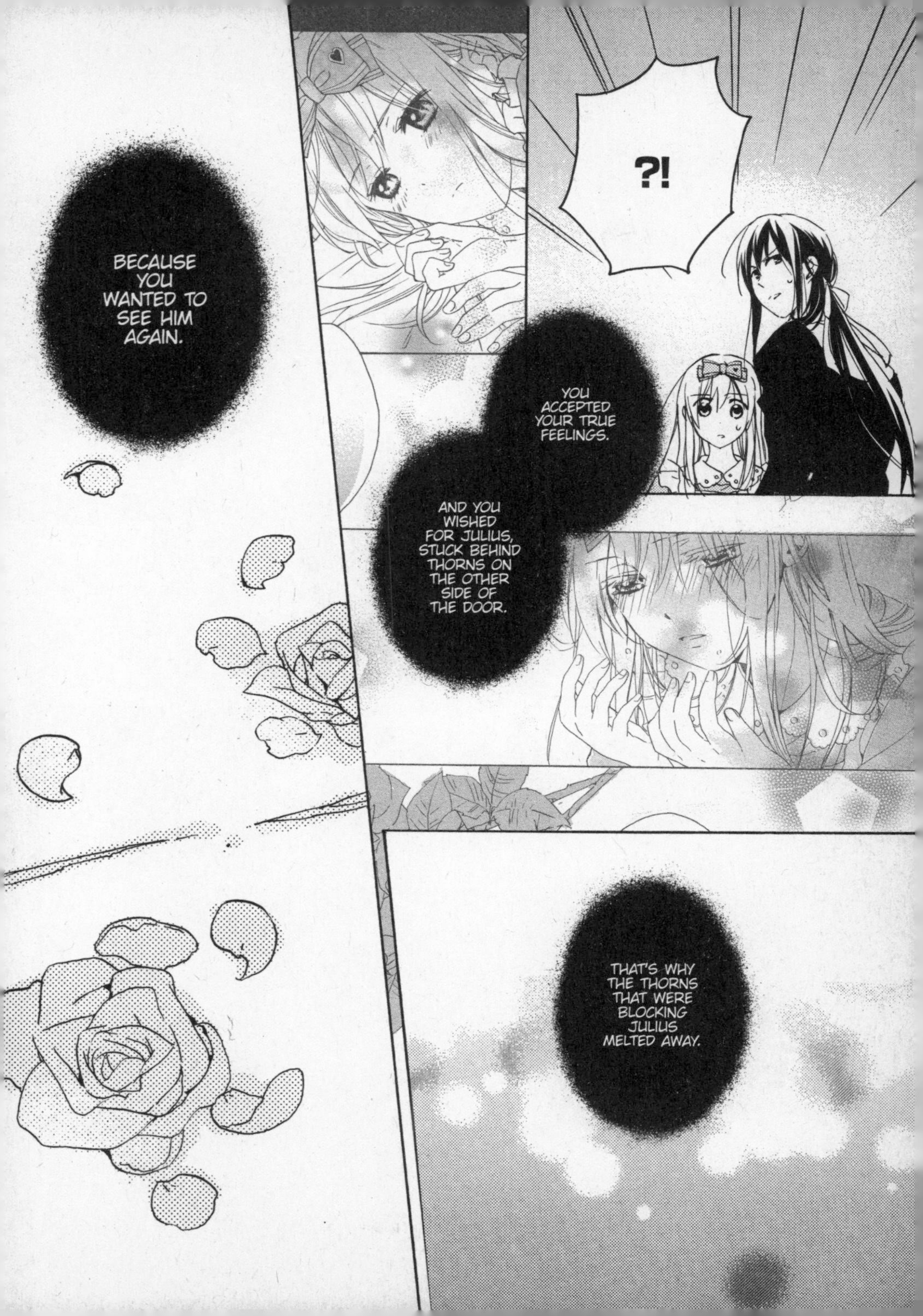
?!
YOU ACCEPTED YOUR TRUE FEELINGS.
AND YOU WISHED FOR JULIUS, STUCK BEHIND THORNS ON THE OTHER SIDE OF THE DOOR.
THAT'S WHY THE THORNS THAT WERE BLOCKING JULIUS MELTED AWAY.
BECAUSE YOU WANTED TO SEE HIM AGAIN.

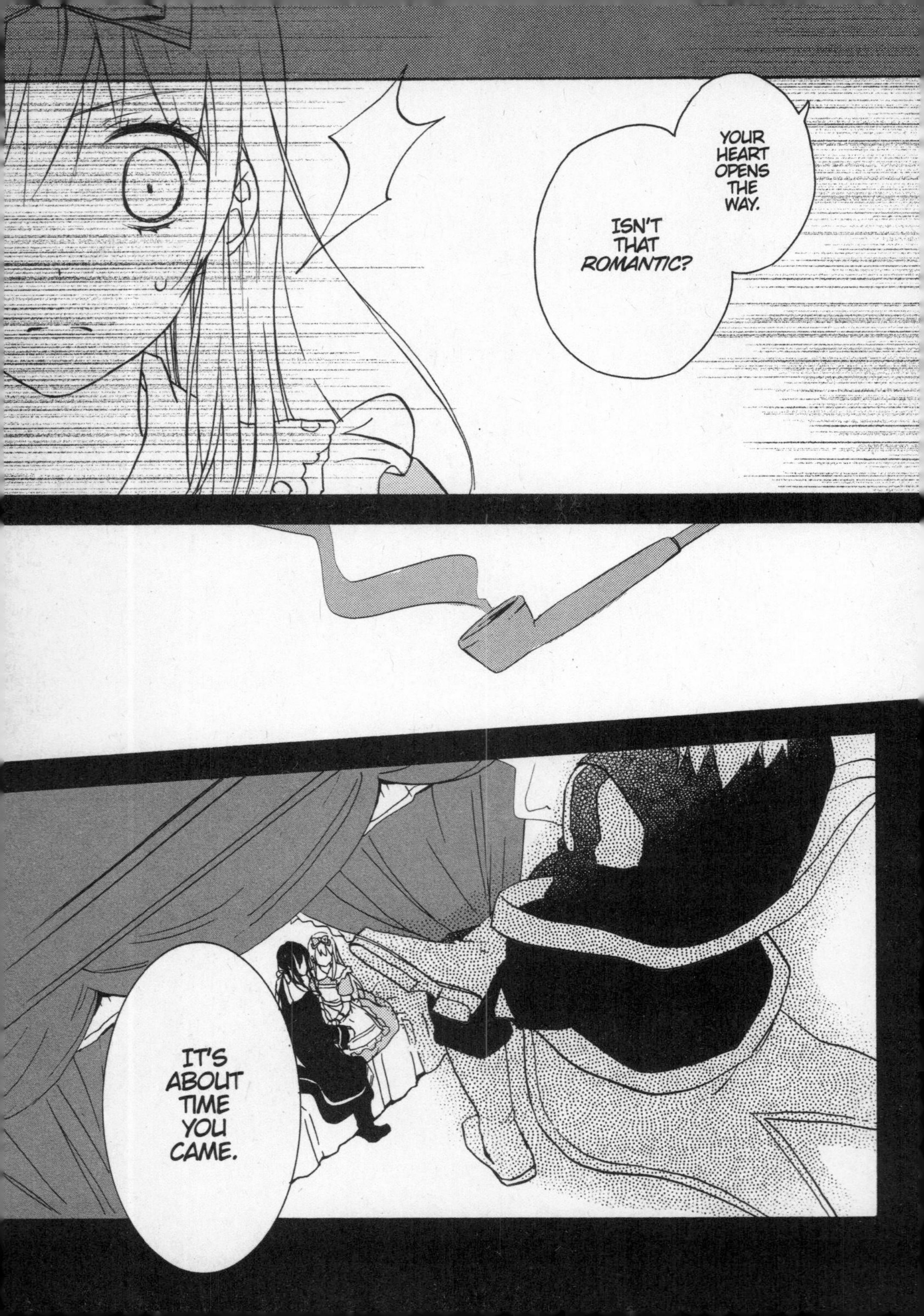
YOUR HEART OPENS THE WAY.
ISN'T THAT *ROMANTIC?*
IT'S ABOUT TIME YOU CAME.

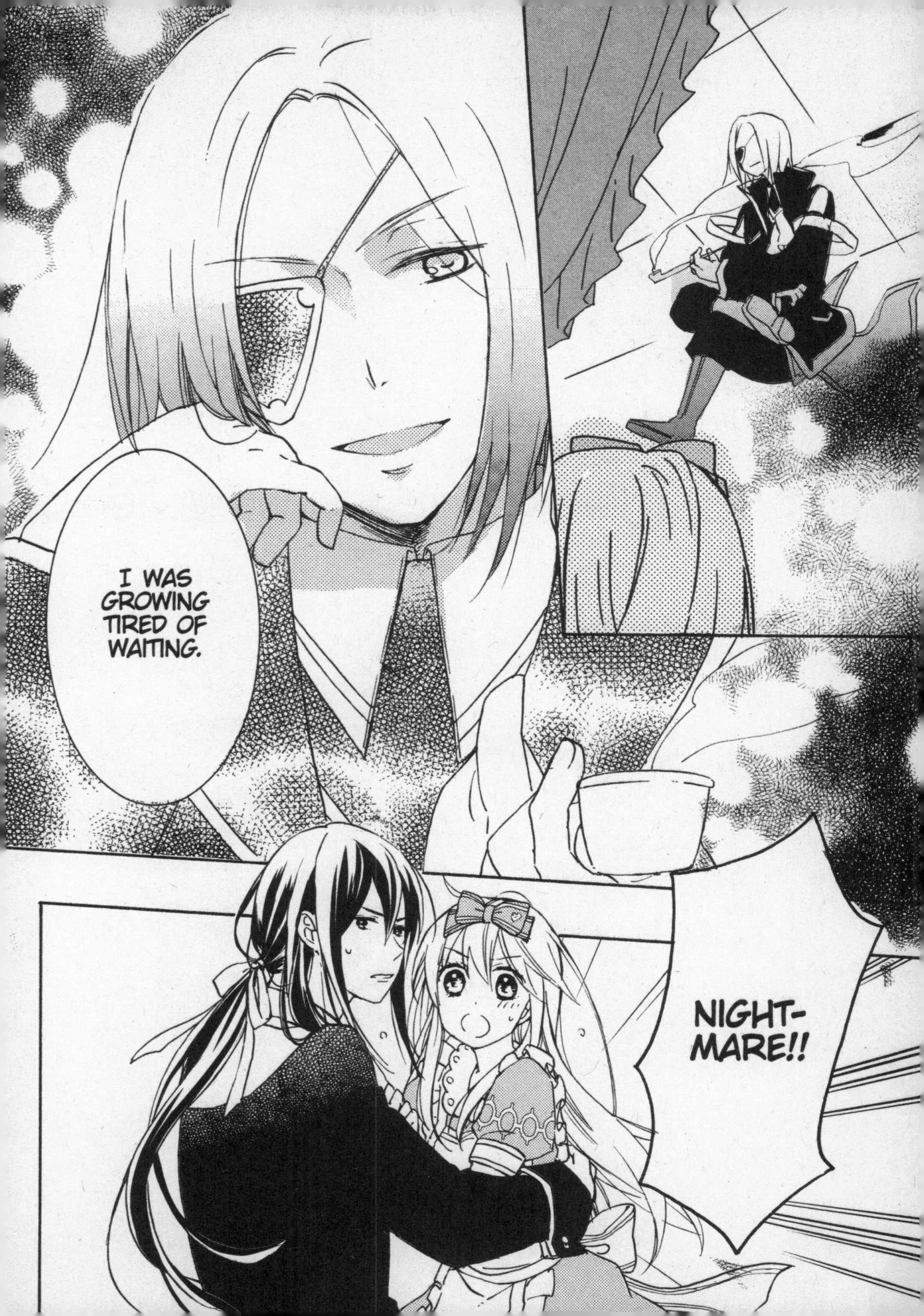
I WAS GROWING TIRED OF WAITING.
NIGHT-MARE!!

ハートの国のアリス
恋する茨の迷宮

Alice IN THE COUNTRY OF Hearts

Love Labyrinth of Thorns

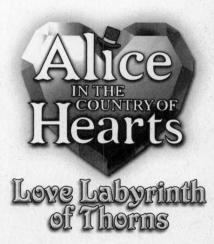

Chapter 5

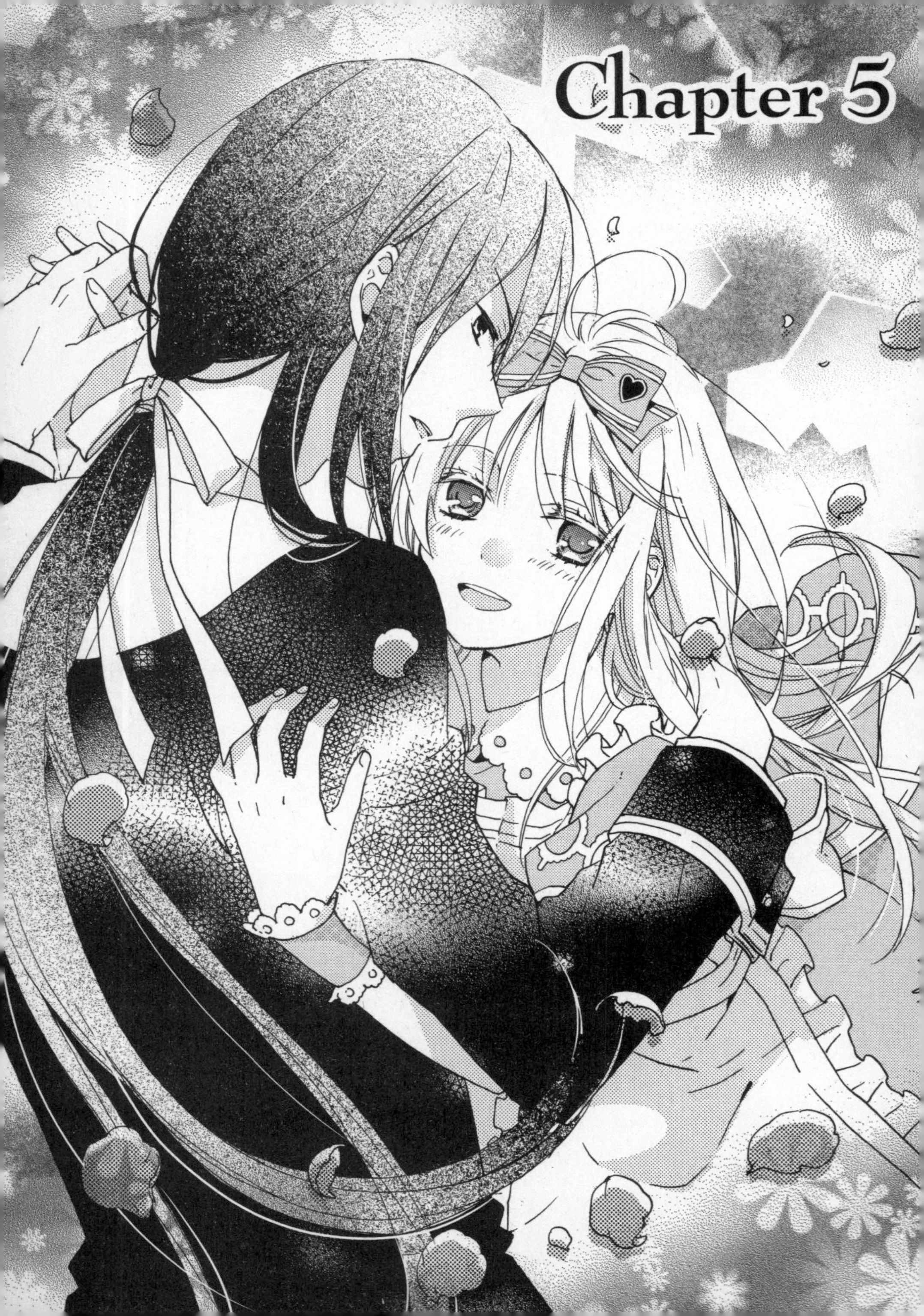

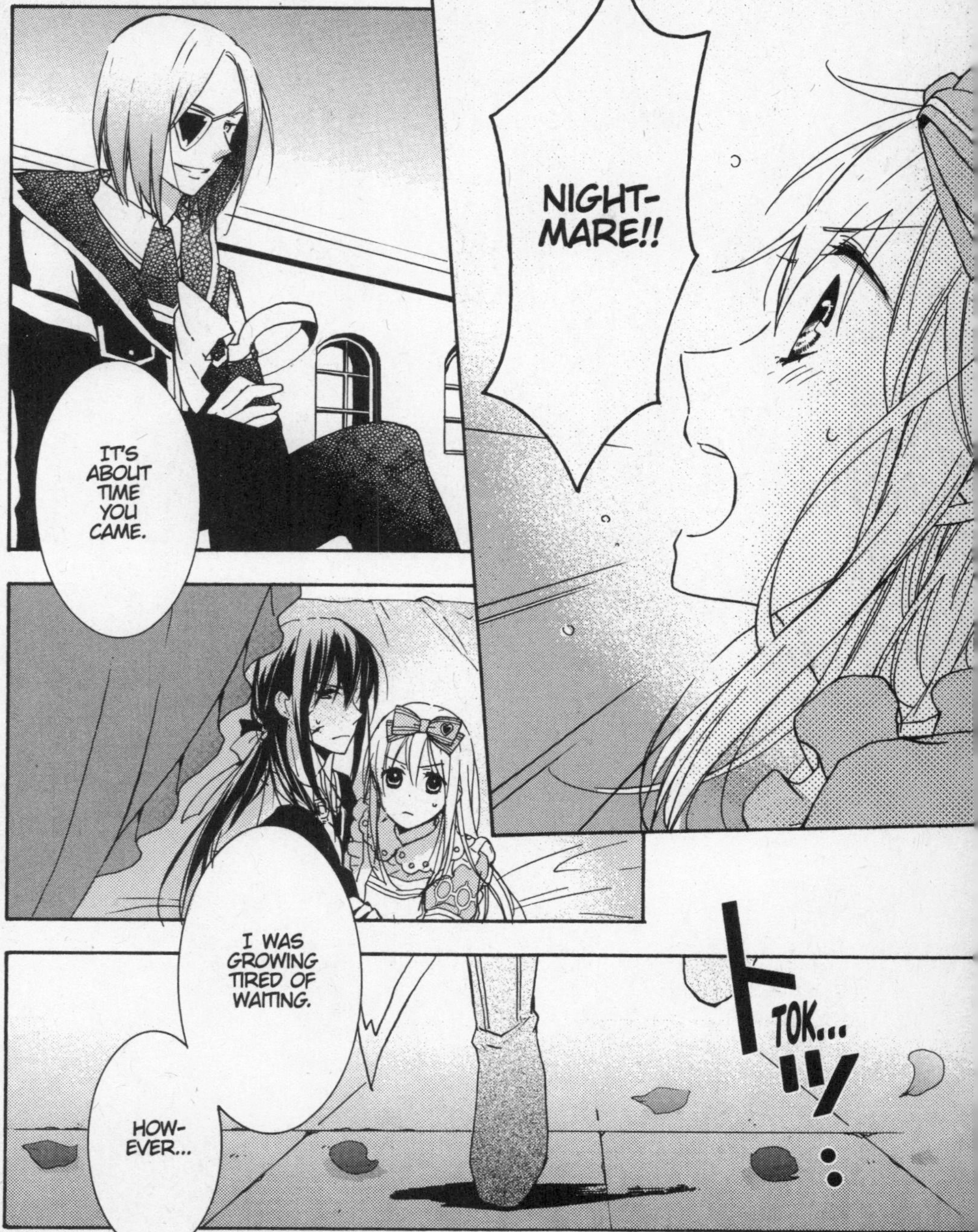
NIGHT-
MARE!!
IT'S ABOUT TIME YOU CAME.
TOK...
I WAS GROWING TIRED OF WAITING.
HOW-EVER...

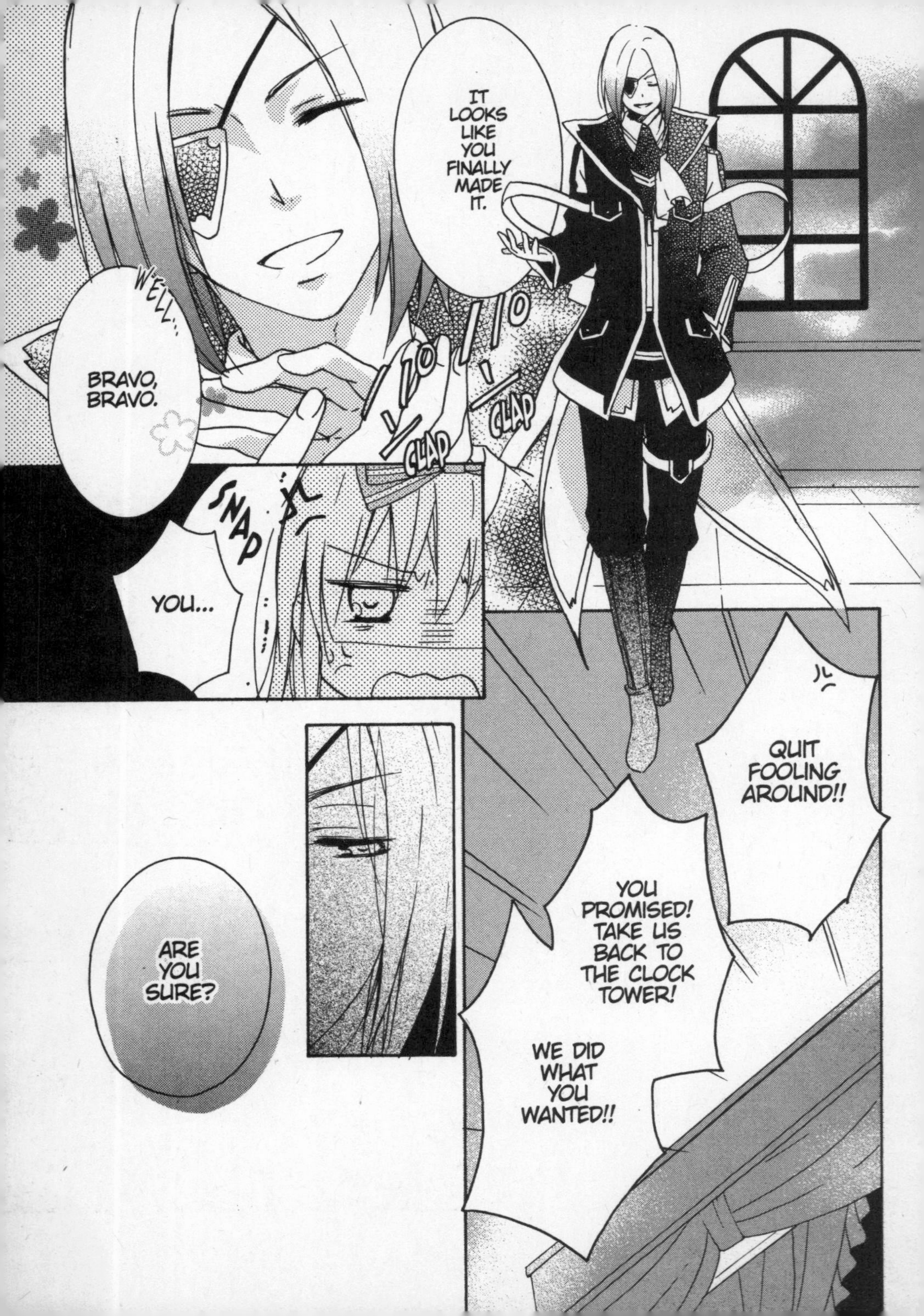
IT LOOKS LIKE YOU FINALLY MADE IT.
WELL...
BRAVO, BRAVO.
CLAP
CLAP
SNAP
YOU...
QUIT FOOLING AROUND!!
YOU PROMISED! TAKE US BACK TO THE CLOCK TOWER!
WE DID WHAT YOU WANTED!!
ARE YOU SURE?

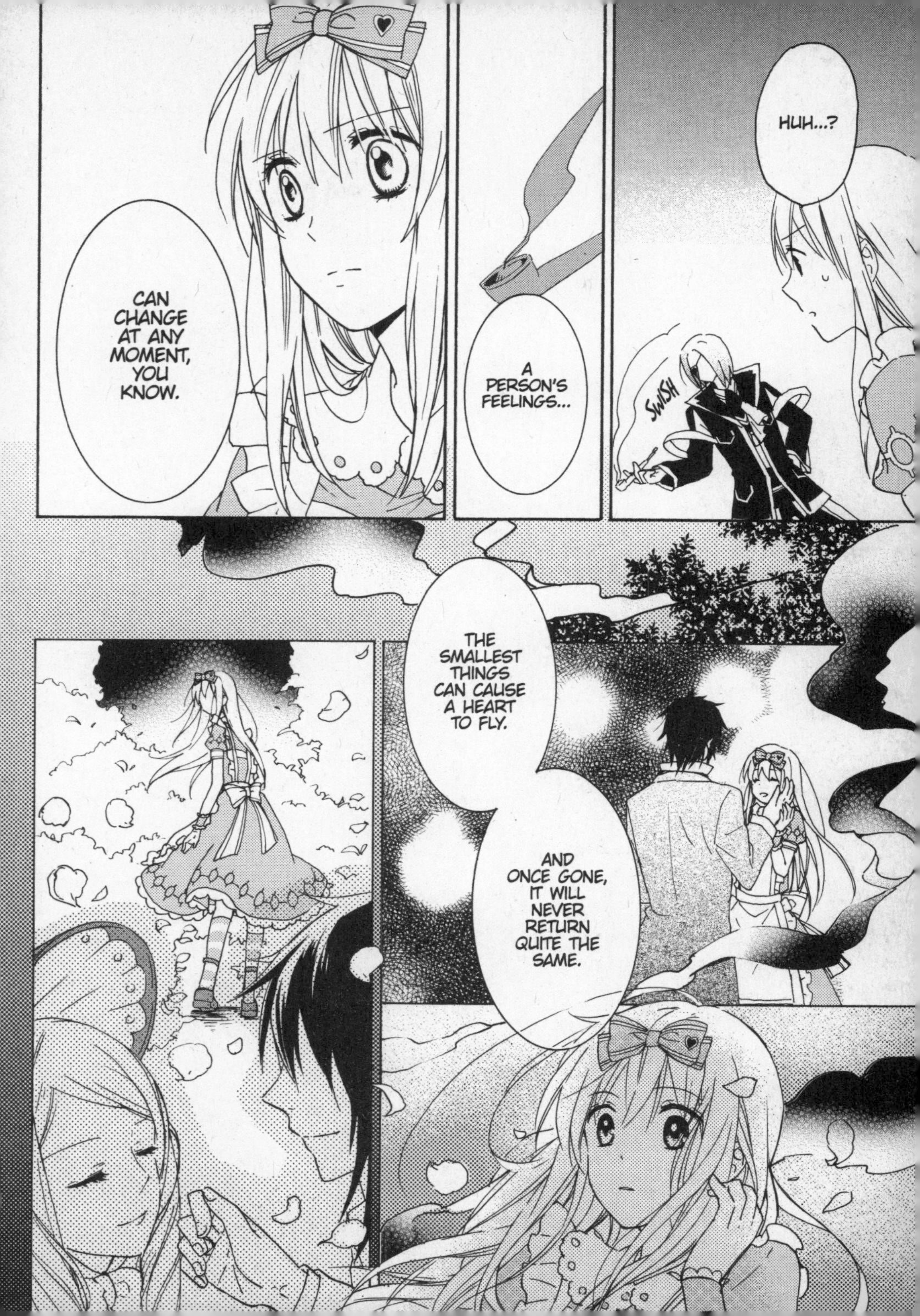
HUH...?
SWISH
A PERSON'S FEELINGS...
CAN CHANGE AT ANY MOMENT, YOU KNOW.
THE SMALLEST THINGS CAN CAUSE A HEART TO FLY.
AND ONCE GONE, IT WILL NEVER RETURN QUITE THE SAME.

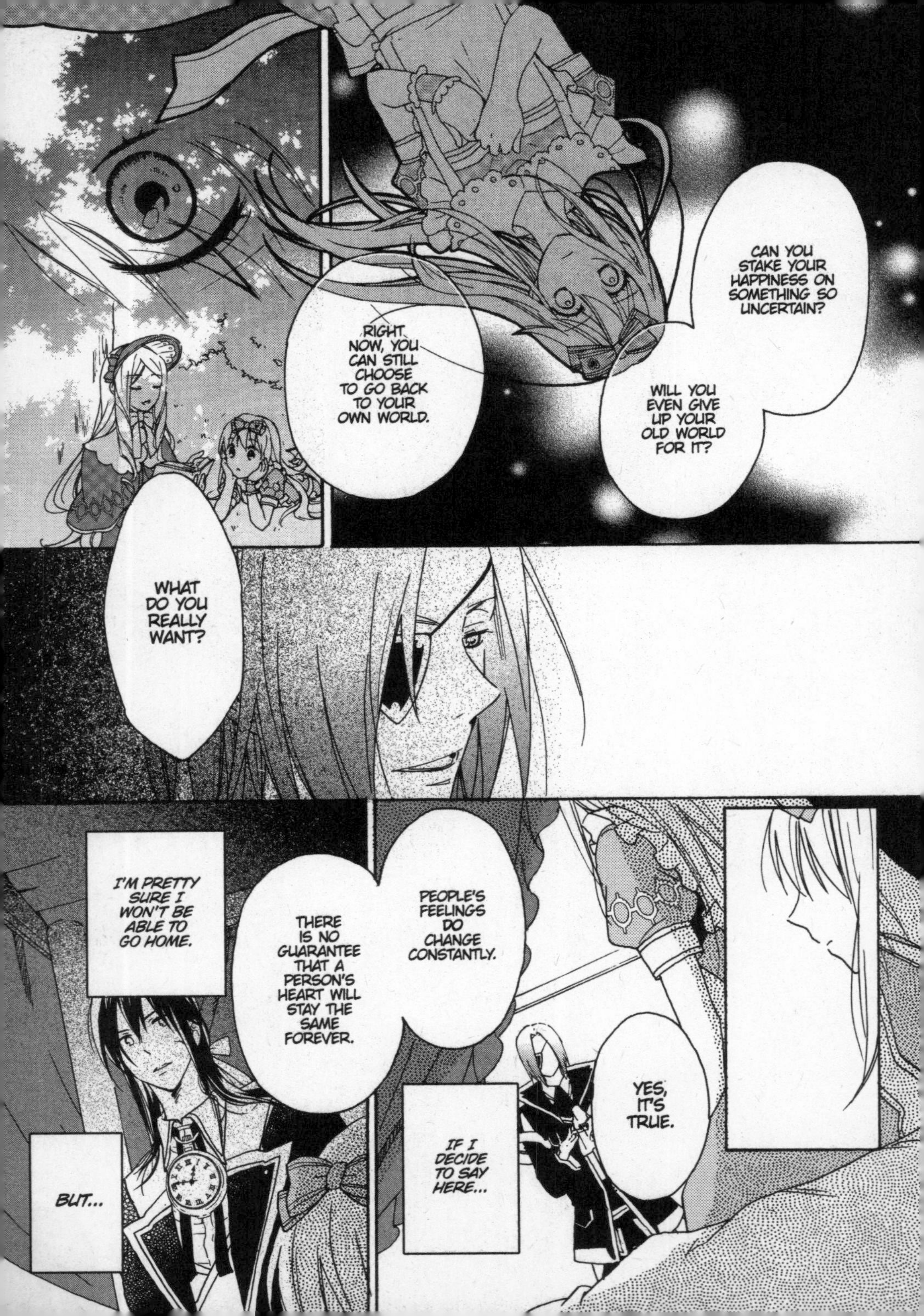
CAN YOU STAKE YOUR HAPPINESS ON SOMETHING SO UNCERTAIN?
WILL YOU EVEN GIVE UP YOUR OLD WORLD FOR IT?
RIGHT NOW, YOU CAN STILL CHOOSE TO GO BACK TO YOUR OWN WORLD.
WHAT DO YOU REALLY WANT?
YES, IT'S TRUE.
IF I DECIDE TO SAY HERE...
PEOPLE'S FEELINGS DO CHANGE CONSTANTLY.
THERE IS NO GUARANTEE THAT A PERSON'S HEART WILL STAY THE SAME FOREVER.
I'M PRETTY SURE I WON'T BE ABLE TO GO HOME.
BUT...

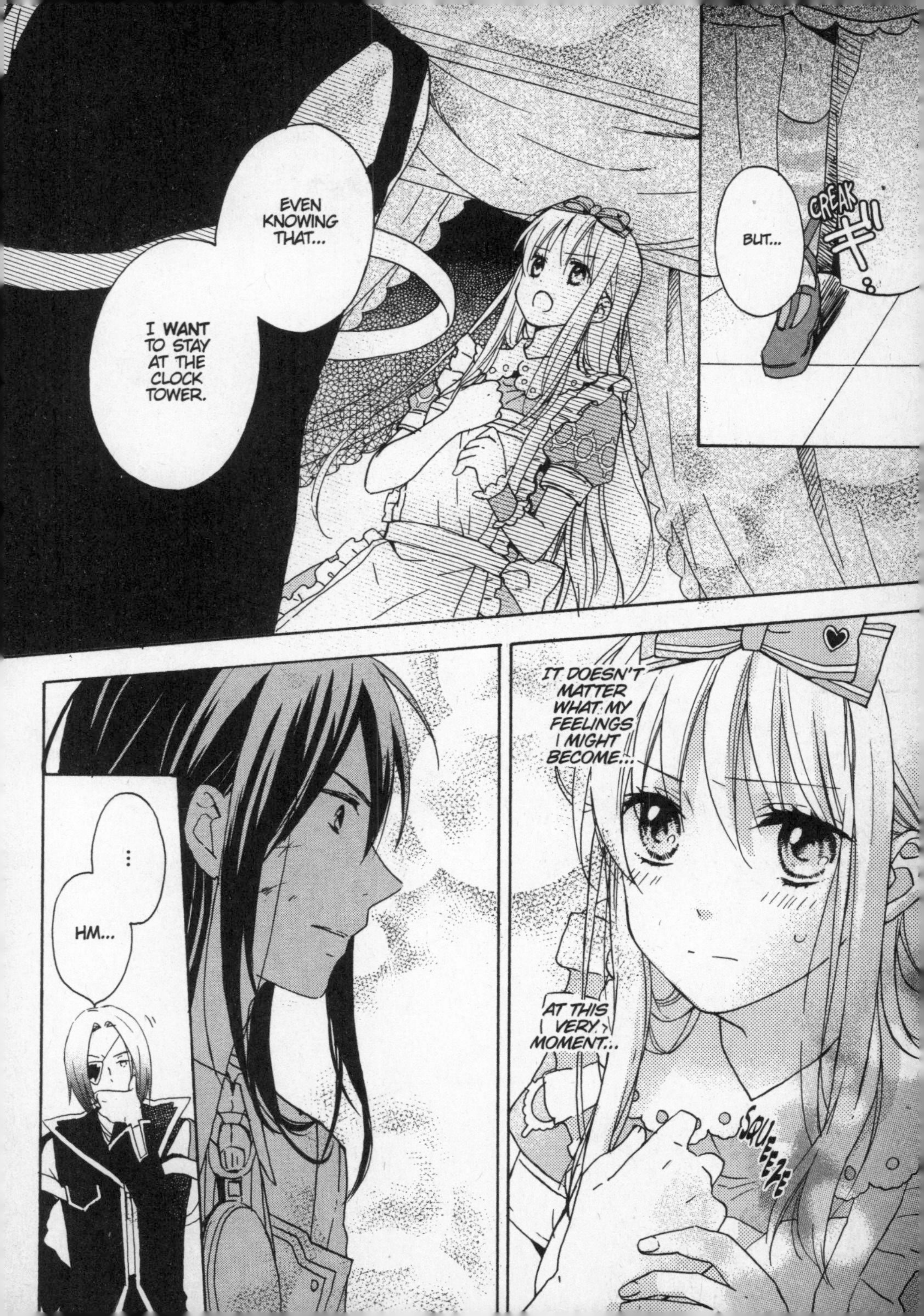
BUT...
CREAK
EVEN KNOWING THAT...
I WANT TO STAY AT THE CLOCK TOWER.
IT DOESN'T MATTER WHAT MY FEELINGS MIGHT BECOME...
AT THIS VERY MOMENT...
SQUEEZE
...
HM...

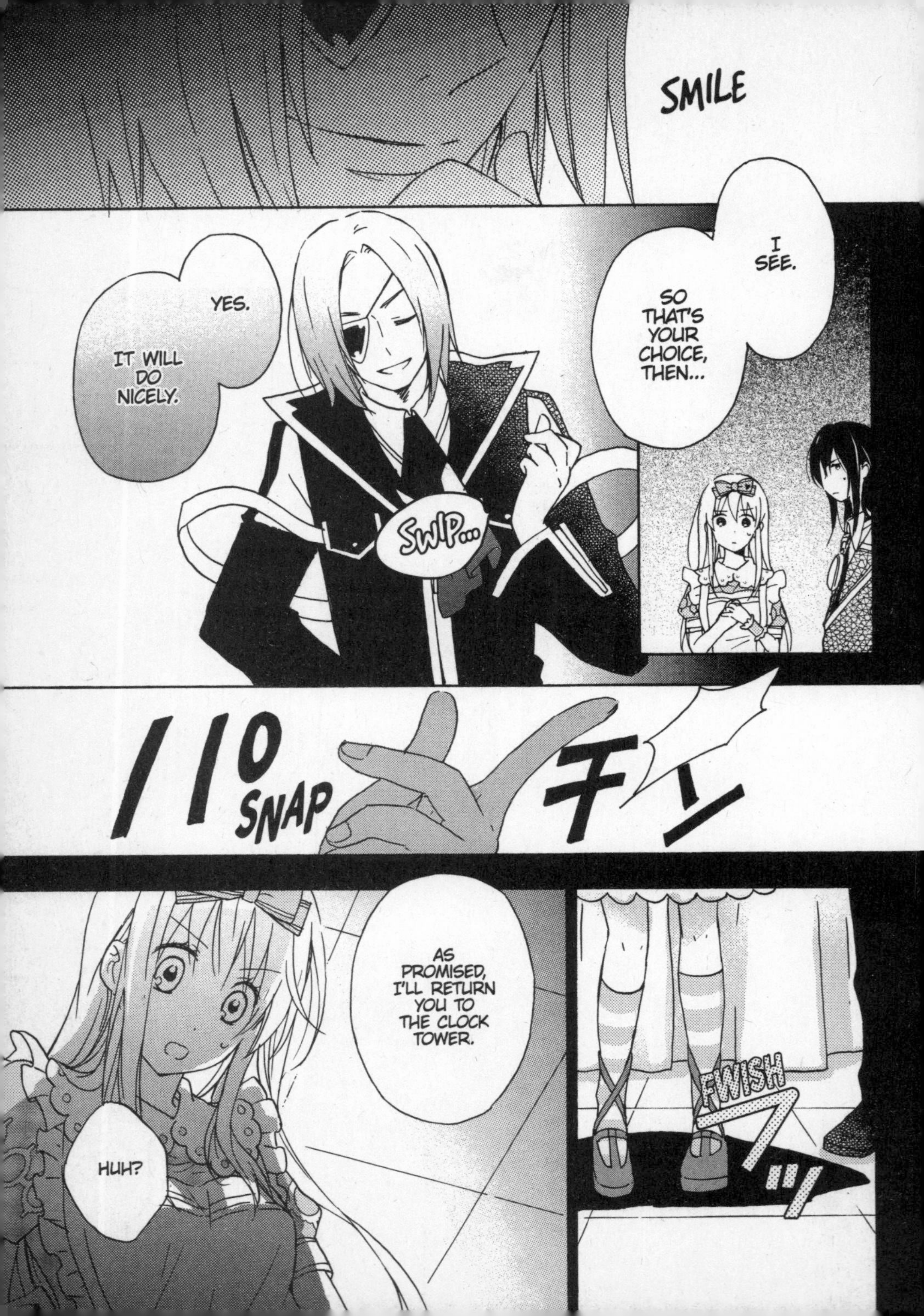
SMILE
I SEE.
SO THAT'S YOUR CHOICE, THEN...
YES.
IT WILL DO NICELY.
SWIP...
SNAP
パチン
FWISH
AS PROMISED, I'LL RETURN YOU TO THE CLOCK TOWER.
HUH?

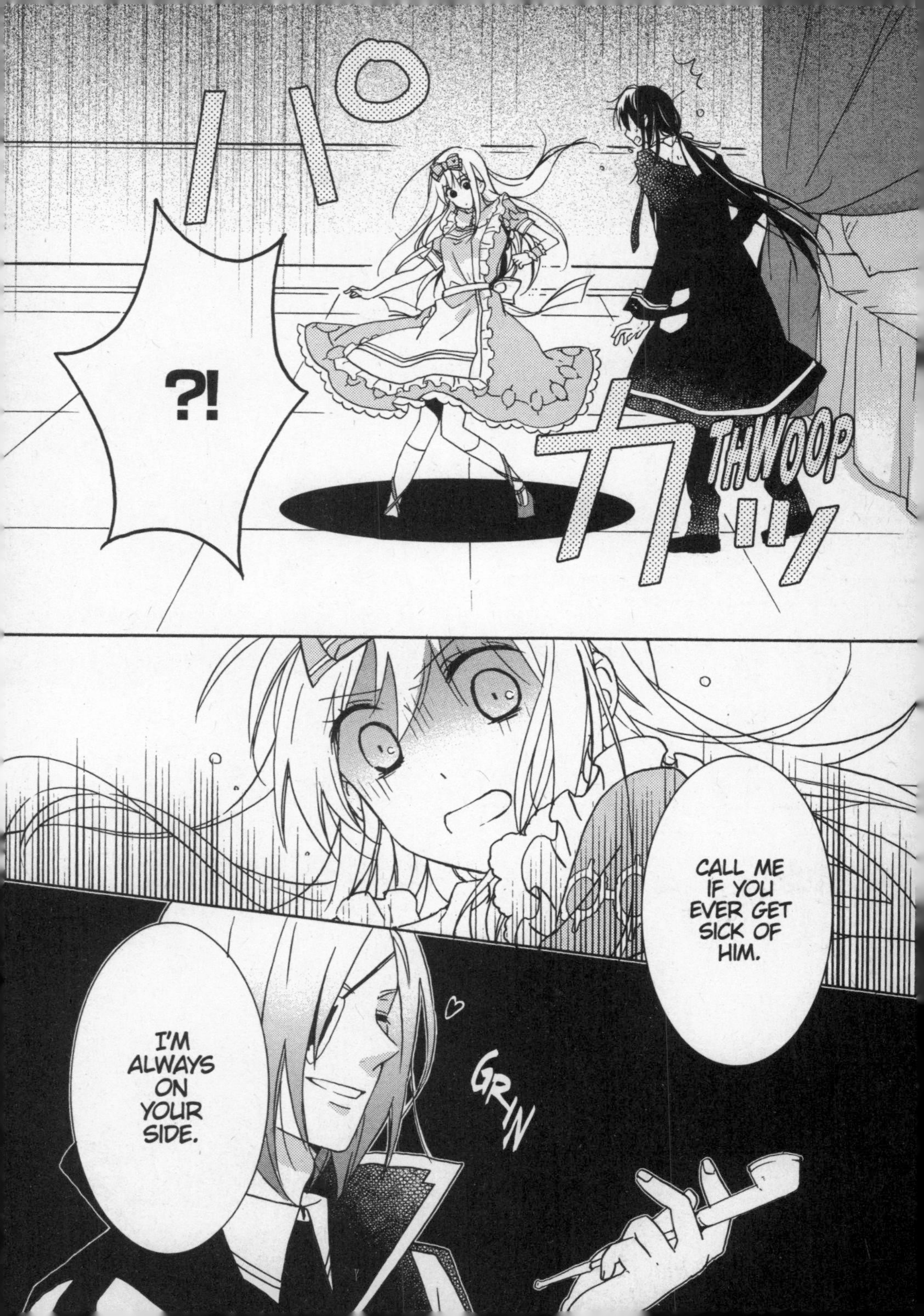
THWOOP
?!
CALL ME IF YOU EVER GET SICK OF HIM.
GRIN
I'M ALWAYS ON YOUR SIDE.

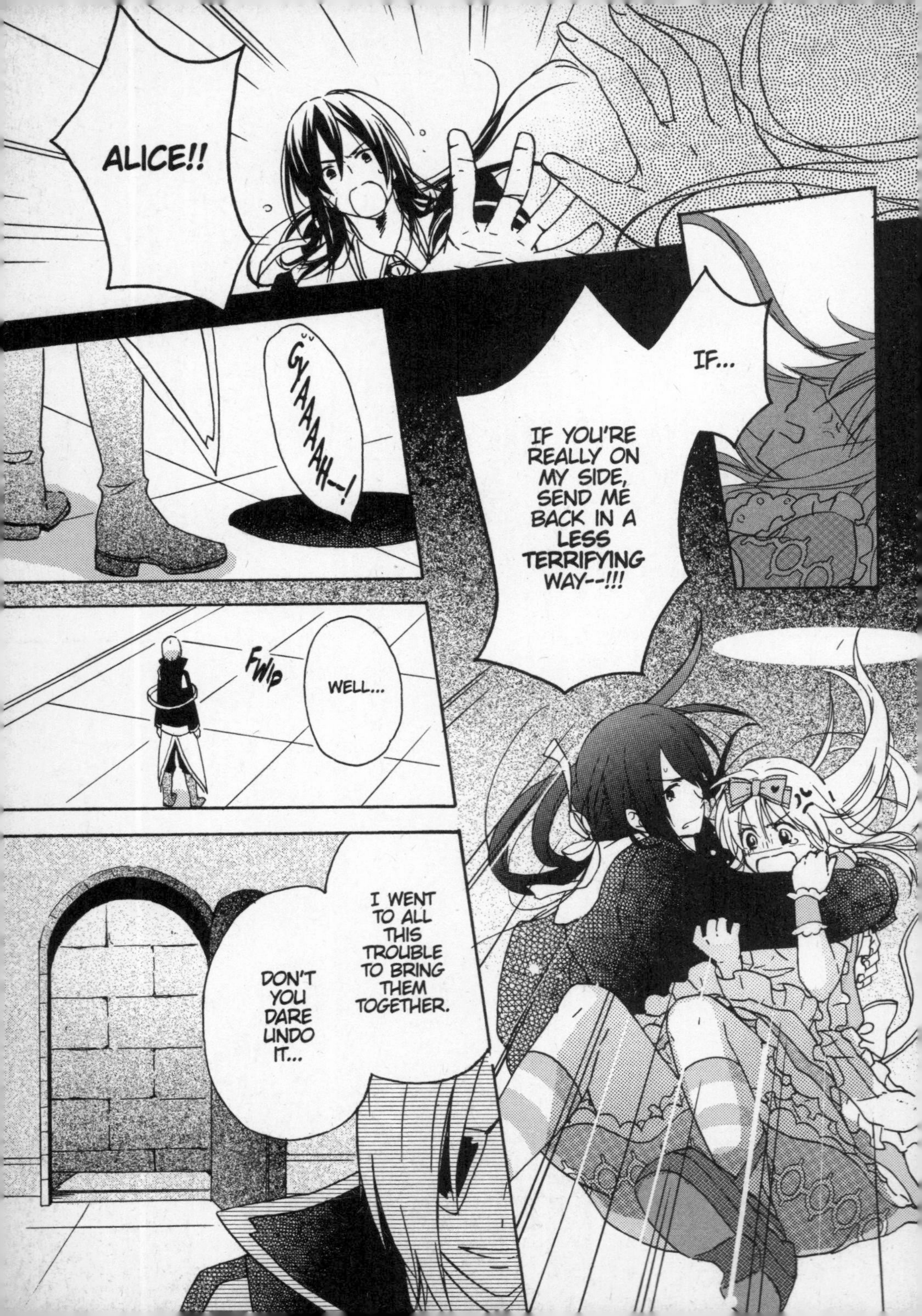
ALICE!!
IF...
IF YOU'RE REALLY ON MY SIDE, SEND ME BACK IN A LESS TERRIFYING WAY--!!!
GYAAAAAH--!
FWIP
WELL...
I WENT TO ALL THIS TROUBLE TO BRING THEM TOGETHER.
DON'T YOU DARE UNDO IT...

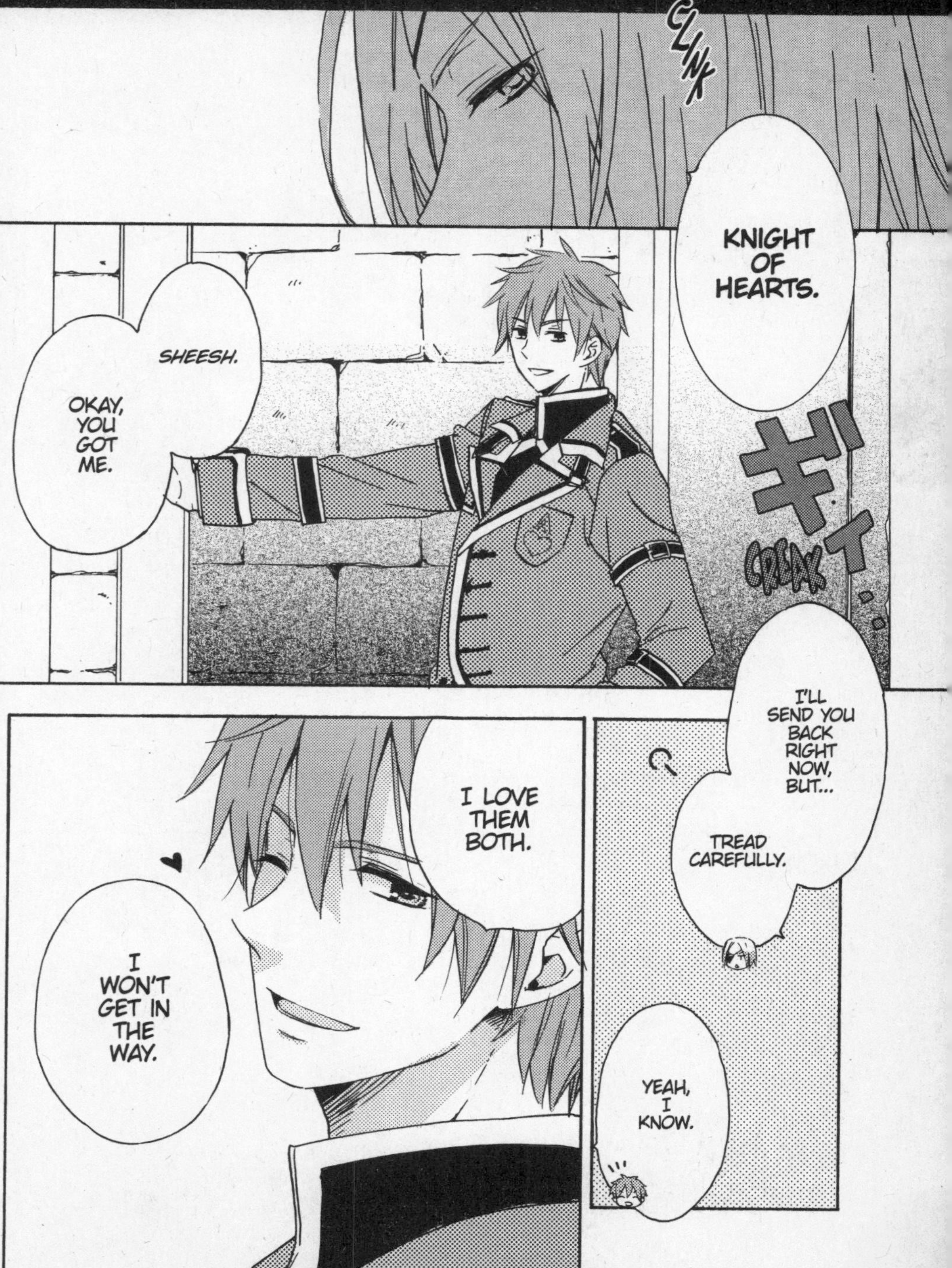
CLINK
KNIGHT OF HEARTS.
ギイ…
CREAK
SHEESH.
OKAY, YOU GOT ME.
I'LL SEND YOU BACK RIGHT NOW, BUT...
TREAD CAREFULLY.
YEAH, I KNOW.
I LOVE THEM BOTH.
I WON'T GET IN THE WAY.

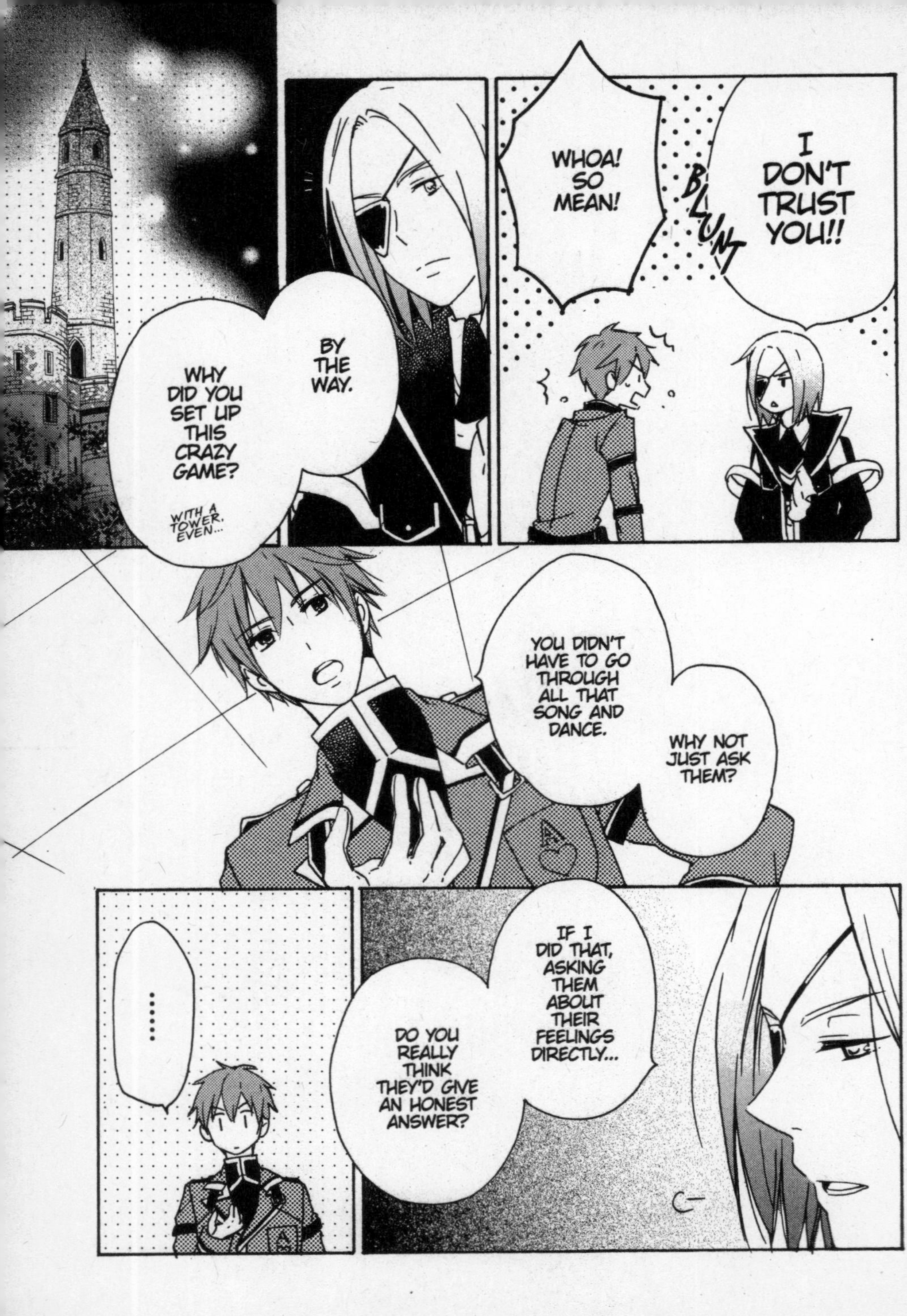
I DON'T TRUST YOU!!
BLUNT
WHOA! SO MEAN!
BY THE WAY.
WHY DID YOU SET UP THIS CRAZY GAME?
WITH A TOWER, EVEN...
YOU DIDN'T HAVE TO GO THROUGH ALL THAT SONG AND DANCE.
WHY NOT JUST ASK THEM?
IF I DID THAT, ASKING THEM ABOUT THEIR FEELINGS DIRECTLY...
DO YOU REALLY THINK THEY'D GIVE AN HONEST ANSWER?
......

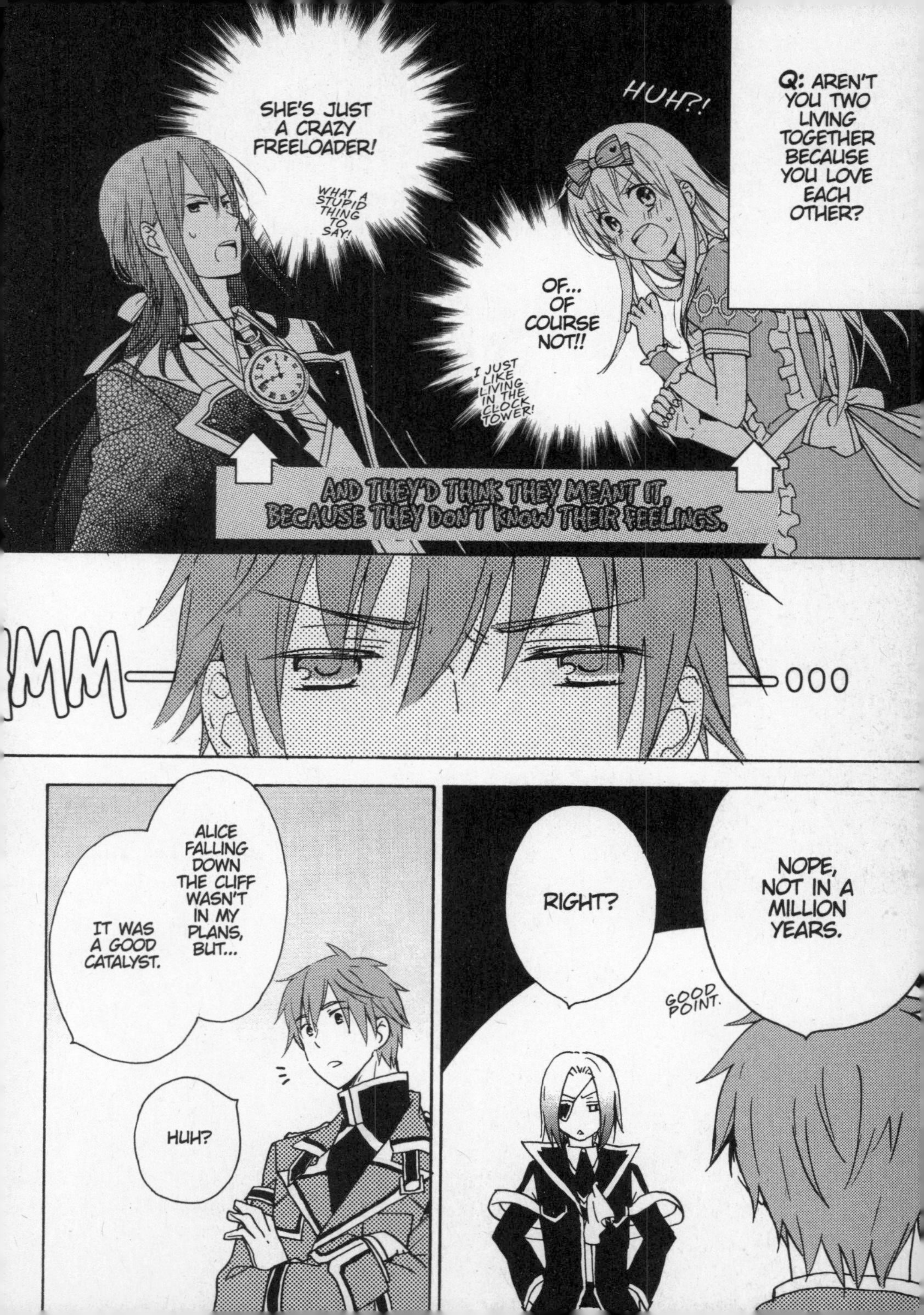
Q: AREN'T YOU TWO LIVING TOGETHER BECAUSE YOU LOVE EACH OTHER?
HUH?!
OF... OF COURSE NOT!!
I JUST LIKE LIVING IN THE CLOCK TOWER!
SHE'S JUST A CRAZY FREELOADER!
WHAT A STUPID THING TO SAY!
AND THEY'D THINK THEY MEANT IT, BECAUSE THEY DON'T KNOW THEIR FEELINGS.
MM—
—OOO
NOPE, NOT IN A MILLION YEARS.
GOOD POINT.
RIGHT?
ALICE FALLING DOWN THE CLIFF WASN'T IN MY PLANS, BUT...
IT WAS A GOOD CATALYST.
HUH?

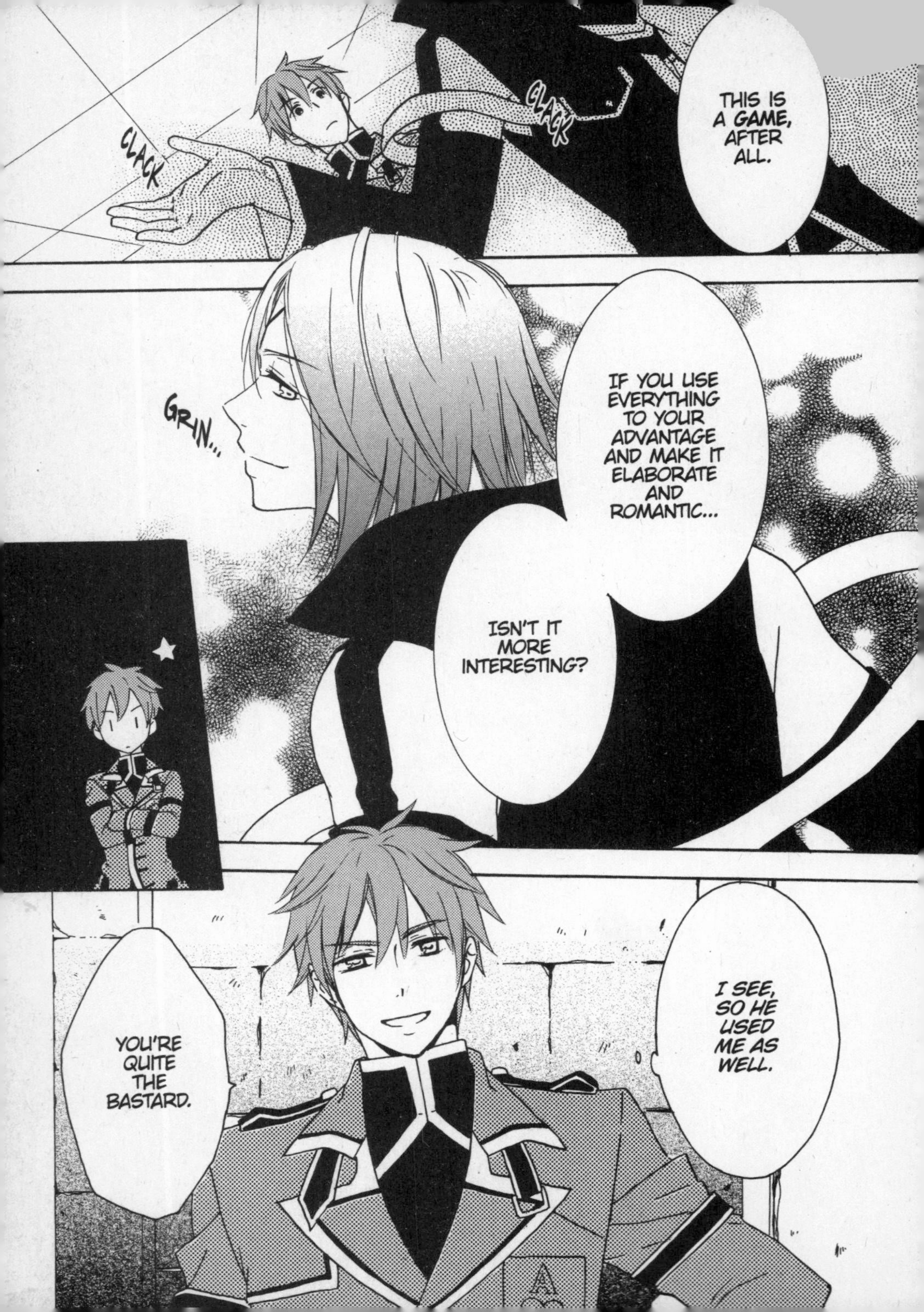
THIS IS A GAME, AFTER ALL.
CLACK
CLACK
IF YOU USE EVERYTHING TO YOUR ADVANTAGE AND MAKE IT ELABORATE AND ROMANTIC...
ISN'T IT MORE INTERESTING?
GRIN...
I SEE, SO HE USED ME AS WELL.
YOU'RE QUITE THE BASTARD.

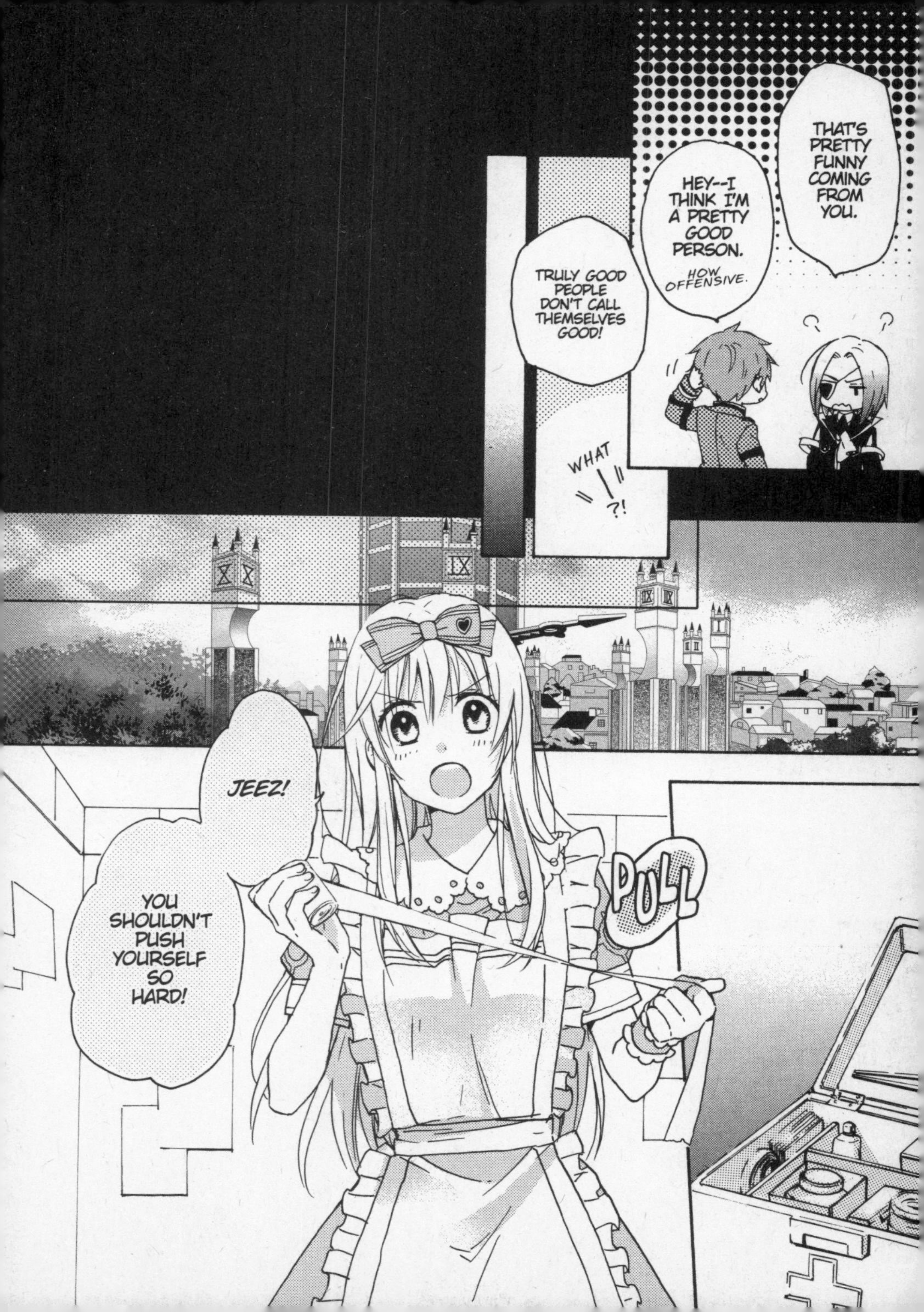
THAT'S PRETTY FUNNY COMING FROM YOU.
HEY--I THINK I'M A PRETTY GOOD PERSON.
HOW OFFENSIVE.
TRULY GOOD PEOPLE DON'T CALL THEMSELVES GOOD!
WHAT ?!
PULL
JEEZ!
YOU SHOULDN'T PUSH YOURSELF SO HARD!

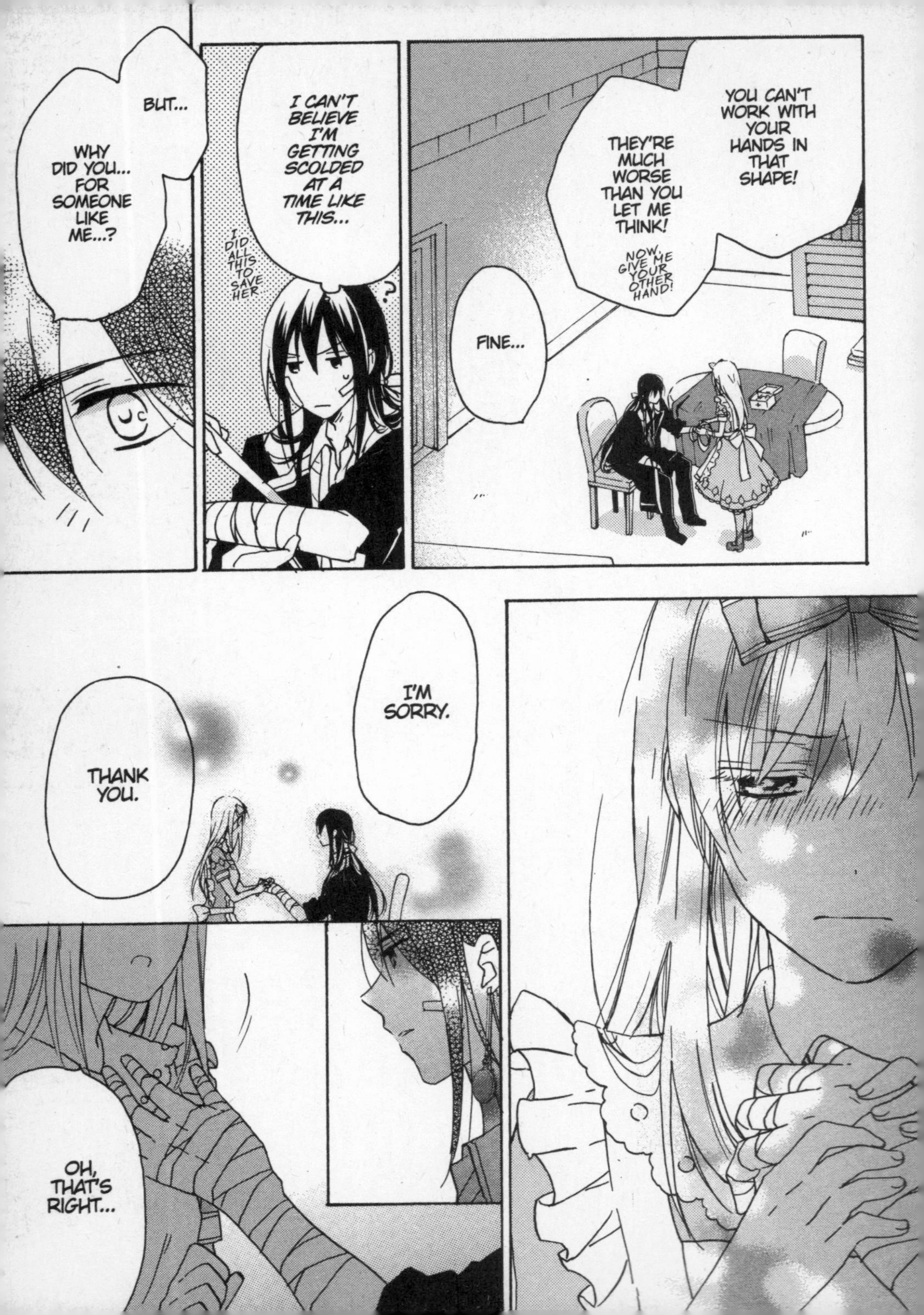
YOU CAN'T WORK WITH YOUR HANDS IN THAT SHAPE!
THEY'RE MUCH WORSE THAN YOU LET ME THINK!
NOW, GIVE ME YOUR OTHER HAND!
FINE...
I CAN'T BELIEVE I'M GETTING SCOLDED AT A TIME LIKE THIS...
I DID ALL THIS TO SAVE HER
BUT...
WHY DID YOU... FOR SOMEONE LIKE ME...?
I'M SORRY.
THANK YOU.
OH, THAT'S RIGHT...

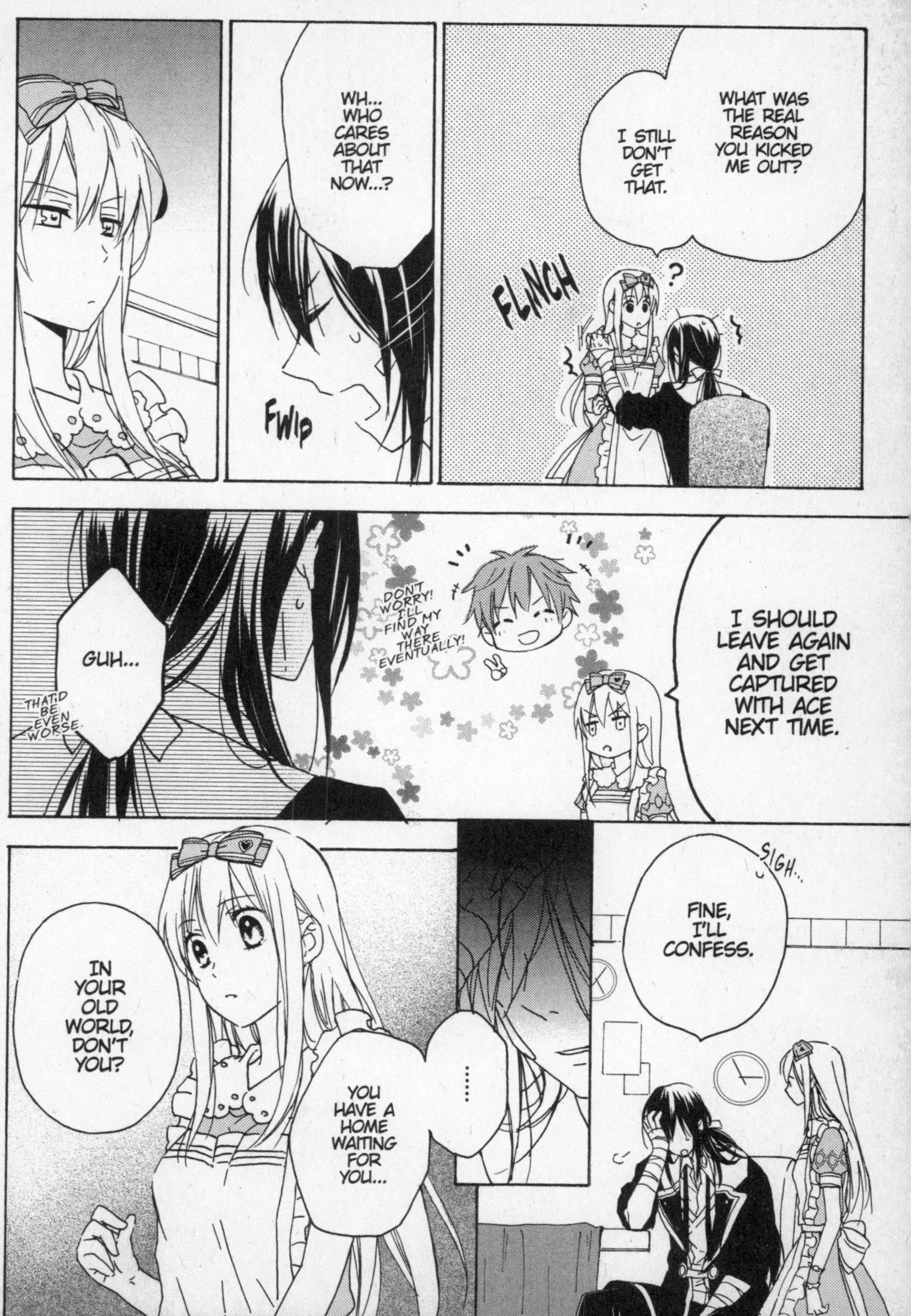
WHAT WAS THE REAL REASON YOU KICKED ME OUT?
I STILL DON'T GET THAT.
?
FLINCH
WH... WHO CARES ABOUT THAT NOW...?
FWIP
I SHOULD LEAVE AGAIN AND GET CAPTURED WITH ACE NEXT TIME.
DON'T WORRY! I'LL FIND MY WAY THERE EVENTUALLY!
GUH...
THAT'D BE EVEN WORSE.
SIGH...
FINE, I'LL CONFESS.
......
YOU HAVE A HOME WAITING FOR YOU...
IN YOUR OLD WORLD, DON'T YOU?

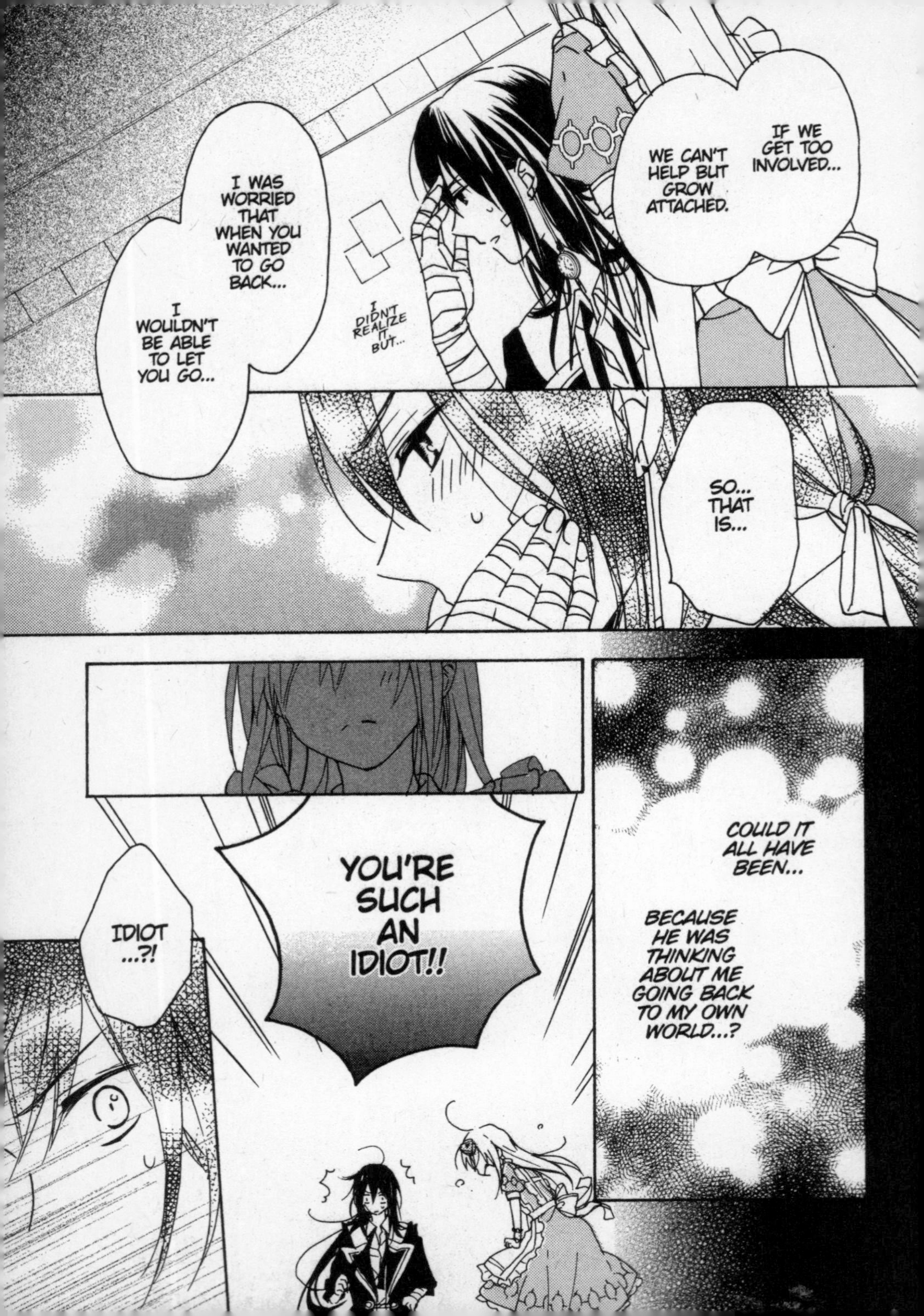
IF WE GET TOO INVOLVED...
WE CAN'T HELP BUT GROW ATTACHED.
I DIDN'T REALIZE IT, BUT...
I WAS WORRIED THAT WHEN YOU WANTED TO GO BACK...
I WOULDN'T BE ABLE TO LET YOU GO...
SO... THAT IS...
COULD IT ALL HAVE BEEN...
BECAUSE HE WAS THINKING ABOUT ME GOING BACK TO MY OWN WORLD...?
YOU'RE SUCH AN IDIOT!!
IDIOT ...?!

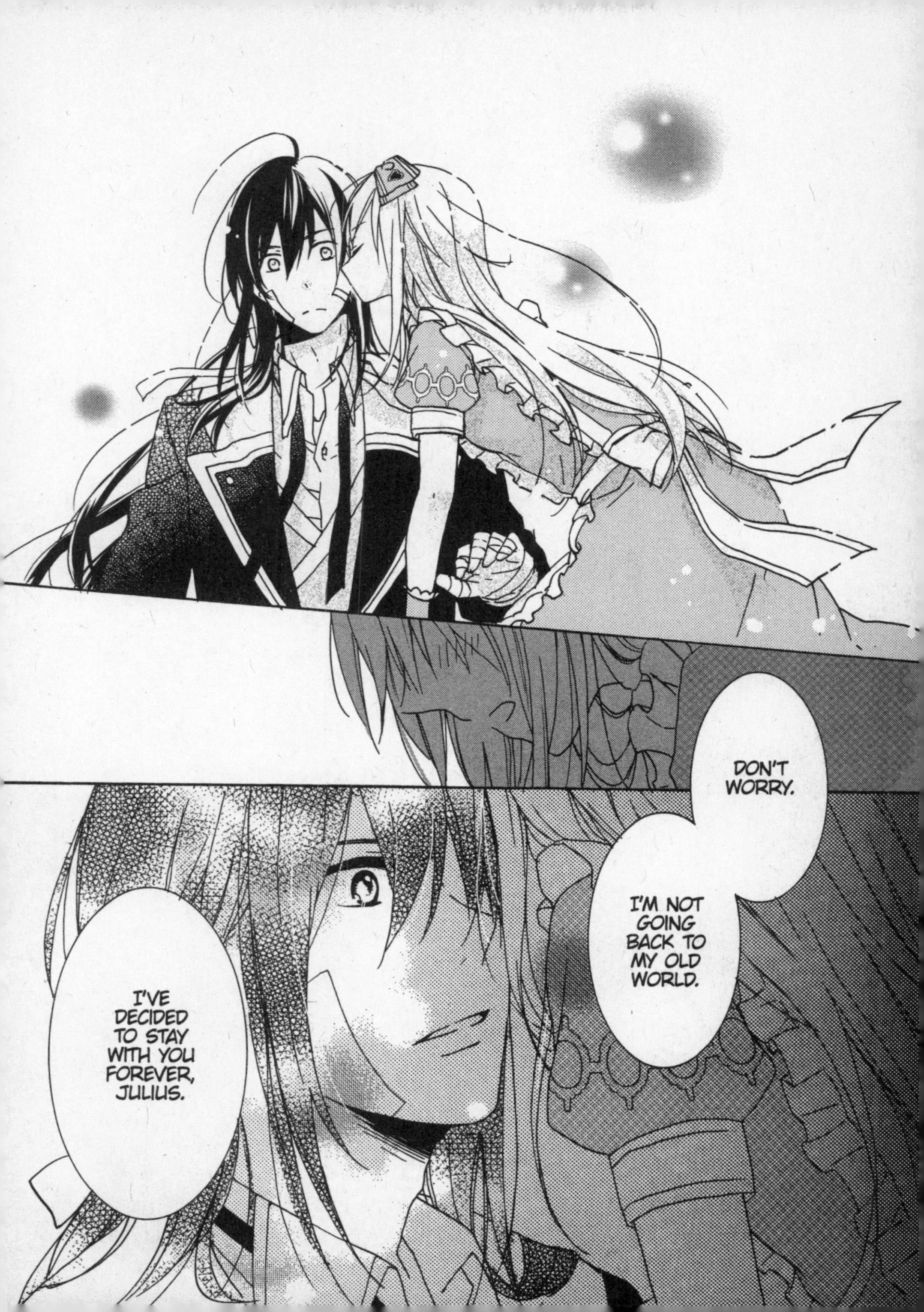
DON'T WORRY.
I'M NOT GOING BACK TO MY OLD WORLD.
I'VE DECIDED TO STAY WITH YOU FOREVER, JULIUS.

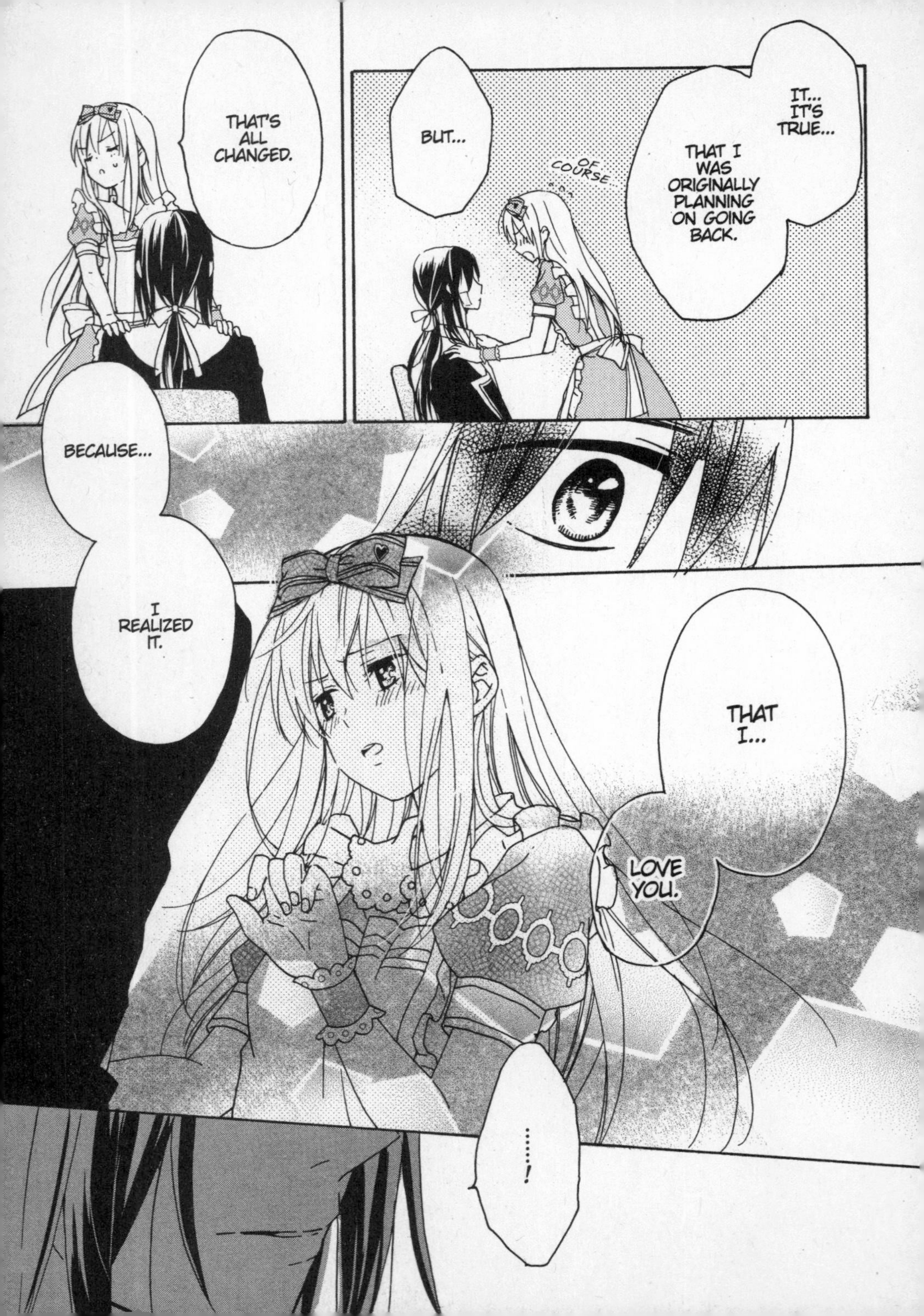
IT... IT'S TRUE...
THAT I WAS ORIGINALLY PLANNING ON GOING BACK.
OF COURSE...
BUT...
THAT'S ALL CHANGED.
BECAUSE...
I REALIZED IT.
THAT I...
LOVE YOU.
......!

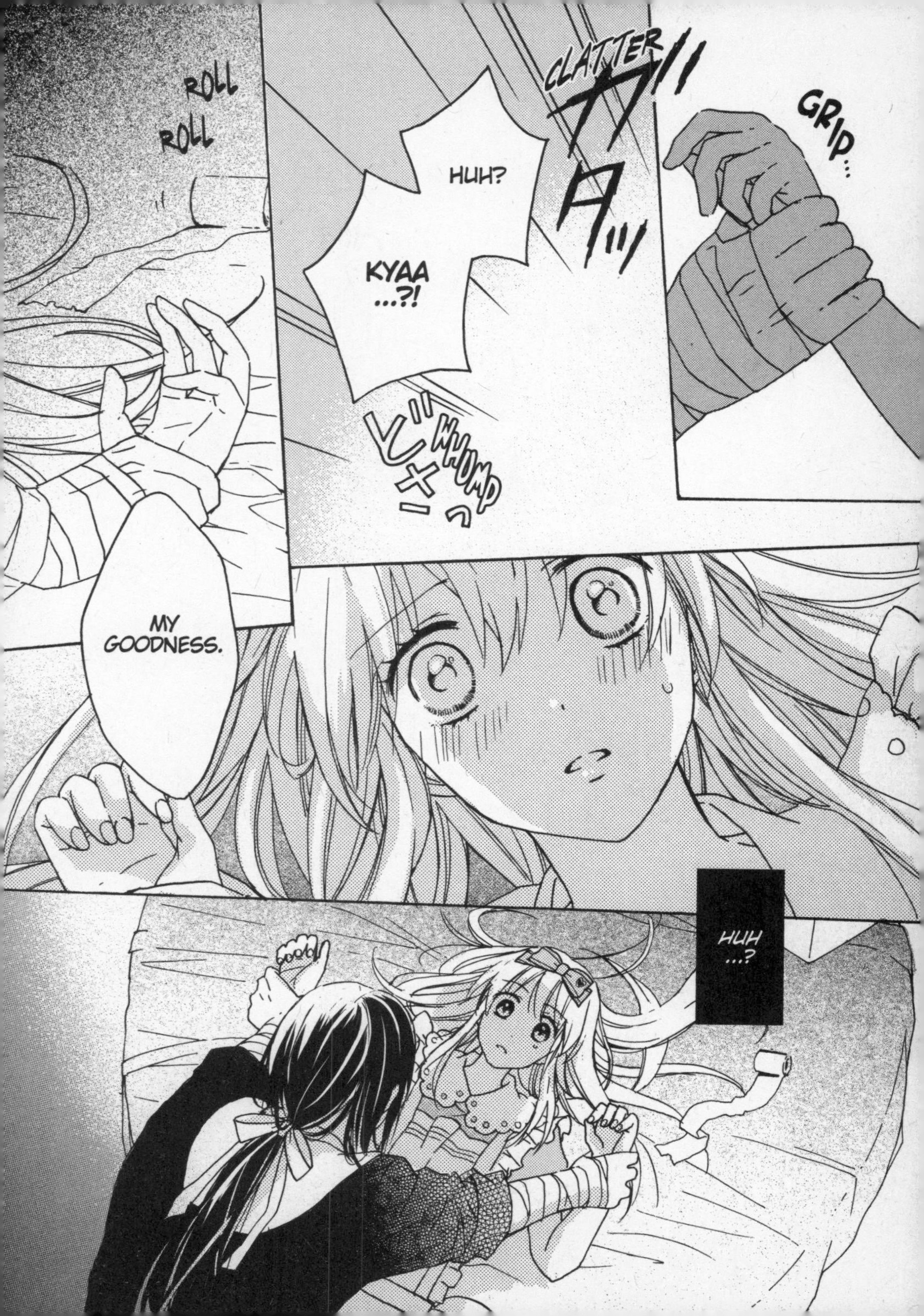
GRIP...
CLATTER
HUH?
KYAA ...?!
WHUMP
ROLL
ROLL
MY GOODNESS.
HUH ...?

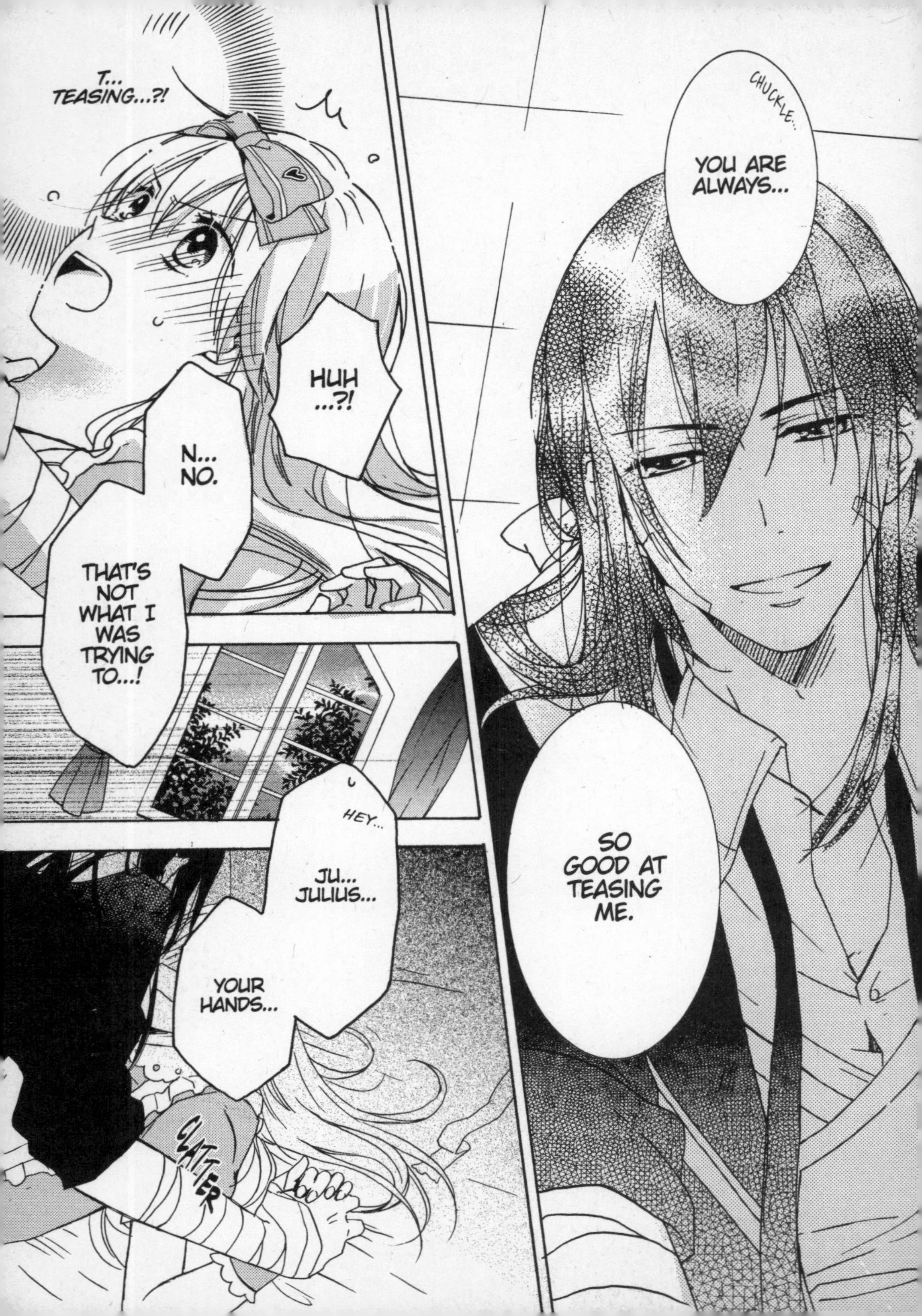
CHUCKLE...
YOU ARE ALWAYS...
SO GOOD AT TEASING ME.
T... TEASING...?!
HUH ...?!
N... NO.
THAT'S NOT WHAT I WAS TRYING TO...!
HEY...
JU... JULIUS...
YOUR HANDS...
CLATTER

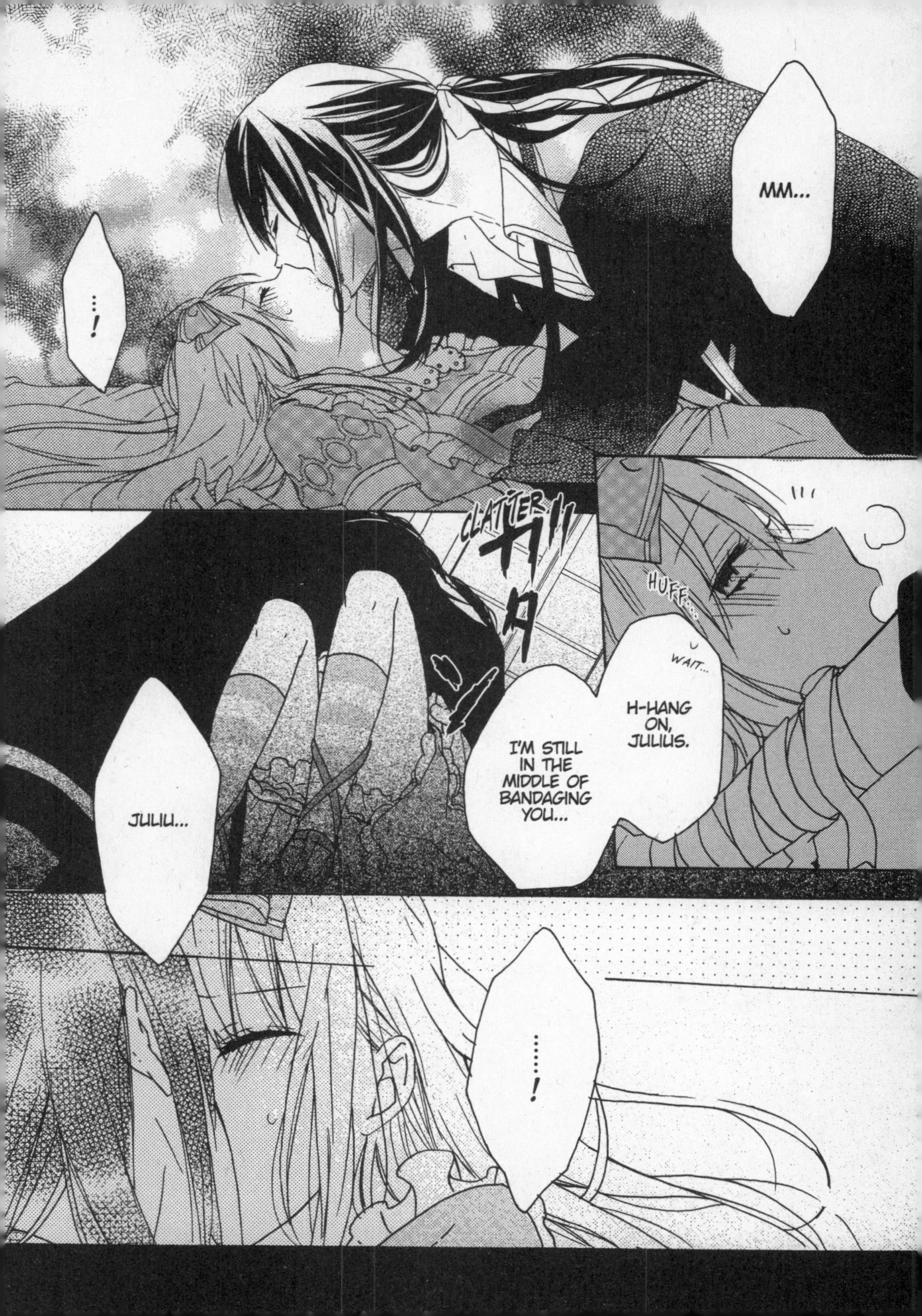
MM...
...!
HUFF...
WAIT...
H-HANG ON, JULIUS.
I'M STILL IN THE MIDDLE OF BANDAGING YOU...
CLATTER
JULIU...
......!

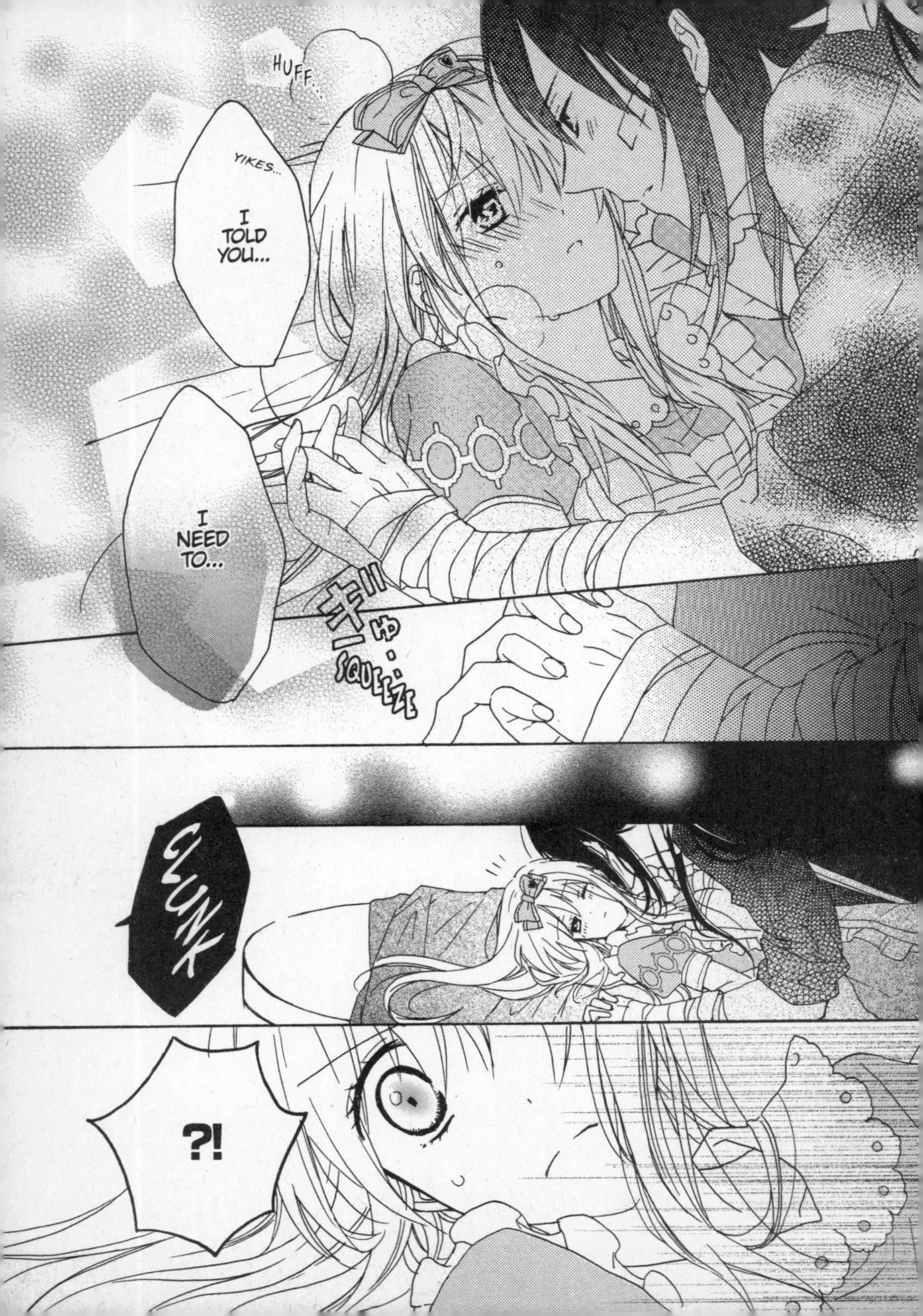
HUFF...
YIKES...
I TOLD YOU...
I NEED TO...
ギュ...
SQUEEZE
CLUNK
?!

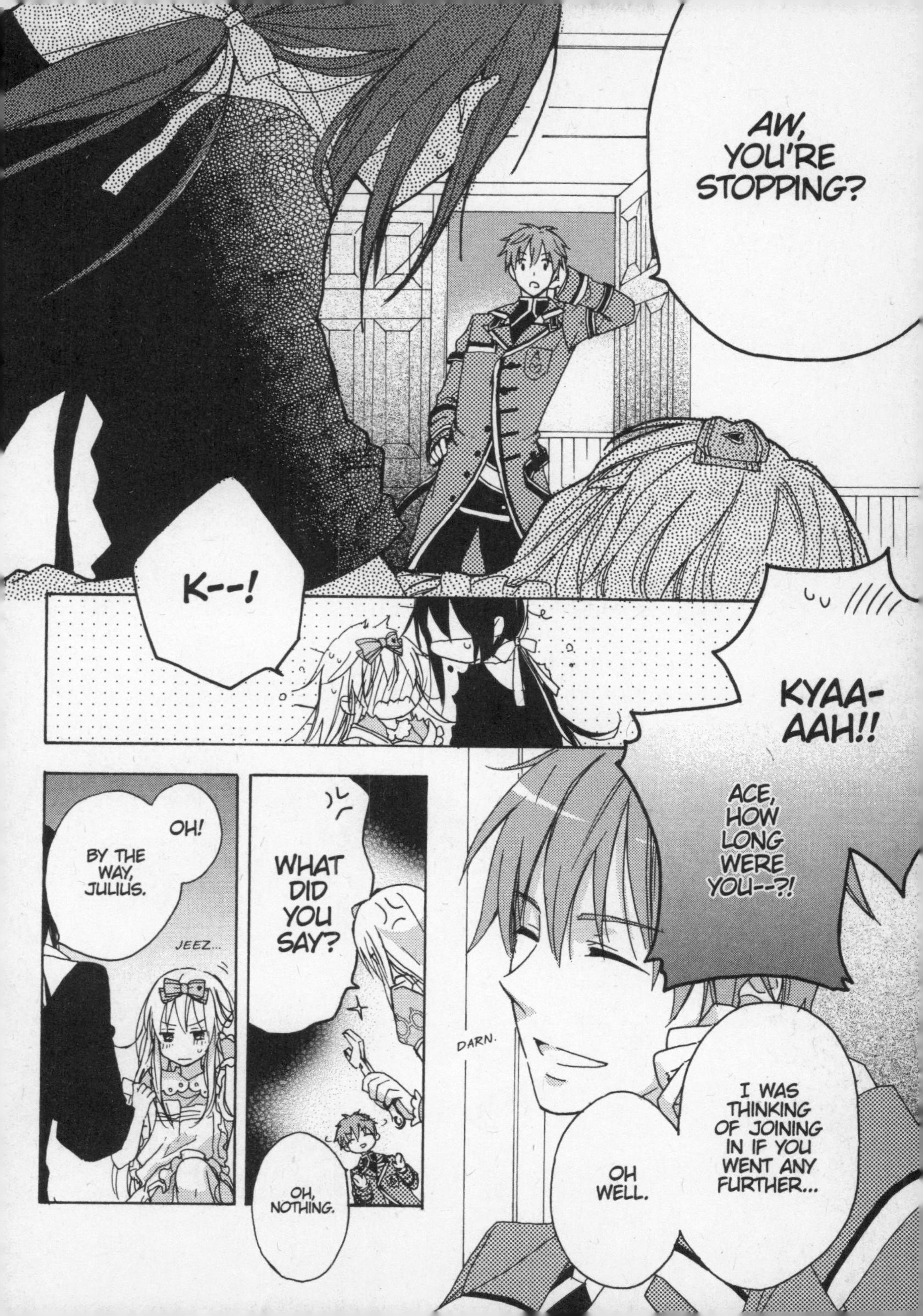
AW, YOU'RE STOPPING?
K--!
KYAA-AAH!!
ACE, HOW LONG WERE YOU--?!
I WAS THINKING OF JOINING IN IF YOU WENT ANY FURTHER...
OH WELL.
DARN.
WHAT DID YOU SAY?
OH, NOTHING.
OH!
BY THE WAY, JULIUS.
JEEZ...

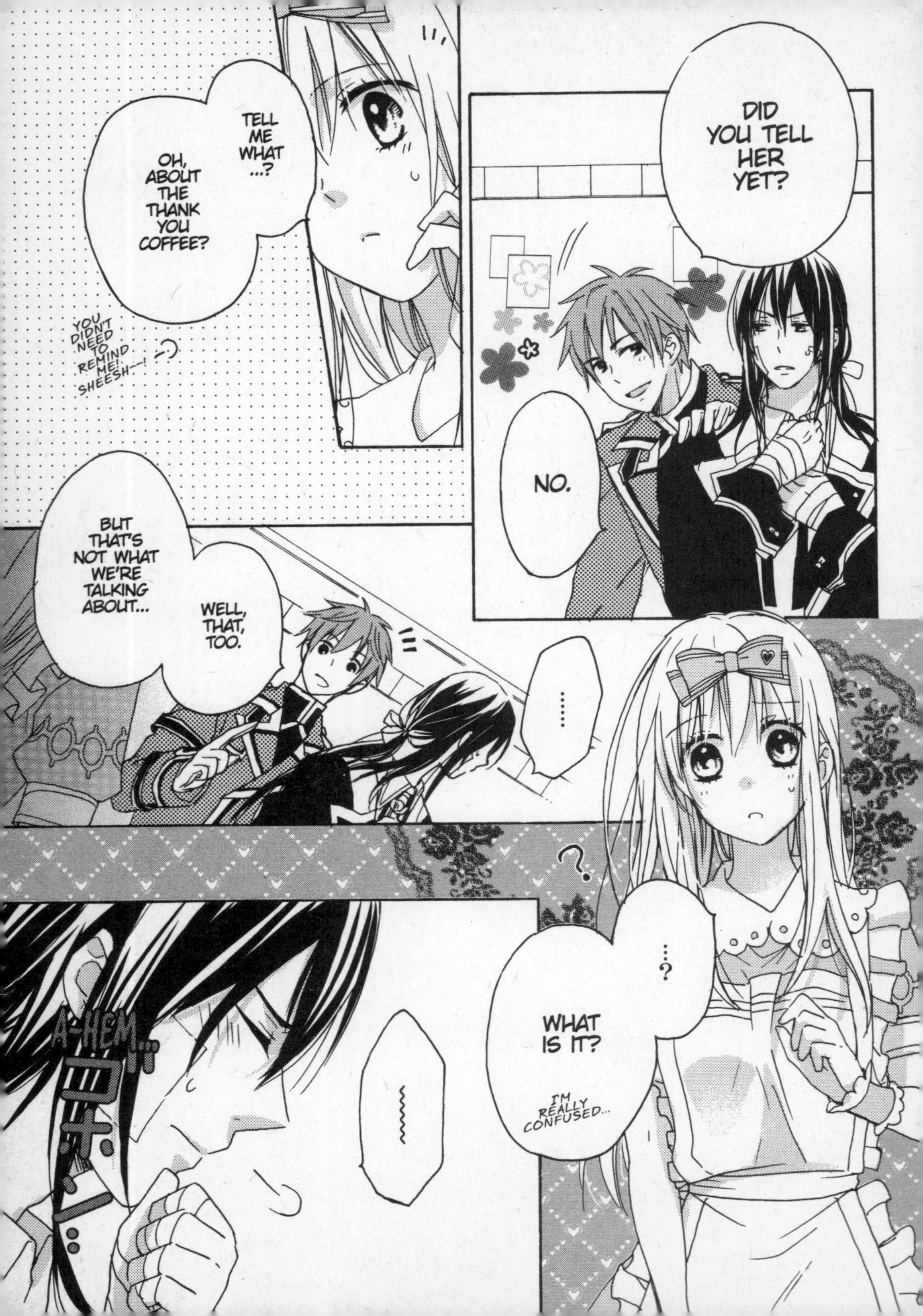
DID YOU TELL HER YET?
NO.
TELL ME WHAT ...?
OH, ABOUT THE THANK YOU COFFEE?
YOU DIDN'T NEED TO REMIND ME! SHEESH...!
...?
WHAT IS IT?
I'M REALLY CONFUSED...
BUT THAT'S NOT WHAT WE'RE TALKING ABOUT...
WELL, THAT, TOO.
......
A-HEM...
......

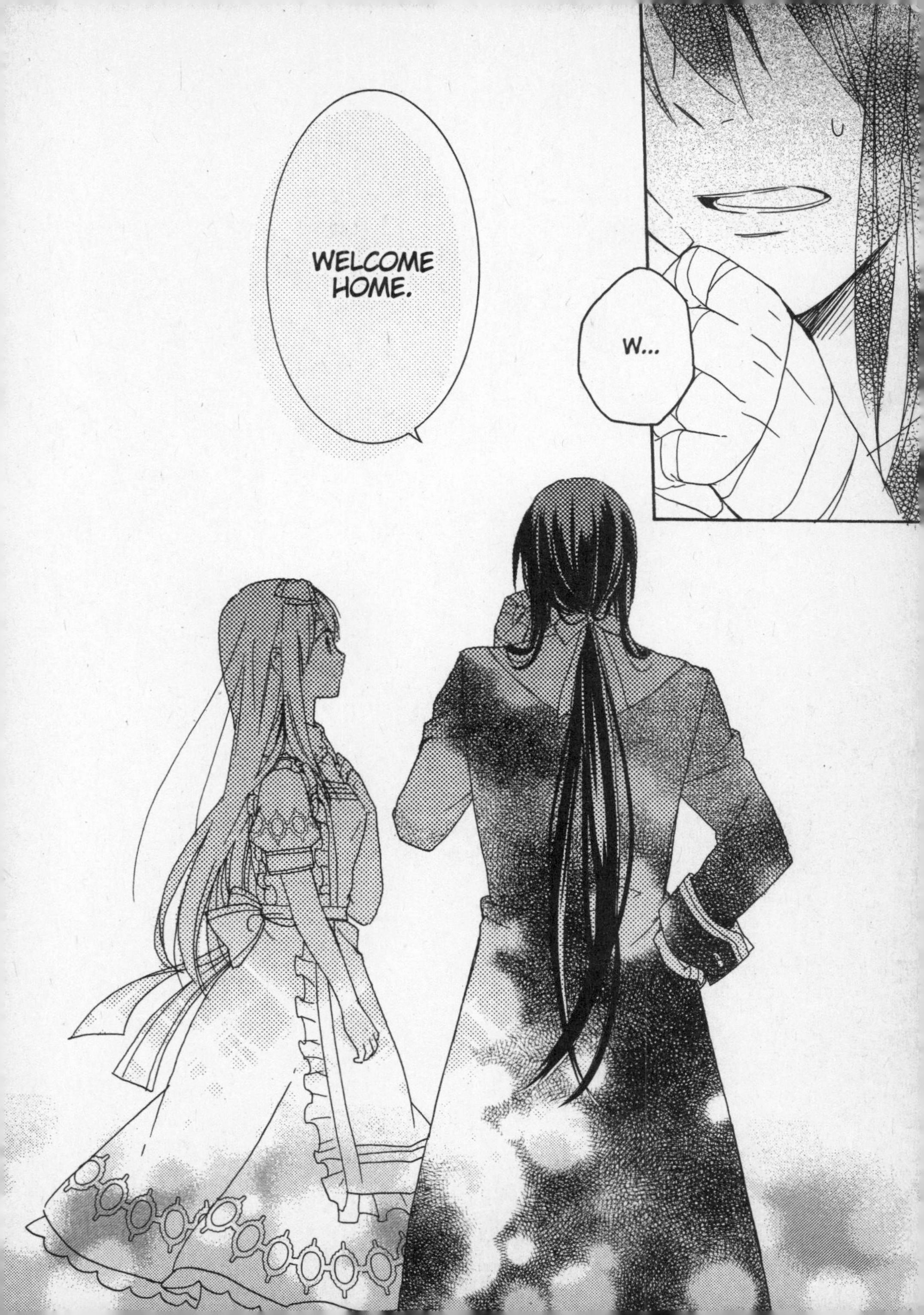
W...
WELCOME HOME.

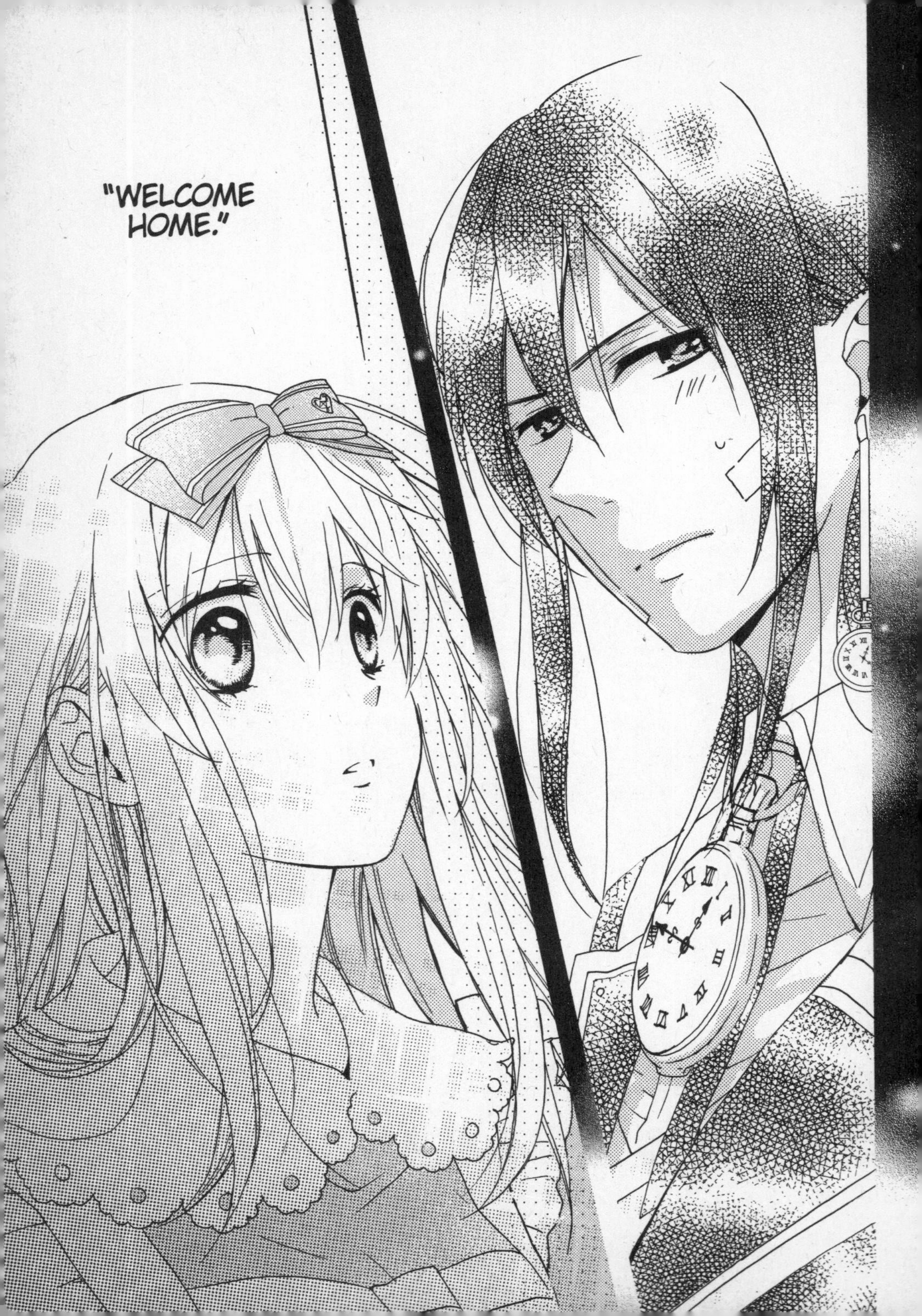
"WELCOME HOME."

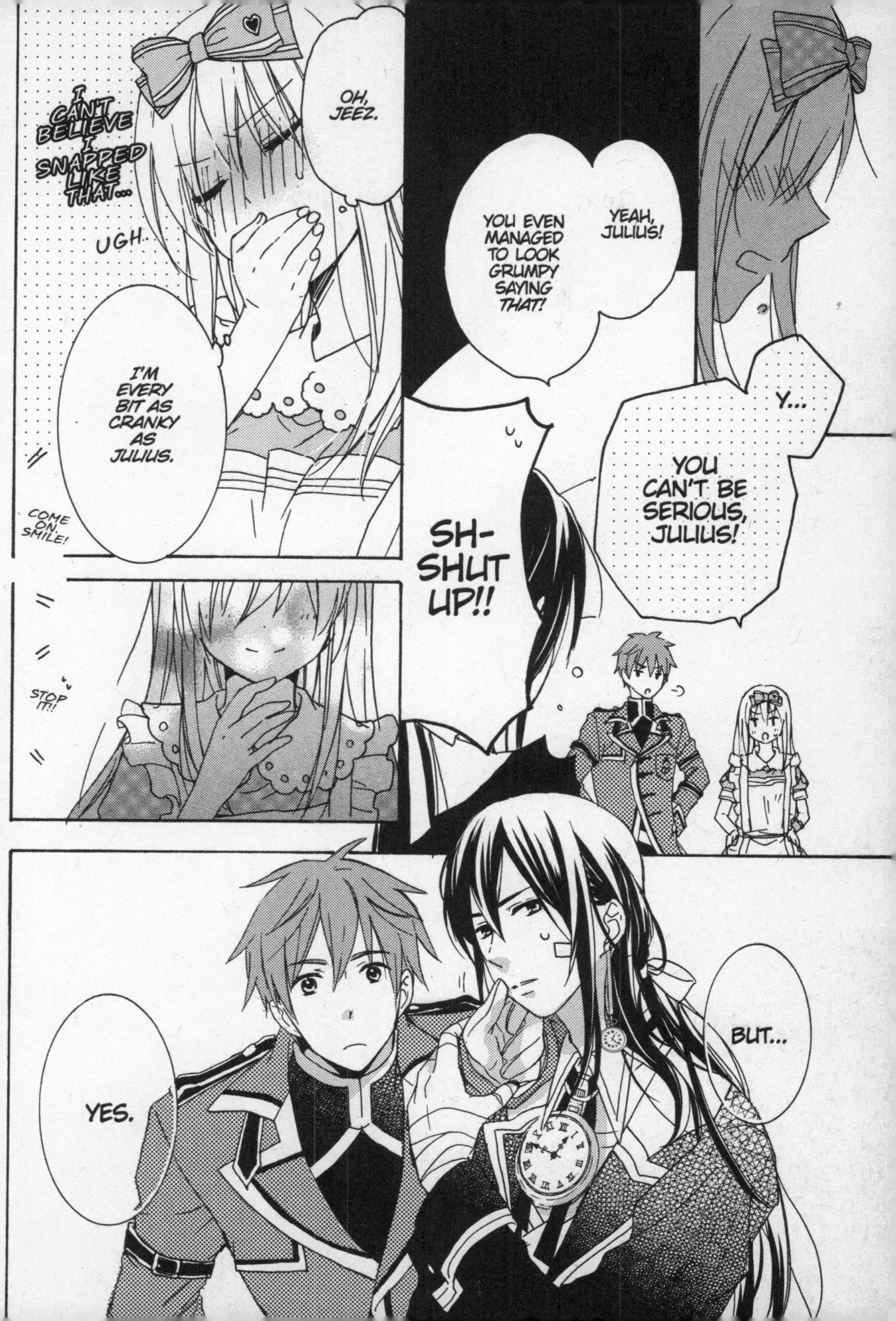
Y...
YOU CAN'T BE SERIOUS, JULIUS!
YEAH, JULIUS!
YOU EVEN MANAGED TO LOOK GRUMPY SAYING THAT!
SH-SHUT UP!!
OH, JEEZ.
I CAN'T BELIEVE I SNAPPED LIKE THAT...
UGH.
I'M EVERY BIT AS CRANKY AS JULIUS.
COME ON, SMILE!
STOP IT!!
BUT...
YES.

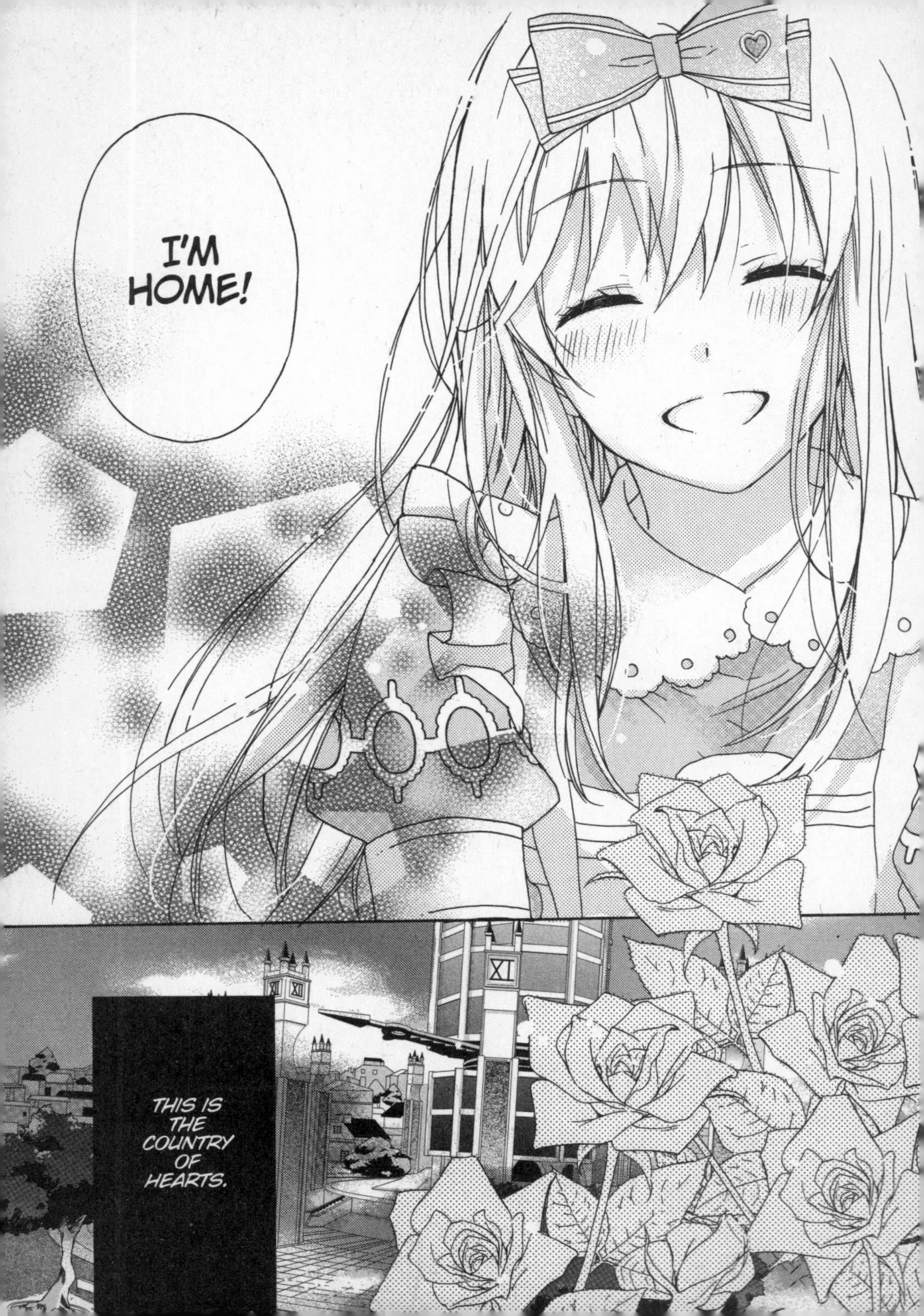
I'M HOME!
THIS IS THE COUNTRY OF HEARTS.

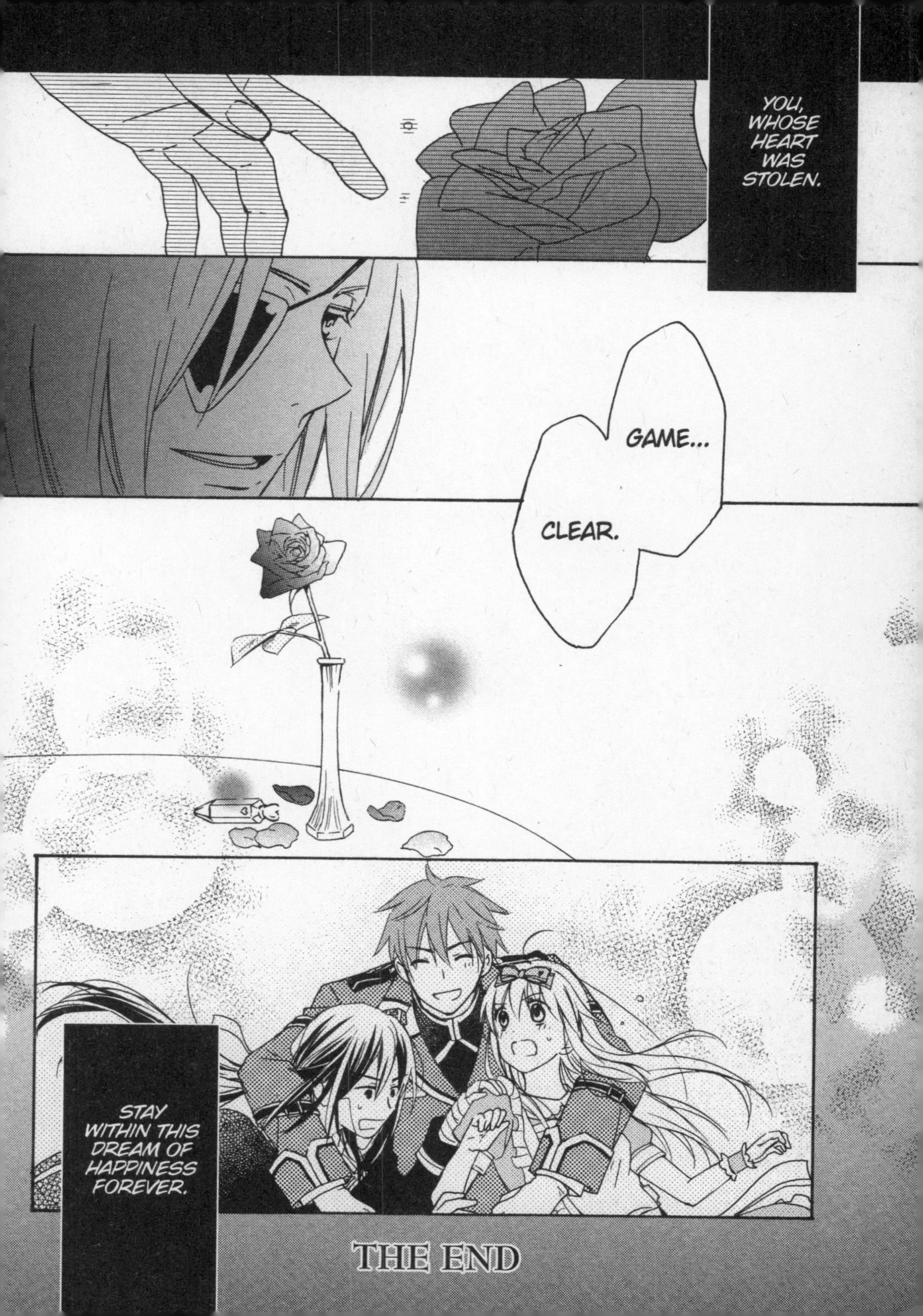
YOU, WHOSE HEART WAS STOLEN.
GAME... CLEAR.
STAY WITHIN THIS DREAM OF HAPPINESS FOREVER.
THE END

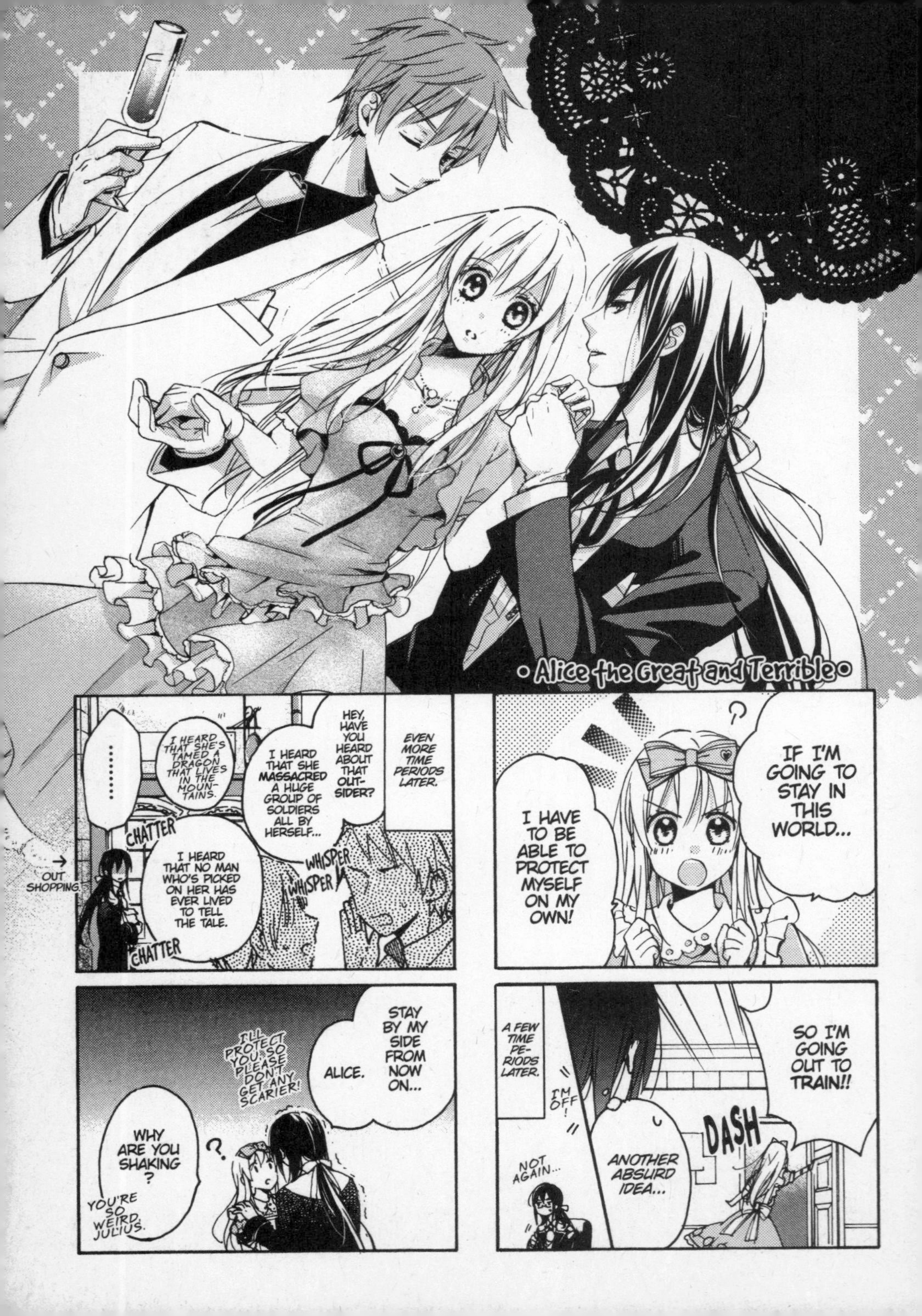
• Alice the Great and Terrible •
IF I'M GOING TO STAY IN THIS WORLD...
I HAVE TO BE ABLE TO PROTECT MYSELF ON MY OWN!
EVEN MORE TIME PERIODS LATER.
HEY, HAVE YOU HEARD ABOUT THAT OUTSIDER?
I HEARD THAT SHE MASSACRED A HUGE GROUP OF SOLDIERS ALL BY HERSELF...
I HEARD THAT SHE'S TAMED A DRAGON THAT LIVES IN THE MOUNTAINS.
......
CHATTER
WHISPER WHISPER
I HEARD THAT NO MAN WHO'S PICKED ON HER HAS EVER LIVED TO TELL THE TALE.
OUT SHOPPING.
CHATTER
A FEW TIME PERIODS LATER.
SO I'M GOING OUT TO TRAIN!!
I'M OFF!
DASH
ANOTHER ABSURD IDEA...
NOT AGAIN...
ALICE.
STAY BY MY SIDE FROM NOW ON...
I'LL PROTECT YOU, SO PLEASE DON'T GET ANY SCARIER!
WHY ARE YOU SHAKING?
YOU'RE SO WEIRD, JULIUS.

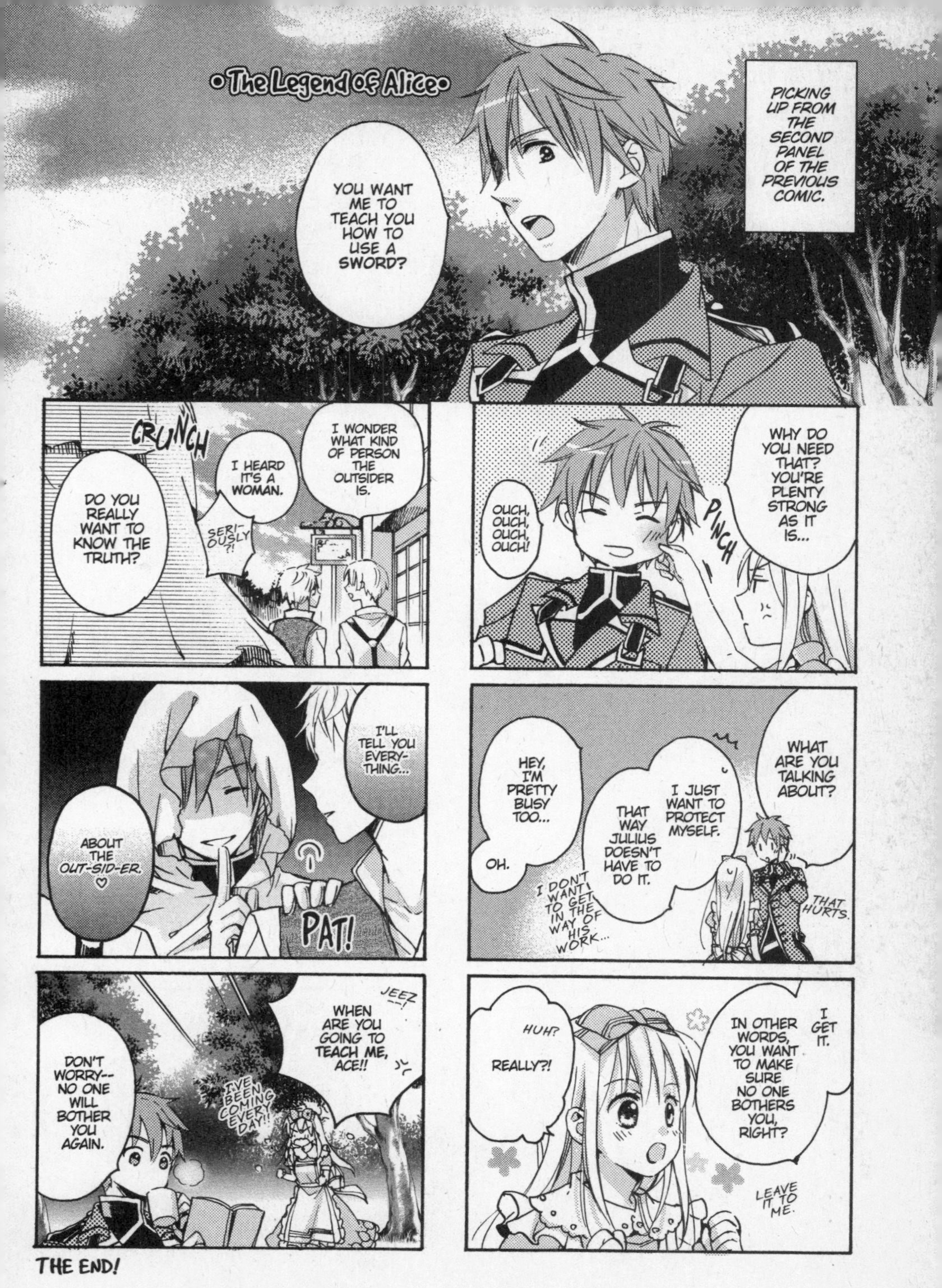
•The Legend of Alice•
PICKING UP FROM THE SECOND PANEL OF THE PREVIOUS COMIC.
YOU WANT ME TO TEACH YOU HOW TO USE A SWORD?
WHY DO YOU NEED THAT? YOU'RE PLENTY STRONG AS IT IS...
PINCH
OUCH, OUCH, OUCH, OUCH!
I WONDER WHAT KIND OF PERSON THE OUTSIDER IS.
I HEARD IT'S A WOMAN.
SERI-OUSLY?!
CRUNCH
DO YOU REALLY WANT TO KNOW THE TRUTH?
WHAT ARE YOU TALKING ABOUT?
THAT HURTS.
I JUST WANT TO PROTECT MYSELF.
THAT WAY JULIUS DOESN'T HAVE TO DO IT.
HEY, I'M PRETTY BUSY TOO...
I DON'T WANT TO GET IN THE WAY OF HIS WORK...
OH.
I'LL TELL YOU EVERY-THING...
ABOUT THE OUT-SID-ER. ♡
PAT!
I GET IT.
IN OTHER WORDS, YOU WANT TO MAKE SURE NO ONE BOTHERS YOU, RIGHT?
HUH?
REALLY?!
LEAVE IT TO ME.
JEEZ--!
WHEN ARE YOU GOING TO TEACH ME, ACE!!
I'VE BEEN COMING EVERY DAY!!
DON'T WORRY-- NO ONE WILL BOTHER YOU AGAIN.

THE END!

✿ AFTERWORD ✿

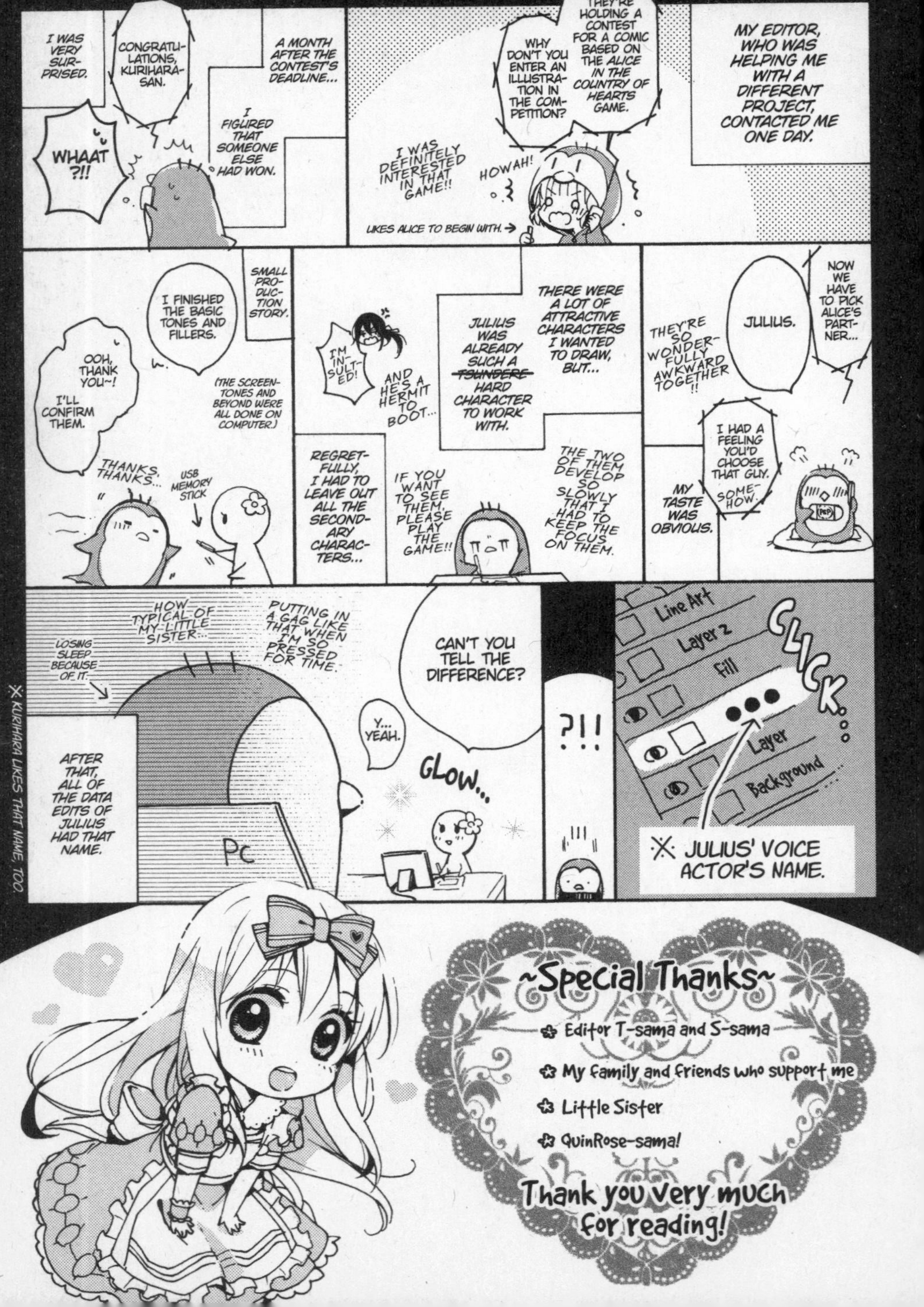
MY EDITOR, WHO WAS HELPING ME WITH A DIFFERENT PROJECT, CONTACTED ME ONE DAY.
THEY'RE HOLDING A CONTEST FOR A COMIC BASED ON THE ALICE IN THE COUNTRY OF HEARTS GAME.
WHY DON'T YOU ENTER AN ILLUSTRATION IN THE COMPETITION?
HOWAH!
I WAS DEFINITELY INTERESTED IN THAT GAME!!
LIKES ALICE TO BEGIN WITH. →
A MONTH AFTER THE CONTEST'S DEADLINE...
I FIGURED THAT SOMEONE ELSE HAD WON.
CONGRATULATIONS, KURIHARA-SAN.
I WAS VERY SURPRISED.
WHAAT ?!!
NOW WE HAVE TO PICK ALICE'S PARTNER...
JULIUS.
THEY'RE SO WONDERFULLY AWKWARD TOGETHER!!
I HAD A FEELING YOU'D CHOOSE THAT GUY. SOMEHOW.
MY TASTE WAS OBVIOUS.
THERE WERE A LOT OF ATTRACTIVE CHARACTERS I WANTED TO DRAW, BUT...
JULIUS WAS ALREADY SUCH A ~~TSUNDERE~~ HARD CHARACTER TO WORK WITH.
I'M INSULTED!
AND HE'S A HERMIT TO BOOT...
THE TWO OF THEM DEVELOP SO SLOWLY THAT I HAD TO KEEP THE FOCUS ON THEM.
IF YOU WANT TO SEE THEM, PLEASE PLAY THE GAME!!
REGRETFULLY, I HAD TO LEAVE OUT ALL THE SECONDARY CHARACTERS...
SMALL PRODUCTION STORY.
I FINISHED THE BASIC TONES AND FILLERS.
OOH, THANK YOU~! I'LL CONFIRM THEM.
(THE SCREENTONES AND BEYOND WERE ALL DONE ON COMPUTER.)
THANKS, THANKS...
USB MEMORY STICK
CLICK...
Line Art
Layer 2
Fill
●●●
Layer
Background
※ JULIUS' VOICE ACTOR'S NAME.
?!!
CAN'T YOU TELL THE DIFFERENCE?
Y... YEAH.
GLOW...
PUTTING IN A GAG LIKE THAT WHEN I'M SO PRESSED FOR TIME.
HOW TYPICAL OF MY LITTLE SISTER...
LOSING SLEEP BECAUSE OF IT.
AFTER THAT, ALL OF THE DATA EDITS OF JULIUS HAD THAT NAME.
PC
※ KURIHARA LIKES THAT NAME, TOO.
~Special Thanks~
✿ Editor T-sama and S-sama
✿ My family and friends who support me
✿ Little Sister
✿ QuinRose-sama!
Thank you very much for reading!

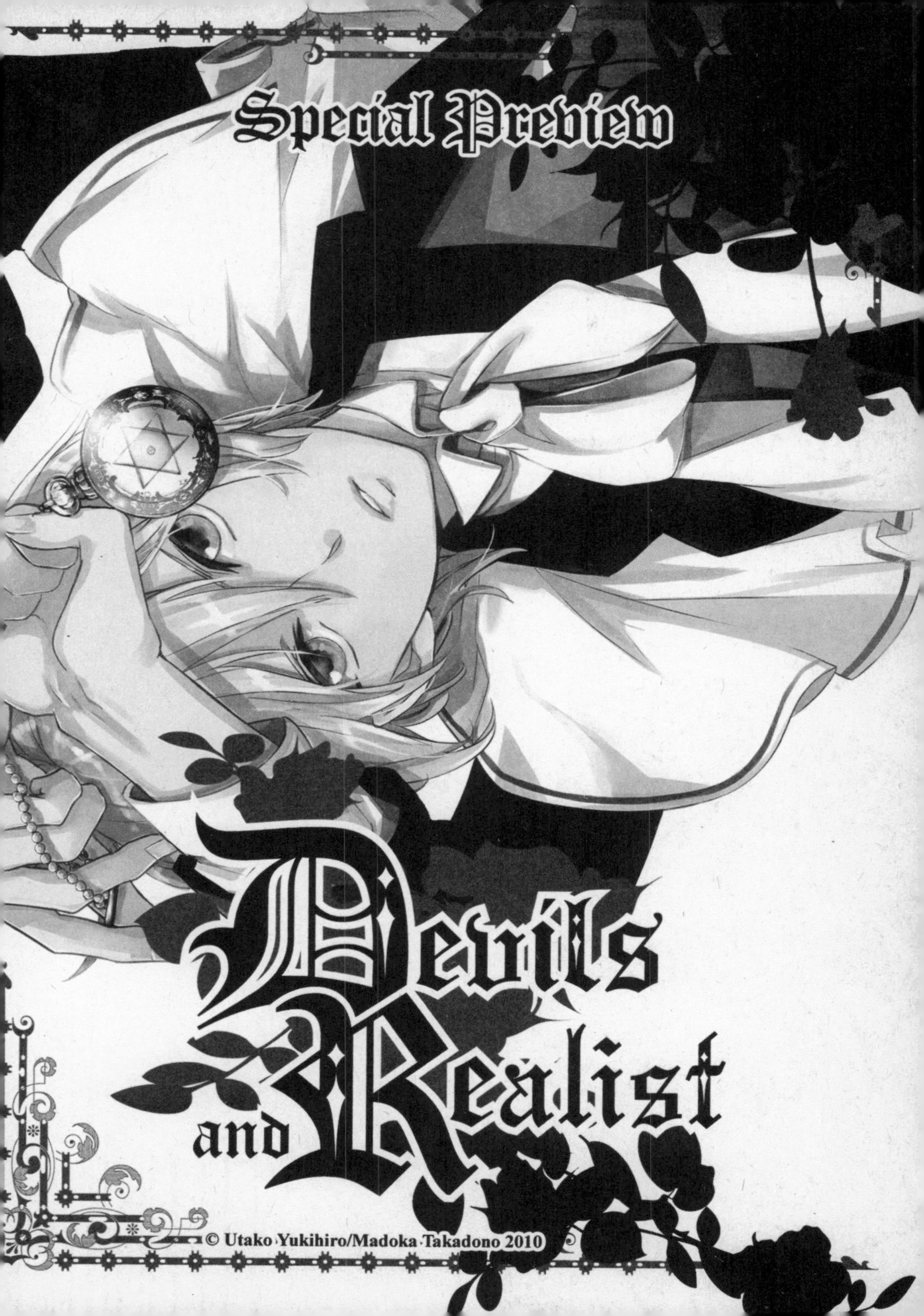
Special Preview
Devils and Realist
© Utako Yukihiro/Madoka Takadono 2010

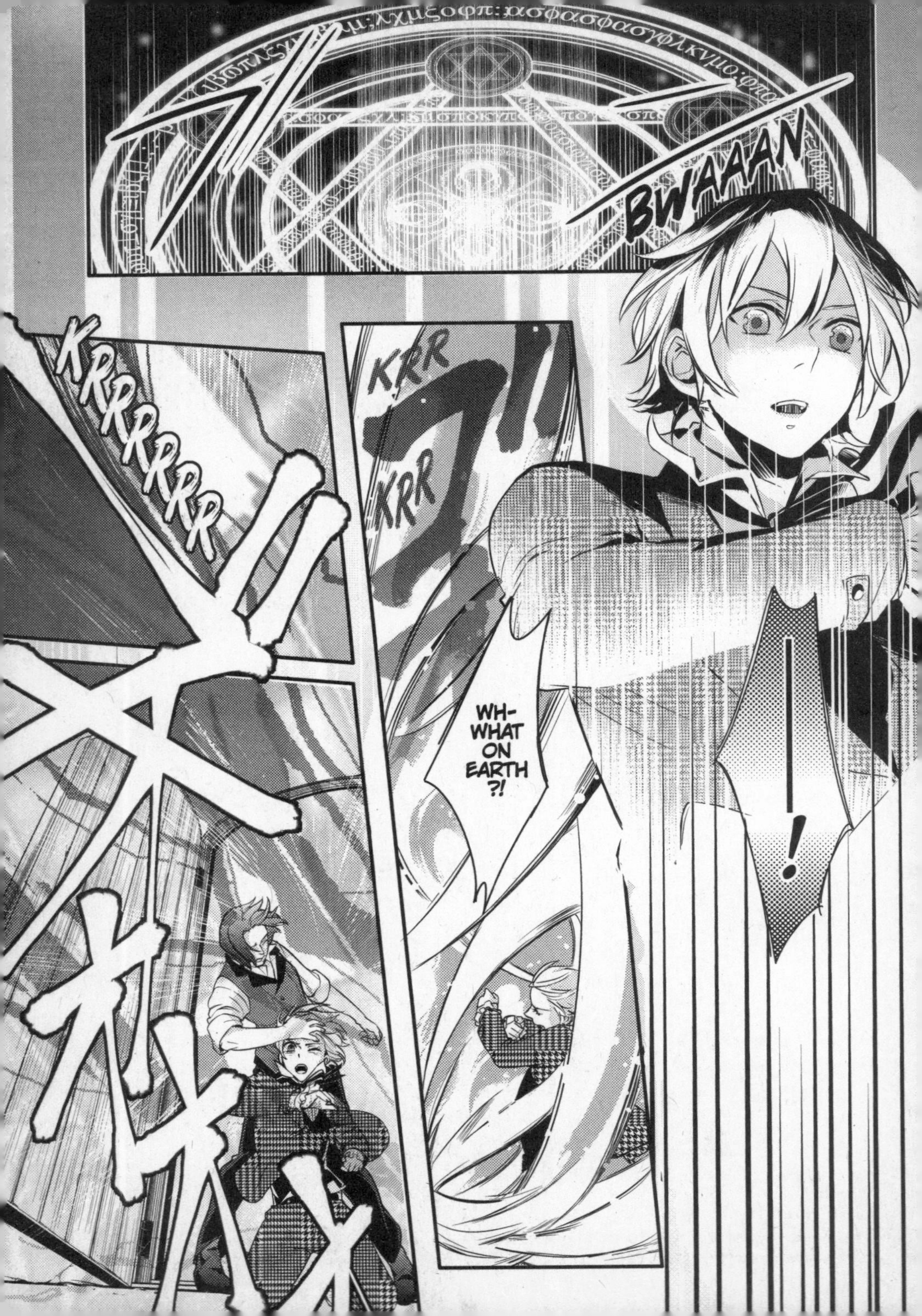
BWAAAN
!
KRR KRR
WH-WHAT ON EARTH?!
KRRRRRRR

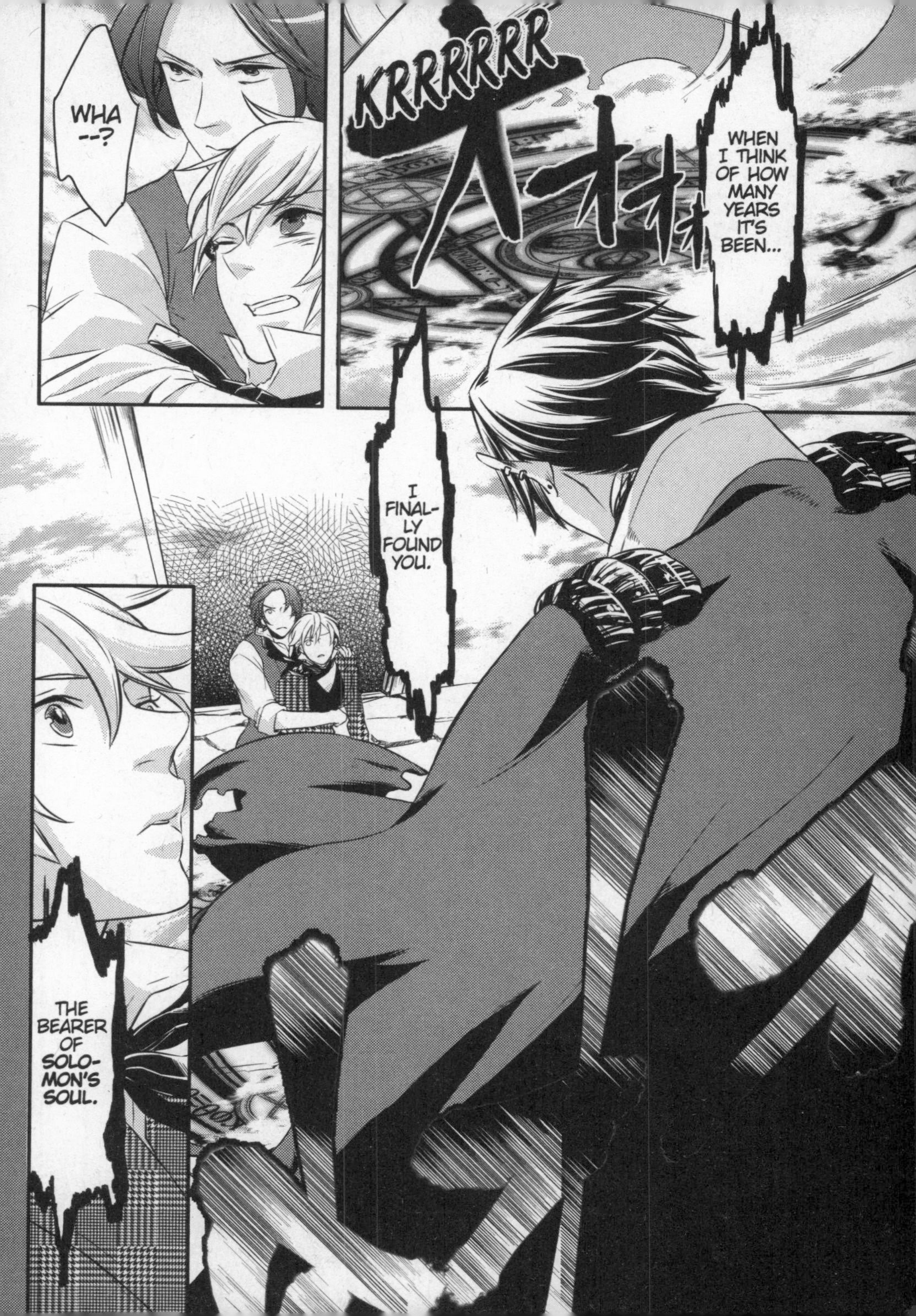
KRRRRRR
WHEN I THINK OF HOW MANY YEARS IT'S BEEN...
WHA--?
I FINALLY FOUND YOU.
THE BEARER OF SOLOMON'S SOUL.

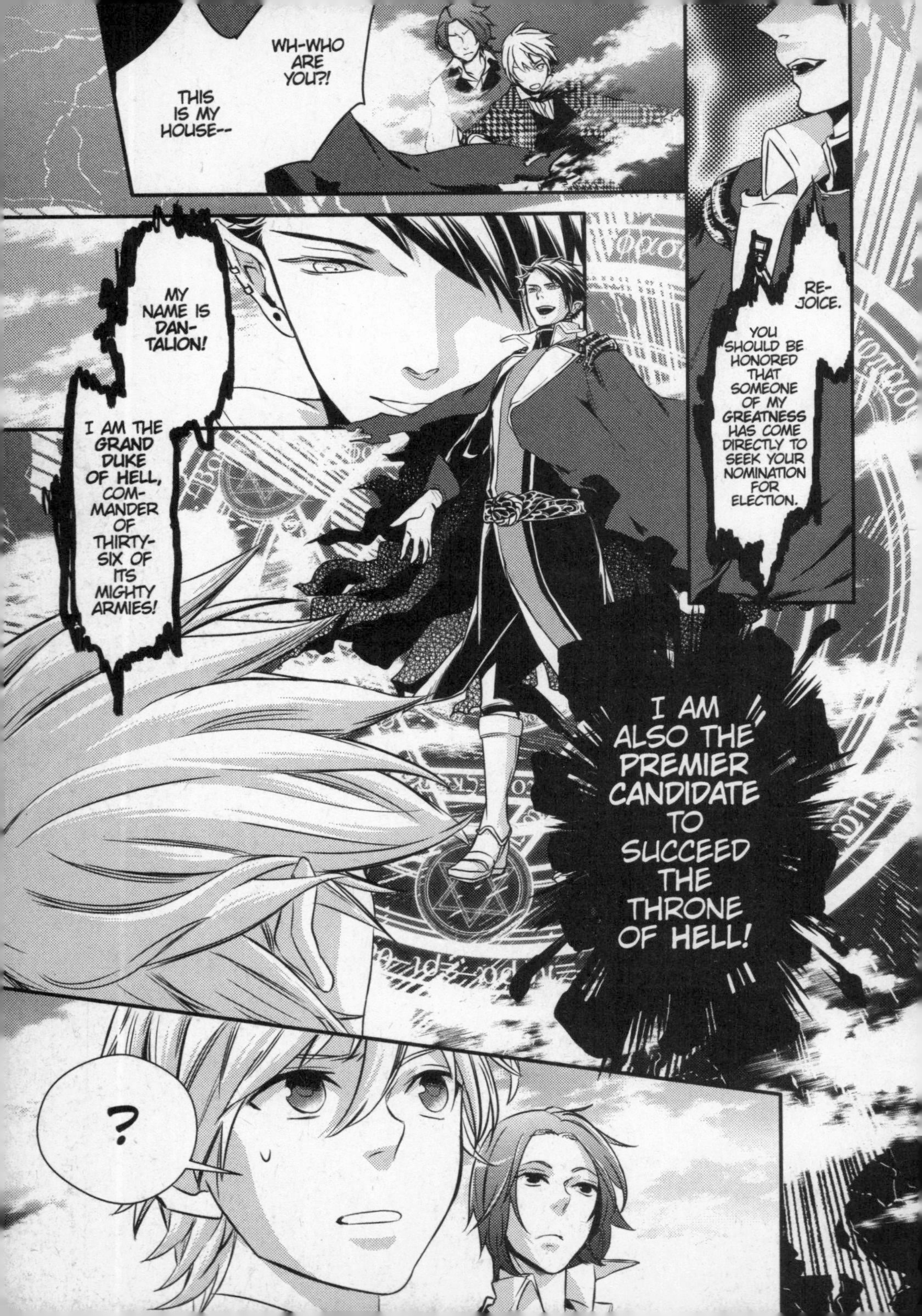
REJOICE.
YOU SHOULD BE HONORED THAT SOMEONE OF MY GREATNESS HAS COME DIRECTLY TO SEEK YOUR NOMINATION FOR ELECTION.
WH-WHO ARE YOU?!
THIS IS MY HOUSE--
MY NAME IS DAN-TALION!
I AM THE GRAND DUKE OF HELL, COM-MANDER OF THIRTY-SIX OF ITS MIGHTY ARMIES!
I AM ALSO THE PREMIER CANDIDATE TO SUCCEED THE THRONE OF HELL!
?

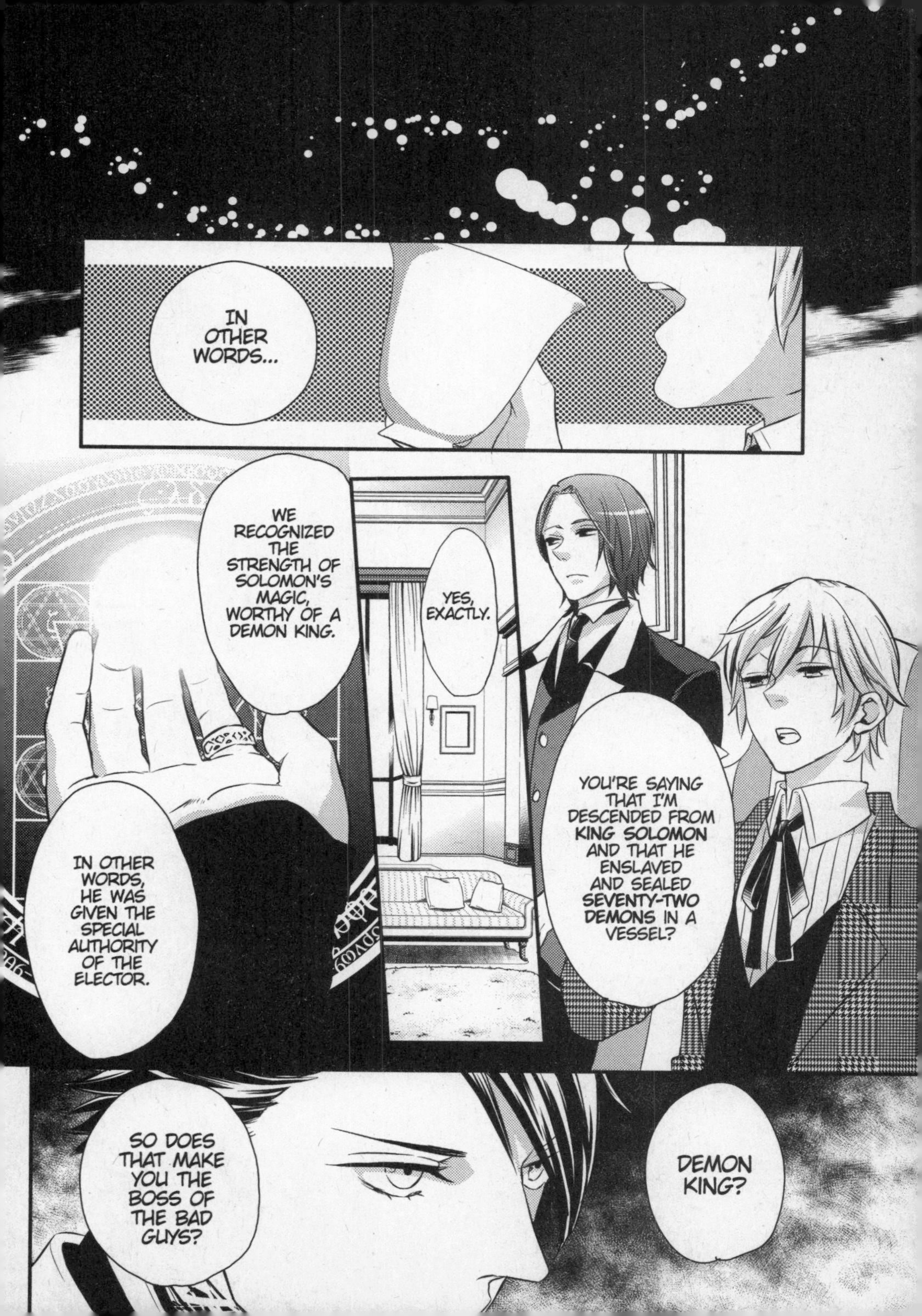
IN OTHER WORDS...
YOU'RE SAYING THAT I'M DESCENDED FROM KING SOLOMON AND THAT HE ENSLAVED AND SEALED SEVENTY-TWO DEMONS IN A VESSEL?
YES, EXACTLY.
WE RECOGNIZED THE STRENGTH OF SOLOMON'S MAGIC, WORTHY OF A DEMON KING.
IN OTHER WORDS, HE WAS GIVEN THE SPECIAL AUTHORITY OF THE ELECTOR.
DEMON KING?
SO DOES THAT MAKE YOU THE BOSS OF THE BAD GUYS?

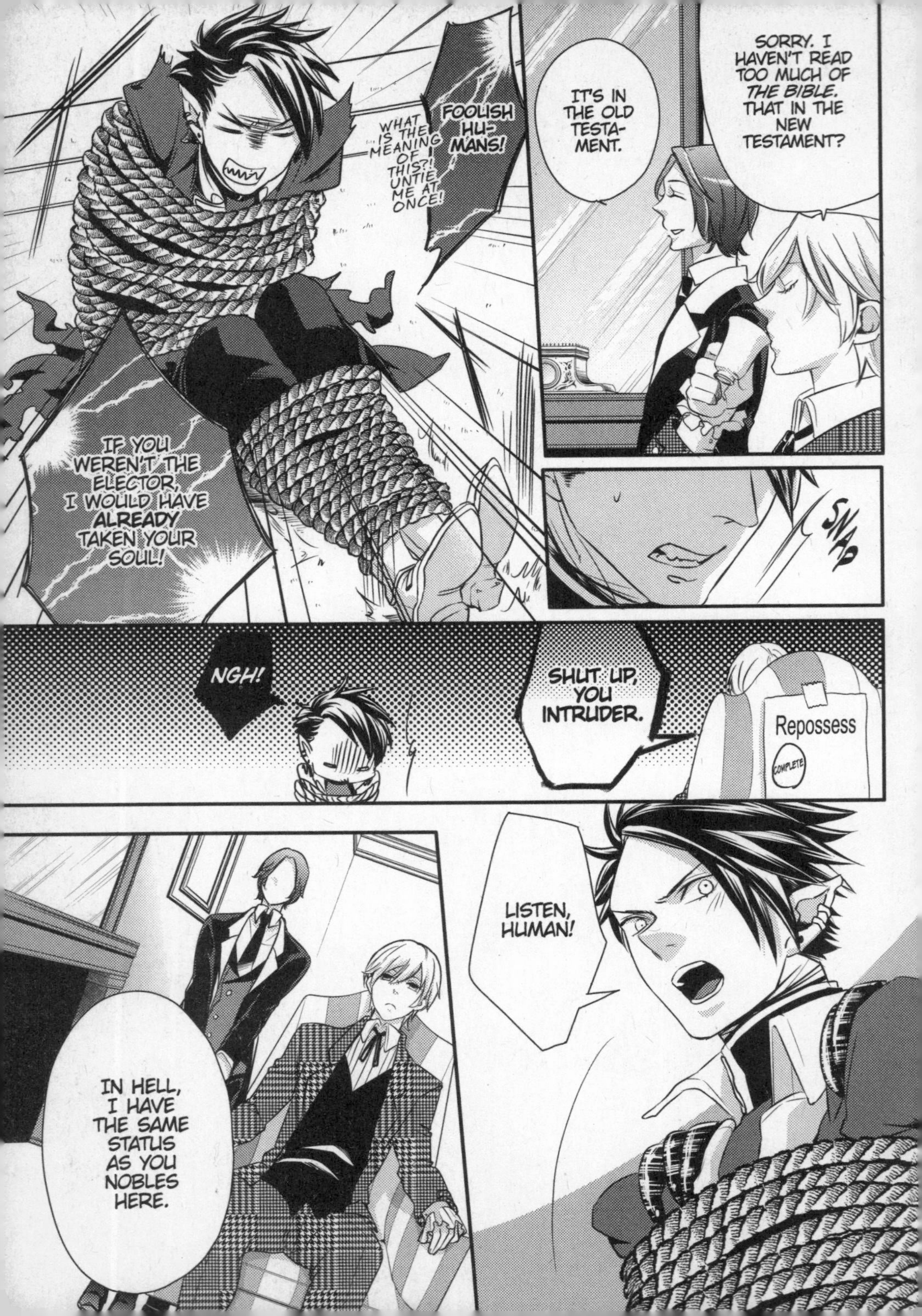
SORRY. I HAVEN'T READ TOO MUCH OF *THE BIBLE*. THAT IN THE NEW TESTAMENT?
IT'S IN THE OLD TESTAMENT.
SNAP
FOOLISH HUMANS!
WHAT IS THE MEANING OF THIS?! UNTIE ME AT ONCE!
IF YOU WEREN'T THE ELECTOR, I WOULD HAVE **ALREADY** TAKEN YOUR SOUL!
Repossess
COMPLETE
SHUT UP, YOU INTRUDER.
NGH!
LISTEN, HUMAN!
IN HELL, I HAVE THE SAME STATUS AS YOU NOBLES HERE.

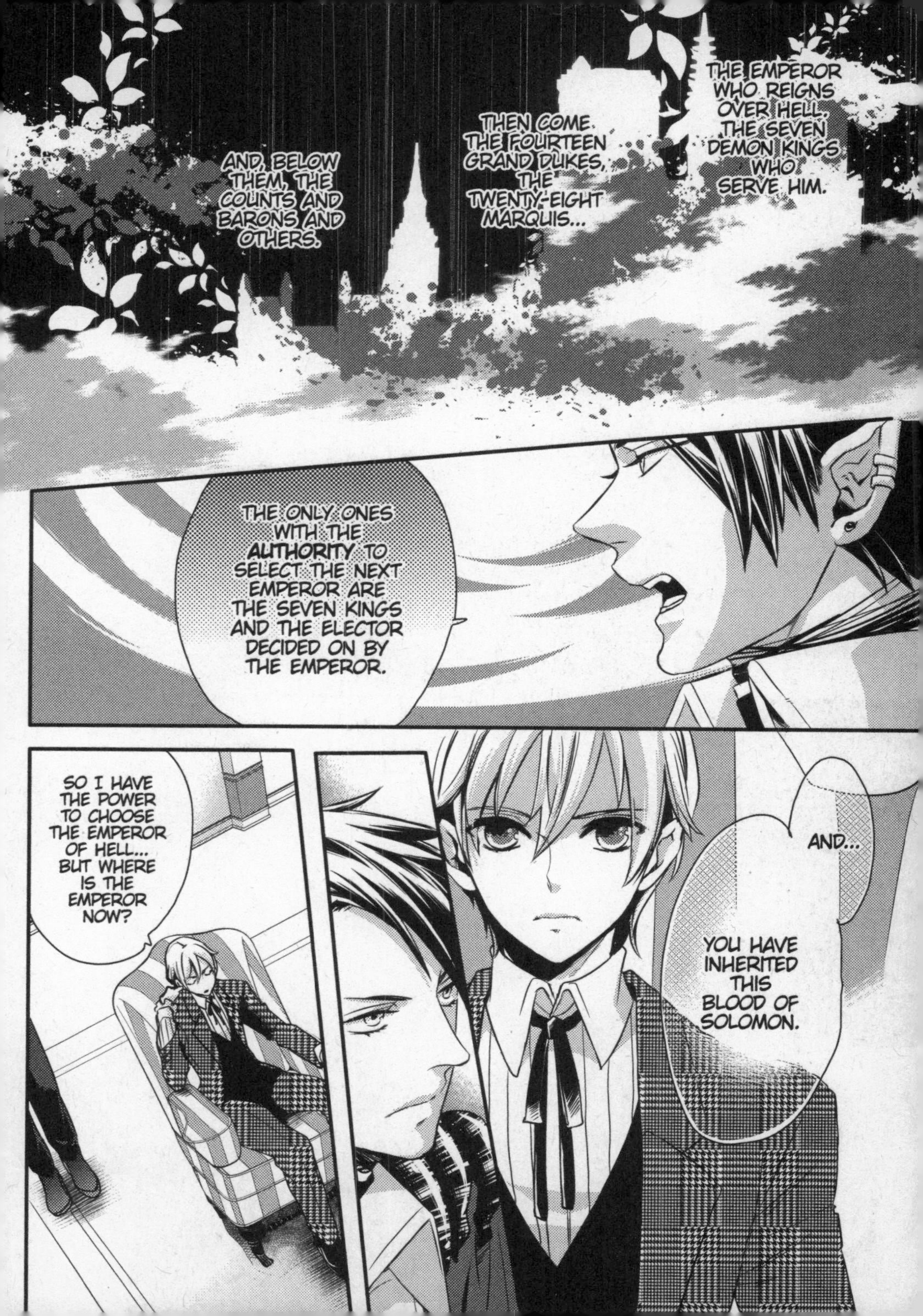
THE EMPEROR WHO REIGNS OVER HELL. THE SEVEN DEMON KINGS WHO SERVE HIM.
THEN COME THE FOURTEEN GRAND DUKES, THE TWENTY-EIGHT MARQUIS...
AND, BELOW THEM, THE COUNTS AND BARONS AND OTHERS.
THE ONLY ONES WITH THE **AUTHORITY** TO SELECT THE NEXT EMPEROR ARE THE SEVEN KINGS AND THE ELECTOR DECIDED ON BY THE EMPEROR.
AND...
YOU HAVE INHERITED THIS BLOOD OF SOLOMON.
SO I HAVE THE POWER TO CHOOSE THE EMPEROR OF HELL... BUT WHERE IS THE EMPEROR NOW?

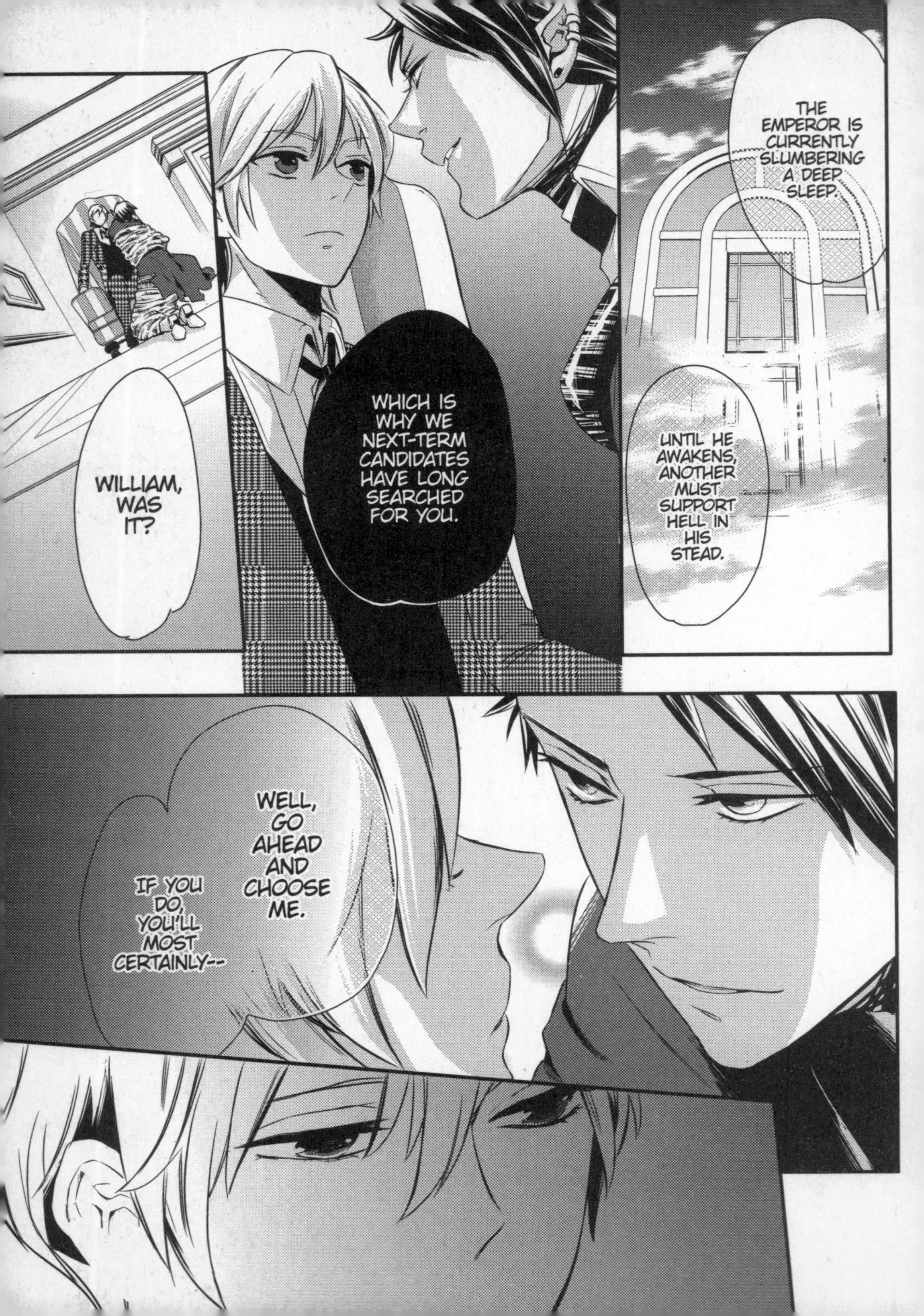
THE EMPEROR IS CURRENTLY SLUMBERING A DEEP SLEEP.
UNTIL HE AWAKENS, ANOTHER MUST SUPPORT HELL IN HIS STEAD.
WHICH IS WHY WE NEXT-TERM CANDIDATES HAVE LONG SEARCHED FOR YOU.
WILLIAM, WAS IT?
WELL, GO AHEAD AND CHOOSE ME.
IF YOU DO, YOU'LL MOST CERTAINLY--

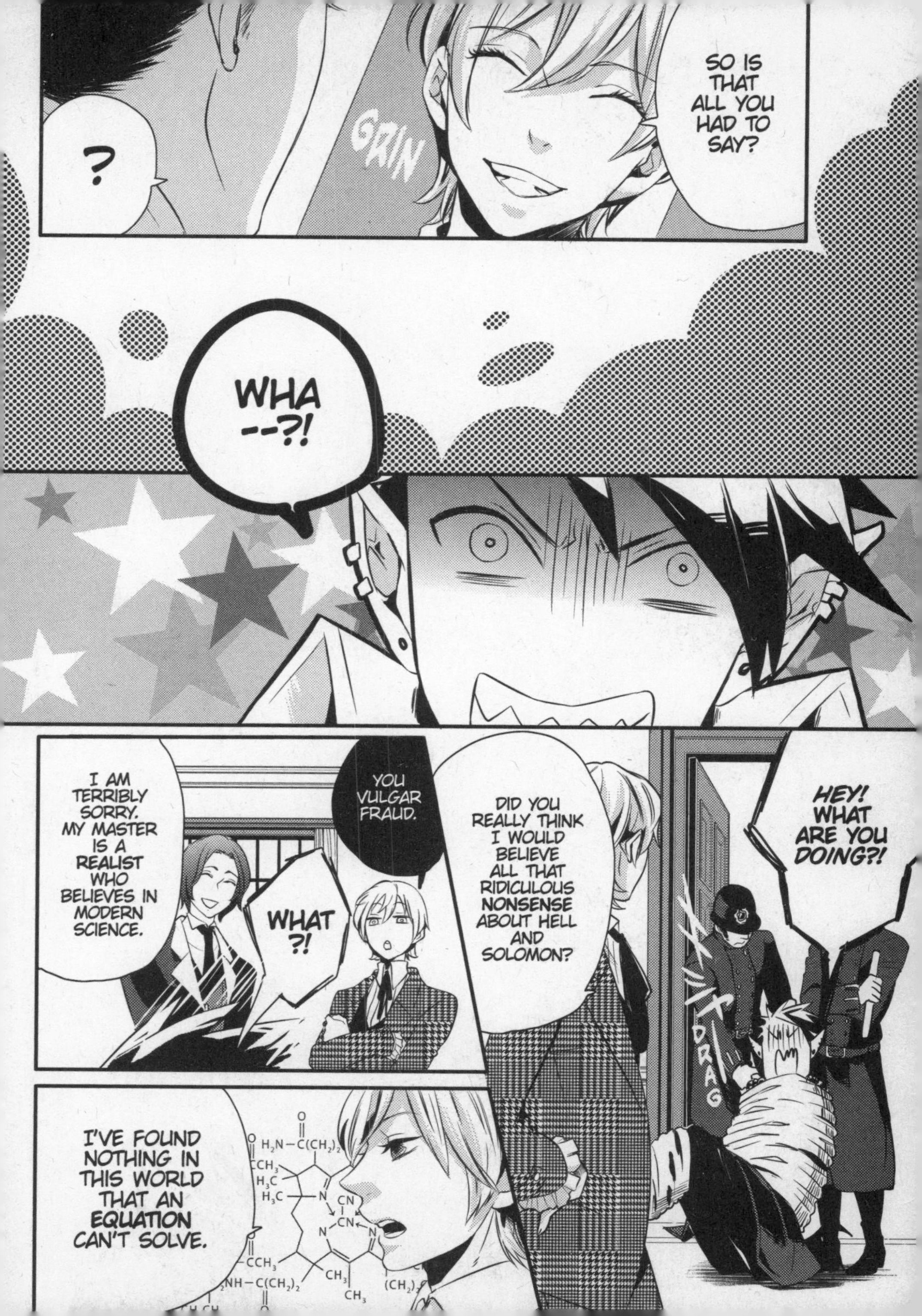
SO IS THAT ALL YOU HAD TO SAY?
GRIN
?
WHA--?!
HEY! WHAT ARE YOU DOING?!
DRAG
DID YOU REALLY THINK I WOULD BELIEVE ALL THAT RIDICULOUS NONSENSE ABOUT HELL AND SOLOMON?
YOU VULGAR FRAUD.
WHAT?!
I AM TERRIBLY SORRY. MY MASTER IS A REALIST WHO BELIEVES IN MODERN SCIENCE.
I'VE FOUND NOTHING IN THIS WORLD THAT AN EQUATION CAN'T SOLVE.

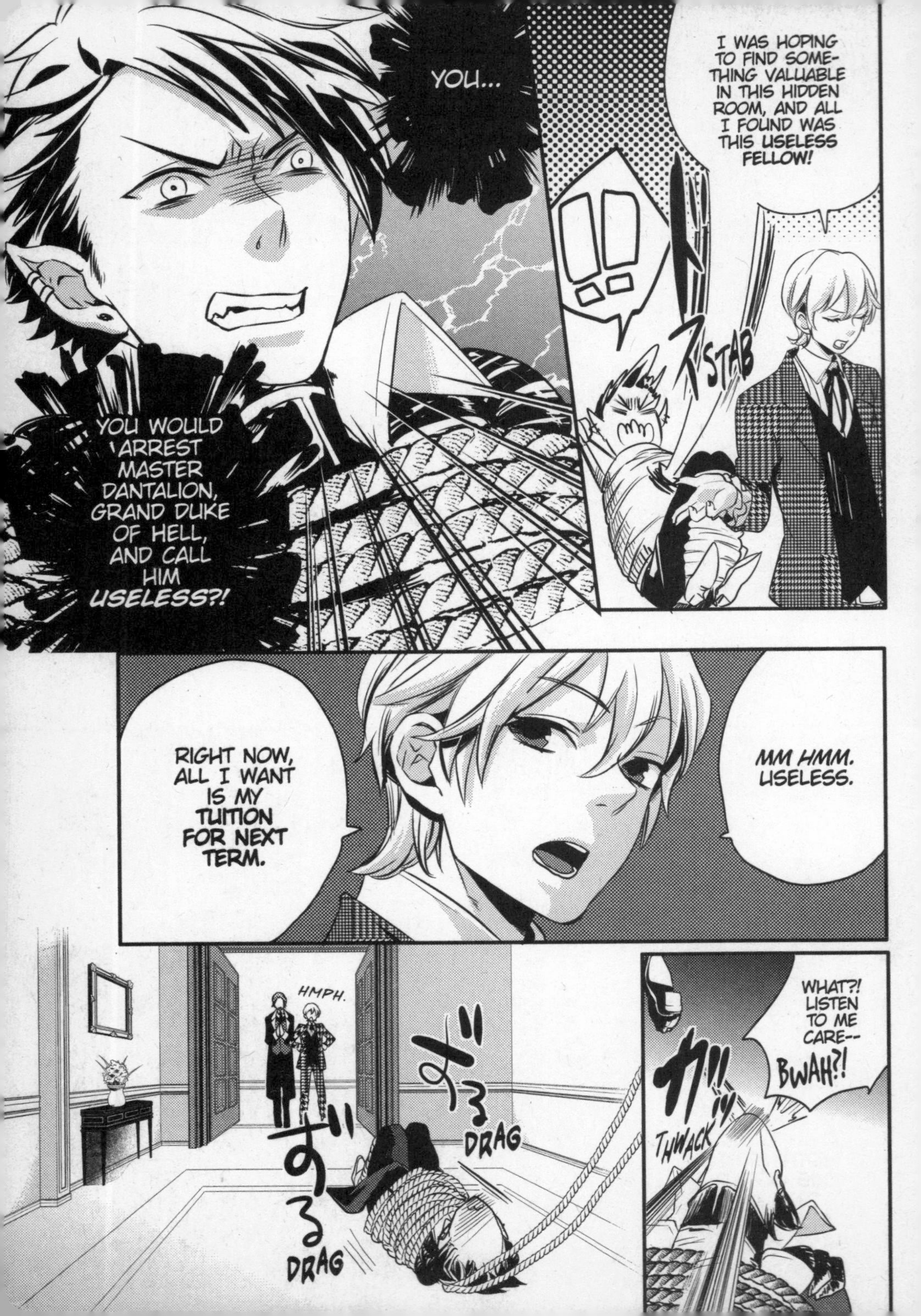
I WAS HOPING TO FIND SOMETHING VALUABLE IN THIS HIDDEN ROOM, AND ALL I FOUND WAS THIS USELESS FELLOW!
!!
STAB
YOU...
YOU WOULD ARREST MASTER DANTALION, GRAND DUKE OF HELL, AND CALL HIM USELESS?!
MM HMM. USELESS.
RIGHT NOW, ALL I WANT IS MY TUITION FOR NEXT TERM.
WHAT?! LISTEN TO ME CARE--
BWAH?!
THWACK
HMPH.
DRAG
DRAG

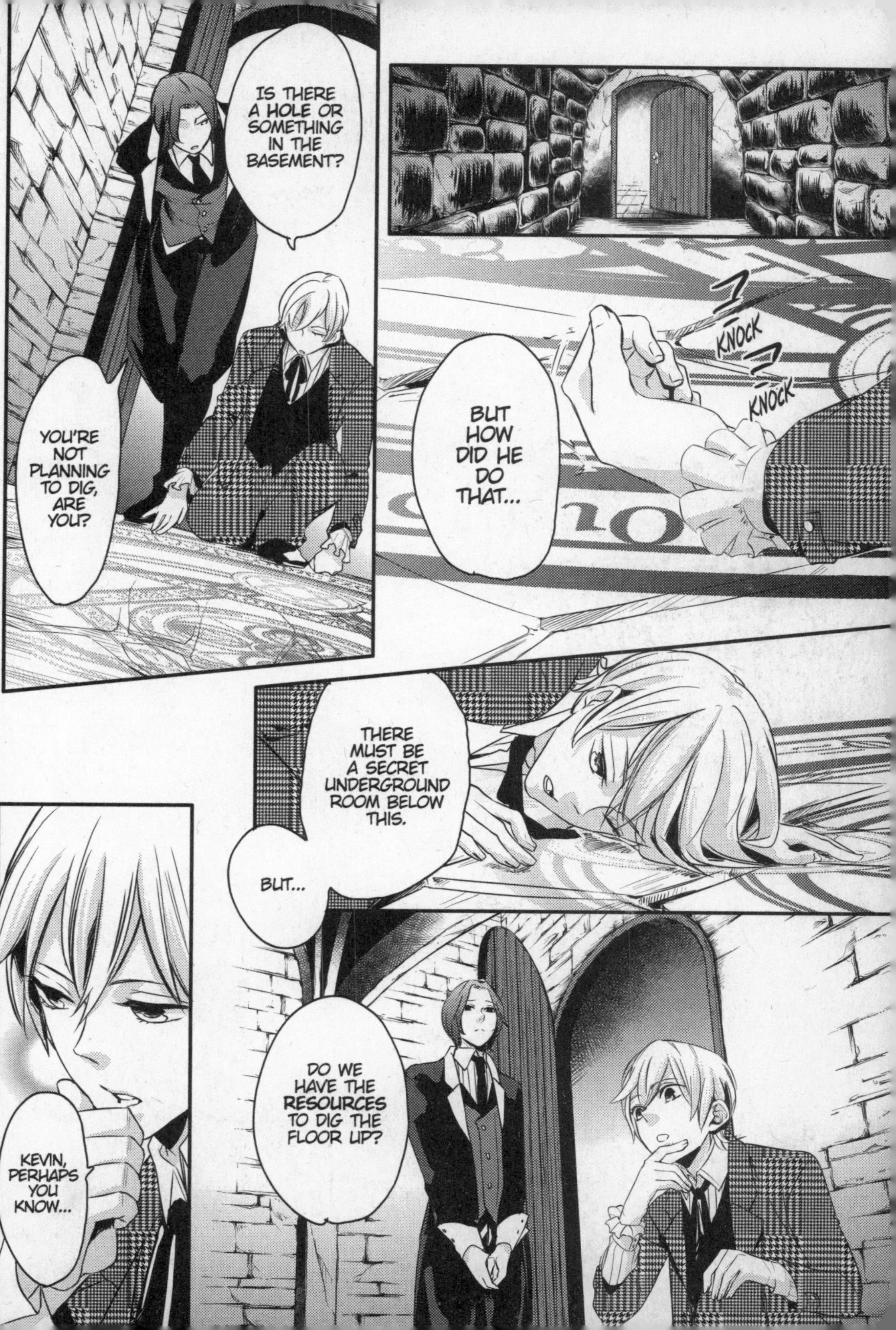
KNOCK
KNOCK
BUT HOW DID HE DO THAT...
IS THERE A HOLE OR SOMETHING IN THE BASEMENT?
YOU'RE NOT PLANNING TO DIG, ARE YOU?
THERE MUST BE A SECRET UNDERGROUND ROOM BELOW THIS.
BUT...
DO WE HAVE THE RESOURCES TO DIG THE FLOOR UP?
KEVIN, PERHAPS YOU KNOW...

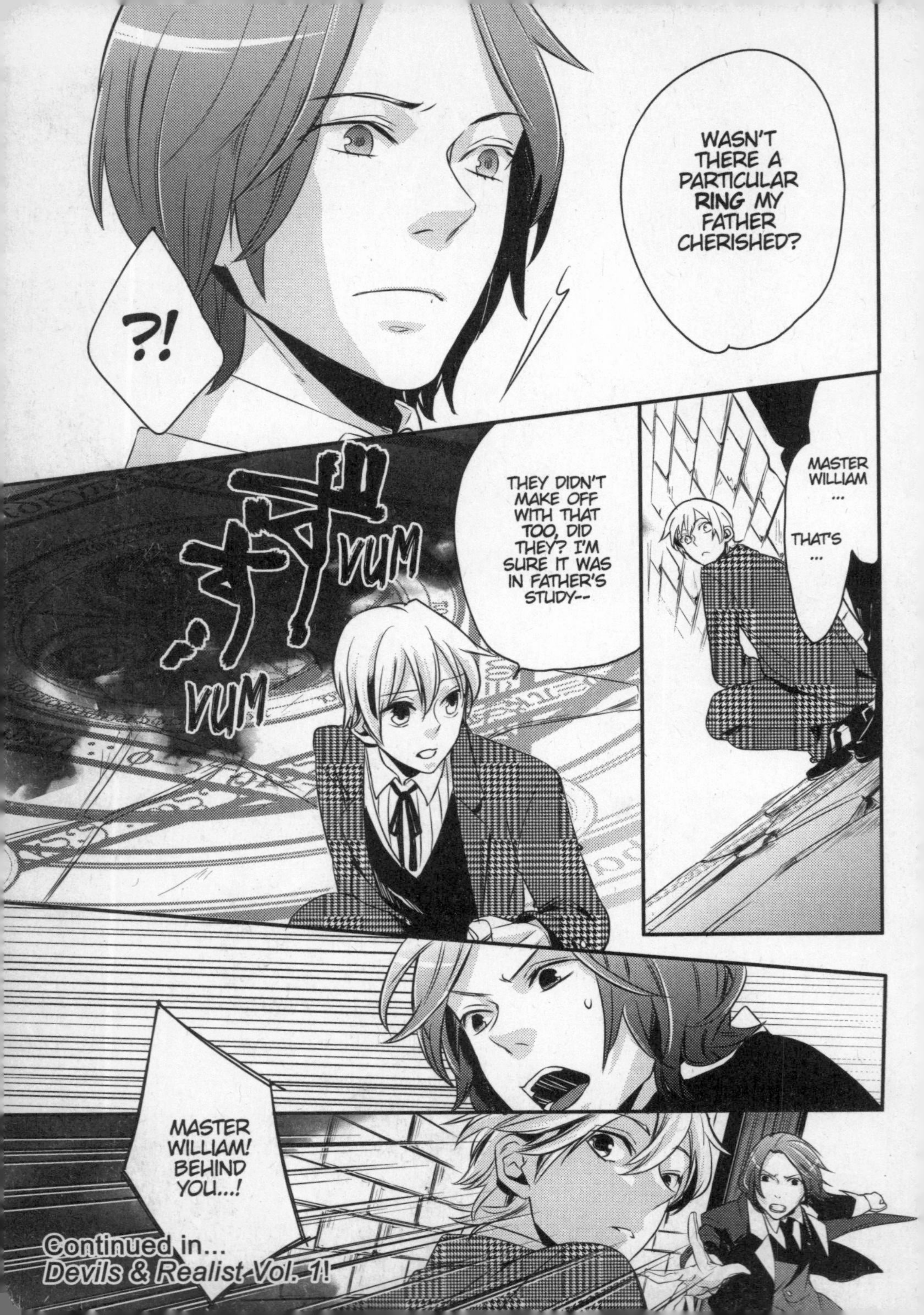
WASN'T THERE A PARTICULAR RING MY FATHER CHERISHED?
?!
MASTER WILLIAM ...
THAT'S ...
THEY DIDN'T MAKE OFF WITH THAT TOO, DID THEY? I'M SURE IT WAS IN FATHER'S STUDY--
VUM
VUM
MASTER WILLIAM! BEHIND YOU...!

Continued in...
Devils & Realist Vol. 1!

COMING SOON

JUNE 2014
Alice in the Country of Joker: Circus and Liar's Game Vol. 5

JULY 2014
Alice in the Country of Clover: Knight's Knowledge Vol. 1

AUGUST 2014
Alice in the Country of Joker: The Nightmare Trilogy Vol. 1

SEPTEMBER 2014
Alice in the Country of Clover: Knight's Knowledge Vol. 2

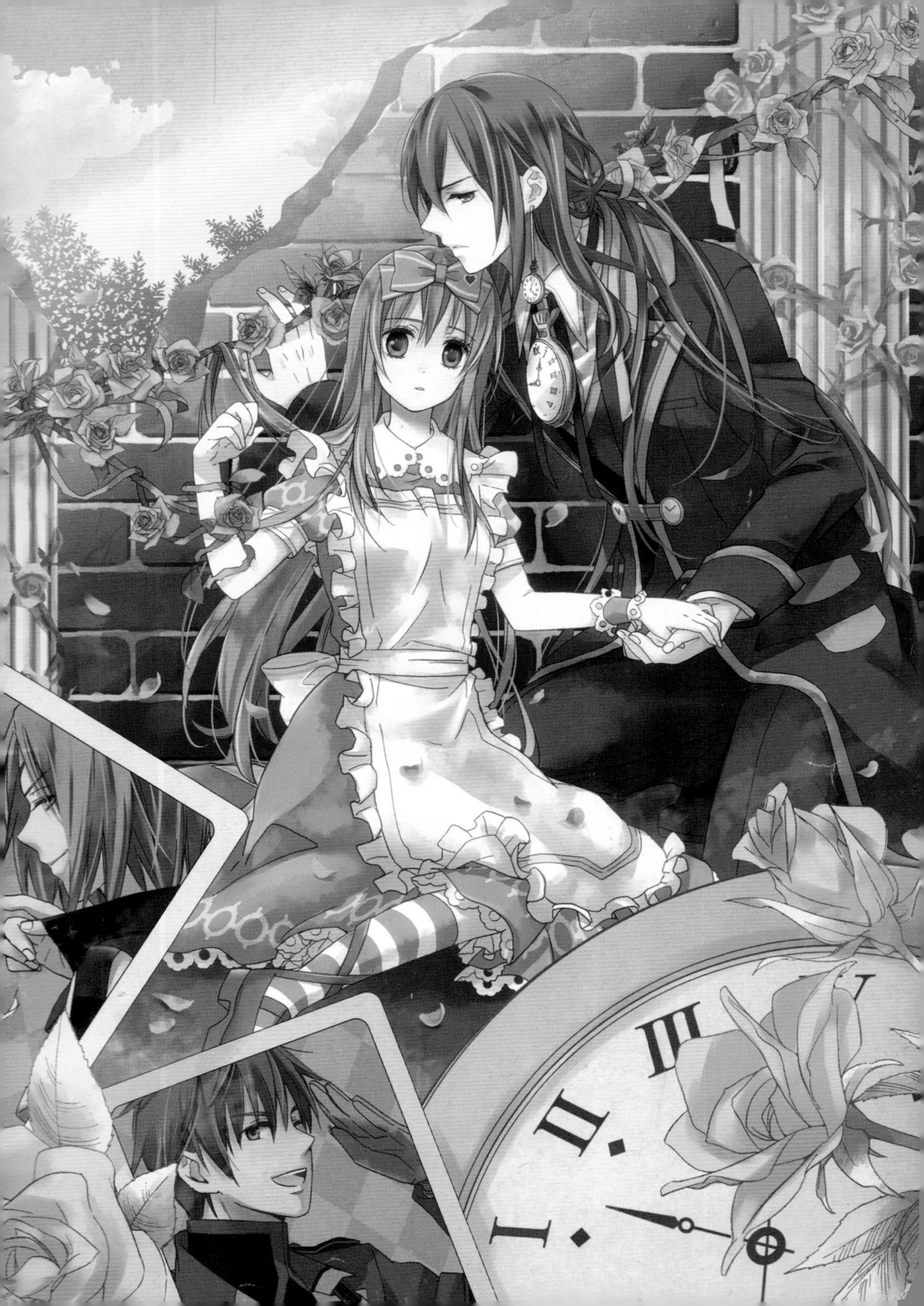

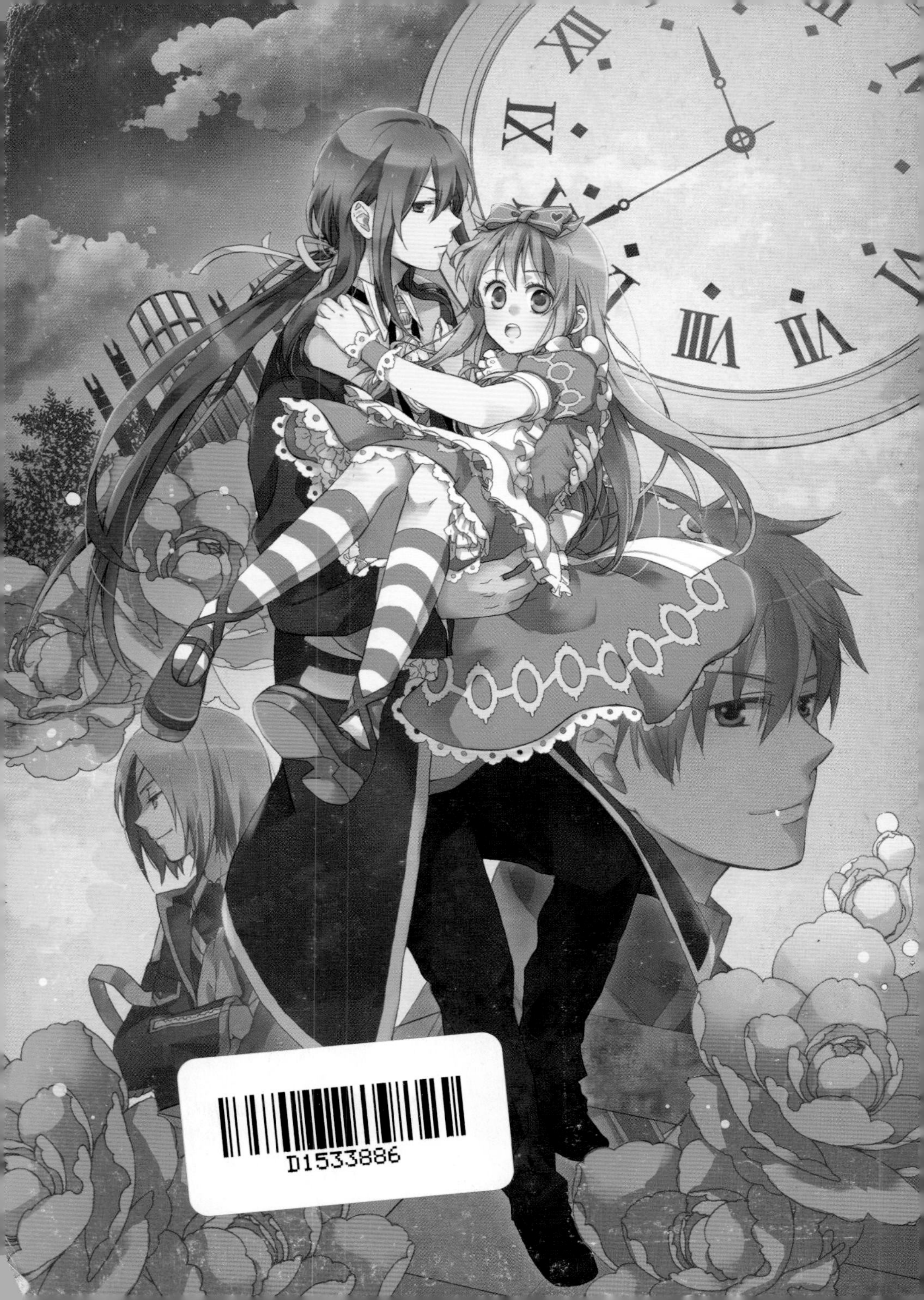